GOLDBERGER'S WAR

GOLDBERGER'S WAR

The Life and Work
of a Public Health Crusader

ALAN M. KRAUT

HILL AND WANG

A division of Farrar, Straus and Giroux

New York

Hill and Wang
A division of Farrar, Straus and Giroux
19 Union Square West, New York 10003

Library of Congress Control Number: 2003104265

ISBN: 0-374-13537-1

Designed by Jonathan D. Lippincott

www.fsgbooks.com

1   3   5   7   9   10   8   6   4   2

Frontispiece: Portrait of Dr. Joseph Goldberger by artist Walmsley Lenhard

To my friend and editor
Dr. Sarah Larson

Contents

I first met Dr. Joseph Goldberger via television in my parents' living room in the Bronx. The encounter occurred on a spring evening when I was nine. I was sitting next to my late father, Harry Kraut, and watching *Cavalcade of America*, a half-hour historical dramatization, on our nine-inch black-and-white Admiral television. The program, sponsored by DuPont in the 1950s, specialized in an idealized version of American history typical of the era, usually focusing on a particular hero or act of heroism. The scripts were soapy and chock-full of the social stereotypes that my generation of historians would debunk a decade or two later. But this was the 1950s. My father, a factory worker and a World War II veteran, a charter member of Tom Brokaw's "greatest generation," respected heroes and loved history. He wanted his son to do the same. We rarely missed the show. It was entertaining, and my dad found it useful; each week it provided him with yet another lesson his son ought to learn. That evening in April 1954 we learned together about Goldberger's war on the often fatal disease pellagra and specifically about the Rankin prisoner experiment. After the show, I suffered my father's attempt to link Goldberger's story to why I should study hard at school in preparation for doing noble deeds. Then I crawled under the covers and called it a night.

Some thirty-five years later, I found myself watching television late one evening as Dr. Anthony Fauci of the National Institutes of Health addressed Ted Koppel's *Nightline* audience. In a voice lightly seasoned by his Brooklyn roots, Fauci told viewers that the AIDS story had not changed since the early 1980s, when the disease first appeared on the public's screen. The bad news was that there was not yet a vaccine to prevent human immunodeficiency virus (HIV) infection or a therapy for those already infected. The good news: that the risk of HIV infection through blood transfusions had been greatly reduced through careful monitoring of the nation's blood supply and that the risk of infection could be further minimized by avoiding certain high-risk sexual behaviors. Public health officials supporting clean-needle programs in the 1990s as a means to prevent rampant HIV infection in the intravenous-drug-user population were sending the same message—prevention through behavioral change. Those hoping to avoid HIV infection must make different choices concerning their habits of life.

My research on immigration and its relationship to public health had taught me that individual choices are often not enough. Broad social and economic factors condition public health, making some individuals or groups more vulnerable to particular diseases than others. Just living their lives can make people sick. Achieving public health is an ongoing struggle.

And so I was reminded of Goldberger and his quest in the early decades of the twentieth century to discover why some Americans—particularly southerners—were falling victim to the disfiguring, and potentially deadly, disease pellagra. When I decided to follow Goldberger's trail, I fancied that I would be tracing the work of a master epidemiologist, a solver of medical puzzles. Certainly he was that. But I learned over the course of researching this biography that Goldberger was above all a crusader. He argued cogently and passionately for the authority of medical science to demand change, using pen and podium to make the case for putting public health first.

The debate over reconciling the demands of public health with other economic, social, and political priorities has echoed across the twentieth century and into the twenty-first. Goldberger's story continues to be fresh and pertinent to a society juggling individual liberties, evaporating medical resources, and the specter of disease as a weapon of mass destruction. In memory of my father, I invite each of you to meet Dr. Joseph Goldberger, and to enlist in Goldberger's war to make public health a path to social justice.

Historians are routinely distanced from their subjects by time and space. Although I could not meet and interrogate Goldberger, I found his son Joseph H. Goldberger, M.D., to be a valuable window on his father's life and career. With a smile and firm handshake, he greeted me at the Austin airport on a warm August morning. Then in his eighties, he so closely resembled his father in photographs that finding him at the busy security gate was easier than I had anticipated. For a full day, with tape recorder rolling, I sat at his table and peppered him with questions, scribbled notes, looked at family memorabilia, and made a new friend. Since then, Joe and his wife, Floylee, have been enormously kind and generous with their time and family photographs. So, too, have other members of the Goldberger family, including Donald Sharp, M.D., who followed in his grandfather's footsteps and is a Public Health Service physician at the Centers for Disease Control and Prevention in Atlanta. Another Goldberger grandchild, Linda Keiter, sent valuable family photographs. Though a more distant Goldberger relative, Eric Bloch generously shared his genealogical material with me, as did Robert Seymour Goldberger.

I have acquired many other debts in the course of my research. As my interest in Goldberger and his crusade against pellagra blossomed into a book project, I received gratifying support from other historians of medicine. Dale Smith, chair of the History of Medicine Department at the Uniformed Services University of the Health Sciences (USUHS), has been my friend and mentor ever since I decided to pursue my interest in the history of medicine. In addition to reading a draft of my manuscript, he has offered valuable research advice and encouragement every step of the way. Robert Joy, now retired from USUHS, remains a valuable source of bibliographical and research strategy for all who sit around the small table where he holds forth over lunch.

In the autumn of 1996 I was the DeWitt Stetten Jr. Senior Fellow at the National Institutes of Health with support from the National Institute of Diabetes and Digestive and Kidney Diseases (NIDDK) and the National Cancer Institute (NCI). Victoria Harden, director of the Office of NIH History and director of the DeWitt Stetten Jr. Museum of Medical Research, was my sponsor. I learned a great deal from Dr. Harden, an accomplished author and expert on public health issues, as well as from Alan N. Schecter, chief of the Laboratory of Chemical Biology at NIDDK, and Peter Greenwald, director of the Division of Cancer Prevention of NCI. Conversations with Evan DeRenzo of the Clinical Center's Office of Medical Ethics and Mark Levine of NIDDK were intellectually stimulating. I shall always be grateful to Vicky Harden for the opportunity to spend time at NIH and for her generous support of my research.

Over the years I have benefited greatly from the support and warm friendship of John Parascandola, historian of the U.S. Public Health Service. John's knowledge of life in the PHS in the early twentieth century and his generosity in giving me access to early-twentieth-century PHS personnel files and photographs assisted me greatly. His associate Alexandra Lord has also been most helpful. Suzanne White Junod, historian at the Food and Drug Administration, generously shared information about Milledgeville, Georgia, and her own fine publications on food enrichment.

Many other historians offered their research and expertise. Harry Marks of the Institute of the History of Medicine at Johns Hopkins University sent me material on Goldberger's mill studies and his own insights about their significance. David Oshinsky of the University of Texas at Austin shared his research on the Rankin experiment acquired for his own fine study of Parchman State Penitentiary. Jon Harkness of Cornell offered valuable observations about the ethical implications of Goldberger's human experimentation. Elizabeth Etheridge shared her considerable expertise on pellagra and the sources for studying it in a telephone conversation with me.

Bert Hansen of Baruch College introduced me to the wonders of eBay and with characteristic generosity helped me to acquire a copy of the issue of *Real Life Comics* that featured the Goldberger story, as well as a copy of the Parke, Davis and Company image of Goldberger investigating pellagra at an orphanage that adorns the cover of this volume.

In the spring of 1995 I was steeped in southern state health department reports in Harvard University's Countway Library of Medicine.

Coffee with the visiting researcher and much-respected historian of medicine Saul Benison was always a welcome break. His good humor and vast bibliographical knowledge never failed to refresh and inform. June Alexander of the University of Cincinnati generously took time to translate from the Slovak the description of Goldberger's birthplace, Giralt, so kindly sent to me by the Office of Cultural Affairs of the Embassy of the Slovak Republic. The genealogist Shirley Langdon Wilcox used her exceptional skills to locate the ship manifest listing the Goldberger family on their journey to America. Historian Joan Cashin offered information on Mary Goldberger's family lineage. The historian John Barry offered his considerable expertise on the Mississippi flood and shared his notes on Goldberger, and the novelist Daniel Akst e-mailed interview material and correspondence with Goldberger's family. Samuel Hynes of Princeton not only recalled that pellagra was mentioned in the song "It's the Same Old South," recorded by Count Basie in 1940; he sent me the lyrics. Shelby Shapiro took time away from his doctoral research and teaching to read the finished manuscript and offer valuable suggestions. I relied on his considerable language skills for the translations of the Goldberger obituaries in the Yiddish press.

Many archivists and librarians assisted me with my research. These include John White at the Southern Historical Collection at the University of North Carolina, Chapel Hill; Randy Jones, Mary Teloh, and William J. Darby in Historical Collections at the Eskind Biomedical Library at Vanderbilt University; Stephen J. Greenberg in the History Division at the National Library of Medicine; Jane Brown and W. Curtis Worthington of the Waring Historical Library at the Medical University of South Carolina in Charleston; the former archivist of the City College of New York Barbara J. Dunlap and her successor, Sydney Van Nort; Robert Shearer of the Tulane University Archives; Anne E. Smith Case at the Howard-Tilton Memorial Library, Tulane; Caron Capizzano and Diane Levy of the New York University Medical Center Archives; David Patterson, deputy historian of the State Department's Historical Office; H. T. Holmes, Sandra Boyd, and Anne Webster of the Mississippi Department of Archives and History; Aloha South, formerly of the National Archives, and the current guardian of Record Group 90, Marjorie Ciarlante; Nancy McCall at the Alan Mason Chesney Medical Archives of the Johns Hopkins Medical Institutions; and Susan Watson of the American Red Cross Archives.

I am most grateful to the American Philosophical Society for the generous grant that permitted travel and photocopying in Jackson, Mississippi, and New Haven, Connecticut. American University, too, rendered support in the form of a sabbatical leave and research money. Provost Neal Kerwin, Dean of Faculties Ivy Broder, and College of Arts and Sciences Dean Kay Mussell and her predecessor, Howard Wachtel, have been supportive throughout my research. The work-study students Christopher Shanley and Howard Lee made weekly trips to libraries for photocopying, and graduate students, including Matt Clavin and Bernard Unti, and my former student Robert Wilensky all offered timely assistance. My current graduate students helped as well. Mary Ellen Henry shared articles she found in the course of her own research on the South. Teri Hedgpeth, an employee of the Naval Historical Center, helped me track down data on the SS *Joseph Goldberger.*

Many friends and colleagues have been generous with their time and effort. Jon Wakelyn, a distinguished historian of the American South, read the manuscript with great care and insight. Over the years his intelligence and warm friendship have been constants. Howard Gillette of Rutgers University, Camden, and James Gilbert of the University of Maryland offered an early critique of the project. After many valuable suggestions, one of them asked me whether my high regard for Goldberger would permit me to present a balanced view of his life. I hope the pages that follow respond to that concern. The late Janet Oppenheim, my dear friend and office mate for many years, was beginning a biography as I was beginning mine. When she was too weak to get to the office any longer, we chatted about our work over the phone. I shall always miss her sparkling mind and rapier wit. Peter Balbert is not a historian but a professor of English at Trinity University in San Antonio. Although the title for this volume that Peter suggested ended up on the cutting-room floor, our friendship and his many other suggestions have enriched me much over the past thirty-five years. My colleague at American University James Mooney has both a fine editorial eye and a knowledge of southern intellectual history. He is a wonderfully careful reader and a dear friend whose daily concern for me and attention to this manuscript I much value. Lisa Hill gave me a copy of the civil rights activist Pauli Murray's autobiography, marking the pages that referred to pellagra. Rabbi Joan Friedman took time from her teaching to discuss the Kaddish prayer with me. Myra Sklarew shared her material on biochemist E. V. McCollum. Suzanne Michael of Adelphi University has listened patiently to my Goldberger tales. Her considerable expertise in both immigration and health, as well as her support, has long been a mainstay. Her mother, Carola Michael, kindly sent on some information about the portrait painter John Carroll, whom Goldberger employed to document pellagra rashes. Scott Parker is neither a historian nor an expert in public health. However, our daily phone conversations lift my spirits, and his insightful questions on my statistical data never fail to send me scurrying to my notes and photocopies for answers.

Lauren Osborne's enthusiasm for my approach to Goldberger's life and work persuaded me to sign a contract with Hill and Wang, a division of Farrar, Straus and Giroux. When Lauren left FSG, Thomas LeBien took over editorial duties. Working with Thomas has been one of the most delightful publishing experiences I have had as a scholar. Cutting the length of my chapters with a scalpel rather than a hacksaw seems an appropriate description of what he did for this volume in the history of medicine. He has become a valued friend whose opinions mean much to me. His assistant, Kristy McGowan, has skillfully shepherded the manuscript through the last stages of the editorial process with patience and sensitivity. It has been a joy to work with her.

For many years Sarah Larson, my dear friend and former Ph.D. student, has been the first to read what I have written. Her editorial skills and her understanding of my own mind and style make her indispensable to all of my scholarly endeavors. No one has been a more constant fan and contributor to this project than Sarah. Our mutual respect, trust, and warm friendship are so great that a cup of coffee at Sarah's table has always been the best preventive medicine I know for writer's block and the best cure for low spirits. Sarah's marks on a manuscript in pink or green or blue—never red—are surefire signs that help is on the way.

And now for the family. Next August will mark the thirtieth anniversary of my marriage to Debby Kraut. A federal employee of twenty years,

Debby appreciates Goldberger's world as only a fellow federal bureaucrat can. During the writing of this book she has been at my side or, more accurate, looking over my shoulder at the screen and deciding when to blow the whistle for a coffee break and some words of encouragement. I would have it no other way.

My daughter, Julia Rose Kraut, is twenty-two and graduated from college last spring. In addition to our allegiance to the New York Yankees, we share a fascination with American history. She encouraged the completion of this volume with her frequent telephone inquiry, "So when is it going to be done, already?" I am enormously proud of her, and I know that her love of the past and her concern for civil liberties is the legacy from her grandpa Harry—a legacy that has also inspired this book. Happy graduation, Julia.

GOLDBERGER'S WAR

Introduction

"You are what you eat"—this is common wisdom in the modern industrialized world, particularly in those countries where the well-off can choose what they will and will not consume. Today what we eat, even how much we eat, is contested. Current campaigns against obesity, especially those that call for dramatic changes in the lifestyle and diet of individuals, recall earlier movements for vitamin-enriched foods or low-fat-food substitutes—margarine instead of butter. Today's targets of criticism include profit-hungry food corporations, self-aggrandizing Madison Avenue advertisers, colluding or ill-informed political officeholders, and negligent public school officials. However, because most modern societies emphasize individual responsibility, the buck stops at the table, where hungry men, women, and children decide what they will eat. But healthy choices depend on knowing what is healthy, being able to afford a nutritious diet, having access to wholesome and nutritious food, and, finally, being willing to alter old eating habits, many of them deeply rooted in ethnic or regional traditions and ensnared in complicated webs of class behaviors.

In a health-conscious era when the debate rages over the nutritional value of health foods, organic foods, and fast foods, it is easy to forget how recent is much of our knowledge of diet and its relationship to our health and life expectancy. Equally forgotten are those "hunger fighters" who conducted scientific research on the relationship of diet to disease, and then sought to teach the world that humanity could be spared some illnesses if only diets could be altered.[1] Even as today's enemies of obesity resurrect the memory of research pioneers such as Dr. Ancel Keys, whose pathbreaking Framingham study linked diet and heart disease, and support contemporary public health advocates, including the former surgeon general David Satcher, whose 2001 *Call to Action to Prevent and Decrease Overweight and Obesity* has become a rallying cry, we would do well to remember the public health prophets of an earlier time. One such was Dr. Joseph Goldberger.

Near Whitfield Road outside Jackson, Mississippi, is a rusted metal sign pockmarked by bullet holes that has been there since 1964. On it is the name Dr. Joseph Goldberger. And under that the following inscription: "Dr. Joseph Goldberger found the cause and cure for pellagra near here at the Rankin Farm of the Miss. State Penitentiary. His research identified the nutritional deficiencies which cause pellagra." That is not absolutely correct. Goldberger did not identify the nutritional deficiency—insufficient niacin—causing pellagra, the hideous disease that menaced Americans, especially southerners, in the early twentieth century. Nor, for that matter, did the feeding experiment he conducted using prisoner volunteers at Rankin conclude his investigation of this affliction, which caused suffering and death among hundreds of thousands. Further study would be required before Goldberger learned how to cure and prevent the disease. However, this is not the first time that history has taken second place to hagiography or hero worship. And the Mississippi Department of Archives and History should be congratulated for paying public homage to the medical scientist whose pioneering epidemiology and crusading spirit curbed the impact of a dietary disease known as the "scourge of the South." Goldberger's war on pellagra was just one chapter in a much larger saga of his crusade against disease, but it is the campaign for which he is most celebrated. And rightly so.

Standing next to the sign in the quiet of a sun-drenched field, one finds it difficult to imagine the suffering that pellagra once visited on Americans. Pellagra was first identified in early-eighteenth-century Spain and called *mal de la rosa*, because a hideous rash signaled its presence. It killed and caused chronic illness among populations in various parts of Europe, the Middle East, Africa, and Asia. Some of the most significant literature on the disease came from Italy, where it was called *mal del sole* because it seemed to peak with the coming of spring. The Italian physician Francesco Frapolli dubbed it "pellagra," the name referring to the "rough or dry skin" that became the basis for diagnosis and for distinguishing the disease from other conditions.

Not unlike AIDS in the 1980s, pellagra was at first a mystery disease in the United States. It came to national attention in the first decade of the twentieth century, a time, ironically, when Americans were living longer and healthier lives than ever before.[2] As epidemic diseases such as cholera, smallpox, yellow fever, and typhoid had become better understood and more effectively prevented through improved systems of public health, Americans began to look forward to longer, more productive lives. Then, beginning in the early years of the century, tens of thousands of Americans were getting sick, often very sick, from a disease that few recognized. Often as many as a third of those stricken died. No one knew what caused it, how it spread, or how to find the cure. It was characterized as the disease of the four *d*'s—dermatitis, diarrhea, dementia, and death. Those who survived it, and others who witnessed the suffering of those who did not, carried memories of the scourge with them for the rest of their lives.

One such victim was a physician who lived to deliver a paper before his medical colleagues in South Carolina in 1926. Dr. Baxter Haynes contracted the disease not long after he had lost a good deal of investment money during a slump in the price of cotton. His worry about his financial reversal led to insomnia and a loss of appetite. Over the next eight to ten weeks, he "lived on hot chocolate and soda crackers." Soon the symptoms began. He explained, "My mouth, tongue and throat became very much irritated and finally this marked condition extended all the way from my lips to the rectum, involving all the gastro-intestinal tract." Blood began to appear in his stool. His mouth became irritated, "so marked that my tongue became very red, thickened and stiff. My throat was so irritated finally, it became difficult to swallow even water." Haynes felt not himself in other ways too. "I became very melancholic, depressed and illusions were so marked that I wanted to live in exile . . . I was obsessed with the idea that all my friends had forsaken me and that I was fighting the battle all alone." In reality, never "were any more beautiful services showered upon an unfortunate person." But reality was deserting his fevered brain. None knew what had befallen him and how his patterns of life and diet had changed prior to the onset of the disease. On a trip to Florida, seeking to recover his health, Haynes noticed a red rash on the backs of his hands, the unmistakable sign of pellagra. Prepared to die, Haynes was taken by a physician friend to a hospital, where they changed his diet to one rich in animal protein. "My first meal was one-half glass of whole milk." Soon he was "forcing a little more each time until I finally reached one gallon each day and I kept it up for one year," even as he resumed a normal diet. Gradually his symptoms vanished, and he recovered. Not all did. As Haynes observed, in some people advanced pellagra resulted in lesions in their intestinal tract, causing them to die of infection before they could be treated with the diet that had saved Haynes's life: the Goldberger diet.[3]

Who was Joseph Goldberger? An elegant painting of him, handsome, wavy-haired, hawk-nosed, with piercing bespectacled eyes, stands watch next to the office of the director in Building 1 of the National Institutes of Health in Bethesda, Maryland. A photograph of him in the uniform of the U.S. Public Health Service peers at those who pass through the halls of the NIH's clinical center. Americans old enough to remember recall a World War II Liberty ship bearing his name. Those slightly younger read about his adventures in the 1943 issue of *Real Life Comics*, his caricature adorning the cover just below that of Supreme Allied Commander Dwight David Eisenhower's. In science classes of the era, *Hunger Fighters* (1928) by Paul De Kruif (author of *Microbe Hunters*) filled in the details for youngsters who aspired to life in a lab or healing the sick. Still others saw the movie: Metro-Goldwyn-Mayer released *A Way in the Wilderness*, a short subject on Goldberger's life and work, just before the war in 1940. Television's *Cavalcade of America* series brought Goldberger's story into millions of living rooms one spring evening in April 1954. American Jews, especially, claimed him as their hero, "a son of the Lower East Side in the South," as the Yiddish humorist Harry Golden, editor of the *Carolina Israelite*, depicted him.[4] Goldberger stirred Jewish ethnic pride with his accomplishments in the laboratory just as Hank Greenberg did on the baseball diamond. Who, then, was this man Goldberger, whom medical scientists revered and schoolchildren were taught to idolize? And just what was Goldberger's war all about?

Dr. Joseph Goldberger was a public health physician who, between 1902 and 1914, became an expert epidemic fighter. He battled yellow fever in Mexico, Puerto Rico, Mississippi, and Louisiana. He fought typhoid in Washington, D.C., dengue fever in Texas, and typhus in Mexico City. Always he ran risks. On three occasions, Goldberger contracted the disease he was studying: yellow fever, dengue fever, and typhus. Later he did research on measles and battled diphtheria. In 1914 Surgeon General Rupert Blue assigned him to supervise the federal government's pellagra investigation.

At a time when most physicians regarded germ theory as the causal explanation, or paradigm, for all forms of disease, Goldberger hypothesized that pellagra was triggered by a flawed diet. Thus his first battle was against a deficiency of understanding. Through a series of eating experiments in which he manipulated the diets of orphans, mental patients, and prisoners, Goldberger, with the assistance of Dr. George Wheeler, demonstrated that diet, not a pathogen, was at fault. Engaging in self-experimentation, he went so far as to place himself, his staff, and even his wife at risk to show the non-transmissibility of pellagra.

Only half the mystery was solved. Demonstrating that pellagra was not infectious and that prevention and recovery depended on diet did not explain why the disease was so prevalent in the South and why only certain southerners were stricken. One of the most important theaters of Goldberger's war was the southern mill town, where pellagra prevalence was often very high. In collaboration with the economist and statistician Edgar Sydenstricker, Goldberger designed and executed epidemiological studies of pathbreaking detail in order to comprehend a second deficiency—that of the diet. Their thoroughness remains a model of epidemiological inquiry. If pellagra was the result of diet and diet was determined at least in part by lifestyle, especially income and food accessibility, then it was the very lifestyle of some southerners that made them susceptible to pellagra. How did one change one's entire way of life? Not easily.

As late as the 1920s, many southerners remained adamantly opposed to Goldberger's findings. Accepting such a diagnosis seemed tantamount to confessing to a stubborn backwardness at just the moment when the South was scrambling for political parity and anxious to seem economically dynamic to outside investors.

Now Goldberger turned from detective to angry warrior for reform, battling yet another deficiency—poverty. He was outspoken in his criticism of the southern economy. As cotton prices plummeted in the early 1920s, after the boom of the war years, Goldberger blasted sharecropping as an agricultural system that impoverished families and discouraged growing diversified food crops. Likewise, he attacked mill owners for paying such low wages that workers were unable to afford a balanced diet. He condemned a system that had simply transplanted the poor from rented farm to mill floor, where the pressure of the work schedule no longer allowed the time to tend a modest garden and rock-bottom wages made keeping a family milk cow an unaffordable luxury. Arrayed against the South's political and business elite, Goldberger's thunder fell for the most part on deaf ears. Sound science and public health confronted, and nearly lost to, political bias.

Goldberger's war was fought over the suffering to which humanity had been subjected by a disease grounded in a particular way of life. It was not a multifaceted campaign for social change. With data that he collected and analyzed, Goldberger demonstrated repeatedly that women were more often pellagra's victims than men and that blacks had markedly higher rates of pellagra than whites. A man of his era, Joseph Goldberger did not campaign for women's rights or denounce the South's racial bigotry. Like many with progressive sensibilities, he focused more on class than race or gender in his social critique. He cared more about what was going on under the skin than about its hue. His own investigation had shown him time and again that poverty's face had many colors.

All wars have a personal dimension, and this one cannot be recounted without mention of Goldberger's life outside the laboratory, his humble origins as an immigrant, his marriage. Much of what we know of Goldberger's war is due to the extensive correspondence he maintained with his wife, Mary Farrar Goldberger. Goldberger was intelligent and idealistic, and he appreciated the same qualities in Mary. They were devoted to each other throughout their lives and wrote almost daily when he was away on assignment, as he so often was. In his letters Joseph shared with Mary every aspect of his scientific and professional life. However, his aspirations to perfection in science often conflicted with his duties as a husband and father. Their marriage was rocky in ways that epitomized an era when husbands routinely patronized their wives and expected absolute compliance to their own schedules and priorities. A southern woman from an affluent family where a successful and head-strong father ruled, Mary Goldberger was ready to suffer an opinionated husband, but she was ill prepared for the economic sacrifices and lone-liness that her marriage entailed.

Pellagra lingered long after Goldberger had taught the world how to cure and prevent it. The disease became part of the memory of life in the South borne by southerners white and black. In his autobiography the former president and Nobel laureate Jimmy Carter recalled how his mother had encouraged the Carters' tenant farmers—many of them black—to plant small gardens and shared the family vegetables with them, hoping to prevent pellagra. The black civil rights activist and co-founder of the National Organization for Women, Pauli Murray, de-scribed her grandmother's shock when she learned at age seventy-three that she had pellagra. Murray explains that for southern blacks "having pellagra was only a little less disgraceful than having 'the bad disease,' as folks called gonorrhea and syphilis." The reason for the shame, Murray says, is that "people thought it came from dirt and filth and that only ig-norant poverty-stricken country folks got it. They considered it highly contagious and avoided those who had it as they would lepers or small-pox cases. It was a great comedown for us." When a local physician felt inadequate to treat Murray's grandmother, a doctor from Chapel Hill corrected the misunderstanding of the disease and successfully treated her by prescribing a change in diet from "cornmeal and grits, fatback and molasses" to "plenty of red lean meat, fresh vegetables and milk." It was the Goldberger diet with some "Epsom salts baths and some pow-ders for the itching and burning" of her skin rash. Musicians, too, re-called pellagra as one of the reasons why southern life was so oppressive. On December 13, 1940, Count Basie recorded "It's the Same Old

South," and the crooner Jimmy Rushing conveyed the intended sense of mock nostalgia:

> It's the same old South.
> Let the Northerners keep Niagra,
> We'll stick to our Southern pellagra.
> It's the same old South.[5]

Today, at the dawn of the twenty-first century, when some Americans are obsessed with health foods and the effects of caffeine and nicotine on their bodies and others protest starvation in the nations of the Third World, Goldberger's war on pellagra is compellingly relevant. Although pellagra is virtually unheard of in the industrialized world, where diets often include foods containing niacin, it remains a periodic health menace in Africa. The Centers for Disease Control and Prevention reported that in 1990 Mozambican refugees seeking safety in neighboring Malawi suffered pellagra in the refugee camps because of a disruption of groundnut distribution. The groundnuts were a regular preventive of pellagra in Mozambique, and their unavailability produced a brief public health crisis as regular patterns of food consumption were disrupted by political turmoil. More recently, war-torn Angola experienced a pellagra outbreak when more than a hundred thousand people living in Bié Province fled the central high plateau and sought refuge in and around the town of Kuito. Between August 1999 and January 2000, 898 cases of clinically diagnosed pellagra were identified. Doctors Without Borders, the World Health Organization, and local groups that deal with such populations engage in constant surveillance to prevent such episodes.[6]

Dr. Joseph Goldberger was the medical pioneer who, more than any other scientist in the early twentieth century, made economic and social factors central to our understanding of disease causation and prevention. He was the epitome of public health physician as outspoken social critic. Goldberger's investigation of pellagra demonstrated how complex the solution to a medical mystery can be when it is grounded in a social critique of values, attitudes, and beliefs that contradict the victims' way of life and their society's most sacred assumptions.

This type of complexity continues to plague the medical profession today as it battles AIDS, tobacco addiction, the recurrence of tuberculosis, high blood pressure and coronary disorder, and a host of other "lifestyle" diseases. Goldberger's war never really ends. We just send in fresh troops.

ONE

"Another Poor Jew"

On May 7, 1916, Dr. Joseph Goldberger, surgeon in the U.S. Public Health Service, injected into his wife seven cubic centimeters of blood drawn from the general circulation of three patients suffering symptoms of advanced pellagra. Pellagra was a mysterious scourge that appeared frequently but not exclusively in the southern states in the early twentieth century. It was characterized as the disease of the four *d's*—dermatitis, diarrhea, dementia, and death. The dermatitis, which often appeared on the face, buttocks, genitals, arms, and legs, was symmetrical. When the rash spread across a victim's face, it looked like an angry red butterfly.[1] Mary Goldberger was one of six volunteers at the U.S. Pellagra Hospital at Spartanburg, South Carolina, helping her husband demonstrate that pellagra was not an infectious disease. Here and at other sites volunteers received the blood of pellagrins and were exposed to their nasopharyngeal secretions, scales, urine, and feces. Some of the volunteers, including Dr. Goldberger himself, would even ingest samples of the secretions.[2]

Mary was the lone female volunteer at Spartanburg in what Goldberger came to call his "filth parties." Dr. Goldberger had tried to dissuade her, even though he always referred to his research as their work. Now Mary Farrar Goldberger insisted that he live up to his word. If it was their work, then she must risk her life, too. Mary's insistence epitomized a marriage, then just ten years old, grounded in a high-minded idealism about the value of science and medicine in improving lives. And by 1916

13

Goldberger's bold research and experimentation, even at the risk of his own life and reputation, had become the hallmark of his medical career.

The Goldbergers' partnership in both marriage and science began as an unlikely one. Mary was the well-bred daughter of an eminent New Orleans attorney. Her southern family's roots reached back many generations in the United States. However, the most notable of her forebears had tried to shatter the American Republic. She was the grandniece of Confederate president Jefferson Davis. What Davis had once yearned to divide, the Goldberger family had traveled by land and sea to embrace.

Dr. Joseph Goldberger was an immigrant. His informal education began in Europe and continued in the streets of New York City. Joseph's father, Samuel Goldberger, was not a physician. Nor, for that matter, was he a grocer, at least not until he crossed the Atlantic Ocean. Before migrating to the United States and becoming the owner and proprietor of a mom-and-pop grocery store at 102 Pitt Street on Manhattan's Lower East Side, Samuel Goldberger had been in agriculture, a sheepherder and tenant who grazed his flock at the base of the Carpathian Mountains near the village of Giralt in the Austro-Hungarian Empire. It was a small town in the district of Saros situated where two rivers converge, the Topla and Radomka. According to census data, the population of the town in 1869 was 820, of which only a small portion were Jews. A synagogue and a *mikvah*, or ritual bath, did not exist in Giralt when the Goldbergers were there. What the locale did provide, however, was a rich agricultural area alternating between forests and meadows and extending into the eastern Carpathians. Wheat and potatoes were popular crops, and the vast areas were perfect for grazing beef cattle and sheep. When a plague swept through Samuel Goldberger's sheep herd, leaving him financially ruined, the family elected to follow the example of the children of his first marriage and immigrate to the United States. Max and Jacob, Joseph's older half brothers, then peddling in and around Cincinnati, dutifully sent funds for ship tickets so that their father and his new family could make the journey and begin a new life. Nine-year-old German-speaking Joseph, who was born on July 16, 1874, immigrated to America with his family.[3]

The forty-three-year-old former sheepherder and his thirty-seven-year-old wife, Sarah, and their six children departed Hamburg on a German ship, the SS *Lessing*, arriving in the port of New York on November 28, 1883, Thanksgiving Day in the United States.[4] It was more than a decade before the federal immigration depot on Ellis Island was built. Immigration was still a state matter. After passing quarantine inspection, ships continued up the bay to the New York emigration depot at Castle Garden, opened in 1855 and once a fortress that guarded the harbor. Resting on landfill at the tip of the battery, the gray thick-walled round stone structure was where the Goldbergers were inspected, counted, and processed. The family passed under the gaze of medical officers whose job it was to exclude any sick who had eluded the quarantine procedure. The ill were transferred to hospitals on Wards or Blackwells Island. The crippled and the blind were also detained unless a bond was posted by a friend or relative guaranteeing that they would not end up a public charge. None of the Goldbergers was detained. They were next led into the rotunda, "a large-roofed, circular space in the center of the Depot" measuring fifty thousand square feet. As the Goldbergers entered, they may have looked up and seen, seventy-five feet above them, the dome that permitted fresh air into the structure. Officers wearing the uniform of the State of New York processed their entry, asking them a list of questions about their past and their intended destination.[5] None was rejected. America beckoned young Joseph and his family.

The Goldbergers did not have an easy life after arrival. Samuel peddled until he accumulated sufficient capital to open his grocery store on the same street where his brother-in-law Solomon Goodman (Guttman) lived. A photograph shows a heavily bearded Samuel in a *kipah*, or yarmulke, the skullcap worn by Orthodox Jews to suggest the ever present demarcation between man and God. However, those who remembered the grocery proprietor recalled that the Orthodox Samuel sold ham, spaghetti, and sauerkraut, as well as matzo at Passover and a line of kosher goods to his multiethnic trade.[6] In the years ahead their Lower East Side neighborhood would become increasingly crowded. Between 1880 and the 1920s, 23.5 million immigrants arrived in the United States, many of them spending their first days, weeks, or months in New York. The arrival of more than a million Jews between 1880 and 1900, many of them from eastern Europe, suggests that the Goldbergers' choice to come to America was a popular one. Crammed into East Side tenements at night and sweatshops by day, Samuel Goldberger's customers were part of the fabled "huddled masses" that fueled American industry at the turn of the century.

The streets surrounding the Goldbergers' grocery store bore the tell-tale signs of urban congestion and inadequate public health and hygiene. Streets were dirty and littered with trash. Animal waste and the decaying carcass of a horse felled by summertime heat or an accident added to the pervasive smell of poverty. Exposure to epidemic diseases abroad and on the journey to the United States and overcrowded living and working conditions in the immigrant quarter made newcomers vulnerable to tuberculosis, the great killer of the nineteenth century, as well as a plethora of ailments and injuries. Poverty and disease were the newcomers' constant companions.

Running errands for his father, jogging up and down the steep staircases of East Side tenements, walking through their dark halls, lit often by a single gas lamp, to deliver groceries, the brown-haired, brown-eyed, bespectacled and lanky Joseph Goldberger grew up smelling the stench of urban poverty. Family legend has it that he was slower than his brothers in making deliveries because he found ready diversion in books that he stashed beneath his coat. In hallways or on tenement stoops young Joseph gave himself book breaks. Sometimes it was a schoolbook that captured his interest, but just as often it was a novel.

Like millions of other immigrant families, the Goldbergers saw education as the port of entry to American life, and when he was sixteen Joseph received a diploma from Male Grammar School no. 4. His next stop was the College of the City of New York. As far back as the 1820s the Workingmen's Party of New York included in its demands the education of all citizens until the age of eighteen. Some of the city's merchants, especially Townsend Harris, proposed creating a school with a curriculum that would democratize education even as it prepared workers' children in subjects relevant to business and commerce. Founded in 1847 as the Free Academy of New York, the institution conferred its first baccalaureate degrees in 1853. Renamed in 1866, City College was located at 17 Lexington Avenue near Twenty-third Street. It was neo-Gothic in style, a creation of the architect James Renwick, an elegant building with four turrets, a kind of castle in which immigrant youth would joust for admission to the American middle class. Because public funds supported the college, no qualified student need pay a cent of tuition.[7]

At the time Goldberger enrolled at City College, the curriculum combined practical and classical studies.[8] It was a five-year program, combining a sub-freshman year and four years of college. The five-year program was still in place in the 1890s, but the exigencies of a burgeoning industrial society persuaded City College educators to develop a "scientific course" of study for those with inclinations in that direction.

This included Joseph Goldberger, who wanted to become an engineer. The forty-fourth annual register of the College of the City of New York for 1892–1893 lists him as a member of the freshman class in the "scientific course."[9] Like his classmates, young Goldberger was being taught to write well, comprehend basic mathematics and science, and document what he observed by sketching it with his own hand, a skill necessary for students keeping laboratory notebooks.

During his years at City College, Goldberger divided his time between studying and helping out at his father's store. For him CCNY was a launching pad, though never the beloved institution that it was for many other immigrant youngsters. Goldberger was one of the many eastern Europeans who dropped out, but in his case not for lack of good grades or sustenance. Like many college freshmen, this City College student had an epiphany. He wanted to study the ultimate in engineering marvels, the human body. The account of the episode recollected by family members and likely told by Goldberger himself credits a neighborhood friend with introducing him to medicine and planting the idea of continuing his education at medical school.

The friend was Patrick J. Murray, the child of Irish immigrants. Young Murray, a student at Bellevue Hospital Medical College of New York University, eventually became the chief surgeon of the New York City Police Department.[10]

During Goldberger's freshman year at CCNY, Murray persuaded his friend to come with him to visit Bellevue and attend a lecture by Dr. Austin Flint Jr., who had a reputation for exciting his classes. His broad interests were also leading him to apply his physiological understanding to psychiatry, criminology, and forensic medicine.[11] It is no wonder, then, that Flint, possessed of a passion for how the body worked, would inspire Goldberger, a young man who studied engineering because he was fascinated with figuring out why things work as they do.

Following the lecture, Murray introduced the shy Goldberger to Flint.[12] Not long afterward, Goldberger broke the news to his parents: after only two years at CCNY he was heading three blocks north and four blocks east of City College to Bellevue to study medicine. Joseph's half brother Jacob, who had moved to Perth Amboy, New Jersey, in 1888, lent him funds to defray his expenses at Bellevue. Jacob could afford it. He and his brother Max had opened a successful "general grocery and provision store with a foreign exchange department" at the corner of Hilg Street and DeKalb Avenue. Three years later the brothers moved their business to a building they constructed at the corner of State and Washington Streets.[13] In return for the loan, Joseph worked summers at the Perth Amboy grocery. But come autumn, his attention turned to medicine.

Founded in 1861, Bellevue Hospital Medical College, at the foot of East Twenty-sixth Street, was only the second medical college in the United States to be part of a hospital.[14] When Goldberger matriculated in the autumn of 1892, the pattern of discrimination against applicants of eastern European Jewish background characteristic of the first forty years of the twentieth century was not firmly in place. Bright Jewish students were not welcomed with open arms everywhere, but those who demonstrated their qualifications and were able to pay their way could find their place in a class at Bellevue.[15]

In 1892 the thirty-year-old institution was financially strapped, but its faculty was excellent. During the years Goldberger attended, he was taught by talented physicians, including the Flints, father and son; Frederic Dennis, who taught surgery; William T. Lusk, professor of obstetrics and gynecology and clinical midwifery; Hermann M. Biggs, professor of materia medica, therapeutics, diseases of the nervous system, and clinical medicine (and director of the New York City Health Department Bacteriological Laboratory); Joseph D. Bryant, professor of anatomy and clinical surgery and associate professor of orthopedic surgery; and J. Frederick Erdman, chief of the clinic. And Bellevue's fees were modest. In 1895, the year Goldberger received his M.D., he paid forty dollars for the spring session plus a five-dollar matriculation fee and a ten-dollar dissection ticket. Both of the latter were good for the following winter as well. Overall expenses were about two hundred dollars per year.

Goldberger received an adequate education at Bellevue. It met contemporary standards, but classes were large and laboratory facilities were not uniformly adequate in all disciplines.[16] Seniors, including Goldberger, had to stand examination on the practice of medicine, surgery, obstetrics and gynecology, and pathology. The students were kept busy that spring because in addition to going to lectures and preparing for examinations, they attended anatomical demonstrations on Tuesdays, Wednesdays, Thursdays, and Fridays. Members of the senior class also received "practical instructions in Surgical Pathology and Operative Surgery on the cadaver and a course in Obstetrics on the cadaver and manikin." Included in the forty-dollar fee was admission to eighteen individual lectures, clinics, or demonstrations that "form a regular part of the curriculum." There were lectures on such topics as "Disease of the Rectum and Anus," "Dermatology," "Orthopedic Surgery," and "Diseases of the Throat and Nose and the Use of the Laryngoscope, with Practical Exercises for the Senior Class Divided into Sections of Four."[17] At the end of the 1895 spring session, Goldberger graduated with a doctoral degree in medicine.

At twenty years old, Goldberger was over six feet tall. His brown wavy hair, brown eyes, and hooked nose, upon which his rimless eyeglasses rested, gave him a decidedly Jewish appearance. Months before his twenty-first birthday, he held an M.D., a credential he could not legally use until his July birthday had passed. His hard work and intelligence were in evidence when he scored highest on the hospital examinations. Now he had to sharpen his clinical skills on the wards. Two years later, on October 1, 1897, he completed his internship at Bellevue Hospital. The newly minted M.D. needed only patients to get his career off the ground, and so, setting up an office in his parents' new East Seventy-second Street apartment, the young physician hung out his shingle. After three months of trying this arrangement, Goldberger had earned only $17.50. At the advice of a senior colleague, Dr. Henry Frauenthal, who had been a consulting orthopedist at Bellevue during Goldberger's internship, Goldberger decided to relocate to a smaller city, where there would be less competition from other physicians. He chose Wilkes-

Barre, Pennsylvania, opening a small office on South Washington Street.[18]

On the eastern shore of the Susquehanna River, Wilkes-Barre was a bustling small city with shop-lined streets and a population that at the end of the 1890s was climbing toward 55,000. With 165,000 people in the small towns surrounding the city, economic opportunities were ample. Several banks were kept busy with loan applications from businessmen who realized the city's commercial and industrial potential. The factories included the largest wire-rope works in the state and the largest axle works in the country. There were silk factories and ironworks, and the city could claim it was the "centre of the lace curtain industry" at a time when having lace curtains in the windows was a hallmark of middle-class living.

Wilkes-Barre's middle class demanded and got clean water from the Spring Brook Water Supply Company and steam-heat pipes beneath the principal streets. The sanitary engineer George Edwin Waring had been hired to arrange proper drainage. A locally produced sketch could justly claim that "the city death rate is remarkably low, the city enjoying exceptional immunity from diseases of an epidemic character." Goldberger's new home took pride in its physical beauty as well as its increasing wealth and refinement. When Goldberger could break away from his office, he might go for a stroll in Wilkes-Barre's mile-long natural park along the banks of the Susquehanna River or along the boulevard that bordered the river below the city. In his spare time he could read books borrowed from the forty-thousand-volume Osterhout Library or exercise at the YMCA.[19]

Although Wilkes-Barre was prosperous, not everyone shared equally in the prosperity. Approximately a quarter of the city's population was foreign-born, and many of the men worked in mines. The town was located in the heart of the anthracite coal region of Pennsylvania. Miners often suffered accidents and the respiratory ailments common among those who spent their days breathing coal dust into their lungs. Low wages in the mines in the years before thorough unionization left miners and their families vulnerable. Poor diets and inadequate preventive care took their toll and offered Goldberger an opportunity to see a type of poverty different from that which he had witnessed on the Lower East Side of New York.

Goldberger's years in Wilkes-Barre were lonely, made bearable by a close friendship with a local chemist, William Dean. Dean, the city water inspector and a chemistry teacher at the Harry Hillman Academy, encouraged the young physician to join the Luzerne County Medical Society, where, before becoming a dues-paying member, Goldberger read and published his first scholarly papers. On the evening of December 21, 1898, Goldberger addressed his colleagues on "Alcoholism." He began by noting that his presentation was based largely on his "experience with these cases in the reception room and alcoholic wards of Bellevue Hospital," where "not less than 2,000 patients" were treated annually. He denounced the cures for the alcoholic habit offered by many sanatoriums as "worthless." Instead, he defined the alcoholic as a "sick man" who must be "quarantined" in a sanatorium to separate him from the unhealthy circumstances of his life, fed healthy food, and placed in "hygienic surroundings, removed from temptation and his old associates." As he would years later when studying pellagra, Goldberger saw alcoholism in its relationship to a larger set of social circumstances.[20]

His own circumstances were improving financially. His first year in Wilkes-Barre yielded fees in the neighborhood of six hundred dollars, a rather modest sum. However, in the second year he collected almost double that amount and was finally able to begin paying off his debts to Jacob and sending some money to his parents. Emotional circumstances were another matter. Goldberger's presentation of two papers during his first year of membership in the Luzerne County Medical Society suggests that he found being a family doctor in a small city intellectually unfulfilling. His son Joseph H. Goldberger, also a physician, recalled his father's reminiscing that he had always been confused about the business end of being a doctor in private practice and never knew quite what to charge.[21] Temperamentally he was also ill suited to running a small professional office. Goldberger's restlessness, as well as his patriotism, manifested itself in his decision to join the U.S. Navy at the outbreak of the Spanish-American War.

On February 15, 1898, the USS *Maine* was blown up in Havana harbor. Several days after the declaration of war, young Dr. Goldberger filed an application for the Navy Medical Corps. He intended to don the uniform of a naval officer. Goldberger's interest in the Navy was long-standing—his close friends had briefly dubbed him "Sailor Joe"—and he was doubtless deeply disappointed when he received a mimeo-graphed form letter dated May 3 from William K. Van Reypen, surgeon general of the Navy, telling him that the Navy "appreciates your patriotic action and has placed your application on file for due consideration, should your services be required." The Navy increased the size of its force from 12,500 to 24,123 after the outbreak of war, but Goldberger never received a call. Was the young eager physician's recognizably Jew-ish last name the reason for the quick rejection? Although the American armed forces had no official policy of anti-Semitism and many Jews had served with distinction in the Civil War in Union and Confederate armies, Jews in the military faced much informal anti-Semitism in the late nineteenth and early twentieth centuries. Some anti-Semites, such as the Cornell historian Goldwin Smith, alleged that Jewish tribalism and Jews' migration from country to country left them incapable of being patriotic. Others alleged that Jews despised physical labor and therefore would not undertake the rigors of military life. There were allegations and official denials that Jewish applicants to West Point and Annapolis were rejected on religious grounds. Even if there were no of-ficial policies, Jews were often not welcomed as equals in the military. At the U.S. Naval Academy in Annapolis, according to one scholar, "Jews were harassed, excluded, and psychologically ostracized." As late as the 1920s the editors of the Naval Academy yearbook humiliated a Jewish midshipman who ranked second academically by publishing his picture on a perforated page so it could be neatly purged without damaging the rest of the book.[22]

Whatever the reason for the Navy's rejecting Goldberger before ex-amination, he remained committed to leaving Wilkes-Barre. When his friend Dean sent him a clipping about the U.S. Marine Hospital Service (USMHS; the name was changed to the U.S. Public Health and Marine Hospital Service in 1902, and to the U.S. Public Health Service in 1912) from The Journal of the American Medical Association, Goldberger did not waver for long. In June 1899, the USMHS summoned him to New

York City for a week of written examinations, followed by an oral examination on June 27, 1899. The following week, those who passed were taken to a local hospital, where they were required to examine and diagnose patients and to identify bacteria and parasites under a microscope. It was a grueling two weeks. Of the nineteen who came before the board of examiners in New York that year, eight were commissioned assistant surgeons, including Joseph Goldberger. A letter dated July 18, 1899, informed him, "Sir . . . at the recent examination of candidates for appointment as assistant surgeon of this Service, requiring a minimum of 80 percentum to be successful, your general average was 82.22 and your relative standing in the class was No. 4." [23] Goldberger was now commissioned an assistant surgeon at an annual salary of sixteen hundred dollars. He had a new career and a steady, if modest, salary.

Goldberger's first post would be New York. With the passage of the Immigration Act of March 3, 1891, all immigrants were required to undergo individual inspection by a physician, and the USMHS was ordered to cooperate with the Immigration Bureau. Goldberger's assignment was a common one, given to most newly minted USMHS officers to help hone their diagnostic skills. Immigrants passed in a line before the vigilant gaze of the physicians. The USMHS's examination could provide little more than a snapshot diagnosis. However, in an era when sophisticated diagnostic technology was still limited and personal observation was a highly regarded method of diagnosis, the uniformed federal physicians took great pride in their ability to spot illness or disability quickly and with only modest clues.[24] Goldberger's keen eye and the attentiveness he developed in the port of New York would be critical years later when he observed pellagrins in orphanages, asylums, and prisons.

On April 24, 1900, Goldberger was reassigned by Surgeon General Walter Wyman to the Reedy Island Quarantine Station at Port Penn, Delaware, the station responsible for inspecting ships seeking entry to the port of Philadelphia. Far fewer immigrants entered the United States through Philadelphia than through New York, and Reedy Island inspectors were primarily concerned with descending into the holds of cargo ships to kill rats and mosquitoes that could be transmitting diseases to humans. Typical was the written order that Goldberger received dated June 6, 1900. He was sent to board and inspect a small vessel, the

Bessie Markham. His orders were precise: "You will see that any dead vermin found in the vessel are properly disposed of by burning, and will at the same time note the method of disposal and treatment of the cargo with a view to making a report upon the same to this office." The order was signed by "T. F. Richardson, Assistant Surgeon, USMHS, in command."[25]

A few years older than Goldberger, Thomas Farrar Richardson was not only in command of the Reedy Island Quarantine Station; he was already quite expert in quarantine practice. He taught Goldberger much about how to quickly recognize signs of typhus, plague, cholera, and smallpox. Both tireless workers and precise in their habits, Richardson and Goldberger became fast friends, though they could not have been more different in their backgrounds. Richardson, called by friends and relatives by his middle name, Farrar, was from a wealthy and socially prominent southern family. His uncle Edgar Howard Farrar was one of the South's foremost corporation lawyers.[26] Goldberger's debt to Farrar grew, especially when he was introduced to Farrar's seventeen-year-old cousin, Mary, who came to Reedy Island for a visit.

Goldberger and Mary began to correspond casually. However, their courtship formally began years later, in the autumn of 1905. They became reacquainted after a church service on Thanksgiving Day held to celebrate the end of a yellow fever epidemic that had brought Goldberger to New Orleans, where Mary lived. All the members of the U.S. Public Health and Marine Hospital Service sent to battle the epidemic had been invited to attend the service. Neither Mary nor Joseph knew that the other would be there that day. When they met afterward, Mary invited Joseph back to her home for a holiday dinner. He readily accepted. Thanksgivings seemed to mark new beginnings.

When Dr. Joseph Goldberger left church with twenty-four-year-old Mary Humphreys Farrar on his arm that Thanksgiving Day in 1905, he began an encounter with a social world in which he was an alien for more reasons than his place of birth. In the months to come, he would find himself under a microscope as he pursued the woman he loved. He would be scrutinized by her family with as much care as he studied the microorganisms on his laboratory slides. However, even his eventual acceptance by Mary's family hardly concluded this season of examination.

The rich correspondence between Goldberger and his fiancée reveals that in the months before they wed, Joseph and Mary subjected themselves to an intense period of self-exploration. Two bright and highly literate individuals, Mary and Joseph were also seekers, exchanging ideas on religion and spirituality as they struggled to reconcile their very different backgrounds.

Mary Humphreys Farrar was born in New Orleans in 1881. She was the second of ten children, and the first of seven daughters, born to Edgar Howard Farrar and Lucinda Davis Stamps. It was on her mother's side that Mary was related to Confederate president Jefferson Davis. During an era when university degrees were thought unimportant for well-bred young southern ladies, Mary attended but did not graduate from Newcomb College, the sister school of Tulane University.[27] Some cultivation and a lively personality were advantageous, especially if one's family possessed an impressive pedigree and wealth. Mary's family had both. Moreover, she was attractive. Her dark eyes, which required spectacles, her brown hair, and her warm smile made her a pretty woman, though hardly a southern belle of legendary beauty. What seems to have drawn Joseph to Mary was her intelligence and sweet disposition. Her cousin described her as "the most guileless, the purest-minded girl that I know."[28] With Mary, Joseph's shyness dissipated; he could discuss anything with her and usually did. That Thanksgiving in 1905, however, Goldberger hardly said a word to Mary, being, instead, mesmerized by her father.

Mary's father was a pillar of the New Orleans community and a formidable personage. The scion of notable forebears, Edgar Farrar spent much of his youth in the Mississippi Delta, where his father had been born. He was educated in Baton Rouge, Louisiana, receiving his primary education at Magruder's School, and, in the fashion of the South's brightest sons, attended Thomas Jefferson's University of Virginia, graduating with his master's degree in 1871 at the age of twenty-two. That same year he studied law briefly at the old University of Louisiana, but after a quarrel with his professors Farrar applied directly to the state bar examining committee and petitioned for an examination, which he passed. In July 1872 he was admitted to the bar by the Supreme Court of Louisiana.[29]

What was most memorable about Edgar Farrar to those who saw him arguing in court or addressing a public meeting in his prime was not his dark penetrating eyes beneath arched eyebrows or his bald dome-shaped head or even his handlebar mustache. It was his voice and his manner. He was remembered by "the explosive quality of his speech." He put his rhetorical skills to the test on public issues about which he felt especially passionate, including better education, improved systems of drainage and sewage for his beloved city of New Orleans, and the supremacy of state over federal jurisdiction in matters of quarantine to preserve the public's health, especially during the yellow fever epidemics that frequently menaced the South. His emphatic, pugnacious style left one observer with the impression that "sooner or later he would lay violent hands on somebody or some thing, and while he presented his case at the bar in a more moderate fashion, it was always within the possibilities that something would happen."[30]

Whether it was to make amends for having been less than completely attentive to Mary at Thanksgiving dinner, as she later claimed, or simply because he was smitten with her and could not bear to miss an opportunity to see her, Joseph Goldberger sought to make the most of the three weeks he had left in New Orleans before returning to Washington. He and Mary attended the French Opera House, seeing *La Vie de Bohème*—unchaperoned, a rather bold gesture for a young lady of Mary's background. They were increasingly inseparable. Concerts, theater performances, even a trip to his laboratory in New Orleans filled the weeks. In mid-December 1905, they shared their first kiss. Then they decided to get engaged to be married. Mary recalled that *she* made the proposal of marriage one afternoon, during a boat trip on a park lake.[31]

Neither of their families was enthusiastic.

Samuel and Sarah Goldberger were shocked and deeply hurt by their son's decision to marry a non-Jew. Interfaith marriages between Jews and Gentiles were still rare, and while in the decades to come popular plays such as *Abie's Irish Rose* made light of interfaith and interethnic coupling, Orthodox parents were known to perform mourning rituals, to sit shivah for a child who married a Gentile, as if the child were dead.[32]

Others applauded intermarriage, seeing it as the next stop on the road to assimilation. For alien and American alike it was an evocative topic that found a ready audience in theaters. On the stage, Israel Zangwill's play *The Melting Pot* opened in 1908 at the Columbia Theater in Washington, D.C., to President Theodore Roosevelt's ardent applause. However, the Jewish press, especially the Yiddish-language press, was offended and said so. Was sacrificing one's identity on the altar of assimilation the only way to gain acceptance in the United States?

Goldberger's parents had lived and raised their children as observant Jews. They did not understand why their beloved Joseph was rejecting all that they had taught him to embrace. Joseph understood their confusion. However, he was determined to marry Mary. Abandoning a faith that he found overly rigid and a threat to his happiness did not seem a barrier. In a letter to his brother Leo, the rational, analytic physician offered an analysis of the situation almost clinical in tone. As for Mary's worthiness to be his wife, there was no doubt; "in fact the real question is whether I'm worthy of her." As for the question most troubling his parents, Mary's not being a "Jewess," the young doctor offered an answer similar to that put forth by many young Jews whose American educations had loosened their bonds to religious orthodoxy in favor of a broader humanism. Most evident to Goldberger was what they held in common and not what differentiated them: "Although Mary was brought up as a Christian, and I as a Jew, our religious beliefs are essentially identical. In other words, she is as much a Jewess as I'm a Jew, and I am as much a Christian, as is she."[33] He could see no reasonable bar to their marrying each other.

Joseph told Leo emphatically that he would not take their father's suggestion to reconsider his marriage plans and he was not persuaded by the idea that he was setting a bad example for his siblings. The loving son was firm in his loyalty to his beloved. Unswayed by his parents' hurt, he concluded, "Again, I must repeat that I am exceedingly sorry that Mother and Father are grieved, but it is a matter in which I am the one most vitally and primarily involved, and I feel that I must follow my own judgment in the matter."[34]

Seven days later, Joseph asked Leo, an attorney, for more than moral support. Well before his wedding day, he requested that Leo draft a will for him, which stipulated, "First, in case of my death all my property to go to my wife, Mary Humphreys. Second, that my body be cremated and my ashes scattered in some field, i.e., not buried in any cemetery or like place. Third, that my wife be sole executrix, without bond." He concluded in German, "Sonst geht's gut" [Otherwise all's well], and finally, "Mary sends her love."[35] Rejecting burial in sacred ground marked Goldberger's profoundest rejection of traditional Judaism. Manner of burial is so important to Jews that colonial settlers in New Amsterdam had purchased land for a cemetery before they built a synagogue. Cremation, acceptable among some Reform Jews, was still not widely practiced in 1906. However, many liberal-minded Christians and Jews were turning to cremation as a way of expressing their belief that the funeral rituals of their faiths perpetuated a mythology about an eternal life that they could no longer respect.

Equally perturbed by the young couple's decision to marry was the Farrar family, especially the bride's father. Edgar Farrar, although a fair man of liberal temperament, was as determined as the Goldbergers to discourage the match. He had not discouraged the friendship of the young physician and his daughter, but marriage involved complications. It was not just that Goldberger was Jewish, which may have been perceived as awkward, although Farrar, who had a Jewish law partner, appears not to have been especially anti-Semitic. The problem was more complex than that. What was the young man's social background? What were his prospects? Was Mary ready to live with the social ostracism she might well suffer because she had married beneath her? There were always the snide remarks and social slights from which even he, influential as he was in the New Orleans community, could not protect her. Surely she and her husband would not be welcomed in either the posh drawing rooms or the oak-walled clubs in which Farrar and his wife felt at ease.

To gather ammunition with which to dissuade Mary, or perhaps to allay his fears that his daughter had involved herself with a social-climbing ne'er-do-well, Farrar launched an investigation of Dr. Joseph Goldberger. The day after Christmas, he went to his office at the Hibernia Bank Building in New Orleans, sat down at his desk, and penned a series of letters to those who might be able to assess Goldberger. He was not vague about his reasons for wanting to know. He intended to probe the past of his daughter's fiancé.

One of the first responses came on Treasury Department letterhead.

Many decades before the Department of Health and Human Services was created, the U.S. Public Health and Marine Hospital Service (the USMHS's name beginning in 1902) was located in the Treasury Department. The surgeon general of the United States, Dr. Walter Wyman, replied to Farrar's query about the "personal character and standing in the Public Health and Marine Hospital Service of Dr. Joseph Goldberger." After giving Farrar a brief professional history of Goldberger, including his most recent promotion to passed assistant surgeon in 1904, Wyman went on to offer an assessment: "In all the time that Dr. Goldberger has been connected with this Service he has commended himself very highly, both to those under whom he has immediately served and to the Bureau. He is considered one of the most promising of the young men connected with the Hygienic Laboratory of the Service." Of course Goldberger had been more than a bench scientist at the Hygienic Laboratory. By the time he married Mary, he had served some time battling yellow fever in the field, where a man's intelligence and personal courage were on the line. How had the young man done? Wyman thought just fine: "In a number of situations in epidemic duty which have called for great tact and firmness he has displayed both. I have never heard the slightest unfavorable opinion as to his character. On the contrary, in general reputation, both personal and professional, he stands high."[36]

Another member of the U.S. Public Health and Marine Hospital Service to whom Farrar addressed a letter was his physician nephew, Thomas Farrar Richardson, who had supervised Goldberger's work in Delaware and was responsible for the couple's meeting in the first place. Richardson, now chief medical officer for the service in the port of Savannah, wrote not only to his uncle but also to his friend, a letter addressed "My dear Goldberger." Writing in the hearty, masculine, forthright language of the day, Richardson did not waste a pen stroke in letting his former subordinate know how he felt: "I congratulate you from my heart, old man, & I trust that everything may turn out as you desire." Then, addressing the matter of Farrar's inquiry a bit more directly but still somewhat obliquely, Richardson added, "It has given me a great deal of pleasure to vouch for you in every way to her father, because I trust you and know that you are worthy of her, and would make her the kind of husband that she deserves." In his letter to his "dear Uncle Ned," Richardson got right to the point: "I know Goldberger intimately, & have nothing but the highest praise for him. He is as nearly 'sans peur et sans reproche' [brave and reliable] as any man that I have ever known. His habits, his character, his reputation, his standing in the service are all excellent." As for his friend's prospects, Richardson's words echoed those of the surgeon general: "He is pretty generally regarded as one of the coming men in the Marine-Hospital Service." His overall assessment was without qualification: "I, personally, should be proud to have him in the family."[37]

An old adage goes that in the North they ask you what you do, but in the South they ask you who your people are. Farrar was interested not just in Goldberger. He wanted to know about the entire Goldberger family. To find out about the clan, he secured the assistance of another attorney, a New York acquaintance named Charles Levy.

In February 1906, Charles Levy took the train from New York's Pennsylvania Station to Perth Amboy, New Jersey, where Goldberger's parents now resided, and spent the entire day there. He informed Farrar that when he arrived, he "called on the banks" and had "an extensive conversation" with bank officers. He explained to Farrar, "I found that the Doctor has a brother who is a lawyer [Leo], and two half brothers, one a grocery merchant [Max], and the other a private banker and steamship agent [Jacob]. The Banks all consider them among the best Jewish people of that town, and all of them enjoy the highest credit. They [the bankers] also told me that they [the Goldbergers] are the leaders and are at the head of all Jewish affairs."[38]

Levy's next stop after the banks was the rabbi's office at Temple Beth Mordecai, a congregation founded in Perth Amboy in 1897. It is unclear from Levy's letter whether he was honest with Rabbi Ellas Solomon and explained that he was checking to see if Goldberger's background gave him the credentials for an intermarriage with a well-off Episcopalian southern bride. It is unlikely. According to Levy, the rabbi thought the family to be "of the best and . . . in good circumstances, and the leaders of his faith and of his Congregation."[39]

Finished with the rabbi, Levy had yet another stop on his list. He walked into the office of "the brother 'Lawyer Goldberger' and had quite an extensive conversation with him." Whatever his thoughts about Joseph, Levy came away from Leo's office "very much impressed with the frankness of the young man." The comment suggests that Leo confided in Levy the family's opposition to the marriage. Levy concluded nevertheless, "All of my inquiries in every direction have been highly satisfactory."[40]

What appears to have impressed Levy the most about the Goldbergers is that they were exactly as Joseph had characterized them to Mary and her father. A somewhat sympathetic-sounding Levy summarized the family in a final paragraph of his report: "These people . . . came over to this country as poor people, all they have to-day is due to their energy and industry. The father realizing the advantages of an education spent his money liberally towards educating his children. They are not poor people, nor are they rich people, they are people in moderate circumstances, honest, intelligent, and frugal, and enjoy the confidence and respect of the Community in which they live."[41] Written with such empathy, Levy's letter sounds like the prototypical Jewish immigrant story, a tale for which he had much feeling—for it was quite likely in some measure his own.

While Edgar Farrar examined Dr. Joseph Goldberger's past, his daughter and her beau carried on a romantic correspondence, he from his apartment in Washington and she from her home in New Orleans. Between the time of their engagement in December 1905 and their wedding in April 1906, Joseph and Mary wrote many letters. Almost nightly they sat at their desks hundreds of miles apart and re-pledged their love to each other. However, their courtship letters were more than expressions of affection. With pens, stationery, and postage stamps they continued to get to know each other.

From afar Joseph and Mary discussed the issues that all young couples must confront before they take wedding vows. First and foremost was their love for each other. Their daily confessions of affection, often rather syrupy, sustained them emotionally. But differences of class, education, and religion required more than flowery phrases if they really hoped to understand each other by the time of their wedding. They had spent so little time together talking. The absence of telephones and the requirement of committing themselves to paper made their observations more thoughtful and coherent than those of later generations, whose phone chatter might more readily suffer from infelicities of phrase or imprecision of thought. Joseph and Mary took great care in making themselves understood. After all, they were preparing for the rest of their lives.

However confident Goldberger might have been of his ability to be a good physician and a clever scientist, he had many insecurities. These insecurities emerged in his correspondence with Mary in the winter and early spring of 1906. One of his greatest concerns was that her marriage to him would mean a step down in lifestyle because of his modest circumstances. He asked her:

> Do you realize fully all that it means to be the wife of a _poor_ man? You are not rich, you say, but nevertheless almost every desire that you may have may be fulfilled. This will not be so, can not be so, when you are my wife. You will have to do without a great many pleasant things, deny yourself a great many things that perhaps appear to you now as essentials. I wonder whether you have given this any thought? Whether you quite realize all, Mary.

Chagrined at his own somber and preachy tone, Goldberger would soften, seeking reassurance even as he reassured himself: "In any event one thing is certain: Mary loves Joseph and Joseph loves Mary with all his soul. Good night Mary, Beloved. Good night and God guard you. 'Kiss me good-night' dear. Love Joseph." Mary not only reassured him of her love but very likely scolded him for his self-pity, because his very next letter, gushing with gratitude and affection, includes an apology for sounding as if he doubted her steadfastness in the face of his modest means.[42]

Aside from conveying to her that they would not be rich, Goldberger wanted Mary to understand that his work was very important to him and that he wanted to include her in it. Unlike many husbands, Goldberger took pride in his and Mary's discussions of his work. Moreover, he knew that Mary was not frightened or threatened by his intelligence and commitment. In his turn, Goldberger valued her opinion as well as her company. The young couple was in agreement. Work was important, and they would discuss it as equals. He would tell her everything on his mind, and she would offer her opinion of all he said.[43]

If Mary was to be his partner in science, at least emotionally, they must agree on the role of science and religion. Their religious differences rubbed raw the feelings of their loved ones in Perth Amboy and New Orleans. But how did the couple reconcile the differences of faith that so irritated those around them?

In their correspondence dealing with religion, Joseph and Mary shared their disdain for religious dogma. They had been engaged barely a month when he began to send her his own thoughts on the subject and items to read about religion.

Goldberger, a man of science and the son of Orthodox Jews, was a seeker of spiritual wisdom. The ways of his forefathers seemed parochial, antiquated, and inconsistent with his commitment to scientific inquiry and empiricism. And yet, like many physicians and scientists, Goldberger found the wonders he uncovered beneath his microscope too marvelous to be the products of chance. He was no atheist, and he never denied or renounced his Jewish heritage. He was a young well-educated Jew, a man of science and medicine, seeking to connect his intellect with his spirituality. He was seeking a rational religion.

Goldberger was not alone among young Jews in his search for a rational religion. The Reform Jewish tradition in the United States, begun by German Jews, had roots stretching back to the mid-nineteenth century. These Jews hoped to turn Judaism away from rituals and traditions that seemed narrow and primitive while retaining the essence of Judaism as a religion grounded in the God of the Torah. However, even some Reform Jews found their faith insufficiently rational and humanistic. In 1885 at a Pittsburgh convention, these Jews had adopted a platform that, in the words of one scholar, "crystallized the fundamental theological, religious, and moral beliefs of contemporary American Reform Judaism." The words of the platform affirmed belief in a single God, the immortality of the soul, and a morality grounded in the Mosaic code. One Reform Jew in St. Louis wrote to his rabbi asking without tongue in cheek, "Why not take a heroic step and become Unitarians?"[44] It was not entirely a foolish question.

Unitarians, Christians who denied the doctrine of the Trinity, had been a voice within organized Christianity since the Protestant Reformation. Drawing on converts from faiths with more rigid dogmas, they subscribed to a simple covenant: "In the love of truth, and in the spirit of Jesus, we unite for worship of God and in the service of man."[45]

Despite the doctrine's appeal to many Reform Jews who were aware that a merger with Unitarians would smooth the road to social assimilation, differences were too great ever to see it seriously attempted. Jewishness was more than a religious position; it was an ethnic identity. Christian anti-Semitism abroad and at home, even in liberal Christian circles, made a union with Christians impossible. Still, some Jews were drawn to Unitarianism. Some converted. Others had an intellectual flirtation with it for a time, among them Joseph Goldberger.

There is no evidence that Goldberger ever converted to Unitarianism. When he died in 1929, a Reform rabbi officiated at his memorial service. However, his correspondence with Mary prior to their marriage makes clear that he was veering away from Judaism and found Unitarianism especially attractive. Nor was he alone in the family. In 1906 his brother Herman, with whom he was especially close, sent him a copy of the *Christian Register*, a Unitarian publication. After reading it, Joseph forwarded it to Mary along with a letter that encouraged her to read it, saying, "There are some good things in it." He enjoyed an article on Benjamin Franklin and another titled "A Life of Pleasure." However, he was emphatic in his dislike of an article titled "The Fatherhood of God" by Charles E. St. John. Goldberger explained his negative reaction: "I confess I do not see why the writer states so positively that 'all mankind must come to an agreement upon the conception of God as love.'" Convinced of human beings' contentiousness in matters spiritual, Goldberger told his fiancée, "For my part I do not believe that there will ever be a time when 'all mankind' will ever 'come to an agreement upon *any* conception of God.'" He observed, "You are a Christian but I who think precisely as you do am not for the simple reason that my parents are Jews. To be a Christian I must avow a belief in a myth which you discard as no more than a myth—beautiful and useful though it may be. I think it all very curious, almost ludicrously ridiculous."[46]

Goldberger saved his praise for John Fiske, a philosopher and historian whom practitioners of both professions derided but who became one of the most popular and prolific writers and lecturers of the late nineteenth and early twentieth centuries. Fiske made comprehensible the ideas of Charles Darwin and Herbert Spencer at a time when evolution was much contested from lectern and pulpit in the United States. When Goldberger pulled copies of Fiske's books off his shelf, he was especially attracted to the erudite arguments rejecting the supernatural component of the Judeo-Christian faiths. Works with titles such as *Through Nature to God, The Idea of God as Affected by Modern Knowledge*, and the multivolume *Outlines of Cosmic Philosophy* confirmed Goldberger's own beliefs, which reconciled a concept of God with rational inquiry and scientific discovery.

He encouraged Mary to enter into a dialogue with him about the articles in the *Register*: "Let me have your thoughts and ideas Mary; I'd like to compare notes and be corrected where you think I need it. If you write me any comments on anything in the paper, return it to me so that I may see the subject of your remarks."[47]

As for his own ideas on God and religion, Goldberger began by observing the lack of agreement among existing denominations generally. Proceeding as a scientist in search of the single correct answer, he could not accept multiple roads to eternal truths, concluding, "They cannot all be right." And yet as he examined these competing religious traditions, they seemed to him to have "one common root idea—One God—'Hear O Israel! The Lord Thy God the Lord is One!'" Without identifying the source, Goldberger wrote to his Episcopalian fiancée the words of the Shema Yisrael, Judaism's most sacred words, the first words learned by every child in religious school and the basic affirmation of faith in one God. He told her, "Essentially they all mean this and it's all I care anything about. This is monotheism; it is Unitarianism."[48]

Goldberger was seeking a religion that offered him God without dogma. He called his conception of God "Infinite Intelligence." He explained, "I like to think of God as an infinite intelligence immanent in all things, in all nature and manifesting Himself (if I may personify this 'Infinite Intelligence' as a male—there is this unavoidable contamination of language) most palpably to our more or less dull perceptions in the workings of what are called natural laws." Goldberger regarded these natural laws, his "signs of the Infinite Intelligence," as at work in "everything from the smallest particle up to the so called noblest work of God—man." What he rejected was the notion of a personal God, noting that "'the gentle rain from heaven' falls alike upon sinner and saint." He rejected the notion of a God who "loves me in the sense that a parent loves a child."[49]

Goldberger concluded his exposition of the divine by describing the "true priest" of his faith. It was "the patient, open-minded, honest worker in science. It is the latter who is striving with infinite pains to learn some thing." Goldberger cast scientists such as himself as the "priests" of the "Infinite Intelligence."[50]

On a Sunday in late January, Mary wrote him a letter from the New Abita Springs Hotel in Abita Springs, Louisiana, where she had gone to relax, recover from a minor illness, and enjoy the sulfur baths that so many believed had health-giving properties. The spirited Mary, raised by her parents in the Episcopal Church and about to be married by her family's minister, did not hesitate to proclaim her anticlericalism. She confessed, "I have all my life wanted to behead the so called Preachers of the Word who see the hand of God in the most outrageous piece of human negligence." And yet Mary did believe in something beyond the rational, explaining, "Dim, half conscious, futile as this perception may be there is yet omnipresent the virile evidence of things not seen. The more we learn, the more we discover, the more conscious we become of this 'Infinite Intelligence.'" However, Mary rejected attributing the good and the bad that happened to people to this Infinite Intelligence. Instead, she argued that "the more perfectly developed mind reasons the cause of the wrong, rights it if he can, and then bows his head in true humility of spirit before the omniscient."[51]

Agreeing with his sentiments in an earlier letter, she exclaimed, "Yes, my Darling, the true seekers after God are those—as you so beautifully put it—those—'the patient, open minded, honest workers in science.'" She credited her fiancé with helping her to complete a spiritual awakening that had begun when she realized that her "girlhood enthusiasms and 'spasms' of religious feeling were nearly all pure emotion of the most hysterical type." Mary told Joseph that his views on the Infinite Intelligence had caused her own to take form, to crystallize. She concluded with a vision of them on the road to truth together: "So my precious Love, we grope along that dim road hand in hand, soul to soul, and together some day may come into the light of more perfect understanding; for I am sure there is light at the end of the road."[52]

Fast on their way to resolving any lingering fear of differences between them, the happy couple had initially set their wedding date for April 20. Joseph would arrive in New Orleans on the eighteenth. Already the Goldbergers had reconciled themselves to their son's decision. Sarah Goldberger even sent her future daughter-in-law a gift prior to the wedding. Near the end of February, a relieved Joseph wrote to Mary:

> I have been very happy today. I had a letter from brother Leo—he of the laconic habit—in which he writes, "Mother has asked me whether she should send Mary the present which you brought her from Mexico." I don't know just what particular gift he refers to but I wrote him to tell her that I was sure you'd be delighted to get any old thing so long as it came from her with her love. Nichtwahr, Kudchen? Mutterchen?[53]

Having gotten a signal from his mother, Goldberger lost no time in trying to endear her to Mary by explaining the role of women in the Orthodox Jewish home. Desperately wanting the two most important women in his life to respect each other and perhaps even build a bond of affection, Goldberger pushed his fountain pen across page after page of stationery. He wrote:

> I believe that my mother is going to take you to her dear old loving heart. Do you know, she's a dear old mother! How I regret that a knowledge of Hebrew reading was thought sufficient education in her day and place for a girl! I should so like to have her write to you. She is a very simple plain old mother and all she has done in her life has been to slave for her children and she has quite a number to slave for. It is curious this idea of the old fashioned Orthodox Hebrew that a girl is sufficiently educated when she can read her prayers (in Hebrew, of course) and teach them to her children. I wonder whether it has not made the Jewish home what it is? . . . Well, I guess it will be all right. Only I do wish she

could write to you or even speak to you or you to her. You know she speaks practically no English.

However, it requires no great amount of speech to understand love and she is just a very simple, loving dear old mother. God bless her.[54]

Joseph's parents' approval was only half the struggle, of course. Almost two months after Joseph asked for Mary's hand, there still was no word from Edgar Farrar. Affectionate and filled with tenderness for Mary, Goldberger was getting impatient. In a tone that is almost adolescent, he complained to her, "It is seven weeks since I had that interview with your father and like 'a good boy' I'm still waiting to hear from him. I wonder whether in the press of his affairs he has forgotten all about it. If I don't hear from him in another week I'll 'ask' again."[55] Whether or not Edgar Farrar regarded the positive reports he had received about young Goldberger as good news or bad, he was a man of his word, and he had promised the young couple who had asked for his blessing an answer. They had asked in December. It was now February.

On February 16, Goldberger received a telegram at the Hygienic Laboratory. It read, "I give my consent. The matter rests entirely with Mary." A letter addressed very formally to "My dear Sir" followed in the mail. It was all good news. In a tone that he likely did not recognize as patronizing or offensive, although he had long favored candor over tact, Edgar Farrar told the anxious suitor that in a note to Mary he had explained that he was now "fully convinced of your [Goldberger's] personal character & worth & that your family were honorable & respectable people." The next word was "but." Farrar then finally told Goldberger what was at the heart of his reservations about the marriage:

But I have advised her not to accept you unless she is willing to take upon herself and her children that unfortunate and unwise prejudice which exists in the minds of the great majority of people against your race and your creed. She has been brought up in this community where such prejudice is at the minimum, but she will have to follow her husband and it is doubtful whether the lines of his life will run here.[56]

To the telegram Goldberger replied with one line of his own: "Inexpressibly gratified." He then answered Farrar's letter. Goldberger responded neither to Farrar's comment about his family nor to his concerns about anti-Semitism. He wrote, "Words are not at my command to express the satisfaction I feel; rather, I shall endeavor to do so by my future behavior as your son." He then proceeded to discuss the date for the wedding, explaining that it was important to have the ceremony by late April because "it would be difficult to leave my station after the opening of the 'quarantine season,' May the first." The nervous, fluttery groom-to-be probably did not see the irony of mentioning the quarantine season to one of the chief opponents of the federal role in that endeavor.[57]

Joseph lost no time in writing the good news to Mary, describing his own reaction as "as crazy as the vulgar proverb has it of the bed bug." He added with the optimism available only to those madly in love: "So Sweetheart the Sun is shining for us and all will be well." And then, in one of those moments of self-deprecation that so irritated Mary: "Really, I believe if the tables were turned I would object to my daughter marrying such a man—a man of no particular attainments, of no particular merit and of very humble antecedents."[58]

Wanting Mary to come to him with her eyes wide open, Joseph once more set before her the disadvantages in marrying him: "First, then, the question of race: I am a Jew, a Hebrew, one of a race despised and respected—curious paradox!—by many if not all of your people, of your race." He also took the opportunity to reiterate a point he had made in an earlier letter, that his economic circumstances were modest and likely to remain so: "I have nothing absolutely to give you but the humblest of positions and I regret more than I can say, that it will never be less humble. I have a respectable position in my corps but I have reached practically as high as I shall ever rise." Knowing that Mary had been able to afford whatever clothes and accessories she had desired because of her family's affluence, he added, "I fear that your lack of experience in the matter hardly gives you a clear conception of all this means." If she did not know already, he now told her: "It means a life of self denial. It means as my wife you would have to deny yourself many things that may appear from your bringing up as necessities of life."[59]

Aiming to nip in the bud any idea that her life with him would be no worse than that enjoyed by her cousin Farrar Richardson, also a U.S. Public Health and Marine Hospital Service physician, and his wife, Corinne, Goldberger reminded Mary that he would have to contribute to the care of his parents even as he supported their household. Then, revealing the very foundation of his character and worldview, he concluded, "Life, Mary, is such a serious matter, so many elements — some apparently very trifling and immaterial — enter into it to make or mar its happiness that painful as it is[,] I feel I must have you consider the question again before you decide finally and absolutely." He then told her that he knew she loved him and that he loved her. He asked her to wire him her reply to "save [him] three days of suspense."[60]

Mary allayed her very anxious fiancé's concerns, and her father soon made clear that once he had given his word, he intended to stand by it. In a letter to Goldberger ostensibly to assure him that he would be married before the start of the quarantine season, Farrar explained that after consulting with her mother, Mary had fixed April 25 as the wedding day, adding, "I suppose she has communicated that fact to you, so you may consider the matter settled." Eventually they fixed on April 19. It seems likely, though, that in addition to conveying to Goldberger that his wishes for a late-April wedding were being honored, Farrar wanted to say something more, which he stated in the letter's last line: "Sir, now that our dear daughter, who has always been a joy and a pleasure to her parents and to her sisters and brothers, has selected you as her partner in life, you will always be received in my family with the love and consideration of a son and brother."[61] The crusty attorney held true to his word. Joseph Goldberger would be as a son to Edgar Farrar.

Goldberger walked on air, his shoes barely touching the floor as he pranced up and down the halls of the Hygienic Laboratory. Not much was accomplished at his dark wooden lab bench the day the telegram arrived. In the old-boy atmosphere of the Hygienic Lab, Goldberger's impending marriage became the occasion for much good-natured banter. The boys were being boys, and their pal Joe relished every bit of the attention. He bragged to Mary, "The other day they were all teasing me, asking all sorts of questions, finally in reply to one I assured them that I had bought you the ring before I left New Orleans. 'Mc' [McClintic] assuming a tone of the profoundest surprise exclaimed, 'Well I be damned!' (Excuse the masculine vigor) 'And you never asked me!' He was ludicrously funny as he said it. We all had a hearty laugh." In early April, Mary received a wedding gift, a berry dish, with a card signed by the "Officers of the Laboratory."[62]

In the preparations for the big day the groom largely deferred to the bride. However, his desire to see that all was done expeditiously, modestly, and unostentatiously led Goldberger to offer his two cents worth of advice, often to Mary's chagrin. Had the minister been notified? Did there really need to be bouquets and flowers? In the end the wedding ceremony went off without a hitch on the evening of April 19, 1906, at 8:00 p.m.

Goldberger's parents did not attend the wedding, at which an Episcopal minister, Dr. Maurer, officiated. Goldberger's favorite brother, Herman, was in attendance. That the wedding was held in the Farrar home, not in a church, was the price of peace with the Goldberger parents; it also allowed the young couple to sustain their claim that they rejected their parents' religious dogma.

On April 20, 1906, "Mr. E. H. Farrar, Jr.," appeared with Mary and Joseph at the office of P. Henry Lanauze, the deputy recorder of births, marriages, and deaths, in the Cora Building at 820 Common Street in New Orleans. There he paid "One Dollar" to register the marriage of Mr. Joseph Goldberger, M.D., and Miss Mary Humphreys Farrar in book 27, folio 845 of Orleans Parish.[63] The honor was all his. The bride and groom began their honeymoon in Gulfport before taking a boat up the east coast to New York, and then a train to visit Perth Amboy, New Jersey, where they were warmly received by the Goldberger family.

By the time of their wedding, Mary and Joseph Goldberger had prepared themselves to launch their new life as a married couple. Dr. Joseph Goldberger, epidemic fighter and medical researcher, was ready to turn his attention from satisfying his personal need for love and security to aggressively pursuing his career in the U.S. Public Health and Marine Hospital Service. He was armed with Mary's devotion. Because of their exchange of ideas, he now had a clearly articulated understanding of how his dedication to a life in medical research and public health echoed a personal faith in one God, his "Infinite Intelligence," whose will could be understood and done through rational inquiry. Goldberger counted himself among the Infinite Intelligence's priesthood. The U.S. Public Health and Marine Hospital Service's Hygienic Laboratory would become his temple.

Two

Medical Mysteries

On Sunday morning May 6, 1906, shortly after returning from their honeymoon and moving into their new apartment, Joseph and Mary Goldberger opened the newspaper to an alarming story. Washington, D.C.'s *Sunday Star* shocked its readers with a front-page headline: TYPHOID FEVER ON THE INCREASE. There were multiple sub-headlines, including "Until Source Is Discovered But Little Can Be Done." What puzzled Washington health officials, according to the article, was that the costly filtration system the city had recently installed seemed not to be working. Early in 1906 the number of cases had diminished, compared with the previous year. That was the dividend on the city's investment. However, by March the numbers had begun to climb. At the end of the week of April 7, 1906, eight new cases were reported; the week of April 14, six; April 21, nine; April 28, thirteen; and the six days from April 29 to May 4, another nine.[1]

No discernible pattern in the location of the typhoid cases readily emerged, and the municipal health department had thus far found no evidence pointing to the sources of infection. The city's water passed through the slow sand filter that Washington had installed in response to other cities' positive experience with such filters, and subsequent tests spoke to the system's efficacy. Bacterial analyses of the water passing through the Washington aqueduct testified to the water's safety. Could there be a previously unknown insect vector? How would an insect vector explain the cases reported during the winter? Public apprehension was rapidly mounting. Of the 110 cases reported that winter and spring of 1906, 48 were still under treatment. With a mortality rate of 30.6 percent for the rest, it was a life-threatening mystery.[2]

At the turn of the century, typhoid was seventh of the ten leading causes of death in the United States. The disease was understood by physicians as the result of food or water supplies contaminated with ex-cretions—feces or urine—from a carrier of the typhoid bacillus (*Salmonella typhi*). One to three weeks was the usual incubation period. Symptoms were fever, headache, malaise, absence of appetite, spots on the torso, and constipation. Inflammation of the small intestine and the colon occurred, with intestinal lesions developing. As the disease pro-gressed, victims had diarrhea and blood in the stool. Left untreated, the fever abated and many patients got well in about a month. Those who died were often felled by ulceration, hemorrhage, and intestinal perfora-tion. Others, it was believed in 1906, died from attendant conditions re-sulting from the release of toxins by the bacilli.[3] By 1906 typhoid fever had increasingly been brought under control by improved urban sanita-tion, though modern antibiotic treatment, which has reduced mortality rates from typhoid fever to less than 1 percent, was still over forty years off. Frightened Washingtonians followed the progress of the disease in the newspapers and bemoaned that their state-of-the-art filtration plant was not the panacea they had hoped it would be.

By summer the typhoid epidemic had worsened still. On June 26, 1906, newspaper reports confirmed that Surgeon General Walter Wyman had agreed that the U.S. Public Health and Marine Hospital Service must come to the aid of Washington's local health officials. Subsequent reports told citizens that their well water would be tested. Finger-pointing began almost immediately. Letters to the editor of the *Evening Star* defended the healthfulness of well water in the city. Citizens loath to hear criticism of their wells blamed the "personal habits" of the victims. However, by July 12 many Washington residents would have sacrificed their wells and more. The *Star* reported, "Typhoid fever is still increasing rapidly in the number of its victims as the D.C. Health Department's records confirmed." Thirty-eight residents of the District had been stricken since July 1, as against 19 in the same period the year before. When the newspaper went to press on July 12, 85 typhoid patients were under treatment, compared with 47 on the same date in 1905. Since January 1 there had been 240 reported cases, 59 more than in that period the year before.[4]

Human-interest stories penetrated the consciousness of Washingtonians in ways that numbers alone could not. In the Pierce family living on P Street N.W., four of the eight children were struck by typhoid fever. Their cases were so serious that the city sent three trained nurses to assist Mrs. Pierce, who was soon stricken herself. To make matters worse, there was an "ice famine" in the city at just the time when ice was needed to cool the feverish. Even more money "could not persuade the iceman on the route to leave the extra supply which was so urgently needed" at the Pierce residence.[5]

Dr. Joseph Goldberger and his wife had returned to a city that was getting sicker by the week. Soon after newspaper headlines blared the bad news at Sunday-morning readers, the thirty-two-year-old newlywed was called from his laboratory. He clambered up the stairs to Milton Rosenau's office at the Hygienic Laboratory, the same stairs he had scrambled up in a euphoric state several months before to tell Rosenau of his impending marriage. Now he climbed them in a sober mood, ready to be briefed on the city's typhoid outbreak, which was nearing epidemic proportions. The surgeon general wanted Goldberger involved in the investigation.

Goldberger was just the medical detective for the job. During the previous four years, he had shown great talent and energy for medical problem solving. His skills and willingness to challenge received wisdom had attracted the attention of some of the best officers in the service. Heedless of his own safety, focused, and driven by a desire to solve medical mysteries, Goldberger had demonstrated that he was equally at home in the library, at the laboratory bench, or in the field. Moreover, by 1906 he had begun to understand that at the foundation of successful public health work was comprehending the connections among politics, economics, culture, and disease.

His tutorial had begun in 1900 at the U.S. Marine Hospital Service station on Reedy Island. The federal physicians there—the country's frontline defense against infectious disease—inspected cargoes, enforced the quarantine, and conducted medical inspections of immigrants. Infectious disease was a constant threat to the health of individuals in the era before the discovery of penicillin and other antibiotics. At times such infections struck individuals and spread quickly to other family members, often costing the most vulnerable—the very young or the very old—their lives. However, some diseases, such as smallpox, yellow fever, cholera, typhoid, and typhus, engulfed communities in epidemic waves, taking thousands of lives until a change of season or a dearth of vulnerable victims caused the epidemic to "burn out." Before public health officials learned the epidemiology of an infectious disease, only clumsily enforced quarantines fended off the death and destruction that microorganisms could wreak on human beings. Clever medical detectives could offer more precise understanding of diseases, how they spread, and how their advance through a population could be curbed. The work was demanding and risky at times. It was frontline duty of the kind Goldberger had long craved. The young man who once had hoped to pursue adventure in the Navy found that medical sleuthing demanded the combination of courage, intellect, and social sensitivity that he could offer.

Solving the puzzle of epidemic disease was a matter of life and death. One of the most dangerous captains of death in the early years of Goldberger's career was yellow fever, a perennial menace in some parts of the United States. How it spread, its epidemiology, was just beginning to be understood, and without that part of the puzzle there was no hope of preventing yellow fever epidemics. However, the very lure of the yellow fever mystery, and the glory that would accrue to the physician who solved it, drew the attention of ambitious young medical researchers in the late nineteenth century, much as today's generation of detectives is drawn to certain cancers or viruses of obscure origin.

Yellow fever is a viral disease of short duration transmitted to humans by various genera of mosquitoes, especially the *Aedes aegypti*. It is endemic in the tropical regions of Africa and the Americas. However, its most dramatic impact has been in its epidemic, or urban, form. This "urban" epidemiological pattern involves the virus's being taken into the blood of an infected human who is then bitten by a female *Aedes aegypti* mosquito, which then bites another human. The disease can be mild or malignant.

Those who contract yellow fever run a high temperature accompanied by a headache, jaundice, and a high protein content in their urine. There is hemorrhaging in the stomach and intestines. The jaundice was responsible for the disease's being named yellow fever. Those who called the disease "black vomit," or *vomito negro*, were observing results of bleeding into the stomach. In the nineteenth and early twentieth centuries, mortality rates could be high, sometimes as high as 70 percent of those identified as having the disease. Today medical scientists know that the mortality rate was actually much lower, because those with milder forms of the disease were often overlooked and not diagnosed. In the eighteenth and nineteenth centuries periodic epidemics of yellow fever swept through the American South and, at times, northern ports such as Boston and Philadelphia in the summertime, killing tens of thousands.[6]

By the late nineteenth century researchers had finally begun to make progress in their investigation of yellow fever. The *Aedes aegypti* mosquito (also called *Stegomyia fasciata*) was identified as the insect, or vector, that spread the disease from one human to another by Carlos Juan Finlay of Cuba in 1878, a theory confirmed in 1900 with the use of human volunteers in Havana by Walter Reed, James Carroll, Aristides Agramonte, and Jesse Lazear of the U.S. Army Yellow Fever Commission. Identifying the culprit was one thing, controlling it quite another. However, the yellow fever problem was hardly solved. Much remained to be known, including precisely how the mosquito functioned as a vector and how best to rid the environment of conditions in which mosquitoes flourished. These challenges were what so excited young U.S. Marine Hospital Service officers, including Joseph Goldberger.

At stations like Reedy Island, the most recent U.S. Marine Hospital Service recruits could meet the experts in their field, and Goldberger was always quick to take advantage of such opportunities. This is where he met the expert on yellow fever prevention Henry Rose Carter. Carter was another southerner of aristocratic stock. He was born in 1852 on Clifton Plantation in Caroline County, Virginia. A scion of the Old South, he attended the University of Virginia, taking his degree in 1873. Between 1873 and 1874 he did postgraduate work in mathematics and applied chemistry. In 1879 he took his medical degree at the University of

Maryland. Like Goldberger, Carter briefly went into private practice, seeing patients in Baltimore. However, between 1879 and 1919 he donned the blue uniform and served his country in the Marine Hospital Service. In 1898 he had made a lasting contribution to yellow fever studies, demonstrating that the incubation period of yellow fever lasts from three to six days, essential information allowing physicians to determine exactly when and perhaps how infection occurred. Carter's other discovery, that there is an extrinsic incubation of the disease—that is, an incubation prior to infection of a human victim—was a key factor leading Walter Reed to seek confirmation of Carlos Finlay's theory that yellow fever was transmitted by the mosquito. Thus, by the time the Virginian and the New Yorker encountered each other on Reedy Island, the former had already made a major contribution to the studies that the latter hungered to undertake. Too junior in position to request assignment in Cuba, Goldberger settled for Mexico and asked the surgeon general for a transfer. On April 19, 1902, Goldberger was reassigned to the office of the U.S. Consul in Tampico, Mexico.[7]

Tampico was not Havana, but it was an assignment abroad, Goldberger's first. The work did not smack of adventure. Goldberger was to help enforce quarantine regulations, co-signing with the U.S. consular official bills of health for cargoes headed for the United States. Was he excited nevertheless? Certainly he was sufficiently enamored of the possibilities to go to a library. One of the crucial work patterns that Goldberger had developed was to thoroughly brief himself about the place to which he was headed and the problem confronting him there. He was already well familiar with the literature on yellow fever. Before sailing to Mexico, he visited the New York Public Library and immersed himself in whatever he could find on Tampico.[8]

Tampico is a city in eastern Mexico in Tamaulipas State and a port on the Pánuco River, not far from where it empties into the Gulf of Mexico. Upon arrival Goldberger entered a world where local inhabitants navigated the river in dugout canoes.[9] The area was a rich oil-producing region. During the first twenty years of the twentieth century, the oil fields brought an economic boom to Tampico, which became a commercial center and one of Mexico's most important seaports. Being a port, Tampico had wharves, damp sheds, warehouses, old empty oil drums where water collected, and other places where mosquitoes could hide and breed. Hoping to fight the yellow fever epidemic with more than his reading glasses, Goldberger arrived in the city with his eyes open to the opportunities.

He was befriended by a vice-consul and missionary, Neill E. Pressley, who had been appointed to his post in 1882.[10] In an era before the consular service was professionalized and a well-oiled part of the State Department bureaucracy, consular positions were often held by missionaries or others who had professional interests in a region. Pressley threw himself enthusiastically into mentoring Goldberger, even going so far as to offer to help collect mosquitoes for yellow fever study. Unfortunately, neither of them knew precisely how to capture the insects. Goldberger quickly learned to determine which mosquitoes were found in particular environs, whether they, like the *Aedes aegypti*, were transmitters of yellow fever, and in which kinds of locations the mosquitoes were likely to spread the disease. Specimen collection was another matter. His inexperience in such research is revealed by explicit instructions he received in a letter from the U.S. Department of Agriculture entomologist C. L. Marlatt, who suggested that Goldberger "take small pill boxes and put in a small layer of cotton on the bottom and then put in the mosquitoes following with a second very light layer of cotton. They can be sent around the world without injury." Lest the young officer misunderstand, Marlatt quickly added, "Of course they must be killed in a cyanide bottle or by other means before packing."[11]

Perhaps Marlatt should have added the admonition "Be careful." The eager Goldberger approached the challenge of yellow fever with great energy until the evening in October 1902 when he himself started to feel sick. The hunter had become the prey. Goldberger had contracted yellow fever. Aware that he was coming down with the disease, Goldberger began to treat himself as the subject of his own human experiment, feeling that much could be learned about yellow fever victims if the disease could be chronicled in the patient's words. Pressley was asked to take notes on the way Goldberger's body responded to the infection. Pressley duly recorded Goldberger's description of the pain in his calves, knees, and ankles and observed that his features appeared to shrink as his skin and eyes turned yellow and he began to vomit blood from the stomach.[12] If Goldberger had yearned for drama and danger to replace the tranquillity of life in Wilkes-Barre, he found it in Mexico. Thanks to the constant care of Pressley and his wife, Goldberger survived, gaining a lifelong immunity to yellow fever, and resumed his work as quarantine officer in Tampico. Goldberger's only contribution to the U.S. Public Health and Marine Hospital Service's ongoing research on yellow fever was the mosquitoes that he and Pressley had managed to ship back to Washington. However, his behavior during his illness had demonstrated amply his willingness to run grave personal risks while conducting his research.

A little over a month after his illness, the rainy season began in Mexico, and yellow fever temporarily vanished along with the mosquitoes. A frail Goldberger was transferred to Puerto Rico to continue quarantine duties in place of an officer on temporary leave. In Puerto Rico he collected mosquito specimens and raised mosquitoes in his laboratory, but this time not for work on yellow fever. Malaria interested the Hygienic Laboratory director, Dr. Milton Rosenau, and he was encouraging Goldberger to raise anopheles mosquitoes and allow them to bite malaria patients suffering from different kinds of the disease.

Malaria results from infection by one or more of four species of protozoan parasites of the genus *Plasmodium*. Three of the species — *Plasmodium vivax, Plasmodium falciparum,* and *Plasmodium malariae* — exist in many tropical and subtropical environs. *Plasmodium ovale* is confined to tropical Africa. Malaria could be severe and even deadly. It begins with chills, develops into fever, and ends with sweating. The fever then subsides, and the patient can sleep and awakens feeling well. However, there are further episodes, paroxysms of the illness. *Plasmodium falciparum* is especially lethal. In 1897, an Englishman named Ronald Ross, working in India, discovered malaria's extrinsic incubation period in mosquitoes.[13] Rosenau hoped that Goldberger could send back from Puerto Rico dead mosquitoes that had bitten victims of the different plasmodia on the third and the tenth day after the bite. Each mosquito would then be shipped in its own bottle of alcohol to preserve it. Back at the Hygienic Lab, Rosenau would place the mosquitoes under his microscope to study the development of the parasite in the stomach and salivary glands of the mosquito. The research aimed to understand the development of the parasite in order to calculate when the mosquito's bite was most dangerous to humans.

Rosenau was another of those outstanding USMHS physicians whom Goldberger first encountered on Reedy Island and who was taken by Goldberger's intelligence and curiosity. The two had more than science in common. Only slightly older than Goldberger, Rosenau was born in Philadelphia. Like Goldberger's father, Samuel, Rosenau's father, Nathan, was a merchant. Milton Rosenau received his M.D. from the University of Pennsylvania in 1889 and interned at Philadelphia General Hospital. He studied abroad in Berlin, Paris, and Vienna and, like Goldberger, had joined the U.S. Marine Hospital Service, surviving his share of quarantine and sanitation assignments in San Francisco, the Philippines, and Cuba. Their admiration was mutual.[14] Both were Jewish at a time when there were few Jews in the USMHS or any uniformed service. During this era the USMHS attracted young physicians of varied social backgrounds, ranking candidates by examination scores for inclusion in a corps of the nation's finest medical minds. From humble beginnings, Rosenau and Goldberger had made the grade. They became fast friends. In Rosenau, Goldberger found a friend and mentor who would become a moving force in the development of public health education in the United States, both at Harvard and later at the University of North Carolina. In Goldberger, Rosenau found a raw talent and a potential collaborator.

As head of the Hygienic Laboratory, Rosenau was responsible for overseeing the research designed to contribute to solving the nation's public health problems. His admiration for Goldberger's research skills and enthusiasm is suggested by Goldberger's next assignment. In November 1903 he was recalled to the Hygienic Laboratory in Washington from Puerto Rico. He had gained valuable experience in the field and now had the opportunity to see another side of the U.S. Public Health and Marine Hospital Service's assault on infectious disease—laboratory investigation.

At a time when professional specialization was not imposed early in the careers of U.S. Public Health and Marine Hospital Service officers, field duty was complemented by time spent in the Hygienic Laboratory under the tutelage of senior scientists. The younger officers were expected to get a broad range of laboratory experiences under their belts and to contribute to the atmosphere of intellectual inquiry that Rosenau sought to encourage. Through encounters with colleagues and visitors, Goldberger was exposed to the ideas of some of the finest medical investigators of the era. Such luminaries as William Welch, Reid Hunt, and Victor Vaughan visited the Hygienic Laboratory. Edward Francis and Charles Wardell Stiles were on staff at the lab. There were even extracurricular activities, including a journals club, which met at Rosenau's home every Friday evening. One Friday evening Goldberger was expected to report on three German and two French journals because of his ability to read and digest scientific materials in those languages.[15]

During these months Goldberger also prepared for and passed the examination for the grade of passed assistant surgeon, an accomplishment that meant an increase of sixty dollars per month beginning in July 1904. Even with the increase, however, his salary was hardly lavish.

Goldberger's stay at the Hygienic Laboratory was interrupted by a crisis. By the time he received his pay increase, he had returned to Mexico. The poor state of public health there and the careless enforcement of existing hygienic laws by Mexican sanitation inspectors were troubling American public health physicians attached to consulates charged with protecting America's southern border from yellow fever. Arriving in the spring of 1904, Goldberger received a second set of instructions from Surgeon General Wyman. He was asked to go beyond his official orders and engage in a kind of covert medical surveillance that would help Washington officials better to assess the situation.[16] The young public health officer in search of adventure found it in the medical sleuthing that the surgeon general now asked of him.

Diplomatic relations between Mexico and the United States were fragile when it came to public health concerns. In a letter to Goldberger, Wyman explained:

The matter of stationing Mexican inspectors in United States ports and places, and United States inspectors in Mexican ports and places was discussed with the Superior [Mexican] Board of Health on my recent visit to Mexico, but it was deemed inadvisable to make a formal agreement to this end. However, I feel confident that no objection will be raised to your making quiet observations and reporting to me. These reports will be more or less confidential. In obtaining this information you should exercise good judgment and tact.[17]

Confidential public health intelligence was now part of Goldberger's professional portfolio. The courage, composure, and keen observational skills he had demonstrated on earlier assignments well prepared him for this one. He enthusiastically embraced the adventure.

In addition to his old haunt Tampico, Goldberger was to visit Monterrey, Ciudad Victoria, and Linares. Wyman ordered him to "visit the different points on the Mexican Central Railroad when it may be necessary to investigate whether these places are infected with yellow fever, so that you can make full reports to the Bureau on any town on this road which may be infected or suspected of being infected with yellow fever, in order to prevent it being carried across the border into the United States." Officially, the young officer was expected to report to Assistant Surgeon T. B. McClintic, who was in charge of the Public Health Service officers in Tampico. However, the surgeon general told Goldberger that once he got out of the port he was on his own.[18] Confidentiality was a diplomatic necessity. Wyman trusted Goldberger to be both politically discreet and medically astute.

In a handwritten draft of a report to Wyman, Goldberger said he had found no yellow fever in Tampico or in the adjoining settlement of Doña Cecilia. He told Wyman that the Mexicans had formed "an official corps of 24 men," a number Goldberger believed inadequate to the task, to make house-to-house visits on nonimmune residents and "inspect water containers and disinfect houses." However, in Doña Cecilia "private enterprise is accomplishing valuable results." The Mexican Central Railroad had removed "a large number of shacks called *jakales* and in their stead are erecting two room wooden houses." Much to Goldberger's satisfaction, the company had minimized "the water barrel nuisance." Company agents replaced the barrels, where mosquitoes often bred, with a tap of running water that served every three or four houses. Unfortunately, near the houses not built by the railroad were water barrels with "breeding larvae" despite "the inspection and a city ordinance requiring a cover for all water containers." Though the residents tried to prevent the breeding of mosquitoes, their efforts seemed to Goldberger quite inadequate.[19]

An acute social observer, Goldberger noted that part of the yellow fever problem in Mexico arose from "the national custom of using lye water for softening the outer shell of the cover [the unleavened bread] in the preparing of the tortilla and . . . in the use of lye water for laundry purposes." He found lye water receptacles to be "an excellent culture medium for the stegomyiae larvae." He wrote to the surgeon general that when he reported his observation to the firm of stevedores hired by the railroad company to supervise living conditions among railroad workers, they promised to build a "communal laundry or wash house, furnishing lye at a nominal price," and to prohibit laundry work except at the washhouse. He also observed that the use of sulfur to kill the mosquitoes was continuing, but at a pace slower than he would have liked, because of the small number of workers assigned to the task.[20]

With more than a little ethnocentrism in his tone, Goldberger described all the sanitary work being done in Mexico as having a "most serious defect." What was the shortcoming? Displaying a characteristic impatience with those who did not share his insistence on careful, expeditious execution of public health measures, Goldberger explained his complaint as diplomatically as his exasperation would allow: "They [the Mexicans] are too polite to be thorough to which may be added insufficient expert guidance and supervision." His dealings with Mexicans caused him to observe that to avoid disagreement and unpleasantness, they tended to tell those in authority what they thought was expected at the expense of candor. To this was added inexperience and self-interest, such as when assigned doctors gave priority to their private practices over the public's health. Goldberger saved his severest criticism for the national government of Mexico, for its lax communication with infected places and lackadaisical enforcement of the quarantine. He observed, "Vessels and crews are inspected on arrival and hold and steerage compartments are sulfured, but the essence of quarantine, the detention or at least supervision of now immune passengers and crews is observed only on paper."[21]

By November 1904 the crisis in Mexico had abated, and Goldberger had returned to the Hygienic Laboratory. Now he was learning about parasitic worms from Charles Wardell Stiles in the Zoology Division. Because parasites were carriers of infectious disease, medical investigators wanted to know as much as possible about how and under what circumstances they infected victims. Were parasites equally infectious in all stages of their development, or were young parasites less infectious? The answer could have important implications for disease prevention. Stiles and Goldberger co-authored an article in which they described how they were able to infect two rabbits and two dogs with hookworm eggs taken from hookworms in a preadult stage of development. The finding was significant because it showed that the parasite seemed capable of penetrating the skin at a much earlier stage of development than scientists had thought possible. Stiles and Goldberger hoped to determine whether or not the infected animals then played a role in spreading hookworm disease to humans, but their research was halted. At the end of the article the authors explained, "At this point in our observation our work was suddenly interrupted by the yellow fever outbreak, and it may be some time before it can be carried further."[22]

How right they were. Because U.S. Public Health and Marine Hospital Service officers were epidemic fighters as well as laboratory researchers, the slow, steady labors of the lab bench were often disrupted by the alarm bell of a public health crisis. Goldberger was soon sent with many other U.S. Public Health and Marine Hospital Service officers to Louisiana to fight a major yellow fever epidemic devastating New Orleans in the summer of 1905. The assignment not only would test the skills and experience he had acquired but also would add to his arsenal an understanding of the politics of disease.

Yellow fever epidemics periodically swept across the South throughout the history of the United States. After the Civil War major epidemics hit Louisiana in 1867, 1873, 1878, 1897, and 1898. Understanding the disease and how to prevent it through mosquito control made the 1905 epidemic the last major outbreak in U.S. history. However, controversies over how best to battle the disease and to elicit public cooperation gave Goldberger a firsthand look at the difficulty of gaining public compliance with public health measures even in the midst of a virulent epidemic. He had reported on the problem from Mexico, but, as he was to learn, it was no less a problem in the United States.

The results of the Yellow Fever Commission in Cuba and William Gorgas's antimosquito campaign in Havana were admired and embraced in New Orleans by both the New Orleans Board of Health, which had only existed since 1898, and the Orleans Parish Medical Society. In 1901, four years before the epidemic, the chairman of the city's board of health, Dr. Quitman Kohnke, promoted lectures, conferences, and other publicity to educate the citizenry on the *Aedes aegypti* mosquito and its favorite breeding places, especially the cisterns which caught the rainwater that drained from rooftops and functioned as open storage tanks for the water used daily by residents. Kohnke encouraged pouring a small amount of kerosene on the surface of the water in the barrels. It was a clever and economical solution. The kerosene would destroy eggs and larvae but have no effect on the water because it would float on the surface and water drawn through a spigot at the bottom of the barrel would not be affected. He also advised covering the cisterns with wire screening fine enough to exclude the mosquitoes. Publicity and initial enforcement proved, however, insufficient. New Orleans citizens were apathetic in the absence of an epidemic and opposed altering their behavior if it involved inconvenience.[23] Again Goldberger was learning about the social impediments to sound public health practice. Education was not enough when the required behavioral changes were resisted by the public.

Four years later, in 1905, these public health measures took on a fresh immediacy as yellow fever menaced the city. New Orleans's population was 325,000, and only about a quarter of the residents had gained immunity from earlier epidemics. When the first cases appeared, some residents in denial of the dimensions of the public health threat resisted fumigation. Kohnke advised local health workers to use means from "soft persuasion to brutal force" to perform their jobs. At first the U.S. Public Health and Marine Hospital Service was present in only an advisory capacity. Dr. Joseph H. White was sent by Surgeon General Wyman to help with investigations. White, along with Kohnke, signed an address to the citizens, published in the newspapers a day after the official recognition of the epidemic, acknowledging a state of emergency. The city embraced an antimosquito campaign to contain the epidemic. Ministers preached sermons about it from their pulpits. Officers of Italian voluntary organizations in New Orleans appointed special committees to make door-to-door appeals to the immigrants, urging them to report cases and comply with government mosquito-eradication policies.

New Orleans's African-American population was mobilized. Even racial stereotypes were assaulted in the name of public health. The Reverend Beverly Warner, a white Episcopal minister who became an important organizer of community efforts, denounced the myth of black immunity to yellow fever, explaining that blacks would suffer infection "just the same as though a white man had been stung." Rarely was such a rhetoric of equality heard in the South. Kohnke told one racially mixed audience, "There is no difference between white and black . . . We live the same way, we get sick the same way, we get well the same way, we die the same way." Kohnke and others preached the equality of infection, but when it came to organizational cooperation, white leaders proved themselves more biased than mosquitoes. Black citizens were excluded from ward organizations and instead were encouraged to form their own antimosquito groups. In response, African-American leaders formed the Central Sanitary Association to educate black residents of the city.[24]

Pamphlets and circulars were printed and distributed by the thousands on the streets of New Orleans. Even buttons were issued showing a picture of a mosquito and the words "My cisterns are all right; how are yours?"[25] Physicians and health officials hit the lecture circuit almost nightly to educate the public on the facts and to dispel harmful fictions. Speakers wanted the public to know that the stegomyia mosquito alone was the vector of transmission; that the mosquito obtained the yellow fever germ by biting an infected person during the first three days of the illness, suggesting that people must be isolated behind screen material immediately after diagnosis; and that mosquitoes did not transmit the illness for ten to twelve days after acquiring the infection, leaving ample time to destroy them in the environment of an infected person before they went on to infect others.

In this era states protected themselves from disease crossing their borders by enforcing quarantine legislation. Quarantines were potent instruments that required prudent use lest one state cripple another's economy by discouraging the commerce and investment necessary for prosperity. In 1897 Joseph Goldberger's future father-in-law, Edgar Farrar, had expressed his concern about state quarantine powers, eventually delivering a speech before the Quarantine Convention held at Mobile, Alabama, on February 9, 1898, which was later published as a pamphlet.[26]

By 1897 most businessmen in Louisiana had had enough of their counterparts in neighboring states attempting to curb their commercial activities by using yellow fever as an excuse. They called for federal intervention, a federal quarantine, to calm the fears and stay the greed of nearby states. Farrar, in *Louisiana* v. *Texas* (176 U.S. 1), argued before the Supreme Court that Texas was using the quarantine not to protect the public health of Texans but as a weapon in a commercial war against Louisiana. The Court dismissed the case as not offering a justiciable controversy covered by the Constitution. However, *inter alia* the Court suggested that such quarantines were valid exercises of state power until such time as Congress passed a law assuming the responsibility of quarantine.[27] In the end, the only legislation that Congress ever enacted was the 1893 law mandating that states meet federal quarantine standards and eventually surrender maritime quarantine to the federal government. Some states retained their quarantine prerogatives into the 1920s.

Although the federal government only gradually replaced the states in administering quarantines, it had long since established a pattern of sending public health officers into states to assist local health authorities. Thus the U.S. Public Health and Marine Hospital Service was poised to respond when asked for help in the New Orleans yellow fever epidemic. On August 4, 1905, state and local government officials, including the mayor and state and city health officers, as well as New Orleans commercial organizations, a number of prominent citizens, and the president of the Orleans Parish Medical Society, met and asked Governor Newton Blanchard to telegraph President Theodore Roosevelt for help. The governor asked that the federal government assume authority over the battle against the epidemic. Roosevelt contacted Surgeon General Wyman, and the U.S. Public Health and Marine Hospital Service was summoned to take charge.

Inviting the federal government to get involved was not without controversy. The Civil War had ended only forty years earlier, and the last northern troops of occupation had departed in 1877, less than thirty years before. Veterans of what the South still characterized as the War between the States were still young enough to be vocal. Newspaper editorials denounced the decision, certain that it would bring about "Federal domination," with the government in Washington taking over all quarantine powers from the states. However, once the federal authorities were in place, the editorials did not counsel resistance but urged cooperation as a "sacred duty." The editor expressed hope that "the very best result may be obtained, a result that may be worth thousands of valuable lives and countless millions in values."[28] The Civil War was a cherished memory, but one that could be sacrificed in the face of a clear public health crisis.

Dr. White, who had already been on the scene working with state and local health officers and coordinating train and ship inspection and the detention of passengers before they left the city, was now put in charge of the crusade against the epidemic. He established a headquarters and gathered a staff of some forty federal physicians, both commissioned officers and acting assistant surgeons. Among the former was thirty-one-year-old Joseph Goldberger.

Goldberger was about to get a valuable lesson in the politics of disease and disease prevention. He was ordered to set up headquarters in Vicksburg, Mississippi. He was responsible for working on the fringe areas of the epidemic, checking suspected cases and imposing quarantine when necessary to contain the disease. Just before he took his post, a major conflict had broken out between Louisiana and Mississippi over quarantine, a conflict that almost erupted into violence. On July 26, 1905, the flamboyant Progressive governor of Mississippi, James K. Vardaman, perhaps best known for his personal corruption, racism, and generosity to the poor of his state, accused Louisiana political officials of having tried to conceal the existence of yellow fever from neighboring states, including his own. Louisiana's Governor Blanchard denied it and denounced Vardaman.

A Mississippi quarantine boat assigned to patrol the coast had sailed onto Lake Borgne and presumed to interdict Louisiana fishing boats. The Mississippians on the quarantine launch began to turn back all boats coming toward Lake Borgne from Louisiana's Lake Pontchartrain.

One Louisiana newspaper blared the headline VARDAMAN MOSQUITO FLEET INVADES LOUISIANA WATERS. According to the report, armed quarantine officers from Mississippi had crossed the Pearl River and dug into positions on the Louisiana shore, watching for anyone headed toward their state. The press dubbed it an "armed invasion." Blanchard called his fellow governor to task. Claiming that he had ordered his quarantine officers to steer clear of Louisiana territory, Vardaman could not resist adding, "I am going to also see to it that the people of Louisiana are not permitted to violate the quarantine regulations of Mississippi."[29]

A livid Governor Blanchard now ordered the Louisiana Naval Brigade to defend its state from the invaders. He also summoned the Orleans and St. Bernard Parish sheriffs and district attorneys to sail with the Louisiana fleet and seize any armed vessels illegally in Louisiana waters. He ordered that the crews of such ships be arrested and brought before the grand jury of the proper parish for indictment.[30] The hyperbole of journalists described two states on the brink of war. The reality was considerably less dramatic. In the end the Louisiana Naval Brigade captured one Mississippi boat and temporarily jailed its crew in St. Bernard Parish. However, by August 6 the episode had ended. Goldberger and the other members of the U.S. Public Health and Marine Hospital Service squad took control of the quarantine.

Goldberger's duties in Mississippi lasted until late October, when quarantine restrictions in Mississippi and neighboring states were lifted. The Louisiana State Board of Health removed curbs on travel from New Orleans and other infected towns on October 21. By early November the cold weather had arrived, and as the mosquitoes died the fever departed. It had been a deadly summer. In Orleans Parish there had been 3,402 cases of yellow fever; 452 victims had died, a mortality rate of 13 percent. As a whole, Louisiana suffered 9,321 cases and 988 deaths, a mortality rate of 11 percent.[31] The South's last major yellow fever epidemic was over. Several weeks later, Trinity Episcopal Church in New Orleans held a special service on Thanksgiving Day to express its appreciation for having been delivered from the epidemic. Goldberger attended.

Less than two years later, the young lady with whom he left the church that day sat across from him at the breakfast table as they read about the typhoid epidemic bearing down on the nation's capital. However, he would soon be leaving her side. Surgeon General Wyman had appointed a triumvirate to oversee the typhoid investigation: Dr. Leslie L. Lumsden, the service's expert on typhoid; Milton Rosenau, chair of the three-person board and chief of the Hygienic Laboratory; and Dr. Joseph H. Kastle, the laboratory's chief of chemistry. On July 19, Goldberger received specific instructions from Rosenau echoing Surgeon General Wyman's orders that Goldberger be assigned to the investigation.[32]

Goldberger's superiors believed that contaminated Potomac water was spreading bacteria throughout the region, and they needed to know the point at which the water was being polluted. Rosenau instructed Goldberger to make a painstaking, detailed study of the Potomac watershed. In addition, he wanted to know the population of the watershed and its distribution, with "special reference to drainage into the Potomac or its tributaries." Goldberger was also to report on the towns and villages that had direct sewage connection with the Potomac and its tributaries. Was there a greater prevalence of typhoid fever in these towns, villages, and "other habitations"? Had there been many cases of typhoid fever in these communities in years past? What was the connection of nearby farms to the city? In short, Rosenau wanted Goldberger to create an epidemiological study so detailed that the answer must emerge—if there was an answer to be had in these communities and the great river that ran near them.[33]

As it had in the past, Goldberger's search began in the library. Although the Hygienic Laboratory's library staff would not permit certain materials to be checked out, they did not object to Goldberger's remaining after closing and even spending the night in the library on a cot. After compiling charts, maps, and tables dealing with precipitation, temperature, prevalence of typhoid in different localities, and correlations of disease cases with distance from the river, an exhausted Goldberger headed to the K Street stables for a horse and buggy.

This was the first lengthy business excursion he had taken since he and Mary were married. As always, from wherever his duties took him, Joseph wrote to Mary, sharing with her news both personal and professional. On discovering an undocumented source of pollution, he burbled, "I believe I have what the newspapers call a scoop." And between commenting on his surroundings—"This is beautiful country about here—lovely is the word"—the solicitous newlywed inquired if his wife might already be pregnant. He also gently asked her to undertake tasks for the first time that would devolve upon her for the rest of their marriage. He sputtered as husbands often do when they are about to load responsibilities on their wives: "By the way Sweetchen I must ask you to attend to paying the gas bill and the rent. You won't mind will you Sweetheart?"[34] She paid the bills, but there is no evidence whether or not she minded.

In the thick, humid summer air Goldberger continued his travels and his search for an answer to Washington's typhoid outbreak. By the time he returned to Washington, he had learned a great deal, but he had not found the source of the outbreak. Autumn brought relief. Goldberger exchanged his horse and buggy and railroad tickets for a fountain pen and a seat at his desk in the Hygienic Laboratory. Three articles in the next volume of the *Hygienic Laboratory Bulletin* report what he had and had not learned from his investigation. In detailed, specific, and cautious language, Goldberger, while unable to eliminate the Potomac as the origin of the typhoid outbreak, pointed out that the river underwent "more or less natural purification and in addition becomes very greatly diluted before it reaches its endpoint at Great Falls."[35] Goldberger's scoop was barely a spoonful. The mystery remained unsolved, the detective unsatisfied.

When he was done with his field research outside the city, Goldberger inspected the bottled table water sold in Washington, D.C. Washingtonians who could afford it often bought bottled spring water because local sources could leave the imbiber with a nasty case of diarrhea and, perhaps not surprising, they preferred the taste. Abuses abounded. Magnesia Crystal Table Water, described on its label as "the purest and healthiest of table waters," had its office on Anacostia Road in the District. Goldberger not only found the bottles' labels to be misleading but also concluded the firm's uneven sanitary practices resulted in "evidence of sewage pollution." Another brand, Renal Spring Water, was not any better. Located at Eleventh Street and Park Road, the company bottled water, but hardly spring water, and the bottling process was hardly sanitary. "The water is pumped into buckets from which it is dipped out and poured into bottles through a tin funnel, being strained in the process through a piece of cloth to remove any coarse particles." Although there was no evidence of bacterial pollution, "chemical examination gives indications of probable seepage from the nearby barn." In the end Goldberger had to conclude that despite the "objectionable sanitary conditions and methods" he found in some plants and the "practices which are calculated to mislead the consumer as to the source or character of the water" engaged in by other firms, these companies and their products were not responsible for the typhoid fever in Washington.[36] Goldberger's negative results at least made clear that the city's water supply was not to blame.

In a literature review, "Typhoid 'Bacillus-Carriers,'" Goldberger also warned of the public health threat posed by "persons apparently in perfect health," the so-called healthy carrier of the typhoid bacillus. He observed that persons "apparently well may discharge typhoid bacilli in the urine or feces for months and even years after passing through the disease." However, even more interesting to Goldberger was the still mysterious second category of carrier, the individual who never seems to have been sick at all. Grounded in the many hours of library work he had done to familiarize himself with every aspect of typhoid fever, he now cited with characteristic thoroughness the still scanty case literature. Tempting his readers, he wrote, "Of perhaps greater interest and not less importance [than those who had the disease and still carried the bacillus] is a group of persons who have been found to discharge typhoid bacilli in urine or feces for long periods, but have never experienced any clinical manifestations of the disease." Goldberger thought that "most, if not all, of the individuals belonging to this group have at some time been in a more or less close association with persons actually sick with the disease."[37]

Goldberger's article on healthy carriers was most timely. The year before, the New York epidemiologist George Soper had identified a healthy carrier, a female Irish-immigrant cook, Mary Mallon, whose victims included members of the wealthy New York families who could afford her services. Although she did not come to popular attention until June 1909, when she was dubbed "Typhoid Mary" by a William Randolph Hearst tabloid, Mallon's rampage did not end until 1915, when twenty cases of typhoid were diagnosed at New York's Sloane Hospital for Women. The bacillus was traced to the kitchen where Mallon was working under an alias. At the age of forty-eight, she was taken into custody and held in detention on North Brother Island for the remainder of her life. Had a Typhoid Mary or two gotten off the train in Washington?[38]

Goldberger did not solve the typhoid mystery in Washington, D.C., and he was not the first to discuss the definition of a healthy carrier. However, his powers of observation, honed in Tampico, Mexico, and his careful, thorough research, well practiced at his Hygienic Laboratory bench, contributed to a better understanding of typhoid. Perhaps of greatest import, Goldberger's studies of typhoid fever and the water supply were for him an advanced course in field epidemiology. They would shape his epidemiological skills in ways that would benefit his ability to understand how diseases move in populations and how the paths of infectious disease in particular can be traced by the clever medical detective.

Exactly one year after his horse-and-buggy ride through the outskirts of Washington, the medical detective became a father. Joseph and Mary Goldberger's first son, Edgar Farrar, was born on June 28, 1907, at Columbia Hospital. Joseph was chided by his friend Dr. Jules Lazard of New Orleans, who wrote, "It is said that the first child causes a man to realize his responsibilities and reasons for existence, but I sincerely hope it will not corrugate your forehead, or affect that genial smile which could be called Goldbergeresque." Lazard had little to fear. If anything, Goldberger smiled more than ever after the birth of the boy, whom he and Mary usually called by his middle name, Farrar, perhaps in honor of her cousin Thomas Farrar Richardson, who had died tragically in a typhoid fever epidemic in New Orleans and who had introduced Mary and Joseph. What would "corrugate" Goldberger's forehead was not the arrival of his son but how quickly he was called away after the baby's birth. Goldberger departed Washington for Brownsville, Texas, within weeks of the baby's arrival. There had been an outbreak of dengue fever, and local health officials needed help.[39]

Characterized by a high temperature, acute rheumatic pains in the back and joints, and red skin eruptions, dengue had appeared in Charleston, Philadelphia, and Galveston in the nineteenth century. Its nickname was breakbone fever because of the joint pains. Others called it dandy fever from the stiff, dandified gait assumed by victims as they tried to cope with the pain. By 1907 physicians had learned how to treat the symptoms. In the 1905 edition of his widely consulted textbook for physicians, William Osler recommended hydrotherapy to reduce the fever and a strong painkiller, opium, for the back and joint discomfort.[40] Dengue had often been confused with other diseases, especially yellow fever, by local health authorities. Therefore, Surgeon General Wyman wisely sent two experts to Texas: Goldberger, because of his expertise on yellow fever, and Dr. George W. McCoy, a leading authority on dengue.

McCoy and Goldberger were contemporaries. McCoy was only two years younger and had enlisted in the USMHS in 1900, one year after Goldberger. Both now held the same rank, passed assistant surgeon. Nevertheless, Goldberger, well versed in how to begin an investigation of an infectious disease, was in charge. His written orders said, "You are informed that Passed Assistant Surgeon G. W. McCoy has also been directed to take part in this investigation, and that he has been directed to report to you, so that this joint work in the field will be under your direction." Specifically, Surgeon General Wyman wanted Goldberger to tell him if mosquitoes were the vector of the fever in Brownsville, whether the disease was in fact dengue or yellow fever, and "the possible relation of dengue to yellow fever."[41]

The last week in July 1907, Goldberger and McCoy boarded the train in Washington and headed for New Orleans, where they planned to switch to the train to Brownsville. Because their train was delayed by four and a half hours, they were able to have dinner with Goldberger's in-laws. Aiming to "save time and gain in comfort," Goldberger and McCoy "rushed through dinner, rushed back to the hotel and dashed to the depot, got our tickets," and just made the 9:00 p.m. train.[42]

Goldberger and McCoy finally arrived in Brownsville on July 30, 1907. Located "on the left bank of the Rio Grande and about ten miles from its mouth," Brownsville boasted a population of about eight thousand, a large proportion of which was Mexican. It remained enough of a frontier town that Goldberger could write to Mary about a "recent shooting-up." On his way to the post office, he stopped at the hotel where there had been recent gunplay. The wide-eyed Goldberger reported with the golly, gee-whiz excitement of a little boy, "I have seen the bullet holes & marks of that interesting event that dragged the little town out of its calm, serene, obscurity."[43] It was not exactly the gunfight at the O.K. Corral, but for Joseph Goldberger, an avid reader of western novels, it was his fantasy of the West come alive.

Soon Goldberger was in hot pursuit of menacing villains himself, intruders that he could not see, even with the help of a microscope. His initial assessment comforted the local public health officers; he confidently reassured them that Brownsville's population was being threatened by dengue fever, not yellow fever. The symptoms of the two diseases differed slightly. The combination of an acute fever lasting five to six days with severe headache and lower-back pain, a rash peppered with macules, tiny red spots, appearing after the third day of the disease, persuaded Goldberger and McCoy that they were observing dengue. So, too, did the absence of a racking cough, jaundice, and albumin in the urine, common to yellow fever but not dengue. Although dengue was milder than yellow fever—the vast majority of those who contracted it did not die—the best prophylaxis was the same, mosquito control.[44]

As the officer in charge, Goldberger made a public statement to the press about the nature of the disease he and McCoy had identified. It was brief. He read reporters the telegram that he sent to Surgeon General Wyman on the evening of July 31: "The prevailing fever undoubtedly is dengue. Have seen no indications of yellow fever."[45]

Now that Goldberger and McCoy had solved the first part of the mystery, they proceeded to the next stage: determining the reasons for the outbreak. Their arsenal—sharp eyes and years of experience. Goldberger and McCoy roamed Brownsville's back streets and alleys, where they saw the conditions responsible for the town's problems. The city lacked a public water supply, and so river water was kept near homes and businesses in barrels and tanks. The vessels holding the water were ideal breeding places for *Stegomyia calopus* and *Culex pipiens* mosquitoes. The humans with dengue who provided the meal for the hungry mosquitoes were likely migrants from across the Mexican border, Goldberger believed. Based on his time in Mexico, he speculated that dengue had crossed the border on the bodies of Mexicans, the first case occurring about mid-June.[46]

Goldberger's previous experience with infectious diseases had taught him to be alert to social and political contexts. Failure to respect the politics of disease hampered even the most skilled epidemiologist from being able to control its spread through a population. In New Orleans in 1905 the U.S. Public Health and Marine Hospital Service had arrived too late in the epidemic to be anything other than reactive to the factions warring over the quarantine. In Brownsville, Goldberger and McCoy had arrived just as the dispute over quarantine was erupting.

As a precaution against the dengue across its border with Texas, the city of New Orleans, with the cooperation of U.S. Public Health and Marine Hospital Service and Louisiana state officials, decided that all persons arriving from Brownsville were to be kept under surveillance for six days from the time of their departure from Brownsville. Texas State Health Officer Dr. W. M. Brumbry had to move expeditiously to quash rumors that dengue had spread to New Orleans and that other cities in Texas and the entire state of Louisiana had declared a quarantine against Brownsville.[47] As if that rumor were not potentially damaging enough, businessmen in Louisiana had spread the word surreptitiously that the epidemic was really yellow fever. If it had been true, Louisiana could legally have declared a quarantine against Texas, thereby creating a panic—payback perhaps for what Texas had done to Louisiana during the yellow fever epidemic two years earlier, an episode still fresh in the minds of many. Goldberger and McCoy sought to calm fears, but the best news was trumpeted in the newspapers.[48] There was a "marked diminution in the number of cases of fever and everything points to a speedy eradication of the dengue if the present good work of the sanitary department is continued." The press quoted Dr. Brumbry as saying that there was "no fear of any quarantine against Brownsville now."[49]

Later reports offered citizens advice on how to handle the mosquito threat by explaining what had been done in Brownsville: "By covering the surface of the water in the cisterns and the surface of the water in the barrels with a small quantity of coal oil, every place where the mosquitos could go to find water or to deposit their eggs was covered by a poison to mosquitos."[50] Many mosquitoes were killed, and the propagation of the species was practically stopped. However, many Texans lacked confidence that cities in Mexico would follow the example of their northern neighbor, and by the end of August, Texas had declared a quarantine against those cities where Texas health authorities thought the dengue in Brownsville might have originated.[51] A minor international fracas erupted with charges and countercharges that rapidly escalated to the point of threatening the local economies on both sides of the border. The dispute was eventually resolved, and in solving the public health problem in Texas, Goldberger had learned that he must worry about creatures with motives far more complex than the mosquito's. Public health policy was a creature of economic and political priorities that could not always be easily compromised.

If the business communities in Brownsville and San Antonio were all smiles, Goldberger and McCoy had little to laugh about. Both came down with the fever themselves before the end of their assignment. Just as soldiers in uniform sometimes fall in combat, the uniformed officers of the U.S. Public Health and Marine Hospital Service were occasionally felled and even killed by the microorganisms they battled. In the history of the service since 1798 twelve officers had died from diseases they had contracted in the line of duty.[52] Goldberger had come close to making the list when he had contracted yellow fever in Mexico years before.

Dengue was a milder disease than yellow fever, but its symptoms were still debilitating. The two physicians felt the aching in their backs and joints; even their eyes ached. Hardly any part of their bodies seemed without pain. There was high fever with attendant chills and sweats. Lying in adjoining beds, Goldberger and McCoy soon recovered, although the residual weakness lasted for several months. His bout with dengue was one of the few things that Goldberger did not share with Mary until later. Goldberger and McCoy could now add personal observations to the excellent paper on the dengue outbreak in Brownsville they eventually published the following December.[53]

After concluding his work with McCoy on dengue fever in Texas, the anxious father went home to wife and child. For almost eighteen months he was detailed to the Hygienic Laboratory in Washington. Evenings were spent comfortably with Mary and their young son. When a second pregnancy ended in a stillbirth, Joseph and Mary were under the same roof to comfort each other. Days were spent exploring the mysteries of helminthology with zoologist and parasitologist Charles Wardell Stiles.[54]

This research on parasites served Goldberger extremely well when, in 1909, Dr. Jay F. Schamberg presented the U.S. Public Health and Marine Hospital Service with a public health crisis whose symptoms had not yet been connected to a known disease.

Schamberg was already an important figure in the field of dermatology when Philadelphia officials asked him for a consultation about itchy red skin eruptions that had appeared on the bodies of the crew of a yacht anchored in the harbor. He immediately recognized the condition, because he had described it in a 1901 journal article.[55] Indeed, the condition, commonly called Schamberg's disease, appeared periodically in Philadelphia. However, now, eight years after the article's publication, there were many cases being reported in various parts of the city. After about seventy cases in Philadelphia, including a dozen among the staff of a popular vacation hotel near the city, local health authorities asked Schamberg his advice about control. When he could offer them none, they called Surgeon General Wyman.

Joseph Goldberger, accompanied by Mary and Farrar, was on his way to Woods Hole, Massachusetts, where he planned to do research in the laboratory. On evenings and weekends the family would swim and frolic in the warm June sun. In a pattern that would become familiar to the Goldbergers, the trip was postponed. The surgeon general had ordered Goldberger to Philadelphia.

With Schamberg's cooperation, Goldberger began to gather data. The red spots were concentrated on the torso and extended to the arms and legs. When the scratching became intense, the rashes started to bleed, and sleep became all but impossible. From Goldberger's article about the episode, though, it is clear that what most impressed him was that the victims tended to be individuals of modest income. Important, too, was that cases were concentrated in the same household or ship, rarely spreading to nearby houses or ships. In the places where it erupted, the disease lasted for several weeks, and then disappeared with no relapses. In the case of the yacht crew, Goldberger interrogated them all and noted that they had begun to recover after leaving the ship. Now he focused narrowly on their living conditions and habits on the yacht. Had they come in contact with poisonous substances in their food? Were there toxins in some aspect of their immediate environment? Were these red rashes the result of insect bites? Was there an infectious disease present, perhaps some variant of chicken pox?

Gradually Goldberger eliminated the possibilities. Because victims of Schamberg's disease in the same locale seemed to come down with it at the same time, it was unlikely that they were catching it from each other. There seemed to be no period of incubation. The disease occurred between May and October only, and the hospital cases recovered very quickly while those who were not taken to a hospital suffered for weeks longer. Thus it did not seem to be an infectious disease, at least none like any that Goldberger had previously encountered. He also eliminated the notion of a toxin. An industrial poison would not likely fit with the disease's seasonal pattern. Schamberg's disease might be a reaction to a plant or pollen toxin. Certainly Goldberger was open to the possibility that the toxic substance might exist in nature. He was drawn to the idea of an insect bite for two reasons: the quick recovery with an environmental change, and the appearance of the pox-like rash.

Among insects there were various candidates for culprit. The seasonal character of the ailment suggested that bedbugs and lice were probably not involved. Clearly the insect must be very small, because none of the reports included an insect sighting. Nor were insects reported flying anywhere near victims. It might be a tiny insect transported on an article coming in contact with the body. Goldberger had not forgotten the poverty of those with Schamberg's disease. Was there something unique about the clothing or bedding that poorer individuals used? Clothing was a possibility, but those who changed locations and recovered were often wearing the same clothes they had on before they left. A thorough search of the premises where the victims had been living when they contracted the disease yielded one constant. Every victim was sleeping on a straw mattress. Without exception, those who had not gotten the disease were sleeping on non-straw mattresses.

Finding some rather new straw mattresses on victims' beds, Goldberger stacked several of them and thrust his arm between two of the mattresses for an hour. Then three volunteers slept on the mattresses. The next morning, all the volunteers' bodies and Goldberger's arm showed the red itchy rash.

Even as the experiment was proceeding, Goldberger learned about the origins of the straw. The mattresses were manufactured by four companies. However, the companies had all gotten their straw from a location near Pennsville, New Jersey.

Suspecting that there might be a tiny insect present but fearing that he would be unable to see it, Goldberger put some of the straw from one of the victim's mattresses through a fine flour sieve. Returning to his laboratory, he deposited the sifted straw into two petri dishes. One was left untreated, and the other was exposed to "vapour of chloroform under a bell jar" to kill any insect that might be present. Goldberger strapped both petri dishes to his chest with adhesive tape. The skin covered by the dish with the untreated straw began to itch, and later the rash appeared. Goldberger then recovered a "small almost microscopic mite." Next, "five of these mites were fished out, placed in clean watch crystals, and then applied to the axillae of five volunteers. At the end of about 16 hours following this application the characteristic lesions appeared on the area to which the mites had been applied." An entomologist identified the small mite as *Pediculoides ventricosus*, a wheat-infesting acarid mite.[56] Prevention required sterilizing the mattresses by steaming them or fumigation.

The uncommonly innovative quality of Goldberger's experiment is suggested by Schamberg's letter to him gushing with enthusiasm: "I am delighted with the information conveyed in your letter of this morning. The method employed by you to determine the specificity of the little mite is certainly ingenious, and the result appears practically conclusive."[57]

At the end of June the Goldbergers were finally headed for Woods Hole. Summer at the Woods Hole facility gave Goldberger an opportunity to swim and enjoy the beautiful natural surroundings with Mary and Farrar when his day's work was done. Habitually an early riser, he was treated to lovely sunrises, which he could enjoy as he pondered all he had learned about epidemiology inside and outside the Hygienic Laboratory. Given increasing responsibility by Surgeon General Wyman and the laboratory chief, Milton Rosenau, Goldberger could claim a broad range of skills in detecting infectious diseases and experience in controlling their causes. His abilities had earned him an array of impressive mentors such as Henry Rose Carter and Milton Rosenau and collaborators such as Jay Schamberg. He had established a pattern of work that would enrich the rest of his career—from his meticulous preliminary exploration of the existing literature, to his keen powers of observation, to his heedlessness of his own safety in the name of the public's health. And all of it was fueled by a focus and drive rare even for the U.S. Public Health and Marine Hospital Service. Finally, Goldberger had learned that culture and politics could be formidable impediments to public health.

Quarantine duty in Vicksburg and addressing public anxieties in Brownsville had instructed him in the politics of disease. In the classrooms and wards of Bellevue he had become a physician. In the Hygienic Laboratory and in the field he had become a medical detective.

THREE

Disease and Duty

The Washington life to which Joseph, Mary, and little Farrar returned after their summer in the sun had been considerably enriched before their departure by the unexpected delivery of a Steinway piano. A piano in the home was more than a musical instrument; it meant social respectability. An elegant piece of furniture, it was virtually the emblem of middle-class living in the late nineteenth and early twentieth centuries. Steinway was an especially prestigious name.[1] Thus Edgar Farrar, as delicately as possible, was giving his daughter and son-in-law far more than the gift of music.

Edgar Farrar's present, which included a cashier's check for $750, came at the right moment. Goldberger's reputation within the U.S. Public Health and Marine Hospital Service as an ingenious epidemiologist and a fearless epidemic fighter was soaring, but neither his income nor his ability to command his own time kept pace. Duty almost always ran roughshod over domesticity in the early-twentieth-century workplace. And Goldberger was becoming increasingly aware of the politics of the U.S. Public Health and Marine Hospital Service, especially how important it was to position himself to advance. Edgar Farrar's generosity was intended to buffer the costs to Mary and little Farrar of Goldberger's demanding career. The Steinway piano brought music to the household, but the rhythm of Goldberger's career fostered disharmony.

Between the autumn of 1909 and the winter of 1914, Goldberger received a series of challenging assignments that tested his intellectual and physical mettle while offering him additional experience with infectious disease and a deeper understanding of the political and social contexts that nourished disease. The first assignment came in the autumn of 1909 shortly after he got back from Woods Hole and involved a return to Mexico. This time the medical mystery was typhus.

Like Schamberg's disease, typhus fever was often associated with the poor, especially the immigrant poor concentrated in urban slums. The disease, whose origin was still unknown in 1909, was characterized by prolonged high fever, severe headache, and a raised red spotted rash. It had a variety of nicknames, including hospital fever, spotted fever, jail fever, camp fever, and ship fever. Highly contagious, typhus was thought to have an incubation period of about twelve days before onset of chills and fever. A general weakness drove most of those stricken to bed. The tongue was furred and white, while the face was flushed and the eyes glassy and vacant. Vomiting frequently accompanied the other symptoms, and a cough developed. When death occurred, as it did in 12 to 20 percent of cases, most often in those over fifty years old, it was often from exhaustion. The young rarely died. Most of those felled by typhus recovered by the end of the second week of the disease.[2]

Goldberger and his contemporaries did not know that the typhus pathogen, *Rickettsia prowazekii*, is transmitted to humans in the feces of the human body louse. That discovery would be made by French physician and epidemiologist Charles Nicolle in 1909. The feces enter the body through wounds resulting from scratching or, at times, through the mucous membranes of the eyes. Lice that bite febrile patients transmit the disease to other humans.[3] In the first decade of the twentieth century, the similarity of symptoms caused some confusion with Rocky Mountain spotted fever. It was the kind of puzzle that brought out the best in Joseph Goldberger.

Once again Goldberger's skills attracted an important collaborator. Dr. John F. Anderson, who had assumed directorship of the Hygienic Laboratory after Milton Rosenau's departure for Harvard, asked Goldberger if he would assist him in determining whether typhus and Rocky Mountain spotted fever were the same disease. If Goldberger and Anderson could demonstrate that typhus fever and Rocky Mountain spotted fever were one and the same, that would be a triumph. If the diseases turned out to be different and the investigators were still able to produce typhus in monkeys for further investigation, that, too, would be a notable achievement, contributing much to ongoing research. A 1909 typhus epidemic in Mexico required a U.S. Public Health and Marine Hospital Service presence to enforce quarantine. More important, the outbreak offered Anderson and Goldberger the opportunity for study. Surgeon General Walter Wyman ordered Goldberger and a supply of caged monkeys to Mexico immediately.[4]

As he reacquainted himself with Mexico, Goldberger was reminded of the grinding poverty. In a letter to Mary he noted, "The poverty among the masses must be dreadful and of course the incidental or correlated misery is sickening to behold. I don't think one can imagine so much filth and misery as one sees here on every hand." Goldberger's perspective on all he saw was enriched by two contacts. One was Dr. A. N. Goodman, who had been a classmate of Goldberger's at Bellevue and now practiced in Mexico. The other was a journalist. Goldberger could not recall his name when writing to Mary, but the individual was the editor of a local English-language newspaper. He and Goldberger remembered each other from Monterrey when Goldberger had been there five years earlier. With such local contacts, Goldberger was able to get a fix on the conflation of economic and social circumstances that promoted the spread of typhus fever among the urban poor of Mexico City and the political circumstances that sustained such conditions.[5]

Goldberger and Anderson's daily routine was grueling, but the work went well. By the end of November 1909, the two investigators had come to suspect, based on research conducted with guinea pigs, that Rocky Mountain spotted fever and typhus were different diseases. In early December they announced their findings in a preliminary report. Further confirmation using monkeys would be necessary before final results could be published, of course, but now they could focus their attention on typhus. That would take more time, preventing Goldberger from joining his family for Christmas. On November 27, 1909, he and Anderson inoculated the blood of victims of Mexican typhus fever, or "Tabardillo," into two monkeys. As always, Goldberger explained to his wife precisely what was keeping him away at holiday time: "The reason for this prolongation of my stay is that we feel obliged to watch the animals for about 3–4 weeks after the last inoculations—to be sure to cover the most prolonged incubation period."[6] There must be no doubt that the animals had typhus and not any other disease.

Any disappointment at not returning home sooner was likely compounded by the patience required of the bench scientist. Goldberger wrote, "We have struck a dead calm in our work." On December 7 he reported, "We haven't seen a new case in 3 days; and it's now simply a matter of waiting developments." Always hungry for publications that would document his accomplishments and make his name known to other medical scientists, Goldberger rationalized his absence at Christmas to Mary: "We will have gathered a considerable body of valuable stuff for publication—whatever the outcome of the experiments now under way."[7] For the moment, though, all they could do was wait and watch through the incubation period, hoping better to understand the etiology of typhus and why it had been confused with Rocky Mountain spotted fever.

Soon Anderson and Goldberger could proclaim success. They produced typhus in a monkey, and it was not at all the same disease as Rocky Mountain spotted fever. Writing with his usual elation when his work was going well, Goldberger began his December 10 letter to Mary, "Well, the old 'Monk' has made good! One of our monkeys is sick—very sick and it is a strong presumption that the animal has typhus."[8]

Just as satisfying to Anderson and Goldberger as the results of their experiment was that "for once in the history of the Service we have gotten on the scene of action first." Goldberger was exaggerating a bit. The service had taken the lead in research on cholera, hookworm, and a variety of other diseases. However, he was correct to believe that others were hot on their trail with respect to typhus. The University of Chicago, Ohio State University, and Harvard were all either sending or contemplating research expeditions to study typhus. An elated Goldberger chortled, "But my dear old sunshiny wife—'we've got them beat by a mile!'" He and Anderson were at work on a "preliminary note summarizing our results" for publication. They hoped to get it into print before the others even got under way.[9]

A week later, the research was still going well, so well that Goldberger would not be rejoining his family for months. The day after Christmas, he wrote to Mary that he had just received a cable from John Anderson, who was now back in Washington. Fresh monkeys were on the way; six of them had already been shipped and were ready for inoculation. Now the plan was for Goldberger to be back by the end of February. The period of calm was definitely over. A disconsolate Goldberger described his days almost by the hour as solitary and filled with work. He arose at 5:30 a.m., breakfasted at 6:00, and made it to the lab by 6:30. After that, "it's a case of hustle through with the animals—make inoculations and take temperatures & get away in time to be at the hospital by 8:30 am to see cases." He returned to the laboratory at about 10:30 to examine his cultures and "do some staining of smears" for his microscope slides. By noon he found himself "ravenously hungry," so he went back to his hotel for his mail, and then to lunch at a café. After eating, he returned to the hotel, where he wrote up his morning's work and attended to correspondence. By 2:30 he had gone back to the hospital, finally returning to the laboratory at 4:00 or 4:30. After checking the animals, he would end his workday by 6:00 p.m. After supper he wrote to Mary and retired. He concluded his description, "So goe [sic] the days!"[10]

There was good reason why Goldberger needed time at both hospital and laboratory daily. He had been collecting lice and allowing them to feed on typhus patients at various stages of the disease and to bite the shaved bellies of monkeys. The technique worked. They demonstrated that typhus was transmissible to monkeys via lice, just as it was to humans, as Goldberger could attest. One day as he was applying a bottle containing lice to a monkey's shaved stomach, he was stung on his hand and got typhus.

For the third time Goldberger contracted the disease he was studying. The onset of the illness began on the afternoon of January 2, when he complained of a "severe headache and repeated attacks of chilliness." By evening he had become feverish, followed the next day by pain in the eyes, tiredness, and loss of appetite. On January 4 he entered the hospital at 4:00 p.m. and was seen the next morning by Anderson, who had returned to Mexico between Christmas and New Year's Day. Gradually over the next few days Goldberger's condition deteriorated. Anderson wired Washington, calling it enteric fever so as not to panic the staff at the American Hospital in Mexico City. By January 9 Goldberger had developed a red raised rash and a bloody discharge from the back of his throat and seemed to be losing hearing. The log reads, "Patient seems slightly deaf. Does not readily respond to questions. Muscles tender upon pressure." Goldberger was in critical condition. For several days his life hung in the balance.[11]

On January 17 the hospital record finally read, "Patient is in good condition. Sweating has ceased. Spots all disappeared." The bloody discharge from the nasopharynx had slowed, although he was still quite deaf. Not until January 22 was Goldberger "up in a rolling chair and out of room." His temperature, which had been subnormal since January 16, continued that way. His hearing was still impaired and returned only very gradually.[12]

Even as Goldberger retreated from death's door, he could not cease measuring his life by the yardstick of his career. He summed up where he thought he stood:

> Well I've got two notches on my stick now, I mean notches representing what we know about quarantinable diseases—"Yellow fever 1902" and Typhus 1910. We don't count Dengue, you know. I've had the whimsical notion running through my head that I'll have a button made with these legends inscribed on it and give it to Farrar some day when he is bigger. For I feel as proud of these notches as if I had received the cross of the legion of honor.

Realizing what he had just written, Goldberger reasserted his innate modesty. "This is childish of course," he wrote, "but childish or no, I feel that I have some reason for a certain pride in my 'battle' scars and why shouldn't my son learn to take pride in them? After all, they were received in line of duty for my country."[13] With Goldberger in need of further recovery, he and Anderson, their work not entirely finished, left Mexico to join Mary and Farrar at her family's home in New Orleans.

After a brief visit and being treated to some home cooking—gumbo, a dish Goldberger had grown to love—all four returned to Washington. Goldberger recovered, though he remained weak for quite a while.

In February 1910, Anderson and Goldberger published a lengthy article describing their research in Mexico and how they had demonstrated that they could produce typhus in monkeys. In March they trumpeted their achievements at the invitation of the Society of Alumni of Bellevue Hospital, the institution where Goldberger had seen his first patients as a medical student and intern. The Bellevue alumni heralded one of their own whose research was of increasing importance to the world of infectious disease.[14]

If Goldberger's body and reputation were quite whole, his relationship with Mary was in need of mending. Mary was pregnant again when her husband was ordered to Mexico, and although she had some modest household help with Farrar, now a rambunctious two-year-old, the prospect of doing without a husband for so long was not appealing. Goldberger's announcement in December 1909 that he would not be home for Christmas shook Mary especially hard. Whatever he and Mary had agreed on in terms of rejecting religious dogma, the colorful decorations, gift exchange, and general merriment of Christmas were hard to ignore. It was unthinkable that Mary was not celebrating Christmas like all her relatives. In America, Christmas was a time for families to gather. When Joseph wrote that the earliest he might be able to leave would be a day or two after Christmas, "bringing me to you and the kiddy for New Year's day," it was little comfort, especially since he would soon renege on that promise as well.[15]

In fact, Mary was beginning to tire of waiting for Joseph. She informed him that she wanted to take Farrar home for the holidays. Goldberger balked. Writing somewhat stiffly, he explained, "I know how much pleasure it would give you to go home with our little boy and I hope you will believe how deeply I regret that circumstances, as they appear to me, make that trip a very unwise and impractical one." He cited two reasons. Since she was pregnant, the trip might fatigue her. However, the far more compelling reason seemed to be money. He reminded her, "We are far from being in a position to afford the expense of the trip and I know that if you will think it over carefully you will agree with me. Unless we are mighty careful I feel certain that we will be in serious financial difficulties."[16]

Salary schedules in the U.S. Public Health and Marine Hospital Service were modest, and most officers made less than they might have in private medical practice. As an officer at the rank of passed assistant surgeon, Goldberger was making slightly more than two thousand dollars per year in 1910. As he had reminded Mary time and again during their courtship, he came with no inherited wealth and, in fact, made regular contributions to his parents' support in Perth Amboy. Joseph and Mary's savings consisted of one thousand dollars. While hardly large, it was more than many young married couples with a child could boast. Still, Goldberger felt compelled to lecture Mary, largely because of his own anxiety that their resources were insufficient to afford a second child. He pressed his point, calling their savings not to be "despised," but "pitifully small when you consider that we are already drawing on it and that our little family is growing and the cost of its maintenance will soon begin rapidly to increase."[17]

Mary was very disappointed. Goldberger pleaded for patience, explaining that he would not know until mid-January whether he would receive another shipment of monkeys to inoculate. He begged indulgence: "I'm forced to beg of you to be patient and brave." Because mail took seven to ten days between Mexico City and Washington, the couple cabled each other when matters could not wait. In an exchange of such cables Joseph relented on her desire to go home. In fact, he now suggested that she remain with her family until their next child arrived.[18] One factor that might have changed his mind was that money was no longer an obstacle. Edgar Farrar had learned of the situation and sent his daughter funds to come home.

Whatever tensions had arisen between husband and wife, Joseph's life-threatening illness helped the young couple reassess their priorities on their reunion. Mary and Joseph returned to Washington a family, which on April 24, 1910, got bigger. The Goldbergers had their second child. The hoped-for daughter turned out to be a healthy baby boy, whom they named after his father, Joseph, and Joseph's favorite brother, Herman. Little Joseph H. Goldberger, who would one day become an ophthalmologist, added to his parents' joy and his father's ongoing concern about income.[19]

While Goldberger was recovering his full strength in Washington in the company of his wife and two young sons, Columbia University's Professor Nathan Brill published an article in *The American Journal of the*

Medical Sciences claiming identification of a new disease that he called "an acute infectious disease of unknown origin." As early as 1898, Brill had described an illness that resembled typhoid fever. Thanks to a blood test developed by French physician Fernand Widal to differentiate the often misdiagnosed typhoid fever from typhus, Brill knew that his mystery disease was not typhoid fever. By 1910, he was also convinced that the disease was not typhus, although it was characterized by "a short incubation period (four to five days), a period of continuous fever, accompanied by intense headache, apathy, and prostration," as well as a "profuse and extensive" red raised rash.[20] These symptoms lasted about two weeks, whereupon the fever abruptly ceased either by crisis within a few hours or gradually, over about three days. Despite similarities, Brill thought that the disease he had identified was not typhus because it was nonepidemic and had a much lower rate of mortality. Goldberger and Anderson suspected otherwise. Another puzzle concerning the specificity of a disease demanded U.S. Public Health and Marine Hospital Service attention.

On May 27, 1910, Surgeon General Wyman ordered Goldberger to New York City to investigate an acute outbreak of Brill's disease. In the official written orders, Goldberger was told that determining whether or not Brill's disease was distinct from typhus was of the utmost importance. He was also told, "On account of the importance of the question, it will be given no publicity." He was instructed to make periodic reports to the bureau and, as usual, a final report.[21]

Having brought back some typhus-immune monkeys from Mexico, Anderson and Goldberger tried to obtain access to a case of the disease Brill had identified in hopes of obtaining blood for an immunity test. If the monkeys were immune to Brill's disease, then Brill's disease and typhus were the same. Unfortunately, the investigators were unsuccessful and turned their attention to their ongoing research on typhus. In August 1911, however, Brill published another article, which reported monkey inoculations and seemed to confirm his hypothesis of a new disease. Anderson and Goldberger could do little to refute the claim until September 20, 1911, when they finally saw their first case of Brill's disease, a Russian immigrant in a ward at New York's Mount Sinai Hospital. Goldberger drew the man's blood and returned to Washington. Over the next six months he propagated the infection from monkey to monkey through more than fifteen generations. Now that he and Anderson had proven to their own satisfaction that the monkey was susceptible, they prepared to test the relationship of Brill's disease to typhus fever by a series of cross-immunity tests.[22]

Because the monkeys that Goldberger had brought back from Mexico two years earlier had died, it was decided in October 1911 that he should travel to Mexico City, where typhus was endemic, and test the susceptibility of Brill's disease–immune monkeys to typhus and the susceptibility of typhus-immune monkeys to Brill's disease. With his portable laboratory and rhesus monkeys, Goldberger boarded a train and headed south of the border once again.[23]

Initially hampered by bureaucratic delays and a lack of healthy monkeys on which to experiment, Goldberger soon had to rein in his enthusiasm for "attempting too much at a time." He wanted badly to "try a series of experiments at one time—something that would be easy enough if I had enough animals and one good man to help. It would be such a saving of time." As it was, Goldberger limited his efforts to one experiment at a time. Still, he could exclaim, "we're off and on the way." By November 22 he had good news. The results were exactly what Anderson and he had hoped. The monkeys that had recovered from Brill's disease were resistant to typhus, and those that had recovered from typhus were resistant to Brill's disease. The results would not have been possible unless Brill's disease and typhus were the same. He wrote to Mary, "As a preliminary and in <u>strict confidence</u>—though you may tell that precious Daddy of yours—the indications are developing that Brill's disease & typhus are one & the same disease. That means that typhus is endemic in New York City, and probably in some of our other large cities and is not & has not been recognized." Expecting to return by the end of January 1912, he was counting the days and promised to apply for a ten-day leave, not just seven, as he had first told her.[24]

Whatever Goldberger had learned about disease, he was about to get a lesson in the politics of research as well. On November 25 he assured Mary with even greater certainty and "in <u>confidence</u>" that "Brill's disease is a synonym of typhus." However, even as he wrote, presses were churning out copies of the early-December issue of *The Journal of the Ameri-*

can Medical Association. In an open letter to the editor in the December 2, 1911, issue, Nathan Brill, well aware that Goldberger and others were seeking to disprove the distinctiveness of the disease he claimed to have discovered, wrote that he would accept that the disease was typhus if certain conditions were met. He must be shown a typhus outbreak of low case fatality, he must see successful inoculation of animals as had occurred with typhus, and he must be persuaded that the disease was communicable. Otherwise, he would persist in calling it "an infectious disease of unknown origin."[25]

When the letter appeared, Goldberger pronounced it a "joke." He explained to Mary that in the letter "Brill states more definitely than heretofore that he considers 'Brills Disease' distinct from typhus & then lays down certain requirements as proof of their identity." Having already shared with her his certainty that his monkey inoculations had proven the diseases to be the same, he now boasted, "I think we can more than fulfill his requirements." Practically bubbling with excitement at the opportunity to deflate the arrogant Brill, who had thrown down the gauntlet in no lesser place than the pages of the eminent *Journal of the American Medical Association*, Goldberger relished a belief that "the trail is growing so hot that we will have to publish soon."[26]

Goldberger and Anderson published their results in the February 12, 1912, issue of *Public Health Reports*. They were polite but devastating. They managed to meet every one of Brill's conditions with data from their monkey experiments on susceptibility and immunity or with data collected by municipal health officials. They concluded that "the disease described by Brill is identical with the typhus fever of Mexico, and inasmuch as the New York strain is undoubtedly of European origin, we may also conclude that the typhus of Europe and the tabardillo of Mexico are identical." On March, 19, 1912, the two collaborators delivered their coup de grâce to Brill in a paper presented to the New York Academy of Medicine.[27] In June, Goldberger was invited to Atlantic City to address the annual convention of the American Medical Association on the subject "Some Recent Advances in Our Knowledge of Typhus." He had fully arrived as a medical scientist.

———

With his career now in high gear and his research taking him in new directions, Goldberger had become a recognized expert on typhus. Whenever he spoke to the issue of prevention, he stressed the relationship of typhus to broader societal conditions, acknowledging that crucial economic reform is "a very slow process":

> Typhus emphasizes, perhaps better than any other disease, the fact that fundamentally sanitation and health are economic problems. In proportion as the economic condition of the masses has improved—that is, in proportion as they could afford to keep clean—this notorious filth disease has decreased and disappeared. In localities where it still prevails its further reduction or complete eradication waits on a further improvement in, or extension of, the improved economic status of those afflicted. Economic evolution is a very slow process, and while doing what we can to hasten it, we must take such precautions as existing conditions permit, looking to a reduction in or complete eradication of the disease.[28]

From the perspective of Goldberger's professional development, his typhus research deepened his understanding and broadened his experience of infectious disease. His self-confidence soared.

While Goldberger was away from Washington, changes were occurring that were beyond his control but that would have an important impact on his career. Mary's letter of November 21, 1911, brought the news that Surgeon General Wyman had died. In answer to her query, Goldberger speculated that Wyman's death would not make "any difference so far as this [his typhus] work is concerned." Nor did he think that "Anderson will be affected by any change in administration." Anticipating her next question, he wrote, "Of course the interesting question now is who will be appointed S-G."[29]

Answering his own question, Goldberger offered his wife his preference, at least at first blush: "My present inclination would be to vote for Dr. [Joseph H.] White." Goldberger thought that while White, a veteran epidemic fighter, had "greater ability in some respects than Wyman had; he has some of the same faults—principally, I think, that he is not a good judge of men and I think permits his prejudices to influence him too much." By December 11 rumors had reached even Mexico City that White and Dr. Rupert Blue were the two contenders to succeed Wyman. Goldberger described his relationship to Blue as "intimate—casual," but he did not feel that he knew Blue well enough to assess his fitness for the position. Pondering from afar a choice that was not his to make, Goldberger still preferred White, because Blue did not possess White's "moral courage." However, knowing full well how political the surgeon general-ship was, Goldberger admitted that "in such a position as that of 'S-G' a flexible moral-courage is rather an advantageous article of equipment."[30]

In the end Rupert Blue received the presidential appointment over Joseph White. Goldberger explained to Mary that Blue had very likely gotten the appointment because he was a Republican and there was a Republican, William Howard Taft, in the White House. Although Gold-berger expressed some personal sympathy for the disappointed White, he wrote:

> I am a wee bit inclined to the view that the more suitable man of the two was appointed . . . Blue has—as equipment for his posi-tion—the advantage of comparative youth, and I hope also that he may have the modern spirit of action—the desire to do things and keep at the head of the procession rather than to just drift with the current and be content with making a *bluff* at leading— Wyman's great role.

Optimistic about the future, Goldberger added, "The position of S-G of our Service has great possibilities[;] whether Blue has the vision and the executive ability to make the most of it remains to be seen. If he has, I predict that in 5 years the Service will be quite a different institution. However, let us wait and see what we'll see."[31] In addition to getting a new surgeon general, Goldberger's agency changed its name. The Pub-lic Health and Marine Hospital Service became the U.S. Public Health Service in 1912. The shift reflected the broader scope of the agency's mis-sion. Treating merchant seamen in Marine Hospitals was still part of the service's mission, but responsibility for the public health of the American people through action in lab and field was now so clearly the service's chief responsibility as to warrant the name change.

There was a new face at the Goldberger home as well as at the office. In the autumn of 1911 Mary was pregnant with their third child. Once again the Goldbergers were hoping for a girl, whom they planned to name Mary. The mother-to-be with her two youngsters in tow headed for her parents' home in New Orleans. On December 10 she wired Joseph in Mexico that "'little daughter' is a boy." Goldberger admitted to being "a bit disappointed"; however, he also observed, "They say that three of a kind is a strong hand in poker." Mary told Joseph that she would name the baby Benjamin Humphreys Goldberger. Benjamin was the name of her beloved uncle as well as that of Joseph's brother. The new father wrote back, "That suits me and hope it may suit him."[32]

As had happened before, Joseph was absent when Mary gave birth. He wrote that while he was confident all was well, "it's mighty hard to be away from you." Perhaps as a result of their earlier arguments over money and bills, Mary now had her own, separate checking account. Practical as always, he told her that he was transferring one hundred dollars to that account for immediate expenses, and in a postscript added, "Please don't forget to have the baby operated on at the end of a week or 10 days . . . Don't put it off. Its best done right away." He was referring to circumcision, of course. Although it is doubtful that Goldberger regarded the ancient Hebrew injunction as any more compelling than the idea of the Immaculate Conception, he likely was persuaded, as many were in his generation, that the operation had hygienic advantages.[33] Regardless, seeing that the operation was performed fell to Mary.

Once again Goldberger spent Christmas and New Year's apart from wife and children. And once again his absence resulted in frayed nerves.[34]

In the early months of 1912 Goldberger returned to a long-neglected project. The investigation of Brill's disease had interrupted research on measles begun in the late spring of 1910 and continued only sporadically. A common childhood disease, measles was not well understood in the first decade of the twentieth century, although the symptoms, which developed seven to eighteen days after exposure, were familiar. Youngsters with measles had an inflammation of the mucous membrane lining the

upper respiratory passages accompanied by malaise, fever, chills, cough-
ing, sneezing, conjunctivitis, spots resembling tiny grains of white sand
surrounded by inflammatory areolae on the inside of the cheek (Koplik's
spots), and finally, three to five days after the other symptoms, a raised
red rash beginning in front of and below the ears and on the side of the
neck. The rash lasted two to five days after onset. Although the germ
causing the disease was as yet unknown, physicians knew that the disease
was highly contagious and that it was among the most deadly of childhood fevers. Death was most often the result of bronchial pneumonia or
tuberculous bronchial pneumonia developing during convalescence.
All too often physicians heard from mothers that "the child caught cold
after measles." Therefore, they advised parents to keep children in bed
for a few days even after the fever subsided.[35]

Goldberger and Anderson's recent success in transmitting typhus to
monkeys offered them hope that they could do the same with measles
and make some significant strides in discovering what caused the disease
and how it was spread. In the early autumn of 1911 Goldberger took time
from his typhus studies to go to New York, where he inoculated monkeys
with measles.[36]

His source of measles for these inoculations was the contagious-
disease wards on Ellis Island. The measles wards were typically among
the busiest, the beds filled with children of every nationality coping with
this common childhood disease.

On returning to Washington, Goldberger, working with Anderson,
infected rhesus monkeys with measles by injecting them with blood
from a human case in the eruptive stage. The monkeys proved most susceptible if infected with blood from a patient in whom the rash was only
about fifteen hours old. Turning from the issue of susceptibility to that of
transmission, Anderson and Goldberger demonstrated that buccal and
nasal secretions also could transmit the disease to monkeys. Having access to a boy on whom the rash was just beginning, they sprayed his nose
and throat with salt solution and encouraged him to blow his nose and
spit out the solution into a sterile glass. Then they inoculated the monkeys subcutaneously with the solution. The monkeys fell ill, and their
blood was used to infect other monkeys. Anderson and Goldberger also
demonstrated that the robust disease organism would pass through a

Berkefeld filter and could be dried for twenty-five hours and frozen for the same amount of time and still remain infectious.[37]

Some of their final measles work was performed at the immigration depot on Ellis Island. Swabbing the noses and throats of immigrants with measles who had been confined to the contagious-disease wards, Goldberger was able to demonstrate that infectivity lessened as convalescence proceeded. On a practical level, this finding suggested that measles patients who were being kept under quarantine for two weeks after the appearance of the rash were being kept isolated longer than they needed to be.

Ludvig Hektoen, Charles Nicolle, and others engaged in measles studies admired Goldberger's work. Hektoen, who had been trying to induce measles in monkeys himself, was somewhat embarrassed by Goldberger and Anderson's success. His attempt to save face, an article in the December 1911 issue of *The Journal of the American Medical Association*, amused Goldberger. "I have just enjoyed a hearty 'chuckle,'" he told Mary. "There is a paper by Prof. Hektoen of the University of Chicago on 'Experimental Measles in the Monkey with Special Reference to the Leukocytes.'" According to Goldberger, the joke hinged on the "with special reference etc." part of the title. Goldberger explained, "The fact is that the paper is primarily a confirmation of our work showing that the monkey is susceptible to measles where inoculated with blood early in the disease. Poor old Hektoen 'fell down' in this problem and he is letting himself down easy." Still, Goldberger wrote, "It is extremely gratifying . . . to have this confirmation of our work come from this source—He is a man who stands very high."[38]

Goldberger, too, was beginning to stand high in the winter and spring of 1912. In August 1912, having served the American people for more than twelve years, he asked to be ordered before the Board of Examiners to ascertain his fitness for promotion to the grade of surgeon. He appeared before the board on December 10, 1912. On January 15, 1913, he was informed that his score of 82.19 percent had earned him his promotion. On March 8 he was told that he would receive a registered letter with his commission as surgeon.[39]

While Goldberger was busy putting in the time and energy that earned him such professional adulation and promotion, Mary was dealing with successive family tragedies that further eroded her happiness and left the couple as emotionally distant as they were physically separated. In October 1910 Mary's younger sister Lucy had committed suicide. Goldberger's description of Lucy as a "loving but evidently troubled spirit" suggests she may have suffered from depression. Perhaps her own psychological demons, with which she would wrestle in the years to come, drove Mary to a grief even beyond that expected upon the loss of a beloved sister. Mary took the children and rushed to New Orleans while Joseph, unable to leave his laboratory animals and attend the funeral, confessed to being more affected than he thought possible by Lucy's death. He wrote, "You may think it strange—I do myself for that matter—but it is so nevertheless—that I have been so deeply depressed by thoughts of poor, dear suffering Lucy. I suppose my being alone here has had something to do with it." But he made the generous gesture: "I want to repeat that while I miss you and the kiddies dreadfully and want you here with me, nevertheless if your longer stay would be a comfort to your dear mother and you would like to stay till Christmas why stay, by all means."[40] Mary took her husband up on his offer and remained in New Orleans.

Although he had encouraged Mary to remain, her doing so left Joseph feeling sorry for himself and, in fact, fuming. In a cruel twist from a man routinely away from home for months, he suggested she was evading her responsibilities by staying away so long, especially her responsibilities to him. In some of the harshest words he had ever addressed to her, Joseph wrote:

> I am sorry to hear that you find it so trying to manage Farrar, and sorry that I can't help. If it were not for your mother & father I'd have you come straight <u>home</u> right away. After all this is where you belong—and I know that you feel the same way about it; I don't see how any "normal" woman can feel otherwise. It's all well enough to want to see ones [sic] mother & father & brothers & sisters, etc. That is quite a healthy desire, but 2 or 3 or 4 weeks is as much as one wants of that after one has started one's own nest. And you, my dear, have started your own—you're a precious little

wife and mother and your husband begrudges every minute of separation. That's the way I feel about it—and I have no apologies either. And what's more you will start for Washington the day after Christmas, namely Dec. 26 at 8 pm. This is <u>settled</u>.[41]

Mary did not rush home in response to his complaint, and although Joseph continued to sign his letters to her "affectionately," a coolness prevailed. As in the past, money was an issue, but he also resented what he regarded as her inattentiveness toward him:

> You poor child! You must be very busy indeed. To be sure you haven't written how your time is occupied but I can easily imagine that your days are full of the cares of your two children, of the nurse and—of a thousand other important matters always pressing on your attention from morning to night. I keenly regret that I can not help you, relieve you, so that you might be more free to think and to do the things that I know you long so much to be free to do. To be so busy as to be unable to finish a letter for three days is to be busy, indeed—and that letter to one's husband![42]

Although Goldberger persisted in his demand that Mary return the day after Christmas, he withdrew his offer of coming to get her to help with the boys and to see her parents unless an assignment materialized that would require the service to send him to New Orleans. With an uncharacteristic coldness he wrote of the trip: "Aside from the fact that it would give me the chance to bring you & the boys home I don't care at all about it. I've gotten into some work that interests me and I should prefer not to be interrupted. I'd like to get something done before spring."[43]

With the return trip scheduled for the evening of December 26, Joseph and Mary tried to mend fences both realized were in serious disrepair. Throughout the remainder of December 1910 they struggled in their daily letters to express their frustrations with each other and to resolve matters. It was not gracefully done. Letters that commenced with protestations of love and affection often deteriorated. Joseph's efforts to be conciliatory too often concluded in the patronizing manner that had come to characterize his tone with her: "Now Sweetheart, be a sensible child and write me frankly and fully just what if anything has been wrong." He reminded her, "I took you home because you thought you would get a good rest; if you are not getting it, I must insist on your returning at once. I believe that you will be better in every way in your own little flat here in Washington. Please understand this is no child's game." Having been away from the family the previous Christmas because of his work, he now offered her the image of a Christmas together: "It would be pleasant to have Christmas dinner right here in our own home. I don't want to be hasty but if I did what I'm impelled to do I would take tonight's train for New Orleans & bring you back at once. I am anxious & worried and very much dissatisfied about you."[44]

Nearly a year after Lucy's suicide, on November 1, 1911, tragedy struck the Farrar family once more. Goldberger was in Mexico. Almost as soon as he arrived, he got the news: his brother-in-law, Edgar Howard Farrar Jr., only thirty-two years old, had been murdered in cold blood on a street in New Orleans by what one writer described as a "common malefactor" named René Canton. René and Lucien Canton, twenty-two and nineteen years of age, respectively, had attempted to rob young Farrar's residence, and when the young lawyer tried to detain the thieves, he was shot to death by the older brother. Again Mary and the boys headed back to New Orleans.[45]

The murderer was quickly apprehended, tried, and sentenced to death. The death sentence was commuted to life imprisonment after Governor Luther Hall received a letter from the victim's grieving father. Explaining that he spoke for his family, including his widowed daughter-in-law, Farrar wrote:

> We feel that this young brute is the product of our system of society, for which all of us, particularly persons of our position, are to some extent responsible. His father and mother are honest, hard working people. With them the struggle for existence was too bitter and exacting to permit them to devote the time and personal care necessary to develop good and repress the evil in their son, who thus grew up amid the malign influences that surround the children of the poor in a large city. We believe that he shot my son as instinctively as a snake would strike one who crossed his path;

and while his act was murder in law, yet it lacked that forethought and deliberation which make a crime of this sort unpardonable. The man is now in no condition to be sent into the next world. We hope and pray that time and reflection will bring repentance and that his soul may be saved.[46]

The same broad, liberal perspective that informed many of Farrar's views, including his embrace of Joseph Goldberger as a beloved son-in-law, compelled him to intervene. No wonder that Goldberger and Farrar found each other so agreeable. Even as the physician had come to recognize some diseases as products of poverty and ignorance, his attorney father-in-law saw urban violence in the context of the social conditions that nurtured it.

From his post in Mexico, Goldberger penned his heartfelt condolences to his wife and in-laws as once again the end of the year found Joseph and Mary apart. He visited with Mary and the children in New Orleans on his way back to Washington. However, little Joseph was ill, and Washington was in the midst of a cold snap. The conquering hero returned from many months in Mexico to a frigid and lonely house.[47]

Unlike the last time Mary was away and he remained in Washington in 1910, he did not whine or complain, at least not as often. Still, he told Mary how much he missed her and that despite his delight with how well his work was being received, he would be "much more pleased and gratified, aye, delighted! To have you with me again." Much of Goldberger's ensuing marital bliss was the result of his promotion in March 1913 and assignments that did not take him far from Washington. He and John Anderson published their remaining papers on typhus and measles. Goldberger spent the summer and early autumn of 1913 on routine tasks. In July he participated with his colleague Joseph Schereschewsky in the reexamination of four immigrant children of a resident alien in Washington, D.C., who were in danger of being deported on health grounds. A typhus scare in Rochester, New York, caused him to be sent there to collect samples for testing and to advise local health officials.[48]

The year's biggest challenge was an outbreak of diphtheria in Detroit. Surgeon General Blue telephoned Goldberger on November 20, 1913. The call was confirmed in writing on December 1. Blue ordered Goldberger to "take immediate steps to start intensive investigation."[49]

Diphtheria, although hardly confined to the young, was often called the "scourge of childhood" in the nineteenth and early twentieth centuries because of a 30 to 50 percent fatality rate among children. Called the Klebs-Löffler bacillus in the early years of the twentieth century, the organism responsible for the disease (*Corynebacterium diphtheriae*) was generally spread to others in excretions from the nose or throat of one who had it. After an incubation period of one to four days, those infected noticed a mild sore throat and had difficulty swallowing. These symptoms were accompanied by a low-grade fever and increased heart rate. Children often also experienced nausea, vomiting, chills, headache, and fever. Gradually a fibrinous membrane, which becomes greenish black, developed in the upper respiratory tract. Heart and neural tissue are often damaged by toxic secretions, but most children who died suffocated because the airway was blocked by the diphtheritic membrane. An epidemic left unchecked could seriously threaten an entire city's health. Diphtheria antitoxin was available, but control of the disease in 1913 relied on isolating those who had it from those who did not—quarantine.[50] Why the sudden epidemic in Detroit?

The medical detective had been called on to solve another mystery. However, this time the solution was derived not from pursuing a microscopic organism but from tracking the irresponsible behavior of a human culprit. Within a few days of arriving in Detroit in late November, Goldberger had helped city officials to uncover a municipal fraud that was likely perpetuating the diphtheria epidemic.

The Detroit newspapers quoted Public Health Service reports showing that on November 19, there were 157 reported cases of diphtheria in Detroit. But previously the figure had reached as high as 300. From January 1 to November 19, 1913, 266 people died from the disease. Those stricken with diphtheria who reported to the Detroit Board of Health were required to submit throat swabs for culturing. The cultures were placed in an incubator overnight and checked at 7:30 the next morning.

Only when the culture was clear could the victim be released from quarantine. Goldberger, who arrived in the city on a Friday morning, concurred with local health officers that the board of health laboratory should be moved from the Board of Health building on St. Antoine Street to the Herman Kiefer Hospital on Hamilton Boulevard. The work of testing the cultures began on Saturday morning. Goldberger quickly determined that those in quarantine were being released prematurely because of improperly handled cultures. Neglect and dishonesty were at the root of the problem. The culprit was exposed on the following Monday.[51]

On November 26, 1913, *The Detroit News* ran the front-page headline OUSTING OF HAYWARD DUE TO DIPHTHERIA. The *Detroit Free Press* trumpeted, CITY BACTERIOLOGIST FORCED TO RESIGN BY HEALTH BOARD EXPOSÉ. The newspapers were reporting that the city's chief bacteriologist, Dr. Edward H. Hayward, had been recording fraudulent results on culture examinations, allowing individuals to leave quarantine who might in fact have been infectious. A bored Hayward, who had been in his position for nine and a half years, had signed releases without examining the diphtheria throat cultures. He then discarded the cultures. The result was a major health crisis.

Goldberger's work prompted the Detroit Board of Health to establish a new policy for release from quarantine. Now two cultures were required. These would have to be taken not less than two days apart. If both were free from diphtheria, the patient could be released.

The mystery was solved, but the detective's work was not yet done. From December 22, 1913, to March 4, 1914, Goldberger and his staff took 9,489 cultures from throats and noses of 4,093 persons who appeared to be healthy and 95 diphtheria patients. Newspaper publicity and house-to-house visits allowed examination of a representative portion of the population. Goldberger's work showed that approximately 1 percent of the general population were carriers of diphtheria bacilli and that about one-tenth of 1 percent had diphtheria. Approximately five thousand carriers existed among the healthy population of Detroit in 1914.[52] Goldberger also demonstrated that throat cultures alone allowed a certain percentage of carriers to escape detection and that the use of separate nose and throat cultures for each individual tested would double the number of carriers detected by throat cultures alone.

The diphtheria work was yet another infectious-disease experience for Goldberger. The scandal over the municipal bacteriologist who had falsified his data angered Goldberger, always the model of scientific integrity.[53] However, it was also another lesson in how matters that have nothing to do with scientific inquiry can shape the public health of a population.

In February 1914 Surgeon General Rupert Blue, in whom Goldberger had so much faith, expressed a similar sentiment about him. He wrote to Goldberger in Detroit asking him to take over the pellagra studies from Claude Lavinder, who had requested reassignment. Blue made the case simply and directly, explaining that in recent weeks he had been subjected to considerable congressional pressure to deal more energetically with pellagra. He confided to Goldberger, "It is undoubtedly one of the knottiest and most urgent problems facing the Service at the present time."[54]

Goldberger was ready. His early life had attuned him to the poverty he would see in the South, where most of the pellagra cases were concentrated. His early career experiences fighting yellow fever and typhus in Mexico had prepared him to recognize the epidemiological connection between that poverty, the broader social and economic patterns causing it, and particular diseases.

Most recently Goldberger had perfected his ability as an infectious-disease expert. At the time that Dr. Rupert Blue penned his order to Dr. Joseph Goldberger to accept the pellagra assignment, the surgeon general knew that Goldberger had the rare combination of experience and imagination required. Blue, then, had reason to be confident when he wrote, "I am . . . under the necessity of selecting an officer who will take charge of these studies and who will take them up from a broad and energetic standpoint. After going over the entire field, I feel that you are preeminently fitted for this work and that it could be placed in no better hands."[55] As he lifted his fountain pen to write to Mary and tell her that his work was about to separate them yet again, Goldberger did not disagree with Blue's assessment.

FOUR

Scourge of the South

Appearances can be deceiving. Dispatched south by the surgeon general in the early spring of 1914, Dr. Joseph Goldberger saw miles and miles of cultivated fields rush past his train window. One could hardly tell that it was a region undergoing wrenching economic and social transformation.[1] Before the Civil War the southern economy was firmly rooted in the soil and dependent on the weather. Agriculture, especially commercial agriculture, was its bedrock. Cash crops like tobacco, sugar, rice, and particularly cotton allowed growers to realize fairly steady if often modest profits. There was rural poverty but not much pellagra, at least not enough to attract widespread attention. War shattered southern economic life. Slaves were free, railroads were in ruin, many rivers were littered with the debris of battle, towns near the theater of war were often in shambles, and the once robust agrarian economy was at a standstill.

In 1914 the Civil War was fading into memory, but when Goldberger went seeking the solution to the pellagra mystery, most southerners, black and white, still made their livings on or near the soil producing cotton.[2] In place of the slave-labor system the post-Reconstruction South had become dependent on tenant farmers and sharecroppers—white and black—to revive southern agriculture. Tenant farmers paid in cash to rent the land they cultivated. Sharecroppers paid for the privilege of bending their backs over others' soil with a percentage of the crop they produced. When the weather did not cooperate or insects consumed crops before the harvest, tenants and sharecroppers had no choice but to take out loans against what they would produce next season. A few bad seasons in a row could tie a farmer to his soil with cords of debt and obligation so sturdy he could never break free. There was much talk of diversification of agriculture and diversification of the economy generally with a greater attention to commerce and manufacturing, but the high prices that could be garnered for cotton curbed the momentum for change. If cotton was what sold, then cotton was what the owner wanted, and cotton was what sharecroppers and tenant farmers grew.[3]

The pressure to grow more and more cotton, especially when prices were low, left little land for grains, vegetables, or livestock. Photographs of the period show cotton growing right up to the rickety front porches of tenant cabins. Food came from local general stores, where landowners had lines of credit for their tenants, whose diets declined as their debts rose. An increasing number of southern workers—men and women— left the land for cotton mills and tobacco factories. Taking advantage of their proximity to the cotton supply and a ready source of cheap labor with no immediate prospect of unionization, textile entrepreneurs grew their industry. By 1900 the South had surpassed New England as the nation's textile hub.

The South was switching to a production-based economy. Just as tenant farmers and sharecroppers were expected to devote their land exclusively to cotton production, textile workers were expected to devote their time exclusively to the mill. Like tenant farmers tied to their general stores through lines of credit and mounting debt, factory workers were often paid in trade checks redeemable only at the company store or a store with which the company had a special arrangement. Workers bought what the stores stocked, and low wages meant little money for good cuts of meat and fresh fruit and vegetables. Corn bread, molasses, syrup, fatback, and coffee were the staples of the mill worker's diet.

As bonds of community were shattered by the migration of labor from farm to mill town, orphanages, insane asylums, and prisons financed with philanthropic dollars or minimal tax support became essential. Here, in institutions public and private, routines of hard work and poor diet were the lot of those who had committed crimes but also of those whose only crime was to be sick or without parents. The verdure of the fields passing before Goldberger belied a region mired in poverty.

Well before boarding a southbound train, Goldberger was aware of the scope of the pellagra problem. Federal physicians had been studying pellagra for almost five years, and still the disease was rampaging across the map, especially in the South. By 1912 South Carolina alone had reported thirty thousand cases, with a case fatality rate of 40 percent. As if the data were not grim enough, the increasing number of pellagra cases and the rising rate of mortality were accompanied by a wave of "pellagraphobia." Writing in the prestigious *Journal of the American Medical Association* in 1912, the Atlanta physician George Niles warned that "a little ripple of fear, if encouraged, may grow into a billow of huge proportions, engulfing a whole neighborhood or community."[4] As cases and corpses multiplied, fearful southerners demanded answers. Surgeon General Blue faced mounting pressure to discover the cause and provide a cure; the forty-year-old Goldberger, newly promoted to the rank of surgeon, was called on to provide both.

Within days of his arrival back at the Hygienic Laboratory from Detroit, Goldberger received orders to head south, where the federal government had already established a research presence under the direction of Dr. Claude Lavinder at three sites: the Marine Hospital at Savannah, Georgia; the Georgia State Sanitarium at Milledgeville, Georgia; and the Pellagra Hospital at Spartanburg, South Carolina. Lavinder had burned out on the project and requested reassignment.[5] Now it was Goldberger's turn.

Goldberger headed first for the Hygienic Laboratory's library. Seeking to illuminate a mysterious disease that grotesquely disfigured its victims, he came to his research with a basic knowledge of what pellagra symptoms looked like and some doubts about whether it was an infectious disease. Pellagra, he knew, was characterized by a symmetric photosensitive red rash, which in older individuals was often dry and scaly, acute diarrhea, and mental aberrations. In the disease's earliest stages, the victim experienced weakness, a confusion or malaise, and crimson skin, which looked like sunburn. Eventually the red skin crusted and peeled. Underneath was smooth, glossy red skin. In some cases there were blisters that ruptured, leaving moist areas. The general appearance was not unlike a third-degree burn. Characteristic of the disease was the distribution of lesions at particular places on the body. Sunlight produced a red rash around the neck known as Casal's necklace, named for the Spaniard who had identified the disease in 1735, and butterfly-shaped lesions on the face. Similar rashes appeared on the backs of pellagrins and on the scrota of males. The rash also appeared on the feet and ankles, hands and forearms, a configuration sometimes called "pellagra gloves."[6]

Goldberger's research began with the basics and explored prevailing theories of pellagra's etiology in the existing literature, much of which had been written by western European scholars in languages other than English.[7] He then proceeded to what had been observed by private physicians and state and federal public health officers, including Lavinder. By the time he was finished reading, he hoped to have the most complete picture of what physicians knew or thought they knew about pellagra.

Among the more insightful material that Goldberger read were 1913 reports by Dr. Rudolf M. Grimm, who had been examining cases of pellagra in South Carolina, Kentucky, and Georgia. Grimm was accomplishing what state and local health officers had failed at doing—counting and mapping cases—basic epidemiological work. His data told a story that raised more questions than it answered, though he did seek to interpret some of what he saw. Pellagrins, or those who contracted the disease, all worked hard and experienced stress connected with their economic responsibilities, and they often lived in an environment rife with insects. But their dietary habits were equally impressive to Grimm, even though the precise linkage remained vague. Was food perhaps only a preconditioning factor? Toward the end of his lengthy report Grimm stated, "From my observations the relationship between food and pellagra seems to be a real one, but whether the character of the food may act only in predisposing to conditions which favor the development of pellagra, or whether certain articles of food act as the real exciting agent, or whether they act only as exaggerators of the symptoms (as the sunlight, for instance), is an open question." He concluded, "No investigation of the etiology of pellagra can entirely ignore the character of the food supply."[8]

A privately funded study reached a different conclusion. Two northern philanthropists, Colonel Robert M. Thompson of New York and J.H. McFadden of Philadelphia, donated fifteen thousand dollars to sponsor a pellagra investigation. The investigators' initial reports derived from the study of Spartanburg in the summer of 1912 and were published in

1913. No firm conclusions were reached. Pellagrins were poor, but so were many non-pellagrins. And although the diets of the two groups appeared to be the same, the report leaned toward regarding pellagra as an infectious disease. By the time of the second national meeting on pellagra held at Columbia, South Carolina, in November 1912, sentiment had begun to build in favor of the belief that pellagra was a germ disease, perhaps the result of poor hygiene and inadequate sanitation.[9]

Goldberger found the conflicting opinions voiced at conferences and in papers frustrating, and he was also uncomfortable with pellagra's being described as the South's problem despite state health reports indicating cases well north of the Mason-Dixon line. In 1909 Dr. George A. Zeller, the superintendent of the Peoria State Hospital in Illinois, admitted he had misdiagnosed pellagra because he had refused to entertain the possibility that the disease could be contracted in a well-run northern institution such as his. Nevertheless, from August to November 1909 he identified 130 cases.[10]

Goldberger was quite prepared to believe that pellagra was as much a problem in Illinois as it was in parts of the South. His restless pencil makes clear that he was seeking to learn about pellagra's etiology and epidemiology from the Illinois experience, and his scribblings and underlinings map his thoughts. In a section dealing with the occupations of pellagra victims, the report, as marked by Goldberger, observes that "herdsmen in pellagra regions are exempt." Goldberger drew an arrow from the sentence to the left margin of the page and wrote, "Milk!" Reading about the diet at the Illinois insane asylums, Goldberger underlined, "Meat is given only twice a week. On the whole it may be said that the food supply is satisfactory except that the general diet is somewhat deficient in proteids." In the summary of the 1909 report Goldberger marked three passages with his pencil to make certain that he would not forget what he considered the most important observations: No physicians, attendants or employees were affected"; "Mild cases recovered without therapeutic aid"; and "The disease impressed us as an intoxication rather than an infection."[11] Again and again he dwelled on the research findings that suggested pellagra was not an infectious disease. And he could not resist being attracted to data that suggested a dietary dimension to the pellagra drama.

Two years later, in November 1911, the State of Illinois had issued *Report of the Pellagra Commission*. The complimentary copy sent to the surgeon general for the Hygienic Laboratory's library contains telltale pencil marks by the detective collecting promising clues. Repeatedly Goldberger returned to diet. In a section of the summary dealing specifically with diet, he boldly marked a section that reminded readers that at the Peoria State Hospital, the diet was markedly deficient in "protein constituents and <u>especially in animal protein</u>."[12]

Goldberger marked the entire last paragraph of the report. Understandably so. The report noted that the Italian peasantry suffered more from pellagra "than any other people and their diet consists almost exclusively of maize in the form of polenta." European scholars who studied pellagra had long made the association between pellagra and corn consumption. Some, such as the nineteenth-century French physician Théophile Roussel, were convinced that pellagra was caused by eating only maize. Others, such as the Italians Lodovico Balardini and Cesare Lombroso, blamed moldy corn, while Giovanni Marzari thought most corn consumed was harvested prematurely and was not adequately nutritious anyway.[13] Such theories focused more on what pellagrins ate than on what might be missing from the diet, the direction that most intrigued Goldberger. The report was honing in on not spoiled maize but the corn-based diet, because of its absence of animal protein: "They [the Italians] eat practically no meat, fish, milk or eggs." However, the Italians were hardly alone, because, as the report noted, "meat becomes a luxury in all conditions of poverty." Maize had a protein value, but "this apparently cannot satisfactorily take the place of animal protein altogether." Having made this point, the report credited a diet low in animal protein as a "predisposing factor to infection with pellagra." What, then, caused the disease, according to the Illinois investigators? Wrapping themselves in the mantle of germ theory, they concluded, "Our impression is rather that pellagra is due to infection of the body with some micro-organism. It does seem possible, however, that a diet deficient in animal protein may so alter the body that the infecting organism has a better chance to grow."[14] His pencilings suggest that the report's concern with food nourished Goldberger's increasing curiosity about pellagrins' diets.

The notion that eating certain foods prevented specific illnesses was known to Goldberger. As early as 1753, well before scurvy was fully understood as a deficiency disease, James Lind discovered that citrus fruit could prevent the condition, and by the end of the eighteenth century British sailors were being issued lime juice to prevent the disease when they were at sea.[15] Similarly, beriberi was being successfully treated with extract from rice bran before anyone truly understood why it worked. And even as Goldberger pondered the relationship of diet to pellagra, others were wondering whether the skeletal malformities of rickets were not the result of a dietary deficiency, too.

Biochemists were beginning to learn more about noninfectious disease as they learned more about the chemistry involved in how the body works, but investigation of the biomedical aspects of chemistry was still in its infancy.[16] However, there had been significant breakthroughs, to which Goldberger had access through the journal articles he read in the Hygienic Laboratory library. Among the most intriguing was Dr. Casimir Funk's discovery of the "vitamine [sic]." Funk, a Polish Jew working in London, discovered that beriberi was a protein deficiency that occurred only in those who ate polished rice and that thiamine (later named vitamin B_1) was the cure. He suggested that other such nitrogenous substances—one for scurvy (vitamin C) and one for rickets (vitamin D)—existed. Although not all vitamins, as they came to be called, contained nitrogen, Funk had demonstrated that not all diseases need be caused by pathogens. Some could be caused by the absence of minute amounts of substances usually found in food. In a 1913 article Funk cast his lot with those who hypothesized that pellagra resulted from a problem in the milling process of corn, just as the milling process of rice caused beriberi.[17] It was a possibility, but there were many others, and Goldberger needed to know much more, insight that could only be gained outside the library.[18]

His homework completed, Goldberger boarded the train, one of the many he would be riding back and forth across the South in the months and years to come. Even as he answered the train conductor's call of "all aboard," he prepared himself to examine with his own eyes the telltale signs of pellagra on the bodies of its victims. He was anxious to visit institutions housing large numbers of pellagrins, to observe how they lived and what they ate. Only then could he test his hypothesis that the pellagra germ was a phantom, that corn was not the culprit, and that the root cause of this scourge was secluded in the dietary of its victims.

Forty years old and determined to solve the puzzle of pellagra, Goldberger gathered his belongings and stepped off the train at his first stop, Staunton, Virginia, in March 1914. There he visited the Western State Hospital, one of Virginia's several insane asylums. In the post–Civil War South patients were assigned to an institution by race, although some large institutions had wards segregated by race as well as gender. Western State received "exclusively white patients."[19] In the months ahead Goldberger visited asylums, orphanages, and prisons—places where pellagra frequently appeared. At the bedsides of pellagrins, white and black, his visits were brief. Because he was always on the move, the rhythms of his weeks were dictated by train schedules. From Virginia he went to Georgia, Alabama, Florida, and Kentucky, then back east to Columbia, South Carolina, and Atlanta, and on to New Orleans, and again to Alabama, and then on to Mississippi. Everywhere he went, he asked institution superintendents for data on pellagra incidence, diets of inmates and staff, especially corn consumption, and permission to inspect sanitary conditions. As he had done in the alleys of Mexico, Puerto Rico, and Brownsville, Texas, he hunted for insects that might be carrying the disease from victim to victim. However, what struck Goldberger most was that in all the institutions he visited, not a single staff member had pellagra. No infectious disease selects victims by status. For the rest of the spring he scrambled and scribbled. By day he made brief entries of his observations in a pocket notebook. At night the weary physician penned hastily written letters to Mary from his hotel room before drifting off to sleep.

In May, Goldberger was in Jackson, Mississippi. There he encountered the orphanages that would become crucial sites for his field studies. On May 11 and 12 he visited the Mississippi Orphans' Home of the Methodist Episcopal Church South. Of the 214 inmates, 60 to 70 were pellagrins. Goldberger was struck by the fact that some of them had been at the institution for "several years" but only now were presenting symptoms. He also visited Jackson's Baptist Orphanage, where 240 children were in residence. The Baptist Orphanage's superintendent, reluctant to admit there were cases of pellagra, a disease of poverty carrying the implication that the children were being insufficiently cared for, said staff members had been noticing cases of "sunburn." With persuading, however, the heads of the Methodist Orphans' Home and the Baptist Orphanage turned their institutions over to the Public Health Service for study.[20]

With his usual meticulous work habits, Goldberger lost no time entering into his small notebook all that he knew up to that point about the Methodist Orphans' Home. For breakfast there were generally grits and gravy or rice and gravy along with biscuits and syrup. In the narrow margin of his notebook Goldberger wrote, "Eggs about once a week when cheap enough." Dinner consisted of several vegetables such as cabbages, turnip greens, beets, onions, lima beans, pork beans, lettuce, spinach, or okra. Once or twice a week there was a dessert of pie or pudding as well as apple butter, pickles, and some canned delicacies. Fresh fruit was served only occasionally. Supper included grits and gravy, biscuits and syrup, light bread, and, to drink, iced tea for the older boys and girls. Sunday dinner was special and consisted of boiled ham, light bread, tea cakes, pickles and salad, apples or prunes, and iced tea. When vegetables were scarce, beef was served two or three times a week and, during the winter, fresh pork about once a week. The Baptist Orphanage menu furnished by Superintendent Carter was similar except that, as Goldberger noted, "No mention made of fresh meats."[21] Over the next few months Goldberger and his assistants studied the children and manipulated their diets in an effort to determine whether this alone would cure and prevent pellagra.

In mid-June 1914, several days before Goldberger's first publication on pellagra was scheduled to appear, the twenty-ninth annual meeting of the Conference of State and Provincial Boards of Health of North America was held in Washington, D.C. The chairman of the Committee on Pellagra was Dr. James A. Hayne, the chief public health official of South Carolina. He described pellagra as "the greatest riddle of the medical profession," a "sphinx of which we have asked a reply and gotten none, for nearly two hundred years." To emphasize the urgency of the problem, Hayne observed that in the previous year there had been 500 deaths from pellagra in Alabama alone; thus far in 1914, there were 170 cases in the state, with 114 deaths. The highly opinionated, bombastic Hayne was a staunch advocate of the germ theory of pellagra. Intolerant of alternative theories, he was also impatient with what he regarded as inadequate federal effort in hunting the pellagra microbe he was so certain existed.[22]

On June 26, 1914, Goldberger, for the first time, told the public health community what he thought about pellagra. In a paper titled "The Etiology of Pellagra," he drew on what he had learned in his reading and initial travels, advancing several hypotheses. First, pellagra was not a contagious disease. How did he know? Having observed that in the various institutions he had visited staff members never got the disease, Goldberger posited an explanation: staff and charges had different diets. He added "from personal observation" that although inmates and staff often appeared to be eating the same fare, such was not necessarily the case. He noted that along with opportunities to supplement their diets, "the nurses have the privilege—which they exercise—of selecting the best and the greatest variety for themselves."[23]

As for other aspects of pellagra, Goldberger observed that it was generally believed to be a rural disease and one associated with poverty. He asked rhetorically, "What important difference is there between the elements of poverty in our slums and those of poverty in rural dwellers?" While he claimed not to be prepared for an extended discussion of the difference, he did explain that he thought "on the whole the very poor of cities have a more varied diet than the poor in rural sections." Goldberger also advanced the observation that "a study of institutional dietaries" suggested "that vegetables and cereals form a much greater proportion" in poor populations than they do in the dietaries of well-to-do people, "that is, people who are not, as a class, subject to pellagra." If, as he admitted, there remained "great uncertainty" as to the "true cause" of pellagra, what should be done in the meantime? Goldberger did not waver. Where the disease was most prevalent, improve the afflicted's diet. Specifically, he called for "reduction in cereals, vegetables, and canned foods that enter to so large an extent into the dietary of many of the people in the South and an increase in the fresh animal food component such as fresh meat, eggs, milk." He concluded by reassuring his readers that the PHS assault on pellagra, now under his supervision, was already being pursued "along the lines so strongly suggested by the observations above considered."[24]

Goldberger was too well trained a scientist to expect his peers to believe him without much more systematic proof than he had thus far been able to produce. In fact, he ended his September letter to the surgeon general by saying that there was "grave doubt in my mind as to [his observations'] general acceptance without some practical test or demonstration of the correctness of the corollary, namely that no pellagra develops in those who consume a mixed, well-balanced, and varied diet."[25] What might that "practical test or demonstration" be? Because no animal equivalent to pellagra was known, any test must involve the use of human subjects. Accordingly, Goldberger began feeding experiments at the Methodist Orphans' Home in Mississippi in September 1914. He hoped that he would cure sick children and that his success would persuade doubters that his dietary hypothesis was correct.

On September 21, Goldberger carefully explained to the surgeon general the feeding experiment begun three days earlier and its cost: "As originally planned, and in accordance with the agreement entered into with the [Methodist] orphanage authorities, the [Public Health] Service supplements the ordinary diet of the institution by supplying fresh meat, milk and eggs." Goldberger estimated that the cost would not exceed $700 per month, $300 less than his original estimate. The experiment would be closely supervised by Dr. C. H. Waring, who had been working at the Baptist Orphanage in Jackson. Goldberger argued that the overall expense was not unreasonable and that "the value of the test now being conducted at the Methodist Orphanage would be enormously enhanced, more than doubled, if duplicated at the Baptist Orphanage." Optimistic and confident, Goldberger predicted to his boss: "A successful outcome, and we have ample reason for anticipating the most complete success, of two such simultaneous tests or demonstrations would practically eliminate all doubt as to the nature of the disease and the means of its prevention and eradication."[26] Expenses would double, because supplying the Baptist institution with food and a nurse would be the same, boosting the overall cost to $1,520 per month, but the payoff would be significantly greater. Rupert Blue was persuaded. He dashed off a letter to the secretary of the Treasury justifying all extra expenses, using language taken directly from Goldberger's letter to him.[27]

His research funded, Goldberger was content for the moment. He took the time to write longer letters to Mary, to apologize for the shorter ones, and to catch up on family matters. He was pleased that his eldest son, Farrar, was doing well at school. As for the youngster's piano lessons, which seemed to be going less successfully, the hopeful Goldberger suggested they reserve judgment. "We'll see what we'll see," he wrote.[28]

Even as his thoughts turned to his own son, the sight of the orphanage children eating wholesome food and enjoying better health cheered him. One day that autumn, in 1914, Goldberger described himself and his assistant as walking across the grounds of one of the orphanages when they were confronted by a boy of seven or eight years of age, the same age as Farrar. The "bright-faced, interesting looking boy" asked the two physicians, "Are you all giving us all the things to eat?" Goldberger said yes and asked the child whether he did not like the food. Very quickly the youngster replied, "Oh! Indeed we do, I hope you won't stop!"[29] Goldberger assured him, as well as Mary, he had no intention of stopping. He shared the moving episode with her because, as he had told her so many times, it was not just his work. It was their work.

His own days, except for such encounters with the children, Goldberger described as not newsworthy: "It is just a daily round of grind, going over the records and verifying data." However, the grind was not without its satisfactions, namely, the process of seeing his hypothesis confirmed. He wrote, "The thing works out with almost the precision of a mathematical problem." He then offered Mary an illustration. He explained that the records relating to a certain child suggested that the boy should have had pellagra a year earlier than he did, because at that point he would have left the youngest group, which got milk on a regular basis and was pellagra-free, and joined the middle group, where most of the pellagra cases were clustered. Why was this child's pattern different? After a careful check of the records, Goldberger discovered that the pattern wasn't different at all. The child had left the "baby" group a year later than the records showed, according to a nurse's testimony. A satisfied Goldberger buoyantly reported to Mary, "Whenever we get a fair test of the 'theory' it works just as it should if it is right. And it is right, there can be no doubt about it after seeing the data we have."[30]

Equally exciting as understanding the epidemiology of the disease was understanding its prevention and cure. Goldberger marveled that both might be "relatively a very simple and cheap matter—BEANS! This and nothing more is essential." As he subsequently wrote to Mary, "I'm well nigh convinced that Beans and peas will do the trick for pellagra. If we can get our people to eat these legumes in winter, Pellagra will be dissipated like a mist before the Sun. It's easy and cheap." Careful even in letters to his wife, he confessed, "Of course I'm not quite sure of this but it looks very much like it, very, very much. If it proves up, it will be a very great strike." As he had so many times before, he cautioned her to keep silent about his work.[31]

Although the orphanage experiment was still in progress, Goldberger was so confident that he knew the answer to the pellagra mystery he published another report co-authored with Assistant Surgeon Waring and their technical assistant, David G. Willets. Titled "The Treatment and Prevention of Pellagra," the report emphasized Goldberger's three preliminary conclusions: first, that pellagra was not an infectious or contagious disease but a disease of dietary origin; second, that it was dependent on a still unknown fault in the dietary in which the animal or leguminous protein component was disproportionately small and the nonleguminous vegetable component was disproportionately high; and, third, that no pellagra developed in those eating a "mixed, well-balanced, and varied diet." As an example of the latter, he referred to the fact that there was no pellagra among the "enlisted men of the Army, Navy, and Marine Corps."[32]

On the basis of these conclusions Goldberger, Waring, and Willets proceeded to recommend "that as long as clinical evidences of pellagra are manifest the patient should be given and urged to take (if necessary tube fed) an abundance of fresh milk, eggs, fresh lean meat, beans, and peas (fresh or dried, not canned)." Hedging their bets somewhat, Goldberger and his colleagues made clear that they were not claiming automatic and complete recovery in all cases as the result of dietary change. They feared that "there will always be patients who even in their first attacks are and will be beyond hope of recovery."[33]

The biochemistry of food was just beginning to be understood and the report's authors had not conducted biochemical analysis of all foods' protein content, but they knew that animal protein in the diet cured pellagra. They explained in considerable detail the foods rich in animal protein for the recovering pellagrin. Milk they described as "the most valuable single food." They urged adults to drink "not less than a pint and a half to two pints in 24 hours." They recommended four eggs per day and fresh lean meat. Confessing that all their experience had been with beef, Goldberger, Waring, and Willets encouraged adults to take "at least a half pound of lean meat a day in addition to the milk, eggs, and legumes." Where chewing was painful, meat juice could be substituted. The beans or peas could be served in soup or eaten in any other form. Even if the patient experienced diarrhea, the full prescribed diet should be continued. Although Goldberger and his colleagues did not subscribe to the corn theory of pellagra, they recommended excluding corn. Corn was a wholesome and nutritious food, to be sure, but because they did not yet know what if any role corn played, they advised excluding it and similarly reducing the amount of other "carbohydraceous articles, such as the newer cereal breakfast foods, molasses, jams, or starch." Once the pellagra symptoms disappeared, corn consumption could be resumed so long as the diet continued to include "an abundance of milk, meat, or legumes."[34]

As for medications, Goldberger did not think that any medication was of value in curing pellagra, although the pain and insomnia that some victims experienced could be treated. In general, though, diet and rest were all that he prescribed, except in acute cases where the sensitivity of the skin made staying out of the sun wise.

If changing the diet offered a cure, a well-balanced, varied diet rich in animal protein was also the best prophylaxis. Goldberger explained that while the poor often had the most difficulty maintaining such a diet, they might be able to obtain the required protein from preserved legumes. Noting the seasonal rhythms of the condition, he observed, "The evidence is daily becoming stronger that the eventual eradication of pellagra from our South will depend largely on the successful introduction of our common dried legumes into the late winter and spring dietary. A valuable step in this direction would be an increase in the cultivation of some of the varieties of beans and peas and their preserva-

Joseph Goldberger's father, Samuel Goldberger, who brought his family to the United States from Giralt, Hungary, in 1883. (Courtesy of Dr. Joseph H. Goldberger)

Joseph Goldberger's formidable father-in-law, Edgar H. Farrar, circa 1906. (Courtesy of Dr. Joseph H. Goldberger)

Bride Mary Humphreys Farrar and her groom, Joseph Goldberger, on their honeymoon trip from Gulfport, Mississippi, to New York City, April 1906. (Courtesy of Dr. Joseph H. Goldberger)

Dr. Joseph Goldberger in the full-dress uniform of the U.S. Marine Hospital Service shortly after receiving his commission in 1899. It was the only time in his career when he sported a mustache. (Courtesy of Dr. Joseph H. Goldberger)

Group portrait of Public Health Service officers who battled yellow fever in 1905. Goldberger is in the second row, fourth from left. (Courtesy of the Southern Historical Collection, University of North Carolina, Chapel Hill)

Dr. Joseph Goldberger at his laboratory bench at the Hygienic Laboratory, being assisted by Dr. William H. Sebrell, Jr., circa 1927. (Courtesy of the Office of the U.S. Public Health Service Historian)

Joseph Goldberger (1906) at age thirty-two, the year of his marriage to Mary. (Courtesy of the Southern Historical Collection, University of North Carolina, Chapel Hill)

Mary Humphreys Farrar circa 1906, at the age of twenty-five.

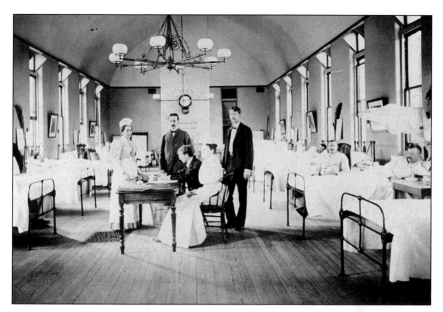

Young Dr. Goldberger circa 1896, seated in a ward at the Sturges Pavilion of Bellevue Hospital. (Courtesy of Dr. Donald Sharp)

Joseph Goldberger and his three sons, probably at the Farrar summer retreat at Biloxi, Mississippi, circa 1915. From left to right: Joseph H. Goldberger, Joseph Goldberger, Edgar Farrar Goldberger ("Farrar"), and Benjamin Goldberger. (Courtesy of Dr. Joseph H. Goldberger)

The Hygienic Laboratory (later the National Institute of Health) was located at Twenty-fifth and E Streets, N.W., in Washington, D.C., from 1904 to 1938. (Courtesy of the Office of the U.S. Public Health Service Historian)

The Pellagra Hospital at Spartenburg, South Carolina, in 1916. It was there that Goldberger and his associates studied the effects of diet on pellagra. (Courtesy of the Office of the U.S. Public Health Service Historian)

tion in the dried state for winter and spring consumption." As he had on earlier occasions, Goldberger reiterated his belief that although some institutions claimed that sufficient fresh meat was "allowed" to prevent pellagra, inmates at such institutions did not always consume an "ample allowance" because they did not always eat what was on their plates or because it was stolen by another inmate. At asylums, measures needed to be taken to see that the inmates actually ate what they were served. As for the rich, who had access to a balanced diet, Goldberger again contended that pellagra erupted when a "personal idiosyncracy" caused the individual not to eat a well-balanced diet: "To have a good, rich, mixed, well-balanced, and varied diet 'on the family table' is one thing; to eat it is quite another."[35]

As 1914 came to an end, Goldberger wanted to give as many southern physicians as he could reach "something to think about." Like the southern evangelists who pitched their tents in open fields and measured success by the number of converts who had accepted Jesus by the end of a warm summer evening, Goldberger proclaimed victory one doctor at a time.[36] In December he was notified that he would soon have the opportunity to pitch his tent in Cambridge, Massachusetts, and seek converts among the nation's medical elite at Harvard University. He was invited by his former colleague Milton Rosenau to present one of the two prestigious Cutter Lectures on Preventive Medicine for 1914–1915.[37] The other presenter was the eminent Dr. Victor Vaughan of the University of Michigan, an expert in infectious disease and toxicology.[38] Goldberger could hardly contain his delight: "I need not say how pleased I am nor how deeply I appreciate the compliment, but I am at the same time completely 'flabbergasted'; this comes 'so sudden' that it takes my breath away." The title he proposed was simple: "Diet and Pellagra."[39]

In early April, Goldberger traveled to Cambridge and delivered his lecture. He began by explaining the enormity of the pellagra problem, citing a figure of "not less than 50,000 cases" for 1914, with 11,000 in the state of Mississippi alone. He summarized the research to date, including his own. Although pellagra cases were found in the North, Goldberger explained that the overwhelming number of them were in the

South, where, he asserted, "pellagra is essentially a rural disease, and a disease of poverty." Always thorough in his scientific observations, Goldberger reported the differences his data revealed between men and women, blacks and whites. Women were at greater risk than men, Goldberger noticed, and "there is a remarkably close coincidence between the period of menstrual life and the curve of maximum incidence of the disease in the female." Blacks were also at greater risk. He noted that in Mississippi "the death rate for 1913 was 55.6 per 100,000 for the negro, and 25.5 for the white people," a ratio in excess of two to one. However, he rejected the notion that different sanitary conditions in the black and white communities were to blame.[40] Wherein lay the cause and the most likely means to a cure?

Diet was the answer that Goldberger offered his listeners in Cambridge. He articulated the view that he had already published, namely, that in a pellagrin's diet a substance was lacking. It could be found in the animal-protein foods, meat or milk or both. Goldberger stressed that he was hypothesizing not that pellagra was due to a lack or deficiency of animal-protein food but rather that it was due to "a 'fault,' brought about in some yet undetermined way in diets of a certain type (largely corn or other cereal or starchy food, or combination of them) and that this 'fault' is capable of being corrected or prevented by including in such diets a suitable proportion of animal protein foods."[41]

Animal-protein foods were not the only solution. Goldberger told his listeners, "Epidemiological observations and therapeutic experience have led us to believe that the common legumes (beans and peas) are of value in this respect and we think it quite probable that there are still other classes of foods capable of serving the same purpose."[42] As he had elsewhere, he added that having the diet available and eating it were not necessarily the same. In cases where individuals who had access to a mixed diet contracted the disease, Goldberger postulated that they had not eaten the healthy diet. As for why women and blacks were more vulnerable, it would take years of more research for him fully to uncover the complex epidemiological pattern at work. However, thanks to Rosenau's invitation, Goldberger had placed his theory before some of the top medical men in the country. Now he must offer scientific evidence to prove his claim.

The Cutter Lecture behind him, Goldberger could return to his research. However, he could not ignore the suffering that had grown progressively worse since the outbreak of World War I the previous summer. According to the *Savannah Morning News*, Goldberger attributed the current crisis to "the fact that the cotton crop was a failure last year [1914] on account of the war, this causing farmers to restrict themselves on diet."[43]

Although the United States would not enter the war until 1917, the hostilities in Europe were having a disastrous effect on the American economy, especially in the South. Disruption of the cotton trade in a year when the South's cotton crop was robust, indeed the largest in history, drove down market prices. Losses in 1914 added up to $500 million, fully 50 percent of the crop's value that year. Major cotton exchanges were dark, remaining closed for months. Prices for the commodity fell below ten cents per pound, the price at which growers could just about survive. However, even after prices dropped by 50 percent to a nickel a pound, there were few customers for the South's most important crop. Many farmers left their cotton unpicked, and many of those who rented were released from their contracts. However, what they gained in freedom, they lost in access to resources. Tenant farmers and sharecroppers released from their agreements had no access to credit at local stores. Their families were without food and supplies for the winter. Fortunately, British purchases of cotton buoyed the price until wartime demand gradually pushed up cotton prices, first to eleven cents a pound, then to almost twenty, and later to as high as thirty-six cents. Between 1917 and 1919 cotton prices averaged twenty-seven cents a pound. There would not be another such crisis for several years.[44] However, for those stricken with pellagra in 1914 and 1915 the future was not bright. For some there was no future at all.

The cotton crisis and plummeting prices in 1914 made even more urgent Goldberger's advice to the South's poor, which he conveyed in press interviews and pamphlets in late 1914 and in 1915. He told southern agrarians to try to own a cow, because a steady supply of milk was crucial in preventing pellagra. He urged tenant farmers and sharecroppers to cultivate five-acre plots in cowpeas or field peas. Addressing himself to those who owned the land that others planted and harvested, Goldberger called for a small portion of land to be kept free from cotton so that there would be room for the peas that he knew to be a pellagra preventive. State health officers and those who worked at the county level in farming regions assisted materially in distributing Goldberger's pamphlets on pellagra prevention in churches, stores, and via the mail. In Georgia alone, eighty thousand copies of the publication were circulated. Some newspapers, such as one in Mississippi, printed it in its entirety.[45]

Having addressed the public, Goldberger turned to his peers and in October 1915 published a detailed description of his eating studies in *Public Health Reports*. The article, co-authored by Assistant Surgeon C.H. Waring and Assistant Epidemiologist David G. Willets, was titled "The Prevention of Pellagra: A Test of Diet among Institutional Inmates." The research, designed to run for two years, was still in progress, but Goldberger's results from the orphanage eating experiments were so dramatic that he could not wait until the experiment was fully concluded to share his findings. Beginning in mid-September 1914, the diets at both orphanages were "supplemented by the Public Health Service." They began by increasing the milk supply. Provisions were made to give every child under twelve years of age a seven-ounce cup of milk twice a day. Those under six got the milk three times a day. Goldberger and Waring prescribed at least one egg served at breakfast to all children under twelve. And where it had been the custom to serve meat but once a week, now fresh meat was served three or four times a week. Because Goldberger believed that beans and peas could supplement a faulty diet as well as meat, they were made a part of every midday meal all year round.[46] The breakfast cereal was changed from grits to oatmeal, the intent being to reduce the corn component of the diet and to increase milk consumption. But because Goldberger regarded the corn theory of pellagra as highly suspect, he chose not to eliminate corn from the orphans' diets altogether. Corn bread was served once a week, and grits were allowed those over twelve once or twice a week.

Goldberger's methods were imprecise. He was adding more than animal protein to the orphanage diet. Still, the results were gratifying. At the Methodist Orphan's Home, 67 of the 79 victims spent the anniversary of their pellagra episodes under the observation of Goldberger and Waring. Following the change of diet, none of the 67 showed signs of a recurrence. The news at the Baptist Orphanage was good as well. Of the 130 cases cited during the summer of 1914, 105 completed the anniversary of their attack under observation, and of these only one had a recurrence.[47] The orphanage studies and similar efforts at institutions throughout the South gave powerful if not scientifically conclusive evidence that Goldberger had cracked the problem.

Certainly the orphanage study seemed to suggest that dietary changes prevented pellagra. The news was also positive from the Georgia State Sanitarium at Milledgeville, where adult inmates were similarly tested. There, two wards had been turned over to Goldberger and his assistant, Willets.[48] Many pellagrins were found among those newly admitted, but there were also many cases that occurred within the institution. The two experimental wards consisted of one ward of "colored" females and one ward of white females. Each ward had a fifty-bed capacity. To each ward approximately forty adult pellagrins were admitted who had experienced attacks during 1914. Few had active symptoms at the start of the experiment, though some bore the marks of their recent attacks.

The same dietary changes made at the orphanages were made at the asylum's two wards. The results compiled as of December 31, 1914, were from the 72 patients ("36 colored and 36 white") who had remained under continuous observation to October 1, 1914, or at least until after the anniversary of their last attack. "Of the 36 colored patients, 8 have histories of at least 2 annual attacks; of the 36 white patients, 10 have histories of at least 2 attacks. None of this group of 72 patients has presented recognizable evidence of a recurrence of pellagra."[49]

The preliminary results of the eating experiments were confirming Goldberger's suspicion. Still, he was well aware that "the ideal form of the experiment would have been, of course, to retain for purposes of comparison a control group at each of the institutions." However, practical considerations prevented him from following such a protocol. He did not specify what made using a control group "impracticable at the orphanages." However, he clearly could not acquire such data without putting some of the orphanage children at risk. Fortunately, another physician had already done research that suggested what might occur among children not eating Goldberger's diet.[50]

Dr. H. W. Rice, a physician at a Columbia, South Carolina, orphanage, reported that "of 31 children who had pellagra in 1912, 18, or 58 per cent, had recurrences in 1913; of the 21 who had it in 1913, 16, or 76 per cent, had it in 1914; and of 75 who had the disease in 1914, 56, or 75 per cent had it again in 1915." Goldberger thought these rates of recurrence consistent with what one might expect at the orphanages where he was conducting research. Therefore, he took as a baseline 50 percent, a rate somewhat lower than the 58 percent reported by Rice, but one that seemed "fairly and conservatively representative." He applied it to the Methodist and Baptist orphanages and found that 33 recurrences at the Methodist orphanage and 52 at the Baptist institution might reasonably have been expected in 1915, whereas none was observed at the Methodist institution and only one among the children at the Baptist Orphanage.[51]

Goldberger did not make explicit his awareness of an ethical tension between his role as physician and his role as scientist at the Mississippi orphanages. However, his behavior suggests some sensitivity to the issue. He had secured the cooperation of orphanage officials with the understanding that his purpose was to get the children well, and curing the children does in fact appear to have been his first priority. As a scientist, he also hoped to collect data that might be valuable in solving the pellagra puzzle. Understanding that an experiment was of limited value without control groups, Goldberger did seek them, but not at the orphanages. Instead, he established his control groups at the racially segregated Georgia State Sanitarium, in "both the colored and white female service." He isolated and monitored these groups. The control group of black female pellagrins in 1914 consisted of seventeen who had been under observation for as long as those who had been moved to Goldberger's special diet. Of those seventeen, nine, or 53 percent, had already experienced recurrences. The control group of white females in 1914 consisted of fifteen women. Of these, six, or 40 percent, had recurrences in 1915. Thus, when the groups were combined, an average of 47 percent had experienced recurrences. The institution's records allowed determination of recurrences in previous years. In the "colored female service" the average rate of recurrence for the four years 1911–1914 was 52.5 percent, the rate in different years varying from 40 to 70 percent. In the "white female service" the average recurrence rate for the same period was 37.5 percent, with variation from 22 to 48 percent. Goldberger wrote that based on such data "a considerable number of recurrences in the groups of insane pellagrins subsisting on the modified diet [a diet rich in animal protein] might reasonably have been expected." Based on the 1915 data alone, one might have anticipated thirty-four recurrences. In fact, none was observed.[52]

Goldberger was well aware that the eating experiments had not been conducted under perfect laboratory conditions. Still, he strongly advocated accepting his results as conclusive:

> Viewing the foregoing results as a whole, bearing in mind that three different institutions in two widely separated localities are involved, each institution being an endemic focus of the disease, and bearing in mind, also, that the number of individuals considered is fairly large, it seems to the writers that the conclusions justified that pellagra recurrences may be prevented and, in view of the condition of the test, that they may be prevented without intervention of any other factor than diet.[53]

In addition to publishing his research, Goldberger argued his position at conventions and conferences. The same month that the orphanage report appeared, October 1915, he took on his critics at the third triennial convention of the National Association for the Study of Pellagra, which, like previous such meetings, was held in Columbia, South Carolina, largely through the efforts of James Woods Babcock, whose articles had first called national attention to the disease. Although African-American physicians were not invited to present papers, they could sit in the gallery and listen.[54] Because Goldberger had only been assigned to head the PHS's pellagra study in 1914, this was his first association meeting. He not only presented his orphanage and asylum data but went toe-to-toe with his severest critics, James A. Hayne, South Carolina's chief public health officer, and the investigators of the Thompson-McFadden Commission, represented on the meeting's program by one of the commission's principal investigators, U. S. Army physician Captain Joseph F. Siler.[55]

Complimenting Goldberger on his paper in a gentlemanly fashion, Siler said he was largely persuaded by his conclusions. Hayne's response to Goldberger was more complicated. Having earlier referred to Goldberger's hypothesis as "an absurdity," Hayne was now faced with responding to extensive studies and data that other physicians were taking seriously. Slated to present a paper on pellagra's communicability, he withdrew at the last moment, saying that it would be best to discuss communicability when the bacillus at fault could be viewed on a microscope slide. He did not deny that diet could banish pellagra's symptoms, and his withdrawal caused Goldberger to dismiss him as having "bleated very gently." However, Hayne did contribute to the general discussion, and his statements were prescient, because they raised the obstacles that public health officers confronted in preventing pellagra if alterations in diet were the only prophylaxis.[56]

Hayne, perhaps moved by anger and frustration at Goldberger's victory, observed that the dietary theory left state public health officers with the dilemma of having to find a way to change the "mode of living" of "the whole people of a state." That, Hayne said, would be "almost impossible." If Hayne was misguided in his commitment to the germ theory of pellagra, he was clever in perceiving that a disease resulting from a social system and economic infrastructure could not easily be prevented by the public health establishment as it existed in most southern states.[57]

Goldberger understood that patience is a virtue and that the gratification derived from public recognition of one's insight and accomplishment is most often delayed. However, unlike scientific researchers confined to their laboratories, isolated from the implications of their research for humanity, Goldberger was a physician, an epidemic fighter who had witnessed human suffering and deplored it. Now, though, his ability to relieve such suffering depended on his ability to banish the skepticism about his dietary theory. Only if he could begin with healthy individuals and alter their diets under controlled conditions to induce pellagra symptoms might he persuade doubters that pellagra resulted from "faulty" diet. Where might he find a healthy population that could be rigidly controlled in diet and behavior? In his Cutter Lecture, Goldberger told his Harvard audience that while pellagra was widely prevalent at "jails," it was "rarely encountered" at "convict" farms. He said that he found such data "particularly striking when it is recalled that many of the convicts are long term prisoners and that these farms are in a very heavily affected section of a severely affected state [Mississippi]."[58] What he did not tell his Harvard audience was that at just such a prison farm he had already begun a bold and controversial test of his pellagra theory.

FIVE

Pellagra, Prisoners, and Pardons

Much big news was coming out of the South in the spring and summer of 1915. And strangely enough, two episodes involved southern governors—John M. Slaton from Georgia and Earl Brewer from Mississippi—invoking executive powers and risking their political careers on behalf of two Jewish northerners. Each governor believed that he was acting on principle, taking a stand that would ultimately redound to the benefit of his state's reputation and to the welfare of the South generally. Both governors became targets of invective for their choices; both are written into the historical record as heroes.

In Georgia, Governor Slaton commuted Leo Frank's death sentence to life imprisonment. Frank, a northerner educated at Cornell University, had married into a wealthy and much-respected southern family. The slender twenty-nine-year-old with his straight dark hair and eyeglasses was managing a pencil factory when he was accused of killing thirteen-year-old Mary Phagan. The daughter of dispossessed sharecroppers, Phagan was employed in the pencil factory fitting metal tips to pencils for twelve cents an hour. On Confederate Memorial Day, April 26, 1913, she disappeared. Her badly bruised body was found slain, lying facedown in the factory basement the next morning. Missing were her purse and $1.20. In an atmosphere charged with anti-Semitism and anti-northern sentiment stirred by a rabid press, Frank was tried, convicted, and sentenced to death. In July 1915, Slaton commuted the convicted felon's death sentence to life imprisonment because he believed there had been a miscarriage of justice that would forever besmirch his state's reputation if Frank was executed.

Slaton had been a successful Georgia politician—until he commuted Frank's sentence. Fueled by the poisoned pen of Populist-turned-bigot Tom Watson, thousands of Georgians carrying guns, hatchets, and dynamite surrounded the governor's mansion. Jewish businessmen boarded up their windows and doors against armed mobs while almost half of the state's three thousand Jews fled temporarily. On August 16, 1915, a mob kidnapped Frank from a prison farm at Milledgeville, Georgia, and lynched him. Frank's name, and with it Slaton's, would not be cleared until the early 1980s, when a witness, wishing to salve his conscience, identified an African-American night watchman as the killer.[1]

Three months after Frank dangled from a tree near Marietta, Georgia, Mississippi governor Earl Brewer put his political career at risk by keeping a promise. He granted pardons to eleven Mississippi prisoners who had volunteered to serve as human subjects in a controlled medical experiment conducted by Dr. Joseph Goldberger. Further testing his hypothesis that pellagra was a dietary deficiency, Goldberger meant to induce the disease in healthy individuals by changing only their eating habits. Success would prove that the presence or absence of pellagra depended on the presence or absence of some aspect of a person's diet.

Conscious that he was taking a political chance, Governor Brewer was committed to helping Goldberger. Failure to support this federal physician with the Jewish-sounding name from the North might mean missing the opportunity to save countless southern lives, many of them in his own state. The incentive to act decisively was great. After all, in 1914, 10,954 cases of pellagra were reported to the Mississippi State Board of Health, compared with 6,991 for the preceding year. The number of deaths reported for 1914 was 1,192, compared with 795 for 1913. Officials could only guess at the number of cases that had not been reported. Mississippi's 32 percent pellagra case fatality rate was the highest in the South.[2]

Brewer knew he would be criticized for offering pardons to hardened criminals, even in the name of science. However, neither his critics nor news of Slaton's political demise dissuaded him from his belief that the

South's future depended on a healthy workforce. From the perspective of the governor's office, the future vitality and productivity of southern workers in mill and field were essential to attracting investment dollars, a precious commodity since the Civil War. Much, then, depended on the success of the clean-shaven, bespectacled, wavy-haired forty-one-year-old physician whom the surgeon general had entrusted with ridding the South of its scourge.

None of Goldberger's professional publications or private correspondence reveals his thoughts about the use of prisoners as human subjects in an eating experiment. The absence suggests that he did not find the use of prisoners a remarkable break with what others had done before him. Goldberger's voracious reading had suggested to him that pellagra might be the result of a faulty diet, not unlike "recent advances in our knowledge of beriberi." Richard P. Strong, an American physician and scientist, had only three years earlier studied the etiology of beriberi and the effectiveness of a cholera vaccine using Filipino prisoners awaiting execution as his guinea pigs. Could Goldberger find prisoner volunteers in the American South? Before he could, he would need the assistance of a southern governor.[3] Governors had the power to offer prisoners sufficient inducement to run a life-threatening risk: pardons in exchange for their cooperation. What were the chances that a southern governor might be persuaded to hazard the political perils of pardoning prisoners in support of Goldberger and the Public Health Service? Better than one might think.

Progressive southern governors, at times a colorful lot that included James K. Vardaman, Theodore Bilbo, James Hogg, and Huey Long, were enacting reforms and taking all sorts of political chances to dispel the popular image of the South as a primitive backwater where few would want to spend their lives or their investment dollars. During the first two decades of the twentieth century, southern states embraced a broad array of reforms, restricting child labor, outlawing the blacklisting of union members, setting safety standards for railroads, financing new roads, making school attendance compulsory, and adopting such democratizing devices as the initiative, referendum, and presidential primary. They were ending the county convict lease system and public hangings.

They were passing state income taxes and using the revenue to build schools, tuberculosis hospitals, charity hospitals, juvenile reformatories, and junior college systems. The South was rising, and a new generation of Progressive governors was leading the way.[4]

On the morning of January 21, 1915, Goldberger met with Governor Brewer for the first time. Dr. E. H. Galloway, secretary of the Mississippi Board of Health and a trusted friend of Brewer's, had laid the groundwork so the meeting could proceed expeditiously.[5] In his diary Goldberger recorded that he had informed Brewer that he had received the surgeon general's "authority to go ahead with the diet test on the convict volunteers." Needed now was Brewer's participation and the promise of pardons. Brewer, not wanting to make the decision without consultation, asked that they be joined by "Mr. 'Bob' Miller and Judge Davis." Brewer's advisers asked Goldberger about the diet, and Goldberger "gave them the proposed bill-of-fare." It would be the typical corn-based diet consumed by the South's poor. Satisfied, Brewer "dictated a form letter to be given to volunteers to sign" and provided Goldberger with letters of introduction to prison officials, including "Mr. Allen, Sargeant [sic] at 'Rankin' Farm, to Mr. Foltz and Mr. Dodds at Oakley and to Mr. O Keefe at Parchman."[6]

Goldberger wasted no time. He immediately visited the Mississippi corrections facilities, beginning with Rankin State Prison Farm, a facility for white convicts about eight miles east of Jackson. The prisoners there appeared strong, robust, and without even a hint of pellagra. It did not take Goldberger long to see why. While the prisoners ate the usual fare of corn bread and syrup, there was usually meat "of some sort" at all three meals, buttermilk "to some extent (not frequent)," and field peas and beans several times a week. At Oakley, too, Goldberger inspected the diet and found it "good."[7] He also found that among the fifty-six convicts there wasn't a single case of pellagra.

Just as Goldberger was about to depart Oakley, he was handed a letter from one of the convicts. It was a signed and witnessed copy of the form letter that Governor Brewer had dictated in his office. Then being distributed among the prison population, it suggested the effort made by the PHS and Governor Brewer to establish that convict volunteers were offering informed consent. It read:

Dear Governor:

I understand that you desire to make certain observations through the state penitentiary by having twelve men volunteer to submit themselves to a diet test that will involve a period of time to be prescribed by physicians in charge, and feeling that this may be of benefit in helping others and that I can thereby accomplish some good to my fellow man I hereby volunteer my service to take this diet test in strict accordance with the rules which you and the authorities may prescribe, and I promise to faithfully and obediently carry out my part of the service with the understanding that at the expiration of the test if I have obediently and faithfully carried out the services that I am to be released from the Mississippi penitentiary or pardoned during good behavior in the future.

Governor[,] I make this proposition and cheerfully volunteer for this service voluntarily of my own free will and accord after having given it due consideration.[8]

Accepting the convict's letter, Goldberger departed for his last stop, the infamous Parchman State Penitentiary, a segregated prison farm known for the unrelenting field labor of its convicts, the austerity of their lives, and the severity with which infractions were punished.[9]

Whatever terrors inmates might face from their captors, Goldberger found Parchman a basically healthy place. The farm was serviced by two physicians, the more senior of whom had been there slightly less than a year but could vouch that during that period there had not been a single case of pellagra. In his diary Goldberger noted how striking it was that there had been no pellagra, though the prisoners had come from all across the state. As always, he asked about the menu and, perhaps not to his surprise, was told that it included "fresh meat every day" and often "sweet milk." Rice and field peas were also part of the regular fare. Dutifully writing to Mary, Jospeh mentioned finding Parchman pellagra-free.[10] However, by the time he next visited with Brewer, Goldberger had decided on Rankin, a white penal farm in the Mississippi prison system, as the best facility for his experiment because its configuration of buildings would permit isolation of the subjects from the rest of the prison farm population while not dramatically changing their environment or daily tasks.

Governor Brewer took care to get the volunteers' consent in writing because he was acutely aware that cooperating with Goldberger exposed him to considerable legal risk. Thousands died of pellagra each year. Goldberger's convict guinea pigs were at real hazard to their lives. As Brewer later recalled, "Some might die and leave us accused as murderers."[11] Why, then, did the governor take the chance?

In Earl Brewer, Joseph Goldberger found a staunch ally farsighted enough to fit the Public Health Service's fight against pellagra into his own vision of southern Progressivism. Although only six years older than Goldberger, Brewer, in his background and cultural baggage, could not have been more different from the immigrant physician in federal service, although neither came from wealthy stock. Born at Midway, near Vaiden in Carroll County, Mississippi, in 1868, Brewer, a Confederate captain's son, was a member of that generation of southerners born after the Civil War but still close enough to the war to bear the burdens of the lost cause and its multiple legacies. Like Goldberger, Brewer had to borrow money for his education, attending law school at the University of Mississippi, where he completed two years of study in six and a half months, receiving a bachelor of law degree in 1892. Unlike Goldberger, though, Brewer grew rich in private practice. Building his law practice around lucrative railroad-accident cases, Brewer plucked hefty settlements from railroad companies' deep pockets while enhancing his public reputation and visibility. In 1895 he was elected to the Mississippi State Senate, later serving as district attorney of the Eleventh Judicial District. In 1906 he unsuccessfully ran for governor, but six years later went nearly unopposed.[12]

Brewer epitomized the Progressive tradition minus the virulent racism and moral lapses that marked the style of the era's notorious southern demagogues, including that of the colorful Theodore Bilbo, who succeeded Brewer in the statehouse and was characterized by some members of the Mississippi legislature as a "moral leper." Still, if Brewer's days as governor made duller newspaper copy than those of his predecessors, such as the "Great White Chief," James K. Vardaman, or his successor, Bilbo, they earned Brewer a legacy as the people's champion. During

Brewer's reign the board of health received increased appropriations to promote sanitation and the prevention of communicable diseases. An assault on pellagra was thoroughly consistent with all that Brewer believed and had tried to accomplish.

The governor and Goldberger dangled the promise of pardons before approximately eighty inmates. All the prisoners had to do was volunteer to spend the next six months eating the traditional southern diet. By all accounts, doctor and politician were candid as to the risks.[13] Moreover, the subjects were encouraged to consult lawyers and family members before entering into the agreement. Nevertheless, the fact that the volunteers were incarcerated when they made the choice was ethically ambiguous. To some, Goldberger's use of convicts could never be anything but coercive.[14] Others argue that to withdraw the possibility of volunteering for medical experiments is an unwarranted denial of decisions about the use of one's body to which even convicted felons still have a right.[15]

Goldberger did not record in his diary his personal view of the convicts who agreed to participate in his experiment. However, in a letter to Mary he refers to the men as "convict 'volunteers.'"[16] The quotation marks may indicate some ambivalence in his own mind about whether accepting pardons in exchange for their participation did not in some way vitiate the prisoners' status as volunteers as compared with those who altruistically offer their bodies to science expecting nothing in return other than the satisfaction of having served humanity. Whether or not Goldberger weighted the convicts' sacrifice differently from that of other experimental subjects on his own moral scales, he never appears to have treated them with anything other than respect and care for their welfare as his patients.

From the many volunteers who came forward, Brewer and Goldberger selected twelve, half of them murderers serving life terms. All were white males, because, as Goldberger and Assistant Surgeon George Wheeler later wrote, "judged by the incidence in the population at large, these [white males] would seem to be least susceptible to the disease." Success with a Caucasian sample, then, would be even more persuasive evidence that pellagra was the result of faulty diet.[17]

There might have been another reason for selecting only Caucasian prisoners. Blacks had frequently been used as the subjects of medical experiments in the South, but participation in experiments involving tangible rewards—such as pardons—was considered a privilege.[18] Although it is unlikely that Goldberger would have allowed Brewer to shape the research design for political reasons, confining the pellagra squad to Caucasians removed at least one potential political burden from Brewer's shoulders. Whatever else he might have to answer for, he would not have to defend to his Mississippi constituents pardons for black lawbreakers.

Between February 1 and February 4, 1915, Goldberger and his staff picked their twelve volunteers, ranging from twenty-four to fifty years of age. Seven were serving life terms for murder. All but one, who developed an inflammation of the prostate gland, remained in the experiment until its conclusion.[19]

The convict volunteers were housed in what was commonly called "the new hospital building." A small screened one-story cottage used as a camp hospital, it was only about five hundred feet from "the cage," where the other inmates lived. Goldberger's volunteers were strictly separated from the other convicts to ensure that they were not contaminated by personal contact with a prisoner who might have pellagra. Scrupulous separation also precluded the possibility that smuggled food could reach the volunteers. Goldberger had planned for a three-month period of close observation with no change in prisoners' daily diet to ensure that none of the men had pellagra, but grumbling among the convicts "to begin and to get through with their ordeal" persuaded him to move up the start date. With daily schedules of "work and discipline" routinized, the prisoners' diet was changed at noon on April 19.[20]

A typical breakfast included what Goldberger recalled seeing orphans and asylum inmates consume: biscuits, fried mush, grits, brown gravy, cane syrup, and coffee with sugar. Lunch generally included corn bread, collards, sweet potatoes, grits, and syrup. Supper did not differ a great deal and included biscuits, mush, rice, gravy, syrup, and coffee with sugar. It was monotonous eating. As Goldberger had seen with his own eyes, it was also what an increasing number of southerners of modest means ate day in and day out for most of their lives, especially the cotton mill workers who had neither cows nor patches of vegetables.

Sharecroppers and tenant farmers often fared no better. Vegetable patches and dairy farming took a back seat to cotton.

The labor that the prisoners performed in the blistering Mississippi sun on a daily basis during the late spring and summer of 1915 was also carefully regulated. Typical were the tasks performed the week of August 8, 1915: whitewashing fences and buildings, two and a half days; sawing lumber, two days; and rest, two and a half days. During the experiment the volunteers kept approximately the same hours and did the same kind and amount of work as they usually did. Any differences were designed to lighten the volunteers' burdens, an easing of the routine that largely occurred late in the experimental period. Similarly, sanitary conditions for the volunteers did not differ markedly from those for the rest of the prisoners, but certain elements of the hygienic environment such as personal cleanliness, cleanliness of quarters, and freedom from insects, especially bedbugs, "favored the volunteers," as Goldberger described it.[21] Netting and clean sheets were the best precautions against insect vectors that some believed transferred pellagra to new victims.

Goldberger and his staff regarded the entire inmate population of the "camp" as their control group. However, Goldberger kept especially close watch on newcomers who were sentenced to Rankin after the experiment began. Twenty such newcomers were kept under what he described as "continuous medical surveillance, comparable to that of the volunteers."[22] If newcomers, freshly adjusted to the lifestyle and diet of Rankin inmates, failed to contract pellagra while the Rankin volunteers became symptomatic, it would bolster his argument that diet alone determined whether or not one got the disease.

Though the experiment was shrouded in secrecy—besides Goldberger, the surgeon general, and Brewer, only prison authorities and state health board officials were fully informed—news of it did leak. According to the press, Brewer was concerned that if the experiment received wide publicity, "relatives and friends of the convicts would institute habeas corpus proceedings or take other legal steps to secure their release from the 'pellagra squad.'"[23] Once the experiment was under way, Governor Brewer found himself the target of complaints and criticism that must have made him wonder whether he was helping Goldberger make medical history or manufacturing a fiasco. Letters addressed to Brewer by those who learned of the experiment ranged from the ridiculous to the outraged.

Among the former was a letter of complaint signed by one of the prisoners selected for the experiment, Guy James. In early August, James, a convicted murderer who thought himself more clever than he was, penned an impassioned, albeit disingenuous, letter to Brewer asking the governor to "come to our relief." According to him, the convicts were being subjected to the "worse [sic] torture" to which twelve men had ever been exposed. James begged the governor to "rescue" the prisoners; conveniently forgetting the terms of the pardon agreements, he asked the governor to "let us go home." Blithely ignoring that the experiment was scheduled to end in mid-October, James warned that if the convicts continued to go "gradually down," they would be "unable to withstand the winter."[24] Governor Brewer was not moved.

Brewer was much more ruffled six weeks later by a letter from an outraged newspaper editor, W. H. Rucker, publisher of *The Itta Bena Times*. Having heard that Guy James was going to be pardoned at the conclusion of the experiment, Rucker wrote to demand that Brewer refuse to put him back on the street. Claiming intense public opposition to James's pardon, Rucker fumed, "If he deserves a pardon there are none deserving of punishment."[25]

While Brewer found himself deflecting criticism for the bargain that he and Goldberger had struck with the convict volunteers, Goldberger seemed unaffected. He focused solely on his pellagra research in Mississippi and elsewhere around the South. From his perspective the weeks and months were filled with anticipation as his assistant Dr. George Wheeler supervised the Rankin experiment on a daily basis.

Goldberger found himself on an emotional roller coaster. The Cutter Lecture in early April had been exhilarating. Two weeks later, on Sunday April 18, the day before the pellagra squad was to be switched to the experimental diet, a tired, slightly morose, and very homesick Goldberger wrote to Mary from his office in Jackson, Mississippi. After a first paragraph professing his eagerness to "get back to you again," he turned to what he held dearest after his family—his work. While the orphanage children were looking "very well indeed," things at Rankin were "not quite as satisfactory as I had hoped for."[26] To homesickness was added impatience as he waited and hoped that once the experiment began, pellagra lesions would appear on the bodies of his volunteers. In the meantime, Goldberger continued to travel almost constantly. He climbed off and on trains, spending many hours each month shuttling between the orphanages in Mississippi, the asylum in Milledgeville, Georgia, the U.S. Marine Hospital in Savannah, the Pellagra Hospital in Spartanburg, South Carolina, and the Rankin State Prison Farm near Jackson. There were also frequent detours to give talks at meetings and local medical societies. Occasionally there was a trip home to see his wife and "the kiddies." Whenever a spare moment presented itself, he scribbled letters to Mary, always on stationery emblazoned with the name and often the image of the hotel where he was staying.

On April 25, Goldberger found himself with "a two hours loaf" at a Birmingham hotel before heading for the train station, just enough time, he wrote Mary, to consume a hasty meal and share some juicy gossip about his assistant, George Wheeler:

> Here is an interesting romance for you—<u>confidential</u>. Dr. Wheeler whom I have to hold things down at the convict farm is to be married May 6. He appears to be a fine fellow. His sweetheart is a Hartford, Conn. girl. On account of the work he can not very well get away so he has arranged for his "lady" to come on to Jackson where he will meet her with a preacher. The three will then go on to Vicksburg where the wedding is to be. They will have a honeymoon of about 24 hours and then return to the convict farm. What a place for a bride! She is a plucky girl, and is getting a worthwhile man.[27]

Chortle as Goldberger might in his entertaining note to Mary, his description suggests that it was precisely Wheeler's self-denial and dedication that he most admired, even expected. After all, if Goldberger was willing to make sacrifices in the name of medicine, so must those in whom he placed maximum trust.

The "two hours loaf" must have been a welcome respite, because he took the opportunity to dwell on what would happen if all went well at

Rankin. The battle would be only beginning. Somehow he would have to convince southerners to change the economic circumstances and social conditions at the root of pellagra's spread.

He momentarily envisioned plans to get his dietary gospel to "the man on the street or the street corner." Pondering the social lines that must be crossed to reach those most at risk, Goldberger wrote of his hypothetical listener, "After all he is the fellow we are after—not the 'high-brow' who is more interested in a hairsplitting discussion of the derivation of the world 'pellagra' than in getting the true faith as to decent diet to the plain everyday worker and his wife."[28]

Such thoughts led Goldberger to consider his own household. Referring to the stresses that his absence from home and family was creating, he asked Mary about the behavior of his eldest son, the ever mischievous Farrar, then about eight years old. Farrar's behavior seems to have caused Mary no end of anxiety. The doctor offered his wife a prescription: "He needs firm and steady control which, I regret to say, you will have to exercise with only such little help as I can give when I'm at home." Goldberger concluded with what passed for husbandly reassurance in an age when few women claimed careers outside the home: "You certainly have a real job. But it's a glorious thing to be a real mother! We all love her so! Adoringly, Joseph."[29] With that, Goldberger left for the train station.

His weeks and months away from his wife and children cost more than he had calculated. Mary, whose sister's depression had resulted in suicide, was now descending into depression herself, possibly the result of a thyroid condition, and was under a physician's care. In late May this southern belle who had so captivated young Joseph with her buoyant, seemingly carefree ways confessed that she had erected a facade of cheerfulness and well-being that would no longer bear the burdens of her life. She wrote to him of how hard she was trying to "get rid of the blue devils." She admitted that from time to time she lied to him "to keep from an angry expression of your disapproval." According to her son Joseph's recollections, the lies often had to do with how much money she had spent at local department stores. She begged his understanding, promising, "I won't [lie] any more, you will help me with my weaknesses and I will not keep what hurts me sometimes about you shut up in my heart." Torn between his war on pellagra and Mary's suffering, he chose to stay the course but continued to reach out to her to the extent that the mails would allow. "Do please write me as often as you can," he implored, "your letters are a very great comfort to me."[30] As she often did, Mary spent the summer on the gulf coast at her parents' comfortable retreat in Biloxi, where her mother could comfort her and servants could help with the children.

Perhaps trying to boost his own spirits as much as Mary's and to make her feel that their long separations were worthwhile, Goldberger wrote, "I think—I have reason to think—that before long we will be able to show that . . . pellagra may be produced in a healthy vigorous adult by a suitable ('unsuitable') change in diet. I am fairly confident that we will be able to present convincing evidence within a comparatively short time that we have the correct solution to the problem of pellagra—for sanitary prevention purposes." He promised her that when the experiment was over, he would take a week's leave so they could relax in Gulfport, where they had begun their honeymoon. He acknowledged how difficult the past two years had been, especially for her. In his letters he cast the imminent "milestone in preventive medicine" as their joint accomplishment. Perhaps trying to lift her spirits, he asked, "Don't you feel a thrill of elation about the success of our years' work?"[31] In the absence of a return letter or diary entry, one can only wonder whether Mary was emotionally well enough to share her husband's sense of accomplishment and impending fame.

Tensions within his marriage caused by Mary's illness were not the only difficulties that Goldberger faced as he traveled the South. By far his biggest disappointment of the summer was due to his unsuccessful candidacy to be head of the PHS's Hygienic Laboratory in Washington, a prestigious position vacated by his former mentor and collaborator John F. Anderson. The job had also once belonged to Goldberger's dear friend and confidant Milton Rosenau. The administrative position would mean an increase in responsibility and salary. However, most important to the Goldberger family, it would mean that Joseph would be on permanent assignment in Washington with limited travel and a stable family life. Goldberger applied, knowing it would please Mary. He confided to her, "No one has peeped except perhaps myself. I took it upon myself to go to [Surgeon General] Blue and tell him to consider me a candidate for the job. So there now!" He quickly cautioned her to keep the matter confidential and not to get too excited because "I haven't got it yet and may never get it, so its [sic] best to be quite calm about it."[32]

Remaining calm turned out to be good advice. Goldberger received the wholehearted support of Rosenau at Harvard and other prestigious figures such as Dr. Victor Vaughan of the University of Michigan and Yale's William T. Sedgwick. In a personal note Rosenau wrote, "I think your scientific achievements entitle you to that position, and if I can, in any way, be helpful in letting the authorities know what a good fellow you are, please tell me what to do." Vaughan echoed the sentiment in a letter to Rosenau: "It seems to me that there would be no question but that Goldberger is the man for the place. I will take great pleasure in writing Dr. Blue to this effect."[33] Still, however eminent the top academics in the field of medicine and public health thought Goldberger to be, the surgeon general did not consider him the best man to head the Hygienic Laboratory. Dr. George W. McCoy was selected.

Goldberger sought to salve Mary's profound disappointment over his rejection. He wrote to her, "I am surely sorry that you are so disappointed over the Director-ship. I'm sorry I ever said I wanted it for then you wouldn't have been hurt and disappointed." He admitted that he shared some of her disappointment but confessed that the pain of rejection was lessened by relief that the decision was now "out of the way" so he could refocus on his work.[34] Undoubtedly, the loss of the directorship was far easier to bear than it might have been because he was about to realize one of the most notable victories of his career. The Rankin experiment was a success.

In calm, declarative, somewhat dry sentences, Goldberger and Wheeler reported the dramatic results of their bold experiment:

> Of the 11 volunteers, not less than 6 developed symptoms, including a "typical" dermatitis, justifying a diagnosis of pellagra. The nervous and gastro-intestinal symptoms were mild and distinct. The dermatitis was first noticed between September 12 and September 24, 1915, or not later than five months after the beginning of the restricted diet. It is of great interest to note that in all our cases, the skin lesions were first recognized on the scrotum. Later

there appeared lesions on the backs of the hands in two cases and the back of the neck in one case.

The control group, the convicts at the farm who were not part of the pellagra squad, showed "no evidence justifying even a suspicion of pellagra."[35] Mindful of the care that must be taken to avoid premature conclusions and accusations that he had seen rashes but not pellagra lesions, the cautious Goldberger had extended the experiment to the end of October. To allay any concerns that his diagnosis of pellagra was self-serving, he had asked a number of outside physicians to examine the prisoners. They all concurred with Goldberger's diagnosis.[36]

It must have been hard for Goldberger to contain his enthusiasm during September and October as he waited for the other physicians to confirm the pellagra diagnosis. Yet his innate caution prevented him from telling even Mary until late October. He sent her a telegram that arrived on October 27, but it simply referred to "great news." Mary knew her husband's definition of "great news" well enough. She immediately scribbled a note back to him. Bubbling with excitement for him, she explained how much it meant to her: "It has done me a lot of good—and only justifies me the more in my opinion that Blues and Politics to the contrary, your light cannot be hid in a bushel." Two days later he could not help gloating over what he could now discuss openly and which he anticipated bringing him no small degree of professional credit: "Yes, Sweetheart, we sure enough have done it. Five [actually six] of the 11 men show clear evidence of the disease. I am, of course, very much tickled and I know how happy it will make you." With tongue in cheek he added, "I presume that the Bureau will not be altogether displeased."[37]

On November 1, 1915, the Rankin prison experiment was ended. Pardons and praise replaced circumspection and secrecy. Newspapers all over the country trumpeted Goldberger's demonstration that he could induce pellagra in strong, healthy men by depriving them of fresh milk, lean meat, and vegetables. True, Goldberger could not yet identify the pellagra preventive, but he knew what kinds of food contained it and what the dire results were when it was absent. Like beriberi and scurvy, pellagra was the result of a nutritional deficiency and not of an errant microbe.

Nowhere was the praise more lavish than in Mississippi. After all, it was a matter of state pride, and journalists made every effort to emphasize the state's role in Goldberger's discovery. An editorial in the *Jackson Daily News* titled "Dr. Goldberger's Great Work" heaped laurels on the federal physician: "Dr. Jos. Goldberger of the United States Public Health Service whose investigations and experiments made chiefly in Mississippi have robbed pellagra of its terrors is entitled to rank with the men of medical science who developed the mosquito theory of yellow fever transmission, the antitoxins for diphtheria and typhoid, the cure for hookworm disease and the eradication of bubonic plague."[38]

The prisoners, too, were heroes in the editorials: "Even though they were only felons, a majority of them being murderers serving life terms, those eleven convicts at the Rankin state farm who volunteered for the experiment showed unusual courage. It required a stern sort of bravery for these men to deliberately subject their bodies to a deadly disease loathsome in its form, and with a high death rate to its credit." Perhaps to quiet those who had implored Brewer not to honor his promise of pardons, the *Jackson Daily News* was emphatic: "It was a successful experiment and the eleven men, even though they were embezzlers and murderers, richly deserve their freedom." Eighteen years later, when he looked back on the experiment and how word of the pardons had gotten out prior to its conclusion, Earl Brewer "laughed" and said that he "caught plenty of trouble when all those pardons were revealed at once without a full explanation. But looking back on the Goldberger experiment I considered it one of the outstanding events of my administration."[39]

Indeed, neither Goldberger nor Brewer wasted any time delaying explanation once the experiment was formally concluded. In a letter to Brewer dated November 1, 1915, Goldberger formally announced the end of the experiment and asked that his subjects be released: "The convict volunteers have faithfully carried out their agreement to submit themselves to the test, and the test being now completed, it is my duty to most strongly urge their claim on the people of the state, through you, for pardon of their sentence and liberation from the penitentiary." Later that day, all gathered in the governor's office, where Brewer signed the unconditional pardons. A reporter captured the dramatic scene when "the eleven men, still clad in prison stripes, entered to receive the precious papers that would restore them to liberty. They were all pale, weak, and emaciated, two or three of the number scarcely able to walk, but all were anxious to get home." Dr. A. W. Borum, pastor of the First Baptist Church, offered a prayer for the men's full recovery, "closing with an earnest appeal to each to become useful and law-abiding citizens." Tears were streaming down the cheeks of most of the men as each stepped forward to the governor's desk to receive his pardon, including the member of the squad whose prostatitis had forced him to withdraw from the experiment in July. After the brief ceremony Goldberger's pellagra squad was marched out of the governor's office to the prison secretary's desk, where each was given a suit of civilian clothing and five dollars. They were once again free men.[40]

Goldberger did not want those prisoners who had developed pellagra symptoms to leave until they were completely well. In his official letter to Brewer declaring the experiment terminated, he made his plea: "These men have been under great physical strain. All are sick men. I would therefore strongly advise that they remain at the farm for a period of at least two weeks to receive the proper diet in order to, at least, start them on the road to health." He predicted dire consequences if his advice was not taken: "Unless this is done there is serious danger of permanent and grave injury to their health."[41] However, only a few of the prisoners took Goldberger's advice. Of the six who had developed pellagra, one was in critical condition, but with care recovered within six months. Three others left with their pardons, and then returned by nightfall to receive the care and feeding necessary. After only a few weeks they, too, recovered.

It was over. Goldberger had done it, but he knew only too well that he could not have done it alone. Even as he heaped praise on Wheeler, his colleagues, and above all on Governor Brewer, friends and family heaped praise on the good doctor. Milton Rosenau's letter was jubilant, though he chided Goldberger, "I have only one complaint about your letter and that is that you insist on calling me 'Rosenau' when I call you 'Joe' and sign myself 'Milton.'" He bubbled over with heartfelt praise: "I almost danced for joy when I read that you had succeeded in producing pellagra through diet in the volunteers. I feel that your achievement in this disease is the equal of any contribution to medical science made in America, and stands on a plane with the results obtained by our European friends . . . really it is great."[42]

Professor Reid Hunt of Harvard's Department of Pharmacology, who described himself as "one of those who have been requested to make nominations for the Nobel Prize," wrote to Goldberger. After congratulating him, Hunt asked for details on some of Goldberger's earlier research, such as his work on typhus, for a letter to the Swedish Academy. He cautioned Goldberger not to be too optimistic about immediately becoming a Nobel laureate, since the nomination was due in January 1916, only two months away: "While, of course, I do not expect your work to be sufficiently well known by that time for you to have any chance of getting the prize, at the same time, I think it only right that your work should be formally placed on file in Stockholm."[43]

As for family, Goldberger's father-in-law, Edgar Farrar, asked Goldberger to visit a hospital established by the Great Southern Lumber Company, a client of Farrar's firm, to discuss the handling of pellagra there. Then the reserved attorney, who had slowly come to respect and even like his Jewish son-in-law, dryly acknowledged what was being trumpeted in newspaper headlines: "I congratulate you on the outcome of your experiment. I did not know, when I saw you last, that the demonstration had progressed so far." Always pessimistic about human nature and what one could expect from one's adversaries, Farrar predicted, "Of course, the infectionists will deny the result obtained and say that the theory of infection is not excluded." If Farrar was restrained in this moment of celebration, his daughter was not. Mary wrote again, "I wish I could have been with you to see the glad faces that surrounded you. No one is more deeply proud of you than I am."[44]

As it turned out, Edgar Farrar was correct. Predictions of the demise of the germ theory of pellagra were premature, and celebration of Goldberger's achievement was by no means unanimous. Goldberger did not have long to wait to hear his work denounced. The arena was a pellagra symposium at the annual meeting of the Southern Medical Association, held in Dallas about a week after the end of the experiment. Newspaper headlines announcing Goldberger's success acted as a red flag to physicians and public health officers gathering to discuss the South's scourge. They lost no time aiming their horns at a theory of causation they refused to accept and a research experiment they found irritatingly audacious.

Goldberger did not attend the meeting. The PHS physician Allen W. Freeman began the symposium with comments about Goldberger's experiment and generally defended it, though he allowed that announcing the results so soon after the conclusion of the experiment was "perhaps unfortunate." Not many of those present joined Freeman in Goldberger's defense. More typical was the vicious attack launched by the chief health officer of South Carolina, James A. Hayne, long a critic of the dietary theory. Only several weeks earlier, at a meeting of the National Association for the Study of Pellagra, a cowed Hayne had avoided a confrontation. Now he was ready to speak. Recalling that earlier meeting to suit his own purposes, he accused Goldberger of waffling on pellagra causation and of ignoring data on the number of new cases when they did not fit his assumptions. Taking full advantage of Goldberger's absence and Freeman's comment about the public announcement being premature, Hayne concluded by taking aim at the newspaper coverage, which he found vexing. He denounced such dissemination as irresponsible, because, as a health officer, he knew "how hard it is to get out of the minds of the people what has been published in the lay press." He then predicted that just as the "bad water" theory of malaria had been discredited, so, too, would the notion that pellagra was caused by a faulty diet.[45]

Goldberger was well aware of the cloudburst of criticism raining down on him. However, he faced it all with "entire calm and peace," as he assured his wife. The criticism was the price of "hitting the publicity line hard," as he had promised Mary he would do. Surely newspaper headlines would catch the eyes of the man or woman on the street ("Mr. and Mrs. chap"), and in such a battle no publicity was bad publicity. Moreover, not every meeting turned into a crucifixion. Shortly after the Dallas debacle, Goldberger attended a conference of state health officers in Little Rock, Arkansas. Afterward an amused and refreshed Goldberger described to his wife one especially enthusiastic supporter who said that he "wanted to confess that he 'swallowed Dr. Goldberger whole.'" However, beneath the humor there was a reservoir of anger toward those he believed were obstructing efforts to rid the South of pellagra. He fumed, "The blind, selfish, jealous, prejudiced asses will only write themselves down in more conspicuous letters by braying forth their so-called criticisms."[46]

As the months passed, the battlefield broadened from the conference podium to the journal page. Although an editorial in *The Journal of the American Medical Association* lauded the Rankin experiment, an article by Dr. Ward J. MacNeal of the Thompson-McFadden Commission, which continued to insist on the existence of a pellagra germ, suggested that Goldberger had not opened the door wide enough for alternative diagnoses of the rashes he took to be pellagra lesions and raised some question about whether the scrotal lesions that he had considered definitive evidence of pellagra were really all that telling. A testy MacNeal concluded his assault:

> It would seem . . . especially pertinent to suggest that Dr. Goldberger should publish at an early date exact and full descriptions of all the symptoms and manifestations, together with available photographs of the lesions on which the diagnosis of pellagra was founded in these cases. Even if it should then appear, as now seems very doubtful, that one or more of the convicts actually had pellagra, the possibility of a preceding attack of the disease would require consideration. Meanwhile, the claim that pellagra has been produced by a restricted diet should be regarded with suspicion, and it would be well for those who have yet acquired a knowledge of this disease by personal observation or by a somewhat comprehensive study of its literature to retain an open mind concerning the essential facts of its causation.[47]

Never shrinking from a fight, Goldberger lashed back. He began his response with a stinging slap at MacNeal: "By reason of the tone and personal character of MacNeal's criticism we have not felt that it required any special notice, preferring to let the record of our work speak for itself." Emphasizing that he was responding primarily out of courtesy to the distinguished biochemist Elmer V. McCollum, who had echoed some of MacNeal's concerns, Goldberger explained:

> The evolution of the eruption on the genitalia was slow and that on the hands and neck very late in appearing, so that the evidence justifying a diagnosis of pellagra was not regarded by us as present until within a very few days of the close of the experimental period, which . . . was abruptly terminated on November 1. We were obliged to limit our invitation, therefore, to such authorities on the diagnosis of pellagra as were quickly accessible.[48]

If Goldberger appeared outwardly stoic as he dodged his critics' brickbats, it was because inwardly he knew that he had provided only a partial answer to the pellagra puzzle. His work at the Mississippi orphanages and Georgia asylum suggested that he could cure the disease's dreadful symptoms and even prevent its onset with a diet that included fresh meat, vegetables, and milk. Now, at Rankin State Prison Farm, he had demonstrated that he could induce pellagra through dietary manipulation alone. However, critics, with some justification, observed that the Rankin experiment might only have proven that bodies weakened by poor nutrition were susceptible to the elusive pellagra germ. He had not eliminated the possibility that well-nourished bodies could contract pellagra. Also, he still could not explain precisely what was missing from pellagrins' diets that the human body could not do without. Was it possible that he had stumbled upon a vitamin that did not yet have a name? Or was the missing nutrient something so obvious that he was overlooking it? More work needed to be done.

The implications of the Rankin demonstration and its critical reception in the medical community left many well-meaning Progressive-minded policy makers in the South confused. How should they respond to the different views of pellagra? Goldberger was an eminent physician who had conducted a bold experiment, but his opponents were trusted medical men as well. Modernity could be especially perplexing when the experts disagreed. Should responsible southerners heed Goldberger's critique and alter their social system so that the poor might be afforded a better diet, or should they join those who denied Goldberger's dietary hypothesis and keep their way of life intact? Medical science and southern culture were at odds. In the autumn of 1915 there were no easy answers.

By the following winter a frustrated Goldberger had come to a decision. He would have to execute an even more dramatic experiment, possibly even putting his own life at risk, to demonstrate that pellagra was not an infectious disease.

SIX

"Filth Parties" and Mill Meals:
Medical Sleuthing in Lab and Village

In 1906, when he was still courting Mary, Joseph told her his conception of God. Natural laws were manifestations of an "Infinite Intelligence," he explained, and scientists such as himself were its "priests," capable of fathoming its mysteries through rational inquiry, including empiricism.[1] Ten years later, hot on the trail of pellagra, Goldberger put every tenet of that scientific priesthood to the test.

At the turn of the twentieth century many American intellectuals came to believe that the path to truth was through the senses. They claimed that factual data derived through careful, attentive observation could be analyzed by the rational mind and expressed in statistics, the language of truth. These assertions were the cornerstone of the Progressive belief in rational, systematic inquiry as the best means of improving the human condition. Many Progressive reformers began their quest by delving into the relatively new disciplines of economics, sociology, statistics, and psychology, collectively called the social sciences. Abandoning the philosophical, theoretical moralizing of the nineteenth century, social scientists gathered data on human behavior in the field. This, then, was the Progressive credo: trained, dispassionate experts should decide what must be done. It was up to others, especially leaders in business and government, to implement the change.[2]

Joseph Goldberger was the consummate, if unself-conscious, Progressive. While he assembled his theories in the scientific laboratory, he tested them in the field, setting himself up time and again as the dispassionate, objective observer. When, as in the case of pellagra, he was unable to persuade colleagues and the public to accept his analysis, he did not lose faith in his theory or in the process of scientific inquiry. He just ratcheted up the level of his fieldwork.

This, then, became the story of 1916 and 1917. Goldberger had convinced himself and an increasing number of physicians that pellagra was triggered by a dietary deficiency. But he had not convinced enough peers to radically change the treatment of the disease throughout the country. Pellagrins were still dying by the thousands. Something dramatic, something conclusive, needed to be done—something persuasive to others, especially open-minded physicians who shared his faith in scientific inquiry.

At the core of the opposition to Goldberger's dietary theory was the conviction that he had not actually induced pellagra at the Rankin State Prison Farm. Instead, he had merely observed the onset of an opportunistic infection in bodies weakened by poor nutrition. Mary's recollection of her husband's state of mind in the spring of 1916 was ferocious in his defense. In an undated typescript essay written after her husband's death, she recalled his resorting to "heroic measures" because he was "badgered, tormented, and unbelieved." According to Mary, at a meeting of the Bellevue alumni Ward J. MacNeal of the Thompson-McFadden Commission accused Goldberger of "faking the prisoner experiment." Goldberger had remained gracious and refused to argue, saying only, "I shall rest on my published works on pellagra." Mary recalled his telling her that when he left the hall that night, a colleague slapped him on the back and said, "Joe, you—a Jew—taught us to behave like Christians." With his quick New York wit, Goldberger shot back, "Wasn't the first Christian a Jew?"[3] However, the exchange of barbs did not resolve the reasonable doubts that MacNeal and other proponents of the germ theory still harbored.

If Goldberger's dietary hypothesis was correct and MacNeal's germ theory was wrong, no effort to infect a host with pellagra would succeed. Contagion and its specificity as well as the means of infection were incompletely understood in 1916. Medical scientists knew more about waterborne bacterial diseases than about airborne ones. They knew that vectors, such as the mosquito that carried yellow fever from one victim to another, were sometimes responsible for carrying pathogens from host to host. They understood the concept of the healthy carrier, one confirmed by the devastation wrought by New York's Mary Mallon, better known as Typhoid Mary.[4] However, they did not yet fully appreciate that a disease could incubate in one host before being communicated to another. Moreover, although the bacterial model was better understood, there was much to be learned about viruses. As for disease that involved diet, everyone accepted that beriberi and scurvy could be prevented and treated by adding certain foods to the diet, but many thought that the diseases were caused by microbes, not a dietary deficiency.

So Goldberger devised a two-pronged attack. First, he would provide a dramatic demonstration to persuade those pursuing a pellagra germ to give up the hunt. Second, he would conduct a field study, a social scientific investigation that would allow him to discover the epidemiology of the scourge. Because such carefully constructed studies were the bread and butter of turn-of-the-century social scientists, he had little trouble enlisting participants. Some nonphysicians as well as physicians offered themselves in the first trial, too, which involved self-experimentation. The real surprise was that his wife was listed among the volunteers.

A Public Health Service spouse, Mary Goldberger never had to deal with late-night calls, the bane of all general practitioners' wives. No, Mary's burden was the months she spent alone, separated from Joseph, shouldering responsibilities different from his. He fought epidemics in faraway places. She kept the family together in Washington. Often he was gone at important moments in her life—when she was ill, when she was giving birth. It is hard to reach out to a man when he is not there. However, if he could not participate in her life, she loved him enough to insist on participating in his.

On May 7, 1916, Mary Humphreys Farrar Goldberger entered the U.S. Pellagra Hospital at Spartanburg, South Carolina, to join in her husband's experiment. She carefully arranged her clothing to preserve her modesty while exposing a spot on her stomach where her husband could inject her with seven cubic centimeters of blood taken from three pellagrins. When the needle went in, a nurse cried "hysterically," fearing that Mary's bravery would soon be her epitaph. Years later Mary recalled her own participation: "I begged to be one of the volunteers . . . This was an act of faith; it took no courage."[5]

Her faith was that of her husband's, for she was not risking an ordeal any greater than that to which he was subjecting himself and other volunteers. Mary's risk involved the injection of pellagrins' blood into her body. Goldberger and the others not only took the blood of pellagrins but ingested their scabs and excreta.

The experiment involved groups of volunteers at four sites: the Hygienic Laboratory in Washington, D.C.; the State Hospital for the Insane at Columbia, South Carolina; the U.S. Pellagra Hospital at Spartanburg, South Carolina; and Charity Hospital in New Orleans. In all, sixteen volunteers participated in the experiment. Each was briefly described by age and occupation. Goldberger was "G.J.—Medical officer, 42 years. Stationed at Washington, D.C. Major part of the time spent in field work in Southern States. Participated in all seven experiments." Mary was "G-MHF—Housewife, 35 years. Resides at Washington, D.C. The only woman among the volunteers. Participated in experiment 3 at Spartanburg, S.C." With the exception of Mary, all were men between the ages of twenty-six and forty-two. Thirteen were physicians. All had been close to the project, and some are readily identifiable, such as "S-E," Edgar Sydenstricker, the highly regarded PHS statistician who would collaborate with Goldberger on epidemiological studies of the mill villages where many pellagrins resided, and "W-DG," David G. Willets, the PHS assistant epidemiologist who had been so helpful to Goldberger in the study of the insane at the Georgia State Sanitarium in Milledgeville. Among those who participated in Washington was "Mc-GW," George W. McCoy, the newly minted head of the Hygienic Laboratory.

The pellagrous matter taken by the volunteers came from seventeen cases of the disease, the patients suffering varying degrees of severity at the time the "materials" for the experiment were taken from their bodies. These "materials" included "blood, nasopharyngeal secretions, epidermal scales from pellagrous lesions, urine, and feces." The pellagrins' blood was administered by intramuscular or subcutaneous injection. Pellagrins' secretions were applied to the mucosa of the nose and nasopharynx with swabs. The scales scraped from the rashes of pellagrins and the excreta taken from their stools were formed into pills and swallowed by the volunteers. Goldberger described the procedure he followed on April 28, 1916:

> The scales [from the rashes] with about 4 c.c. of each specimen of urine and with about the same quantity of the liquid feces were worked up into a pillular mass with wheat flour and in this form swallowed by volunteer G-J, 30 minutes after taking 20 grains of sodium bicarbonate and about 1 to 1½ hours after collecting. After swallowing the mass another dose of 20 grains of sodium bicarbonate was taken. The alkali [sodium bicarbonate] . . . was intended to reduce gastric acidity and thus perhaps favor infection.

Goldberger reported that his stomach felt bloated and that he belched. On the third day after the experiment he got diarrhea, his stool quite watery. That lasted for about a week, but it did not stop him from ingesting scales, urine, and feces on May 7 in Spartanburg, the day Mary was injected with pellagrins' blood. By that time Goldberger "had not yet completely recovered from a rather marked attack of diarrhea following a previous ingestion experiment."[6]

Goldberger did not insist that his subjects alter their usual habits or activities. The data on them would be gathered through interviews conducted by him, reports from the volunteers themselves, whom he trusted because most were physicians, and reports from non-subject medical officers who were asked to observe the volunteers.

Would anyone get pellagra? Would any of the brave volunteers end up sacrificing their lives on the altar of science? The answer was not very dramatic but certainly satisfying for Goldberger. His volunteers experienced lymph gland swelling and other forms of moderate discomfort. However, none developed pellagra. The last of the "filth parties" was on June 25, 1916, with Goldberger, Wheeler, and Sydenstricker "feast[ing] on filth." A relieved Goldberger wrote to Mary, "It's the last time. Never again!"[7]

Five to seven months following the experiment none of the volunteers had developed "evidence justifying a diagnosis of pellagra." Goldberger's conclusion: "These experiments furnish no support for the view that pellagra is a communicable disease; they materially strengthen the conclusion that it is a disease essentially of dietary origin, brought about by a faulty, probably 'deficient,' diet."[8] With that dry report Goldberger's potentially dangerous, and without question disgusting, experiment came to an end.

On November 16, 1916, Goldberger presented his findings in a paper delivered to the Southern Medical Association in Atlanta.[9] If those most committed to the infectious theory of pellagra had not been moved before, Goldberger would move them now.

The discussion following the paper was lively. Although four papers were delivered that day, most of the comments were addressed to Goldberger. Some were now thoroughly persuaded by his hypothesis. But his filth parties didn't persuade all. Many at the meeting continued to believe in a pellagra germ. Vaulting the high walls surrounding germ theory's applicability to all diseases remained difficult. Accepting pellagra as a disease without pathogen, a disease caused by a lack in the diet, was still more than most of these intelligent, responsible physicians could do, no matter how much they respected Goldberger.

Some of Goldberger's critics were moderate in tone, such as one physician from Dallas who found his experiment "incomplete" because it tested only the transmissibility from person to person and not the possibility of incubation in another host (extrinsic incubation) and transmission by "intermediate carriers." Others were outright nasty. Especially offensive were the comments of Alabama's Dr. J. F. Yarbrough, who floridly stated that Goldberger's "advice to discard all drugs and other means other than diet has cast a pall of gloom over our fair Southland and our cemeteries are blooming as do fields of grain after beneficent summer showers." He angrily denounced Goldberger, whom he accused of using his prestige as a "physician of national reputation with the United States Public Health Service" to pursue a theory while treatment lapsed and patients died. He deplored that "physicians all over the South are following his teachings implicitly, crucifying their patients upon a cross of error."[10]

The allusion could be construed as offensive. In 1896 the Democratic presidential candidate William Jennings Bryan, an ardent populist and advocate of a silver-backed currency, had denounced the advocates of the gold standard, which had made borrowing and debt payment so difficult for farmers and workers of modest income. At the National Democratic Convention, Bryan, a fundamentalist Christian, had thundered at his adversaries, "You shall not press down upon the brow of labor this crown of thorns. You shall not crucify mankind upon a cross of gold!" Because some silver advocates blamed an international conspiracy of Jewish bankers for the woes of the poor in the United States, the reference to crucifixion could be taken as an insult. At the Dallas meeting it was unclear whether Yarbrough was inoffensively invoking Bryan's cross-of-gold speech or referring to an earlier crucifixion for which Goldberger's ancient forebears had been held responsible. Either way, some physicians thought Yarbrough had gone too far. Later in the meeting Yarbrough denied any intention to be offensive, assuring colleagues that the attack was made "wholly on Dr. Goldberger's diet theory in the treatment of pellagra—*not on the man*."[11]

In Goldberger's view his critics suffered from a deficiency of scientific imagination. Having once worshipped at the shrine of bacteriology, they were unwilling to reconsider their basic assumptions of disease causation. Physicians knew that beriberi and scurvy could be treated by adding certain foods to the diet. However, the notion that disease might result not from a microbe but from the absence of a substance that the body required, from a deficiency, was beyond the imagination of many physicians. Goldberger's frustration, as it had so often before, transmuted into determination. In particular, he took issue with the remarks of James A. Hayne, a longtime detractor. During the meeting in Atlanta, Hayne announced, "I am as absolutely convinced as I was many years ago of the communicability of this disease, but let us leave that aside as a settled point in my mind which has not yet been controverted by any evidence brought to bear upon it." Hayne did allow that at least one element of curing a pellagra patient was to give him "a diet he can digest, properly balanced."[12] But that was as far as he would bend in Goldberger's direction.

Seizing on that last statement, Goldberger once again sought to persuade his listeners that he meant not that pellagrins were eating too little food but that they were not eating something their bodies required for good health. At issue was not merely an "insufficient" diet, with malnutrition lowering resistance to infection by microbes, but a "deficient" diet triggering disease. As the meeting concluded, it was clear that Goldberger would never persuade certain skeptics to abandon the germ theory of pellagra no matter what experiments he performed, no matter what risks he took. Far more troubling to him, however, were the critics not in attendance who offered up quite reasonable reservations.

Goldberger had been engaged in an ongoing duel, in print, with the Thompson-McFadden Commission and its researchers Ward J. Mac-Neal, Joseph F. Siler, and P. E. Garrison, all of whom were convinced that there was a pellagra germ. Following the latest experiment, Mac-Neal observed that Goldberger had used the wrong population for his test. He believed that Goldberger would have offered a more persuasive experiment had he isolated groups of individuals in the most vulnerable populations, women between the ages of twenty and forty-five and children aged two to ten.[13]

MacNeal was correct. Goldberger had not conducted a carefully controlled experiment under ideal conditions. He did not ensure that his experimental group was the most vulnerable to the disease. He did not isolate his population, as he had done at Rankin. And he did not conduct a double-blind controlled experiment, the procedure that was becoming the yardstick of proficient scientific research. Goldberger, in a hurry to get answers and confident of the outcome, had relied on the methods of infection used on laboratory animals of the era to test the contagiousness of a disease. Then, too, some investigators continued to dismiss his research as irrelevant, tenaciously clinging to the maize theory of the disease.[14]

In addition to these criticisms, public health concerns arose: if Goldberger was mistaken and pellagra was contagious, it could spread with the virulence of a traditional epidemic. Migrants were known to bring disease across oceans and continents, as happened with the great cholera epidemics of the nineteenth century. As in the past, prevailing racial and ethnic biases conditioned contemporary apprehensions. A Chicago physician feared that the relocation of African-Americans to the North, a movement that historians have since called the Great Migration, might result in increasing rates of pellagra in northern cities. African-American physicians such as those on the Pellagra Commission of the National Medical Association did not disagree. However, rather than lay blame on the migrants' condition, they reported that pellagra was "a communicable and therefore preventable disease" and blamed insects nourished in unsanitary environments for incubating and spreading it, especially among the poor, which included so many black southerners. These physicians sought their model in yellow fever, a scourge that had been brought under control through sanitation.[15]

As always, encouragement came from Mary, but also from experts such as Elmer V. McCollum, a renowned University of Wisconsin biochemist who conducted pioneering research leading to the identification of vitamin A, and Cornell University's Graham Lusk, whose work on nutrition was nationally recognized. In New York in late 1916, the nutritionist assured Goldberger that he had the "highest regard" for his endeavors, which Lusk called "convincing" and "conclusive." Goldberger was so gratified by the praise from such an eminent individual that he scribbled to Mary, "If a thing is convincing and conclusive to him what need for worry about what such men as Hayne, MacNeal, et al think! I am telling you this precious Partner, because I know how much this will please you." Responding to some reprints that Goldberger had sent him, McCollum wrote, "I have read your papers—those with which I was not already familiar—with great interest and am fully convinced that your interpretation of the etiology of pellagra is correct. I congratulate you on the thoroughness of your investigation." All echoed earlier praise, such as that of the Massachusetts commissioner of health, Allan J. McLaughlin, who had written, "I consider your discoveries as epoch making and of greater importance in preventive medicine than any discovery since the beriberi problem was solved. Your work in pellagra coupled with your previous work on typhus fever, measles and other diseases stamps you, in my opinion, as the foremost figure in America today in the field of preventive medicine."[16]

His confidence bolstered by the likes of McCollum and Lusk, Goldberger, in 1917, resumed his search for the dietary deficiency that caused pellagra and the circumstances that contributed to its appearance, the disease's epidemiology. The detective had been seeking clues by studying institutionalized populations. Now he turned to the general population.

Goldberger hoped communities where pellagra was prevalent would help him to understand its etiology. Most often such communities surrounded the textile mills that were the great economic hope of the South. To comprehend why residents of mill villages suffered from pellagra disproportionately to the rest of the population, Goldberger turned to the kind of population studies being undertaken by Progressive-era sociologists, economists, and demographers in hopes that they could shed light on the linkages between incidence of pellagra and the lifestyle of those who contracted it. Investigating life in mill villages was not without risks. Inmates of prisons, orphanages, and asylums were generally regarded as marginal populations, warehoused and secluded from view, with few advocates or interests of concern to the broader population. However, textile mills embodied major economic investment and the South's very hope for a prosperous future. Many would be watching Goldberger as he observed life in the mill villages.

The mill village study, which began in April 1916 and continued, in parts, throughout the next two and a half years, is a classic in shoe-leather epidemiology. However, the shoes that would be worn down would not be Goldberger's alone. He assembled a team to assist him. Dr. George Wheeler had been Goldberger's trusted assistant from the beginning of his pellagra investigations. A handsome and personable thirty-one-year-old native of North Carolina, Wheeler knew the South, spoke easily with southerners of every class, and was an excellent observer. It would be his task to visit each mill village in the study every two weeks from April 16 to June 16 and conduct a house-to-house canvass to determine the incidence of pellagra and to inquire about the diet of those who lived in each home.

To tackle the issue of sanitation in mill villages, Goldberger needed to expand his research team. He asked the surgeon general to assign to him a sanitary engineer familiar with the method of surveying sanitary conditions that had been developed by Wade Frost of the PHS. Concerned with stream pollution and its health implications, Frost had developed a system of "weighted ratings for each of several constituent factors" in stream pollution. Ralph Tarbett, a nonphysician sanitary engineer who knew Frost's system, got the assignment.

The data that Wheeler and Tarbett collected would be compiled and analyzed by Edgar Sydenstricker, chief statistician of the Public Health Service. Trained in sociology and economics, Sydenstricker would not only analyze data but also collect it. He supervised a squad of "enumerators" responsible for gathering information on mill village family income and food accessibility.

Brother of the novelist Pearl S. Buck, Edgar Sydenstricker courted fame in a less public arena. A social scientist with statistical skills and the inquiring mind of a journalist, he entered federal service as a special investigator for the U.S. Immigration Commission under the leadership of Senator William Paul Dillingham. The commission was preparing its monumental forty-two-volume study of immigration to the United States. Sydenstricker was in charge of industrial community studies. Gaining valuable experience in collecting data and measuring social behavior, he joined the staff of the U.S. Commission on Industrial Relations in 1914–1915 and in 1915 was appointed to organize the statistical work of the Public Health Service. Among his first assignments was pellagra.[17] For the next thirteen years, whenever Goldberger went into the field to collect social data, Sydenstricker would be at his side.

While Wheeler and Sydenstricker collected data and the latter created a statistical profile, Goldberger traveled from village to village, monitoring the project as well as visiting the PHS hospital at Spartanburg and the other sites conducting pellagra research under his supervision. Periodically he would huddle with Sydenstricker to examine the numbers, and in the end he provided the medical analysis.

Textile mills of the kind that Goldberger and his collaborators visited were not new to the South. The textile industry evolved in New England and came slowly to the South in the nineteenth century. By 1850 two hundred mills had been set up in the South, primarily in the Piedmont of Virginia, North Carolina, South Carolina, and Georgia. As southerners sought to recalibrate their economy in the post–Civil War world, the number of spindles and mills below the Mason-Dixon Line rose sharply in the 1890s. More and more capital was invested in textile manufacture, rising from $22.8 million in 1880 to $132.4 million in 1900. That same year textiles became the South's number-one industrial employer, surpassing New England as the heart of America's textile industry.[18] In 1915, while Goldberger was brooding over whether the Rankin prisoners would present pellagra rashes, the South was embracing textiles, claiming 60 percent of the nation's cotton manufacturing that year.

No southern state was more committed to cotton milling than South Carolina. The state was second only to Massachusetts in number of spindles, and 12.6 percent of its white population were cotton mill workers. After the expansion of the 1890s, 147 corporations were producing yarns and cloth, employing forty-five thousand textile workers. In the twenty years between 1880 and 1900 the number of mills in the state increased forty-five times.[19]

The mill villages in the Piedmont of South Carolina that Goldberger, Wheeler, and Sydenstricker considered for inclusion in their study tended to be similar in appearance. As one historian has described the milieu, "There were the looms, the red-brick factory, the village streets and houses." These were "a given in much the same way as were countryside and plowed fields for cousins who stayed on the farm." Housing tended to be similar as well. In Spartanburg County, where workers' lives were closely bound to the mill village, company housing was designed to attract and retain workers. Dependence on child labor and the family wage system encouraged southern mill owners to build cheap cottages with two, three, or four rooms or duplexes with eight rooms that could be used by two families.[20]

Supervisors and black workers lived in separate neighborhoods from white wage earners. Differences among the mills in general were not great, but some acquired reputations for being especially advantageous to workers. Inman Mills, for example, sought to cultivate a family atmosphere more than most. The local governance at Fairmont Mills was so lax that workers could make ample income on the side dealing moonshine.[21]

The mill buildings visited by Goldberger's team were noisy factories where workers turned raw cotton into yarn and fabric. Workers performed different tasks, although they were sorted into four general departments: carding, or processing the raw fiber; spinning; weaving; and finishing. Each unit had specialty jobs: in carding there were openers, pickers, slashers, and speeders; in spinning there were poolers and doffers; in weaving there were doffers, battery fillers, drawing-inners, and warp tenders; and in finishing there were inspectors, stitchers, and folders. All these production jobs were restricted to whites. The job of "fixer" was the most prestigious, held by men who knew the machinery well enough to be promoted to full-time mechanics responsible for keeping the machines running night and day. Weavers held prestigious jobs as well because of the artistry involved. Few black faces would be visible; blacks were confined to menial jobs such as janitor or boiler fireman.[22] Mill hands in 1890 worked sixty hours a week for wages that varied from 15 cents to $1.25 per day; the average employee made about 85 cents a day. A sectional wage differential operated to the advantage of southern mill owners.[23] In this era northern workers with some skill were making as much as $2.50 a day, far more than their southern counterparts.

Not all the wage earners that the federal physicians saw were turning out cloth and yarn. Because the mill company ran the mill village, there was ample employment for workers in construction and maintenance. Carpenters, painters, plumbers, electricians, store clerks, and teamsters were all essential to life in the villages. Villages also required a small number of professionals, including teachers, ministers, and police. Paying professionals to meet the needs of mill hands in the villages was just one aspect of the industrial paternalism that attracted many poor southerners to the mills.

The mills ran almost around the clock. One mill hand described the situation:

> The day hands commence work at 6 o'clock in the morning and run till 7 o'clock at night. They stop at 12 o'clock for dinner and ring the bell at 12:30 o'clock. I counted that the hands are in actual motion 13 hours per day. The trade check system is used here, and is not as good as cash, at this place or any other place . . . This long hour system is destroying the health of all the young women who work in the mills. The employment of children in the mills at low wages keeps a great many men out of employment.

In a trade-check system salaries are given as trade checks redeemable at the company store and nowhere else. Mill hands consequently purchased goods in a system unregulated by competition. Without cash wages they could not shop for the lowest prices for food or any other commodity. One discouraged mill worker saw himself and others like him on a "grind-stone" but hoped that mill owners would eventually discover that "if they give their hands good houses to live in, pay them cash, and teach them how to live and take care of their earned money, both parties will prosper and grow fat."[24] Although some owners did seek to nurture their workforce, most did not. Rather than "grow fat," many mill hands grew thin and got sick with pellagra. Why? What linked mill life with the misery of pellagra?

Following the accepted protocol, Goldberger used initials to identify the seven villages in his study.[25] However, a glance at county maps of South Carolina makes readily clear which mill villages were selected. Four were in Spartanburg County, Arkwright, Inman, Saxon, and Whitney; two in Oconee County, Seneca and Newry; and one in Chester County, Republic Mill Village at Great Falls. Why these and not others? These villages had been treated before in the work of the Thompson-McFadden Commission. Thus, it would be possible to compare findings. Moreover, these villages were all easily reached from Spartanburg, where the U.S. Pellagra Hospital and laboratory were located. Results could be analyzed conveniently and expeditiously.

The seven villages were similar. They were of average size, all between five hundred and eight hundred inhabitants. Each was a "more or less isolated community" surrounding or adjacent to a "cotton-cloth manufacturing" plant. Almost everyone in the villages was a mill employee, and with the exception of a handful of "Negro families," whom Goldberger chose not to include in the study, all were white, of Anglo-Saxon stock, and had American-born parents. Besides omitting the black families, Goldberger excluded the families of mill officials and store managers. He did so, he said, to yield "a group exceptionally homogeneous with respect to racial stock, dietary custom and also, we thought, to economic status."[26] Because the study extended over many months, village populations varied, but the overall number of individuals included generally remained around four thousand.

When Dr. George Wheeler first knocked on their doors in April 1916, mill villagers were suspicious and uncooperative, but the kind and charming Wheeler won them over. Their reserve diminished, and some even brought pellagra cases to his attention. Because the hours of work in the mills were long, Wheeler varied the time of his visits to use the lunch hour and Saturday half holidays in "different villages and in different sections of the same village in rotation." He always inquired about household members absent at the time of the visit and any "suspicious illness or condition in the village, particularly in members of neighboring households." Any report that he thought "suggestive" was investigated, and he would go directly to the mill to do so. He also conferred with local physicians. Remarking on how few cases were reported via this route, Goldberger speculated that "but a small percentage of the cases occurring in any season come to the attention of a physician."[27]

As for which symptoms would justify a pellagra diagnosis and therefore inclusion in the study, Goldberger's criterion was the same as that used in the experiment at Rankin: "Only patients with a clearly defined, bilaterally symmetrical dermatitis were recorded as having pellagra."[28] Active cases, whether they were initial or subsequent attacks, were included, and onset of the disease was defined by the appearance of the rash. Goldberger and Wheeler made certain that a symptomatic individual had been part of a given household for at least thirty days to ensure that a relationship could reasonably be drawn between the disease and particular conditions of life, especially diet, in that household.

Veteran pellagra fighters such as Goldberger and Wheeler had long been aware that pellagra rashes were more common at certain times of the year. The statistics Goldberger had seen on pellagra morbidity suggested that "the height of the seasonal curve of pellagra incidence in the southern states began in the late spring and reached its peak in June." It took a minimum of several months for a patient to become symptomatic. Based on those data, Goldberger estimated that the "distinctively pellagra-producing dietary season began sometime in late winter or early spring and continued up to or possibly somewhat into June." The earliest he and his team could organize to collect dietary data was April 16, but they ran the collection until June 15, 1916, to make sure they did not miss pellagra's peak season.[29]

Day in and day out Wheeler knocked on doors in the mill villages, chatted with workers and their families, and visited the stores where they shopped. When Goldberger caught up with him, the two would huddle over the data and try to see linkages between one pattern of behavior and another. Try as he might, Wheeler could not be present in the mill workers' households at every mealtime. Therefore, data on household diet were supplemented with sales records from the stores where mill villagers shopped during the fifteen-day period prior to or coincident with the marked seasonal rise in pellagra.

Wheeler noticed that in pellagra-free households the family "enjoyed a more liberal supply of foods of the 'animal protein' group (lean meat, milk, including butter, cheese, and eggs)" than did pellagrous households.[30] Milk or fresh meat was served regularly. Corn and corn products were often part of the diet, too, but their consumption and the use of wheat flour or dried legumes appeared to have no correlation with pellagra occurrence. Goldberger took this as a refutation of the European theory of pellagra. Again the issue was neither corn nor the amount of protein in the diet, because pellagrous households had protein in their diets, but not as much animal protein as non-pellagrous households. Moreover, when Goldberger and Sydenstricker analyzed caloric intake, they found the numbers similar in pellagrous and non-pellagrous households. The proportion of calories derived from carbohydrates and fats was identical. Indeed, the supply of carbohydrates was smaller in the diets of pellagrous households. Too many carbohydrates were thus not the problem.

Vitamins and minerals? Here the results were telling. Goldberger reported, "The diets of the pellagrous households have a smaller average supply of the recognized vitamins than do those of the nonpellagrous, the supply being particularly marked with respect to the 'fat soluble A' factor."[31] Similarly, those in non-pellagrous households had a superior "mineral make-up" to their diets or at the very least showed no mineral deficiency compared with those in pellagrous households.

Goldberger wanted to know more than what was on mill villagers' dinner tables. He needed to know whether sex, age, and occupation affected vulnerability as well as whether an individual's condition, especially a "disabling sickness," affected the picture. His team collected data on 4,399 individuals, among whom there were 115 definite cases of pellagra, a rate of 26.1 per 1,000. In a number of cases the rash was "ill-defined." If these 73 "suspect" cases were recorded, the total would rise to 188, an incident rate of 42.7 per 1,000.[32]

But who was getting the disease? As he came through the doors of villagers' small wooden houses, Wheeler rarely saw a baby with pellagra. Sydenstricker's statistical compilation of Wheeler's data suggested that children two years old and younger rarely fell ill with the disease. Males and females had a similar incidence up to age twenty, although incidence was higher between ages two and ten than between ten and nineteen. The big gender difference came from the age of twenty, when the incidence was many times higher in females than in males. Between ages thirty and forty-four, for example, the rate of incidence for males was 9.1 per 1,000 and for females, a stunning 54.4 per 1,000.

Whatever the age or gender of its victims, pellagra seemed more prevalent at certain times of the year, just as Goldberger had thought. There was a sharp rise in incidence during April and May, reaching a "well-defined peak in June."[33] A broader view suggested that onset was almost always between April and September. Could it have something to do with occupation and the tasks that workers performed at different times of the year?

Not all of Wheeler's hosts were mill workers. Data comparing mill workers with those who lived in the villages but did not work in the mills yielded a surprise. Incidence for both men and women was higher for non–mill workers. Thus, there was nothing about mill work per se that appeared linked to contracting pellagra.

Perhaps the most telling result concerned those mill villagers, especially women, who did not work because of a disabling illness unrelated to pellagra. In this group the pellagra rate among non-mill-working females was "approximately four times as high as that among mill-working females," but the rate for disabling sickness was "distinctly higher in mill-working than in non-mill-working females." Goldberger concluded that the disability indicated by the higher illness rate among mill-working women did not "influence materially the pellagra rate in this group."[34] Their vulnerable health status did not incline them to contract pellagra.

Goldberger's rich experience in studying infectious disease had taught him the importance of sanitation, and he did not neglect the subject when it came to pellagra. He noted that white and African-American southerners shared the same environment and, therefore, presumably the same sanitary conditions. "But few Negroes are employed in or about a cotton mill; these with their families usually live in a quarter somewhat apart from that of the white families," he wrote. "Contact between the two races in the mill is very slight; it is more frequent at the stores, which are patronized in common, and in the houses of some of the white operatives in which colored women are at times employed as laundresses or cooks, or to nurse the very young children while both parents are at work in the mill." Aware that the physical proximity of the populations needed to be taken into account in the sanitary analysis, he wrote, "In evaluating the sanitary factors considered in determining the sanitary rating of a village, conditions in the Negro quarter were taken into account, but the pellagra rates represent the incidence in the white population" of mill villagers.[35] To preserve the homogeneity of this phase of his study, and because it remained unclear whether race or the economic conditions attendant upon being black in the South were at issue in pellagra incidence, Goldberger continued to exclude blacks from the database on which pellagra rates were calculated.

Tarbett, the sanitation expert, surveyed the seven villages in November 1916. Because typhoid fever was caused by fecal contamination, he used typhoid incidence as a "good index of sanitary conditions" and so recorded all cases of typhoid in the course of the canvass for pellagra. There were 38 cases of typhoid, a rate of 8.6 per 1,000 of the aggregate population, 4,399 individuals. The results suggested no relationship of pellagra to typhoid incidence.

Goldberger noted that whether a village had a great deal of pellagra or none, there were no significant differences in the pollution of its water supply or in the incidence of typhoid. Not surprisingly, villages with more water pollution had higher incidences of typhoid. However, there was no inverse relationship between extremes of excreta-disposal rating and pellagra incidence. Of the two villages at the extremes of excreta disposal, Republic Mill Village, which had the highest rating (it was served by an efficient water-carriage system), had a pellagra incidence rate that was negligibly different from that of Whitney Mills, which had the lowest rating (probably because it was served by surface privies).[36] Whether clean or dirty, water quality was not related to pellagra incidence.

As Wheeler, Goldberger, and their assistants roamed the villages, they kept their eyes open for insects that might be spreading the disease. Were there flies buzzing around? Were the food and the milk that families ate and drank protected from airborne infection? There was little difference in either the presence of flies or how well provisions were shielded from them in pellagrous and non-pellagrous households. The same held true with ratings for "control of communicable diseases" and cleanliness of the "domestic environment." Republic Mill Village stood out only because its environment was substantially more sanitary than those of the other villages, but it had an intermediate rate of pellagra incidence, not a low one. Goldberger, admitting that the sample was modest, nevertheless contended that his results "afford no support for the view . . . that pellagra is 'an intestinal infection transmitted in much the same way as typhoid fever.'"[37]

So what was left? Having visited the mill villagers at their dining tables, talked to their grocers, tested their drinking water, and observed how they disposed of their excreta, Goldberger and his associates turned their attention to the pay that the villagers carried away when their workweek was done. If his long nights in the Hygienic Laboratory's library years before had taught him anything, it was that "a close association of pellagra with poverty has been repeatedly remarked since the time of the first recognition of the disease." The Italian Gaetano Strambio, in 1796, had written, "This much is certain, that pellagra is most at home where poverty and misery reign and increases as they increase." The Thompson-McFadden Commission had not neglected the relationship. Citing his rivals in that group, MacNeal, Siler, and Garrison, Goldberger recalled their five categories of economic condition: "squalor, poverty, necessities, comfort and affluence." Using their data, Goldberger noted that of the 277 individuals with pellagra classified by their economic conditions, 83 percent had been found to be poor (squalor, poverty, and necessities) by MacNeal, Siler, and Garrison, 15 percent in the average or comfort category, and a mere 2 percent in the affluent category that designated above-average economic condition.[38]

Goldberger also recalled the work of Vanderbilt University's James Jobling and William Petersen, who had studied "the economic condition of pellagrous patients" in Nashville. Their data were the average rentals for the entire population of Nashville, the weekly income of pellagrins who were wage earners, and the total income of the "pellagrous family." They then determined the amount of money available to each pellagrin per week by dividing the total income by the number of individuals in the family.

What they found intrigued Goldberger. Seventy percent of the white adult male pellagrins were wageworkers. Of these, more than 60 percent earned $10 or more per week. Of the white adult female pellagrins, 22 percent were wage earners, but of these 56 percent earned less than $10 per week. Of the "colored" wage earners, 66 percent of the males earned less than $10 per week, while a similar percentage of the "colored" females earned less than $8 per week. As for the amount of money available to each pellagrin per week, Jobling and Petersen found that of the whites 56.5 percent and of the "colored" 24 percent had an available income of $2.50 or more per week.[39] Still, the work did not satisfy Goldberger, who complained that none of it "affords any basis for a comparison with the economic distribution of the general population . . . [or] any means of measuring in a definite objective manner the degree of association between economic status and pellagra incidence."[40] Sydenstricker would help Goldberger go further than anyone else had with respect to the relationship of poverty to pellagra.

From April 16 to June 15, 1916, a staff of "trained enumerators" under the direct supervision of Sydenstricker collected dietary and economic data from approximately 4,160 individuals in 750 households. They asked villagers about family income, household food supply, and the composition of households. Each household was canvassed for fifteen days because Goldberger and Sydenstricker believed that such a period would give a "sufficiently representative sample of the supply [of food] of the season immediately anterior to the peak of seasonal incidence of the disease." In short, the canvass would occur in what was generally considered "the pellagra-producing season."[41]

What Sydenstricker found in villagers' pay envelopes was the basis for classifying them according to economic status and was secured from a family member and supplemented by mill payrolls, which administrative officials willingly provided. Because the mills paid employees semimonthly, taking the total cash income during a pay period made sense. Also, it coincided with the fifteen-day sample period being used.

With the intention of examining the relation of food availability to income and incidence of pellagra, Sydenstricker supervised data collec-

tion from three sources: household members, peddlers, and store employees. He and his staff asked household members about the "immediate source of every article of food entering into their half-month's
supplies." For example, Sydenstricker wanted to know whether a household's fresh milk came from a family cow or was purchased from a cow-
owning neighbor or from a store. Perhaps it had been given to the family
by a relative, a neighbor, or someone else. If the source was different
from that of most of the households in the village, Sydenstricker wanted
to know how long a family had been using that source. He also talked to
those who sold food in the village, "farmers, hucksters, or 'peddlers,'"
who knew about quantities sold, prices charged, frequency of sale of a
commodity, and the kind of produce sold most frequently in the villages.

Finally, Sydenstricker and his staff visited with the managers and
clerks in the stores, markets, and other retail outlets where mill workers
and their families shopped. These individuals, who were most familiar
with village patterns, supplied food prices during the fifteen-day period
of investigation, price changes during 1916, sources of food they sold (for
example, nearby farms or middlemen who obtained food from regional
markets or other parts of the United States), and brand names and quantities of food sold. Because they sold directly to villagers, these managers
and clerks also knew about credit practices, especially as related to the income of their customers.[42]

As detectives do in criminal cases, Sydenstricker and his staff gathered the facts and testimony of witnesses. However, fact gathering on income and diet was just the first stage of the investigation. Now the
well-trained economist in Sydenstricker emerged to develop schemes of
classification and analysis. From the data he had compiled, Sydenstricker estimated the average annual cash income of the mill village
families at about seven hundred dollars. Few exceeded one thousand
dollars. If almost homogeneous in income, families did vary in size, and
some had boarders, whom Sydenstricker classified economically with
the family where they resided. Needing a common denominator to compare families of different sizes, gender compositions, and age ranges,
Sydenstricker used a food-requirements scale developed by the nutrition
researcher Wilbur Atwater. Values were expressed in "adult male units."
In using the Atwater scale, Sydenstricker assumed that the expenditures

for total maintenance for individuals varied according to gender and age in the same proportion as their food requirements. While acknowledging that such an assumption might not be completely accurate, he argued that since family spending generally equaled total family income and since food expenditures accounted for at least half and sometimes more of these expenditures, it made sense to derive some measure reflecting that relationship.[43]

If most mill workers earned similar wages, what made some better-off than others? Sydenstricker identified three factors: supplemental income, especially from boarders; number of non-wage-earning dependent persons, such as young children, in proportion to adult wage earners; and the wage-earning capacity of individuals because of natural ability, special training, or general health and vitality.[44]

As Sydenstricker and his enumerators went about their business, they saw with their own eyes that poor folks got pellagra and that often in poor families more than one member came down with the disease. In the 747 households analyzed, there were 97 definite cases of pellagra in 61 families. When economic data were correlated with data on pellagra incidence, Sydenstricker observed that "the proportion of families affected with pellagra declines with a marked degree of regularity as income increases." This inverse correlation was even more marked in cases where there was more than one case of pellagra in the family. Further analysis revealed that "with decreasing income it [pellagra] seemed to show an increasing tendency to affect members of the same family."[45] Whatever the course that led to an attack of pellagra, it began with a light pay envelope.

If income and diet were related to pellagra incidence, as Goldberger and Sydenstricker had already demonstrated with data from the seven villages, then the medical detectives needed to know as precisely as possible how income was related to diet in the mill villages. Certain general tendencies became clear as Goldberger and Sydenstricker saw the association of one variable with another emerge.

The more modest the income, the smaller the amounts purchased of all meats with the exception of salt pork. So, too, green vegetables, fresh fruits, eggs, butter, cheese, preserved milk, lard, sugar, syrup, and canned foods. At the lower end of the income range, there was increased purchase of salt pork and cornmeal. Regardless of income, the quantities purchased of "dried peas and beans, potatoes, dried fruits, wheat flour and bread, fresh milk, and rice" showed no discernible trend, or so it first appeared. However, when the extremes of income were examined, "it appeared that the supplies of wheat flour and bread and of fresh milk were appreciably smaller in the poorest households." The investigators drew the conclusion that with differences in income, there were "quite definite differences in household food supplies" overall.[46]

Household circumstances besides salary affected the resources available for food. Diet is affected by how income is managed, and the proportion of the family's income available for food as opposed to other necessities and the general attitude toward thrift were two such variables. Others included "the intelligence and ability of the housewife in utilizing the available family income" and whether or not the family owned cows and poultry and tended its own garden.[47]

Noticing marked differences in pellagra incidence among the villages, Goldberger, Wheeler, and Sydenstricker pondered the reasons. The data suggested that differences in the proportion of low-income families in the villages were negligible. After the researchers considered several variables, the difference that emerged most markedly had to do with "availability of food supplies on the local markets or from home production." This promised to be a complex matter to treat precisely. After all, it took time to track down stores and peddlers and to trace their patterns of stock and sales.

Limitations of time and resources prevented investigation of food availability in all the villages. Instead, the Goldberger team compared availability in two villages: Newry in Oconee County, where there was no pellagra, and Inman in Spartanburg County, where pellagra incidence was 64.6 per 1,000 during 1916.[48] Both communities had company stores and grocery stores in adjacent villages. However, there were marked differences in access to food.

In general, residents of Newry had greater access to those foods that appeared to be required to prevent pellagra. For example, there was a fresh-meat market, which in recent years had been open seven days a week all year round. That same market sold fresh fruit and vegetables. There was also a market about a mile away that operated a wagon and had taken meat orders for delivery to mill workers' homes during the spring of 1916 as well as the preceding fall and winter. In Seneca, a town four miles away, two other fresh-meat markets were patronized by Newry mill villagers.

In sharp contrast, Inman had not had a fresh-meat market since the end of February 1916. There had been a privately owned market in the basement of the company store building, but it was poorly managed, and hours had dropped from a daily schedule to one or two days a week by the winter of 1916, as had the extension of customer credit. In the town of Inman, a mile or so from the mill village, there was a meat market, but because sales were by cash only, few mill workers could afford to shop there. The next-nearest market was in Spartanburg, but that was thirteen miles away.

In the rural South, as Sydenstricker and Goldberger had so often seen, what folks could not buy at the store, they could buy from a neighbor who farmed and marketed his crops from a wagon. Inman village had no regular sellers of farm produce in the spring of 1916. Farmers rarely visited the village, and then usually only to dispose of goods they could not sell in the nearby town of Inman. Newry, on the other hand, was a center for marketing produce from nearby farms. Twenty-two farmers who did retail sales in the village were interviewed for the study.

Why the contrast? One reason was the difference in the kind of agriculture in the vicinity of the two villages. The land near Inman was planted largely with cotton. There was almost no truck farming, few beef cattle, and only those milk cows that individual farmers needed for their own families. Often farmers with cotton planted right up to the doors of their cabins did not even keep pigs or chickens. In contrast to the terrain around Inman, the rolling, hilly land near Newry was less well suited to cotton cultivation. It was no wonder, then, that other crops and truck farming were common. Besides the kind of agriculture practiced, market conditions differed in the two villages. Newry was a hub for surrounding farmers; Inman had little trade with nearby farms.

Mill workers were southerners who had departed the land. Often that departure was partial, and their own produce supplemented what they could buy. Both villages had a similar proportion of cows, but because Newry residents purchased milk from local hucksters, families there had considerably greater access to fresh milk. Newry's more diversified agriculture gave its residents greater access to poultry and eggs. However, Inman had a decided edge in home gardens. Nearly 92 percent of the Inman households had gardens, compared with less than 23 percent of homes in Newry. And yet home gardens contributed little to the food supply in both villages in June 1916. Why?

Goldberger and his associates were more than a little surprised that as of June 1, 1916, the gardens in Inman had yielded no food. What could have gone wrong? When a crop is planted determines when it can be harvested, and the medical detectives learned that residents found it difficult to get the ground prepared early enough for crops harvestable by June. Long hours of work at the busy Inman mill left no available daylight for gardening until well into the spring. Therefore, although the climate would have permitted harvesting some vegetables in late April or May, few mill households could harvest an early crop, and food shortages were frequent in the spring.[49]

What Goldberger, Wheeler, and Sydenstricker witnessed in Newry and Inman echoed what they had learned about diet in earlier studies of the food supply in pellagrous and non-pellagrous households. Community conditions appeared to be paramount in the larger portrait of how family income and food availability affected pellagra incidence. Still, individual factors were involved. After all, the favorable economic status of an individual with pellagra seemed to suggest that diet was not of etiological significance, because well-off individuals presumably had a full and proper diet. Not so, Goldberger learned.

Human eccentricity sometimes played a role in determining who got pellagra. Individual food preferences and peculiarities of taste accounted for pellagra in the well-off. So, too, did "ill-advised, self-imposed, or professionally directed dietary restrictions in the treatment of digestive disturbances, kidney disease, etc.; they may originate as a fad; and in the insane they may arise because of some delusion such as the fear of poisoning, etc."[50]

But individual cases did not alter the basic conclusion: the most "potent factors" influencing the incidence of pellagra in the communities studied were low family income and "unfavorable conditions regarding the availability of food supplies." The families needed higher incomes in order to have adequate diets, and the availability of food, "particularly of milk and fresh meat," needed to be improved. However, Goldberger's team observed, the ups and downs of the cotton industry alone resulted in sharp swings in family income, creating the hard times that they believed were the root cause of inadequate diet leading to pellagra. The hard times "observed in the United States in 1915, following depression consequent on the outbreak of the World War in 1914," were echoing still in the spring of 1916.[51]

The findings of the mill villages study, conducted mostly in 1916, echoed observations made by Sydenstricker in 1915, when he examined earlier investigators' studies, ones not concerned with pellagra, that treated the relationship between economic conditions and diet.[52] Eyeballing the numbers that others had compiled, Sydenstricker had before him a rich cache of data: data on the relation of the white wageworker's family income to diet in the South and the rest of the United States, data on factors governing the availability of food supply in different southern industrial localities, data on differences in the diet of workingmen's families in northern and southern states, and data on factors that *might* have affected the diets of white southern wageworkers in recent years. Included in the latter were the regional origins of white southern workers in factories and mills, the effects of migration on patterns of employment, changes in the character of the migrating white southern wage earners' food supply, changes in the status of white southern wage earners' families, and, finally, the rising retail price of food in the second decade of the twentieth century.

Much of what Sydenstricker had gleaned in bits and pieces from those earlier, broader social scientific studies was now confirmed by the exhaustive investigation of the seven mill villages. The earlier data had left Sydenstricker with a number of conclusions. First, "the lower the economic status of the white American family, the greater is the pressure for sacrifices in diet, particularly in animal protein foods, since animal protein foods are the most expensive." Second, the economic status of wage earners' families in the South, especially mill village families, was lower than that of similar families in other parts of the country. A 1901 Bureau of Labor Statistics cost-of-living study based on the annual income of 25,440 families of representative workingmen in the principal industrial areas of the United States informed Sydenstricker that "the average southern white workingman's family income was between $650 and $690, or approximately 10 per cent lower than in the Northern States and 20 percent lower than in the Western States [across] . . . all occupations and industries." Even in the mills there were differences: "While slightly over half of the workers in New England mills were found to be earning under $7 a week, nearly nine-tenths of the southern mill workers were in that group. The average annual income of the southern cotton-mill family was found to be $822, as contrasted with $1,002 for New England cotton-mill families." The southern family income was 20 percent lower.[53]

Third, Sydenstricker learned that southern industrial communities had a restricted supply of protein foods at affordable prices, a condition not true of industrial areas elsewhere in the nation: "Lean meat, fresh or salt, . . . is not so generally sold in the southern industrial town and village as in similar localities in the North and Middle West." A fourth conclusion he drew was that "the proportion of proteins in the diet of southern families is considerably less and of carbohydrates and of hydrocarbons considerably greater than in the diet of northern families." He observed that crop diversification and beef and milk production had improved in the South since the end of the Civil War. However, there was a decline in beef production nationally between 1900 and 1914. The beef supply in southern urban and industrial centers continued to come from other sections of the country. Thus families in the North generally consumed more protein than those in the South: "In the Northern States the average family was found to consume between 1,000 and 1,100 pounds of proteins, while in the Southern States the protein consumption averaged between 700 and 800 pounds. The southern family consumed nearly a pound a week less of fresh beef, nearly half as much milk, very much less of 'other meats,' and hardly any salt beef as compared to northern families." When it came to fats and hydrocarbons, northern families consumed butter, but families in southern states consumed over 60 percent more lard and nearly three times as much "salt hog products." Southern families consumed "twice as much bacon and ham," and an even greater amount of "lard, suet and dripping." As for carbohydrates, southern families consumed larger quantities of wheat bread and wheat flour than northern families. "Southern families also consumed larger quantities of corn and corn meal, rice, and molasses and sirups than the northern families." Most important, the pattern appeared "true of families of all incomes."[54]

Finally, Sydenstricker found that an industrial depression beginning in late 1907 lowered the economic status of wage earners' families, especially in the cotton and lumber industries, even as the retail prices of food went up. While prices increased everywhere, nowhere was the increase as pronounced as in the South. There the rise in retail food prices was at minimum 40 percent higher in protein foods than in foods rich in carbohydrates and hydrocarbons.[55]

Sydenstricker's sketch indicated that poor workers in the South were less able than their counterparts elsewhere in the country to provide their families with properly balanced diets. He also found a decrease in the availability of animal-protein foods at prices affordable for wage-workers began just around the time that more pellagra cases were being diagnosed and reported. Others' work had offered them important clues and pointed them in fruitful directions, but the Goldberger team had uncovered the gestalt of poverty and deprivation directly related to the incidence of pellagra. Still, the mystery of the diet remained unsolved. Goldberger no longer advised eating beans and peas, but he could not yet tell from the data gathered in the mill villages precisely what milk and meat provided such that its absence yielded pellagra. What was missing from pellagrins' diets? Was it "some amino acid or acids," "the ash or some of its constituents," an unknown essential such as an unidentified vitamin, or all of these, or some yet to be determined combination? Goldberger speculated that one or more of several conditions likely prevailed: "(1) a physiologically defective protein (amino-acid) supply; (2) a defective or inadequate mineral supply; (3) a deficiency in an as yet unknown dietary essential (vitamin?)." The reduced supply of "potential energy and of protein," while likely not the cause, might be "contributory by favoring the occurrence of a deficiency in intake of some one or more of the essential dietary factors," especially when a generally poor diet allowed so little margin for error.[56] Goldberger still had much work to do before the mystery would be solved. However, what he had already learned could save many lives.

In the Progressive tradition, the medical scientist and the social scientist had shared their skills and perspectives to make the underlying causes of pellagra visible to the eye, just as a pathogen might be isolated on a slide and studied under a microscope. The priest of the "Infinite Intelligence" had served his god. Goldberger had struggled to "know something"; what to do about it was another matter. Resolving the social conditions that led to pellagra was a job for businessmen and politicians, not physicians or statisticians. Goldberger, Wheeler, and Sydenstricker had done their part. Now it was up to those southerners who understood the South's stake in the textile mills and cotton production to decide whether they were willing to make the changes demanded by Goldberger's conclusions.

SEVEN

Cotton in Crisis and
the Politics of Public Health

On April 7, 1917, the day after President Woodrow Wilson signed the declaration carrying the United States into World War I, Goldberger uncapped his fountain pen to share his puzzlement with Mary. He was mystified by how little moved most Americans seemed to be. Bending over his desk at the Hotel Cleveland in Spartanburg, South Carolina, he wrote: "Everything seems remarkably quiet here; except for an unusual display of the National flag there appears no surface evidence of the fact that we are at war with Germany." He did suffer "one or two minor unpleasantnesses." He explained to Mary, "On account of the war and the talk of German spies[,] strangers are immediately under suspicion in these mill villages. One of our men had to explain and explain that he had no connection with the Germans."[1]

Far more serious than a case of mistaken identity, though, was the threat of pellagra to the southern population. And war promised only to exacerbate the poverty that was its underlying cause. He observed, "Pellagra is slowly increasing. The prospects are for a heavy crop of this reaction to [economic] want. There are many, many people living mighty hard in this our own country. I doubt if they are any worse off in Belgium."[2]

Goldberger felt surrounded by pellagra, and he felt increasingly helpless as cases multiplied. In mid-June he confessed to Mary how besieged he perceived himself to be: "Pellagra continues to develop; we have recorded nearly 500 cases to date in the villages we are studying. If we had that much typhoid the militia would probably be called out, or something like that." In another letter, several days later, the theme continued: "The pellagra cases are coming in at a great rate. I think we will have a record of fully 600 cases by the end of the week. Probably over 10% of the families have a case or more. When one pauses to think of it the horror of it becomes oppressive. And the end is not yet!"[3]

Politics in Europe had shattered the southern economy before 1917. Landowners were releasing renters from contracts because there was no sense in harvesting a crop that could not be sold. War brought prosperity—in 1917 the price of commodities like textiles, lumber, iron, and coal began to surge—but it was too late to offset the economic devastation that Goldberger was tracking in households across the South.[4]

Having identified the peak season for pellagra as the spring and early summer, when meat, milk, and fresh vegetables were least accessible to poor mill workers, Goldberger breathed a sigh of relief in August 1917, commenting to Mary, "The pellagra season is coming rapidly to a close; we are finding very few cases now and soon there will be none at all." Walking in Spartanburg, between his hotel and the hospital, Goldberger noticed that the streets were unusually crowded: "The town is full of people and when the soldiers come it will be overflowing." Would more people mean greater prosperity for the town or just the opposite? Surrounded by a disease he felt powerless to halt, Goldberger wasn't optimistic: "I am wondering what influence their presence is going to have on local people. I am afraid some of the poor people are going to have a hard time."[5]

A month later, soldiers were pouring into towns near military training camps. In Spartanburg, streets were crowded with men in uniform: "The place is already full of soldiers, although only the Engineers of the [National] Guard have arrived . . . Prices for board & rooms are skyrocketing." And then, with his usual prescience, Goldberger predicted, "I'm thinking Spartanburg will see a big slump after the war." What worried him most immediately was the lifestyle of these mobile men and women: "Eating places are appearing like mushrooms over night. Things are going to be here as I suppose they were in some of the western gold-mining camps—everyone living out of tin cans—fresh vegetables and milk & eggs very hard to get." Haunted by what he had already seen, he explained to Mary what was most on his mind: "I am wondering how the mill people are going to make out."[6] The potential for more pellagra haunted him.

As Goldberger watched the streets of Spartanburg, other physicians were watching him. Surgeon General Rupert Blue asked several prestigious medical experts to visit him and assess the government's pellagra research under Goldberger's leadership. Blue had complete confidence in Goldberger, but he wanted independent confirmation that the government was doing all it could to banish the South's scourge. In July, Goldberger was visited by Dr. David Edsall, the eminent public health expert known for his biochemical investigations of nutritional diseases and his studies of industrial hygiene. Edsall, a member of the medical faculty at Harvard and the medical staff at Massachusetts General Hospital, spent several days with Goldberger visiting mill villages, the U.S. Pellagra Hospital in Spartanburg, and the Georgia State Sanitarium at Milledgeville. He was delighted with Goldberger's accessibility and stimulated by his insight. By his visit's end Edsall had become convinced that pellagra was not an infectious disease and that Goldberger's studies had furnished "most impressive evidence of the probable dietetic origin of the disease." Confessing to the surgeon general that he had been "distinctly skeptical about the latter point," Edsall had "through observation on the ground" come to feel that he needed only a few points clarified to be "wholly convinced."[7]

What did Edsall need to know? "First, a satisfactory explanation for the striking seasonal incidence of the disease. Second, an explanation of the fact that certain villages have shown in past years . . . a curious freedom from the disease. Third, an explanation of the occasional cases in persons who have available a generous and varied diet." By the summer of 1917, when Edsall made his inspection, Goldberger and Sydenstricker were well on their way to satisfactorily answering his queries. However, Edsall made clear that even in the absence of conclusive answers, "the evidence now appears to me to favor very strongly indeed, the dietetic origin."[8] Goldberger had made another convert.

If Edsall was all but persuaded that pellagra was a disease caused by a poor diet, he was even further persuaded that Goldberger's detective work was pathbreaking. He concluded his report to the surgeon general

with praise: "I cannot refrain from saying that I was more deeply impressed with the value of this investigation than anything I have come in
contact with in recent years. Its value in relation to pellagra, wide-spread
and important as that disease is, seems but a fraction of its importance."[9]

What was it about the mill village studies that drew such accolades
from the eminent Edsall? The Harvard professor made clear the tran-
scendent importance of Goldberger's research:

> As an example of the study coincidently of the sanitary, the socio-
> logic, the economic and other important factors influencing dis-
> ease, at the same time investigating accurately the rise and fall of
> the disease itself, this is[,] so far as I know, a unique study in the
> breadth of its conception and in the care and patience with which
> the medical officers and others at work in it are carrying on the
> irksome details of the many times repeated examinations of these
> groups of people.

Predicting that Goldberger's data would yield insight in "a social and
economic way" as well as medical understanding, Edsall correctly fore-
cast that "this study will set standards that will be very welcome and helpful at this time when the social and economic relations of medicine are
becoming clearly recognized."[10]

Even before Edsall wrote his report to the surgeon general, Goldberger knew that he had impressed his distinguished guest. He wrote to
Mary, "Prof. Edsal [sic] 'came to scoff and remained to pray.'" Delighted
with these results, he let Mary in on his technique: "He [Edsall] had a
strenuous time of it. I kept him busy. He was going all the time from the
moment of arriving to the moment of departing. There was not a moment wasted. He visited ten of the mill villages, the hospital and
Milledgeville." If Goldberger ran the good doctor ragged, the result was
well worth the exertion: "He told me that his visit of inspection was one
of the most interesting and profitable ones he has experienced in recent
years." Goldberger not only respected Edsall's professional regard; he
came to like the man. "His personality is very agreeable," he told Mary.
"I enjoyed him very much."[11]

The warm feelings were mutual. Edsall invited Goldberger to bring

Mary and visit him at his home in Boston. However, Goldberger postponed acting on the invitation, making his apologies to his long-suffering wife: "I wish I could go and have you with me—perhaps some day we may go."[12] His schedule was too busy for a trip to Boston with Mary.

A trip to Boston would have offered Mary and Joseph a badly needed vacation together. Even as her husband tramped around mill villages checking the health of her fellow southerners, Mary's own health and peace of mind had been compromised a good deal of late. Two years earlier she had been ill with hyperthyroidism and bouts of depression. In a letter reeling with her own pain and inner turmoil she had assured him then, "I'm trying hard to take care of myself and to do right." She felt herself on the way to getting rid of "all the blue devils" and expressed a strong desire to "be my old happy self once more."[13] Often she went for over a week without writing to him, and then said little about herself. The following year she was robust enough to participate in the "filth parties," and she and her husband were never closer. However, in 1917 the pressures of caring for four youngsters—the three boys and little Mary, born in 1915—with only the help of a "mammy" led her to seek diversion in shopping and socializing with neighbors. Whenever she could, she traveled with the children to her family's retreat in Biloxi.

An educated, well-bred southern woman, Mary was lonely for her husband and hungry for a normal social life. Like many women of her class and background, she depended on her household help to a degree that non-southerners, her husband included, viewed as overly self-indulgent. She received letters from him chastising her for not doing enough. In March, Goldberger expressed his pique, writing, "It has seemed to me that you have been giving your children and house largely over to 'Mammy.' You can hardly have deliberately decided that she is an adequate substitute." Denying his own selfishness, Goldberger continued, "You see I'm not asking for anything for myself but the children have claims that cannot be waived by selfish considerations." He even went so far as to admit that he was not without fault: "I am conscious that I have not given the children the attention that is due them from me. But I have the—it seems to me—sufficient excuse that my work has prevented and interfered." He told her of his own determination "that this will cease . . . by the end of the year, for the field work simply must stop then and the mass of collected data must be taken up for deliberate analysis and study." In the meantime, though, he lightly scolded, "It seems to me that you must carry the whole burden and my fear is that you do not sufficiently realize your duty and responsibility."[14]

Their correspondence in early July 1917 reveals how heavily the burdens of family continued to fall on Mary. Even Joseph expressed concern rather than criticism: "You must be having your hands full to overflowing—Mary [their daughter] with tonsils out, Ben with ear trouble and Mammy crippled with rheumatism." Moreover, relief was not in sight, as he observed: "It is hard to tell just what to expect of mammy's rheumatism; it has unpleasant possibilities of invalidism." He concluded with the lame good wishes that absent husbands sheepishly offer overburdened wives: "I hope that all this hasn't thrown too much of a strain on you."[15]

The following summer little had changed. Now the problem was eleven-year-old Farrar: the eldest son and his mother were not getting along. Mary and the children were in Biloxi for much-needed relief, leaving Joseph in Washington. A bored Farrar wanted to join his father, but Goldberger was having none of it: "I am at a loss to know how to take care of Farrar up here. When I'm in Washington, I am at the laboratory all day. Occasionally I am away from Washington from two days to a week or so." Goldberger, absorbed by his work, bluntly concluded, "I see no practical way of caring here for him in your absence." Unlike earlier times, he did not press Mary to return. Having decided that Farrar would remain with her, he wished her well: "I am glad to learn that you are beginning to relax and enjoy yourself. Keep it up. As for coming home, do it when you get ready; don't cut your visit and vacation short on my account. While I miss you and the kiddies, I am making out quite comfortably."[16]

Throughout 1917 and early 1918 Goldberger was well aware that he, too, was feeling the strain of it all and experienced chronic sleep deprivation: "I do not sleep well when I'm away from home so that I soon get very tired." However, what was keeping him awake at night was more than simply a strange bed: "Added to this I have the work here with its many phases on my mind. The successful outcome of the [mill village]

investigation depends in such large measure on the efficiency of a number of junior officers." At the age of forty-three, Goldberger was hardly a
dinosaur, but his performance standards were high, and while he had
great faith and genuine admiration for George Wheeler, many of the "junior officers" were of unknown "efficiency." The degree of his weariness
was most clearly caught in his desire to move on: "I have pretty well
made up my mind to drop this sort of investigation at the end of this year.
Anyone may have it who wants it—and welcome." Then, realizing that
what he had just said was his stress talking, he scribbled, "I wonder
whether I'm getting old; I fancy this feeling of fatigue, of diminished enthusiasm must be a sign of beginning senility. Well I am tired of it; I feel
I've had enough."[17]

Weary of the investigation, the sleuth continued to press on and to
impress. In early January 1918 further evaluations of his work arrived on
the surgeon general's desk from the eminent physicians Victor Vaughan
and William Welch. Along with Dr. John W. Kerr, the much-respected
assistant surgeon general in charge of scientific investigation, Vaughan
and Welch visited Goldberger and observed the research in Spartanburg
and Milledgeville in late 1917. Both were generous in their praise.
Vaughan accepted not only the dietary theory but also Goldberger's
broader social analysis, writing, "The eradication of pellagra is largely an
economic problem and can be accomplished only by securing for the
people a properly balanced diet." He recommended that the Milledgeville study "be regarded as having fully demonstrated the claim that pellagra can be eliminated from the institution by dietary measures." He
urged discontinuing the study and insisted that state authorities furnish
asylum inmates with "such an improved dietary as Dr. Goldberger's
investigations indicate." However, Vaughan was not suggesting the end
of pellagra research per se. The research at Spartanburg must be continued to learn "more exactly what food principles and how much of each
must exist in a diet in order to prevent the development of the disease or
to prevent its recurrence among those in which it has already manifested
itself." Most of all, he wanted Goldberger to turn to laboratory investigations to find out "exactly what food constituents, either by their presence
or absence or by their abundance or scarcity, are concerned in the etiology of the disease." He also advocated trying to find "some lower animal

in which this disease can be produced by dietary measures." Now was the time to analyze the data collected at Spartanburg and move forward.[18]

William Welch agreed with Vaughan's report on every point but two. He thought it economically impractical simply to recommend that fresh milk, eggs, meats, and so on be added to the dietary of the Milledgeville asylum. Instead, he urged "further experiments to determine the effect in control of pellagra of the addition of individual dietary ingredients less expensive than fresh milk, fresh eggs and meats." Rather than closing down the experimental program at Milledgeville, Welch thought it a fine place for further research, because "conditions could be controlled and the material for observation was abundant." He, too, recommended extended biochemical studies to determine more precisely the role of "individual dietary factors" on pellagra incidence. Echoing Vaughan, Welch wrote to Rupert Blue:

> I desire to record my conviction that the work on pellagra carried out by Dr. Goldberger and his assistants has been admirably planned and conducted, is most creditable to the Public Health Service, and has resulted in most important scientific and practical contributions to our knowledge of this important and perplexing subject. I believe that these results will lead to the saving of thousands of human lives.[19]

Goldberger took Welch's advice. Because the Spartanburg hospital had facilities that Goldberger regarded as inadequate for animal experimentation, he divided up the hospital's laboratory work. Animal experimentation would now be conducted at the Hygienic Laboratory in Washington. The biochemist Michael X. Sullivan in Spartanburg was ordered to discontinue animal experimentation and to focus his efforts on conducting biochemical studies, using clinical material, that might yield answers about what precisely was missing from pellagrins' diets. He would spend his days analyzing the urine, excrement, and other excreta and substances extracted from the bodies of pellagrins.

Still Goldberger yearned for a break or a change of pace. He got it courtesy of two foreign adversaries, the German kaiser and the Spanish influenza. In August 1918 he wrote to Mary in Biloxi that he was involved in "war activities." He and George McCoy, the head of the Hygienic Laboratory, following "much thinking and discussion," had decided to "wrap pellagra in moth balls until after the war and to find something of more war-time importance to do."[20]

Years earlier, when he was bored to death as a general practitioner in Wilkes-Barre, Goldberger had unsuccessfully tried to join the Navy. He tried again, only to be rebuffed again. However, this time he turned to the Army and Colonel F. F. Russell, curator of the Army Medical Museum and professor of bacteriology and clinical microscopy at the Army Medical School, who assisted in developing the typhoid vaccine. Goldberger wrote to Russell "to see whether his division had anything I could do." Much to Goldberger's delight, "he jumped at me at once, said that he could put me to work as soon as I could come or sooner." Now the question was, would the PHS allow him time off to become a soldier? He went to see several senior officers, including the surgeon general. Rupert Blue seemed "favorably disposed" and promised to take the request to the secretary of the Treasury. Goldberger wanted his wife to understand that he had not made the decision lightly but had "come to feel that it is my duty to take up the work the Army has for me, and that, if necessary, I ought to resign from the Service to do so."[21]

Fortunately, the Goldbergers did not have to decide whether with four children they could afford to lose the nine hundred dollars per year of income Joseph's resignation from the PHS would have occasioned. The Public Health Service agreed to detail him to the military, as he requested. Moreover, an increase in PHS pay added fifteen dollars more per month to the family coffers. Sounding like a youth ever so anxious to impress his girl, Goldberger boasted, "You will also be interested to learn that the commissioned officers of our Service are now 'sure enough' part of the 'military forces' of the U.S."[22] The air of weariness and boredom seemed to have vanished. A new adventure loomed before him even as he was enjoying the recognition that comes at midlife.

Later in August, Goldberger left Washington for the South "in order to get things underway for winding the work up and putting it in shape for preservation until after the war." It was also an opportunity for him to sit back and marvel at his successes. He was especially pleased that the PHS's "educational propaganda on pellagra" was making progress. The evidence was an editorial in the most recent issue of the *Southern Medical Journal*, which Goldberger called an "amusing contrast to one there published just about three years ago." Earlier editorials had been critical of the dietary hypothesis. "Now the editorial writer takes the 'unbalanced diet' as a matter of course and admonishes the doctors to take due notice and practice accordingly; three years go he laughed at the idea and in effect stated that diet could not produce such a disease as pellagra! We certainly have made great progress!" A conversation at Camp Meade with Colonel Russell led Goldberger to muse over how ideas become accepted, or, as he put it, "Curious how we are led not only in politics and religion but in Science, too!" When pellagra came up in conversation, the colonel remarked, "Why I thought that it was all settled. Welch told me all about it!" Goldberger was amused: "The conversion of such heavy artillery as Welch, Vaughan, Edsall, and Flexner, practically settles the matter for the profession. All the pop-guns are at once silenced!"[23] He basked in the victory of his ideas, though the war against pellagra was as undecided as the war against the kaiser.

By the end of the month Goldberger had drafted recommendations that allowed his research to be interrupted so that "a number of medical officers and other personnel" might be made available for "other more important duty." The physicians at the Spartanburg Pellagra Hospital were to continue care but cease collecting field data on or about October 1. Data already collected were to be prepared for filing and preservation at Spartanburg "for such period as the present emergency may necessitate, and also permit of their later study and analysis without material loss." Research at the Georgia State Sanitarium at Milledgeville was to be completely discontinued and the records sent to the Hygienic Laboratory in Washington.[24]

At the end of September 1918, Goldberger was assigned by the surgeon general to study "the etiology of influenza with special reference to the transmission of the disease by carriers." However, less than two months after he received his marching orders, at least one of Goldberger's wars came to an end. The war in Europe was over. On the day that an armistice was declared, an excited Goldberger, punctuating almost every sentence with an exclamation point, wrote to Mary, "I wonder whether you were awakened by the 'Xtra' this morning! I heard it shortly after we left the station in New York. It surely is great!" On his way to Boston Goldberger described the scene: "The streets here are full of people with all sorts of noise-making devices. The Governor has declared tomorrow a holiday so that Boston will celebrate on two days."[25] The physician who was making history himself marveled at being enveloped in it.

Goldberger's other war, the one against Spanish influenza, was just beginning. And the enemy was flourishing. Tens of millions died in the pandemic of 1918–1919.[26] In addition to the civilians stricken, large numbers of military personnel were felled. With the United States at war, some 1.5 million American men had been moved to a small number of military camps across the country, many of them moving from camp to camp. It is no wonder that the influenza virus moved with them. Soon American troops at home and abroad were getting sick. So, too, were the troops of other nations. The so-called Spanish flu threatened to fell soldiers more effectively than enemy fire.

By noon on September 20, 1918, the Army had reported 9,313 new cases of flu among troops stationed in the United States. Three days later, there were over 20,000 cases. By September 28, when Goldberger was ordered to Boston, more than 31,000 American naval personnel ashore in the United States had been stricken. The Army reported 50,000 sick and 1,100 dead.[27] This second wave promised to be more deadly than the 1917 flu.

The PHS was ill prepared for an epidemic on this scale. Surgeon General Rupert Blue distributed information on how to recognize the disease. For those stricken he urged bed rest, wholesome food, salts of quinine, and aspirin. He appointed physicians to direct the fight against the flu in each state, and then set about recruiting additional doctors to help them. The Volunteer Medical Service Corps, a kind of auxiliary of the PHS, helped in recruitment. By October 1918 the PHS had placed more than six hundred physicians in the field, and soon Goldberger joined the fray.[28]

Influenza reunited Goldberger with his old friend and mentor Milton Rosenau, who took leave of Harvard to hold the rank of lieutenant commander in the U.S. Navy during the war. With two collaborators, Lieutenant W. J. Keegan of the Navy and Assistant Surgeon Gleason C.

Lake of the PHS, Goldberger and Rosenau conducted two sets of experiments using human subjects to explore influenza. Goldberger was back on the familiar turf of infectious disease.[29] However, this time the subjects did not include himself or Mary. They would be military personnel—volunteers.

As early as January 1916 Rosenau had organized a symposium to explore the idea that the cause of the new influenza was an organism so minute that it could pass through a laboratory filter. The hypothesis that it was a filterable virus, however, had never been proved. In August 1918 one center of the epidemic on the east coast offered the opportunity to do exactly that. Rosenau, former chief of the Hygienic Laboratory, now found himself directing the laboratory at the Chelsea Naval Hospital in Boston. Profoundly ill sailors arrived daily at the hospital; many were dying. Rosenau had enough experience with infectious disease to realize the opportunity in front of him. With these sailors he had the disease in its early and purest form. He had a working hypothesis and, most immediately important, held the rank and position to assemble the equipment and individuals necessary to test it.[30]

With sickness and death seemingly everywhere, Rosenau and Keegan were determined to establish whether the influenza was being caused by a filterable virus. Using throat and nose washings from two flu patients, they filtered the material and swabbed the noses of nine volunteers from the U.S. Naval Training Station on Deer Island in Boston, where influenza had not yet appeared. After ten days of observation, well beyond the usual incubation period, the volunteers still showed no sign of flu. The researchers concluded that influenza was not a filterable virus, and Keegan published the results in *The Journal of the American Medical Association*.[31]

The problems with the experiment were many. Human beings, even under the most controlled circumstances, as in Goldberger's Rankin experiment, are difficult scientific subjects. As the historian Alfred Crosby has quipped, "A bacteriologist conducting experiments with human beings during a pandemic is like nothing so much as a man trying to build a ship model in a bottle during a barroom brawl." Crosby raised numerous questions about Rosenau and Keegan's experiment:

Did the donors of the secretions have authentic cases of the flu? Where had the nine volunteers been the previous spring and summer when the mild variant of Spanish influenza swept across the world? Was Deer Island really still free from all contamination from the epidemic just a short distance away in Boston? Within a few days of flu's first appearance at Commonwealth Pier, nearly everyone at the Naval Hospital must have been exposed to it, including Rosenau and Keegan; were they in contact with the volunteers before the inoculations were made? How long before? Long enough so that the nine volunteers may have had symptomless cases of flu and developed immunity?[32]

Rosenau and Keegan knew the work was incomplete, hence their delight at bringing Goldberger on board and including him in planning the next experiments. The first series of these began on November 6, 1918, and continued until December 23, 1918. The team headed by Rosenau and Goldberger used sixty-two volunteers from the Deer Island Naval Training Station. They ranged in age from fifteen to thirty-four, with the majority of them being eighteen to twenty-one. Thirty-nine had no history of an attack at any time. Fourteen had a history of the disease, and nine had had attacks of a "doubtful nature," which means that they may have had it. All had been exposed in varied degrees to influenza on Deer Island. Eight experiments were conducted using different methods to infect the volunteers from the pool of sixty-two.

In two experiments pure cultures of a bacillus were inoculated into six men by instillation into the nose and spraying of the nose and throat. In two other cases unfiltered secretions were taken from the upper respiratory passages of flu patients at Peter Bent Brigham Hospital and sprayed into the noses and throats of volunteers; in one of these some of the secretions were even introduced into the eyes. In one, filtered secretions from the upper respiratory passages were sprayed into the nose and throat and instilled into the eyes, and in another the same filtrate was injected subcutaneously. In another, transfers of secretions were made from the nose and nasopharynx of flu patients by means of swabs to the nose and nasopharynx of volunteers. Blood taken from flu victims was injected into volunteers. And finally, there was exposure through contact by breath and droplet infection. After these extensive efforts one volunteer developed a red throat, and none developed unmistakable influenza symptoms.

The failure to induce symptoms puzzled Goldberger and Rosenau. Combining their negative results with what they knew about the disease's epidemiology led them to suspect that influenza is most communicable during incubation and that most of their influenza material came from patients in the first, second, or third day of the disease, or long after its incubation. They speculated that discharges from the mouth and throat during incubation were the means of transmission, but they had no evidence.[33]

The following winter, from early February 1919 until March 10, 1919, Goldberger and Rosenau secured another forty-nine naval volunteers for further testing. These volunteers were naval prisoners. They were told the nature of the experiment and that they might get sick. Forty-three were inoculated, receiving eighty-two inoculations in all. The age range was nineteen to thirty-six. From the various inoculations investigators concluded that influenza could be transmitted with secretions of the upper respiratory passages of patients in the early stages, usually within less than twelve hours of the disease's onset. Still the results were inconclusive because the criteria for a positive diagnosis of influenza were not well defined. Many volunteers came down with clear cases of streptococcal tonsillitis. Only a few of them got influenza, and the investigators speculated that it might have been because, "being young male adults in a region where epidemic influenza had recently prevailed," they might have acquired "more than average resistance."[34] The research team had demonstrated how streptococcal tonsillitis could be transmitted, but what they had learned about influenza was modest at best.

The influenza pandemic ended in the spring of 1919 as mysteriously and silently as it had begun. Over 500,000 Americans lay dead, a modest percentage of the 25 million who perished from the disease worldwide but enough to give the pandemic a permanent and dark place in the collective memory of Americans. Like all wars and epidemics, influenza bifurcated time. Individuals referred to an event as occurring before or after the flu. For a while medical scientists could think of nothing else.

Physicians who had dropped other work to study the flu or care for those who had it only slowly returned to what had occupied them before. Goldberger, too, only slowly turned his attention from a disease he knew was infectious to one he knew was not. He resumed his war on pellagra, heading south to yet another scene of medical combat.

During Goldberger's absence George Wheeler had been in charge of the suspended pellagra investigation. However, there was little to do at Spartanburg. The hospital had been converted into a relief hospital for influenza sufferers on October 14 and continued to be used as such until November 19, 1918. By the winter of 1919, however, pellagra studies had resumed. In April the detective Goldberger had turned his attention to pellagra again. He was seeking to perfect the recording of evidence. Specifically, he sought "some satisfactory way [to document] the types and variations" of the disease. Why not simply use a camera? Goldberger explained to the surgeon general that "attempts have been made to do this by photography but this has given only partially satisfactory results so that it is felt that this must be supplemented by colored and black and white drawings."[35] Goldberger wanted the assistance of a portrait artist.

Goldberger recommended hiring John W. Carroll, who lived and painted in Washington. He wanted Carroll assigned to Wheeler at Spartanburg and suggested the painter be paid a salary of one hundred dollars per month and a per diem of four dollars and given travel expenses to Spartanburg and to the Georgia State Sanitarium at Milledgeville. The surgeon general agreed.[36] The twenty-seven-year-old portrait artist, a war veteran who had honed his skills sketching his shipmates in the Navy, produced the kind of illustrations that assisted Goldberger and Wheeler in documenting pellagra rashes on different parts of the body and on individuals of different races and complexions. Goldberger would need all the help he could get because by the summer of 1920 the incidence of pellagra had begun to increase.

In July 1920 Surgeon General Hugh S. Cumming, who had replaced Rupert Blue, received a communication from Dr. R. W. Hall, assistant secretary of the Mississippi State Board of Health, about "a large number of cases this spring in a certain locality in Humphreys County, Mississippi." Goldberger was sufficiently intrigued to investigate personally. What he found did not surprise him: "Neither the cases nor the circumstances surrounding the cases were found to present anything of peculiar interest. In scarcely a single instance was there any difficulty in ascertaining that the individual or the household had been living on a decidedly restricted diet, milk, eggs, lean meat and fresh vegetables being conspicuous by their scarcity or practically absolute absence from the diet."[37]

Of considerably more interest were the cases of pellagra in Holly Bluff, a small village in cotton-plantation country near the Yazoo River. A local physician told Goldberger that there always seemed to be more pellagra after the periodic overflow of the Yazoo. Such episodes had occurred in 1912, 1913, and 1916. And one was occurring then. The flooding had begun at the end of March and continued "with a great increase in June." Flooded roads prevented a visit, but one sufferer happened to be at the physician's office when Goldberger arrived. Goldberger confirmed the diagnosis. Then he put on his detective hat.

He soon learned that floods brought about a restricted diet because "milch cows as well as other stock could not graze and this imposed on the owners an unusual expense for feed which, in the case of the poor household, must have constituted a serious economic drain." When the costs could not be met, cows died of starvation. While the short-term consequence was fresh meat, the long-term consequence was a restricted milk supply. Moreover, the flood disrupted railroad lines and required detours. Freight was delayed, including perishable foods. Gardens were flooded out. The food supply was limited to staples such as "flour, meal, molasses, fatback and a limited variety of canned goods" purchasable at plantation commissaries. However, because the overflow had lasted so long in 1920, even these foods sold out. And because the flood threw into question the quality of the forthcoming crop, planters and merchants quickly limited the amount of credit they extended, decreasing the purchasing power of poor farmers and further diminishing the quality of their diets.[38]

The twelve pellagra cases Goldberger identified in the course of his Mississippi visit involved nine households, two white and seven "colored." According to the board of health records that he checked, seventy-six cases of pellagra were reported in Humphreys County that June, seventy-three "colored" and three "white," indicating to Goldberger "a very marked disproportion of incidence in the two races, even after allowing for the difference in the proportion of the population constituted by the two races." Why the racial differential? Goldberger speculated that it was the result of "the differences in economic conditions of the two races." Now he pulled no punches: "The indications are that a larger proportion of the whites than of the negroes are better to-do; nearly all plantation owners, merchants and professional men are white; the renter for the most part black, though including some white, is mostly very poor ignorant and shiftless, and because of his ignorance and lack of thrift labors under other handicaps of varying degrees of economic importance." The system was flawed, but Goldberger, a man of his times, placed some of the blame on the shoulders of the victims. To his eye the cause for greatest worry was that the incidence of pellagra was "very much higher than the at present available figures seem to indicate." His conclusion: "An improvement in the availability of food supplies particularly milk and fresh vegetables would seem to be a pressing need of the 'delta.'"[39]

His cry of concern came at a time of general optimism concerning pellagra. Overall, wartime production in industry and agriculture made for higher family income among southern workers and farmers alike. Higher incomes allowed for more nutritious diets and resulted in fewer cases of pellagra. Equating patriotism with good nutrition, some southern farmers plowed under their cotton and put in food crops for the war effort. By 1918 the shift had become unmistakable. In Mississippi alone there was a marked decline in both incidence and mortality compared with the prewar period. In 1914 there had been 10,954 cases of pellagra in the state, with 1,201 deaths. In 1918 there were 8,340 cases and 746 deaths.[40] The data and the optimism found their way to Washington.

In Washington the surgeon general decided to close the Spartanburg Pellagra Hospital in light of the declining cases of the disease. To celebrate the closing, Goldberger and his assistant, George Wheeler, were honored at a banquet. A local physician proclaimed from the dais, "We have met for a funeral and an interment. We are here to bury pellagra." Another applauded Goldberger's "courtesy," "tact," and "diplomacy."[41] The praise as well as the memorial for pellagra turned out to be premature.

In his sober banquet remarks Goldberger warned that the return of bad times could mean the return of pellagra.[42] His words were prophetic. By the autumn of 1920 the price of cotton had begun to fall. When tenant farmers and sharecroppers settled their accounts after the harvest, they received 50 percent less than their toil had yielded the previous year. Tobacco profits dropped to a third of what they had been a year earlier. Goldberger had been in Mississippi in the late summer at the request of the state board of health to investigate a spike in pellagra. The situation was bad and promising to turn worse the following year. In the mill villages as on the farms, the wartime prosperity was over, and the return of poverty brought the resurrection of pellagra.

Goldberger, only recently praised at Spartanburg as a diplomat, now more resembled an angry prophet. He linked pellagra to the basic poverty of the South, caring little for the humiliation and resentment that southern leaders would feel or the economic and political fallout that might result. The press release came from the Public Health Service in Washington, but the facts and interpretation were Goldberger's.[43]

On July 9, 1921, Goldberger wrote to Joseph Schereschewsky, assistant surgeon general in charge of the Division of Scientific Research, "I am impressed with the need of arousing public interest in the significance of the very decided increase in pellagra this year and the prospect of a more serious increase next year." He wrote that in the summer of 1921 there were "thousands of people who are starving and dying. There is reason to believe that there will be still more next Spring and Summer." Referring to American aid abroad, Goldberger steamed, "We are feeding the near East and the Far East but we are neglecting our own people right here at home." He recommended a preventive campaign, one consisting of publicity to inform the public of the threat, educate them on proper diet, and convey to the planter and his tenant the need for "a home food supply in order that the failure of the single crop [not] leave [the tenant] practically destitute and dependent on such credit for food as the merchant or banker may feel they can afford." He also stressed the need to improve the availability of food, especially in "smaller isolated industrial communities."[44]

Goldberger's memo offered the surgeon general no numerical projection, but the PHS was quoted by *The New York Times* as characterizing pellagra as one of the "worst scourges known to man" and predicting that in 1921 the disease would claim 100,000 victims, 10,000 of whom would perish. In 1922 it might get even worse. The press release offered a dire image of the South: "A veritable famine has been developing in the rural districts of the South . . . and particularly in those of the cotton belt which stretches from Eastern Texas to the Carolinas. The tenant farmers . . . have been forced by the failure of the cotton market to adopt a starvation diet that is rapidly decimating them." Directly quoted, Goldberger described the worse areas as in Mississippi, the Memphis region of Tennessee, parts of eastern Texas, and the Carolinas. Georgia's fruit crop alone had saved that state from being included.[45]

In Washington, President Warren Harding wrote to both Dr. Livingston Farrand, head of the American Red Cross, and Surgeon General Cumming. In his letter to Farrand the president observed that "due to the depressed cotton market, many thousands of people are unable to sell their one product for money wherewith to obtain a necessary variety of wholesome food, and . . . there is grave threat of an epidemic of pellagra." Demanding a report from the surgeon general, Harding described the South as menaced with famine and plague, "words almost foreign to our American vocabulary, save as we have learned their meaning in connection with the afflictions of lands less favored, and toward which our people have so many times displayed large and generous charity."[46]

Cumming and Goldberger were delighted with Harding's support. In an interview Goldberger explained what he thought needed to be done to save the South. Instead of the $18,000 the PHS had to fight pellagra, $140,000 was required, plus funds for hospitalization and relief supplies for those already stricken. Goldberger also wanted one pellagra expert, one dietitian, and one clinic per state, the latter capable of treating at least one hundred pellagrins each. Once sent home, patients educated as to healthy diet could teach their neighbors. According to Goldberger, pellagra patients could recover if they received even one good meal a day, costing about twenty-five cents each. He concluded ominously, "If economic conditions do not improve I would be loath to prophesy what the 1922 story will be."[47]

Goldberger also called for local relief. He wanted farmers to refocus their efforts from cotton to more vegetables, eggs, cheese, milk, and lean meats. Plantation stores and those that serviced mill workers could assist by carrying cheap canned meats and fish at affordable prices.[48]

Goldberger's advice, which he regarded as pragmatic, seemed to southerners an insulting provocation. The backlash was palpable. Floridians were afraid that the blanket indictment of the South and its poverty would frighten tourists. However, the main offensive was led by South Carolina's young congressman James F. Byrnes. Later a New Dealer and secretary of state under President Harry Truman, Byrnes stood up for the honor of all southerners in 1921. He branded reports of famine and plague in the South as an "utter absurdity." He declined in advance an offer of emergency aid from the Red Cross. Several days later he wrote to Harding again:

> We may be over sensitive, but the average American dislikes to have placed in front of his door a flag indicating the presence of a plague, when . . . there exists within his home nothing to justify that characterization. And likewise, when there is no famine he dislikes to be held up as the object of charity, and compared with the "unfortunates of other lands" for the relief of whose starvation and disease our people have so generously contributed.

Livid, Byrnes demanded that Harding take action against those who had misrepresented the situation to him.[49]

Other senators and congressmen leaped to the South's defense. The Georgia congressman William C. Wright proclaimed that there was no "grim and gaunt spectre of famine . . . walking abroad in the Empire State of the South." Tennessee's Senator Kenneth McKellar carried an invitation from the state's public health officer. He said that all the fearful should come see how healthy Tennesseans treated the rumor of famine. Tennessee, he said, was prepared to ship beef, pork, poultry, and milk to its poorer northern neighbors should they need it.[50]

Comprehending the potential impact on investment in the South, the business community soon weighed in on the side of the politicians. The Atlanta Chamber of Commerce complained that the report was unwarranted by facts. *The Atlanta Constitution* called the report of semi-famine conditions "bosh and poppycock." Businessmen in Memphis protested that President Harding's statement about the South boded ill for investment.[51]

Support for the PHS came from the African-American community. James Weldon Johnson, Harlem Renaissance writer and a founder of the National Association for the Advancement of Colored People, blasted what he called "The Super-Sensitive South." In the summer of 1921 Johnson wrote:

> That section of the country which is known as "The South" offers an interesting field of investigation by both psychologists and pathologists. This fact is again brought out by the outburst of indignation which has come up from Mississippi and her neighboring commonwealths because of the warning issued by the Public Health Service in Washington in which it was asserted that pellagra had made an alarming headway in the South during the year and that it stood in danger of plague or famine.

Johnson observed that many southerners were criticizing President Harding for saying what they had long known to be true. According to him, these critics, well familiar with hunger and pellagra in the South, "nevertheless immediately grew indignant when the matter was stated by the Federal Health Service and the President." Johnson was especially offended by a statement made by R. W. Hall, the statistician of the Mississippi Board of Health, who said, "Of the 2239 cases of pellagra shown in the June morbidity report, fully eighty per cent are among Negroes chiefly in the Delta section." Johnson called Hall's analysis "absurd." "If all of the pellagra victims in Mississippi were Negroes," he wrote, "the fact would be just as damaging to the health and safety of the State and its population. We wonder whether if smallpox was raging in Jackson, the capital of Mississippi, the statistician of the State would say, 'I can see nothing whatever in the situation to cause alarm because eighty percent of the cases are Negroes.'"[52]

President Harding, much to his credit, stood fast with the Public Health Service despite the political heat. He could take comfort in the fact that his stand was unlikely to hurt him politically. After all, he had lost all eleven states of the old Confederacy in 1920. In an effort to resolve the stalemate, the Public Health Service held a conference on August 4–5, 1921, in Washington, with state health officers, agricultural experts, and relief agencies to plan an aid program for those felled by pellagra. However, instead of being constructive, the session degenerated into little more than an opportunity for southerners to vent their anger.

Goldberger, who had devised the estimate reported by the PHS and cited in *The New York Times*, explained how he arrived at the projection of 100,000 cases for 1921. Because of the increasing prosperity, he reduced the estimate of 5,000 deaths that likely occurred in 1920 to 4,000. He then applied to this reduced number a conservative rate of increase, projecting 5,000 for 1921. Based on the studies in South Carolina, he estimated that only 1 in 20 who have the disease dies. "Adopting this factor and applying it to the number of deaths [5,000] estimated for 1921, we get 100,000 as the number of definite cases." Backpedaling slightly, Goldberger said that the number of pellagra deaths for 1922 might be as few as 4,000. He and the PHS denied the 100,000 death estimate some newspapers mistakenly reported.[53]

In response, Goldberger was denounced. An old adversary, James A. Hayne of South Carolina, led the charge. Hayne reiterated his refusal to accept the diet theory of pellagra. He said that he never would and that he was "not the only fool in South Carolina" who had not accepted it. Others, such as Dr. Samuel Welch of Alabama, were equally upset. Welch found the offer of free meat and other food to Alabama such a provocation that he could barely control himself. He said that he would not try to refute Goldberger's projections because "I have never had to verify my statements with letters and figures as some of my neighbors do."[54] Southerners' indignation and preference for what they believed to be true, regardless of the data, echoed the passions Goldberger had witnessed in his earlier battles with yellow fever and dengue; diseases could never be isolated from the social and political contexts in which they appeared.

On August 9, the surgeon general sent a lengthy report on the meeting to President Harding. Revisiting the anger expressed by southerners, he attributed the unintended affront to "some confusion" aroused by the "misinterpretation of the sense in which the term 'famine' was used." Cumming explained to the president that the term used by the PHS "implied a deficiency in certain elements of the dietary, whereas it was generally interpreted as signifying an actual deficit in all food products." Then, just to make certain that Harding understood, he repeated Goldberger's analysis, now the accepted wisdom: "Pellagra is a deficiency disease due to the lack of certain elements in the diet which are found in milk, eggs, and flesh foods." Although the "financial depression in the South" was likely to cause southerners to "sacrifice these elements for a diet which ordinarily does not contain a sufficient amount of pellagra-preventing foods," Cumming was quick to add that the pattern was not exclusive to the South and that bad economic times generally produced "an increase in the prevalence of tuberculosis, pellagra, and other diseases."[55]

Cumming reported that state health officers at the meeting had agreed that there "was no emergency which would warrant the extension of relief on the part of the Red Cross." In fact, representatives of the Department of Agriculture at the meeting suggested that "the South was producing more food crops than at any time in its history, except probably during the period when war-gardens [during World War I] were in fashion." There were three reasons for this optimistic turn. One was the by-product of a perennial disaster visited upon cotton farmers—the boll weevil. Infestations compelled planters to find other uses for their land until the threat passed. The other reasons were the products of education. Cumming credited the Department of Agriculture's "two thousand county agents and home-demonstrators," who taught farmers the importance of crop diversification, and the federal and state health agencies that preached the gospel of the balanced diet as the path to disease prevention. According to Cumming, all present readily agreed "that there was a much larger increase in the food production in the South than there was during the pre-war period of 1908–1914 when pellagra was so prevalent."[56]

What could be done to improve the situation even further? Again, education seemed a popular answer at the meeting. The Department of Agriculture promised to launch a program that would convey the necessity for "fall and winter gardens and increasing the production and consumption of milk, eggs, and flesh foods throughout this country." Cumming wisely took care to emphasize that pellagra was a national problem, not the South's problem. He reported to Harding that the economist Clyde King, attached to the congressional Joint Commission on Agriculture, attributed the problem to the fact that "financial depression had affected the farmers of the United States to a much more serious extent than any other part of the population, especially the farm laborer and tenant classes," who lost purchasing power most dramatically.[57]

Was there a solution besides waiting for the economic cycle to change? No commitment to social change emerged from the southerners at the conference, although they did pass a resolution saying "there is no condition approaching a famine or plague in the South. It is obvious that there is a clear case of misinterpretation of terms, and incorrect analysis, and as a result statements have been made that are erroneous and misleading to the public."[58]

Cumming took the opportunity to place before Harding two courses of action with which few could disagree. One involved funding. Cumming told Harding, "There is urgent need for continuing and extending the financial support to the Federal, State, and local health departments, and a cooperative effort in intensive public health education." The other suggestion involved some reorganization. Cumming suggested consolidating "into one department all of the Federal agencies concerned in the public welfare" and improving coordination between federal activities and those of state and local welfare agencies. However, not until the New Deal and an even greater crisis—the Great Depression—would there be such reorganization and cooperation. In the meantime, Cumming supported the southern state health officers' appeal that PHS officers be "detailed in a liaison capacity to State Health Departments." The goal was to coordinate federal with state and local activities and to work with the states to "forestall, in so far as practicable, the expected increase not only in pellagra but in other diseases."[59]

Cumming's suggestions were sound, but the meeting was a fiasco. Almost nothing was accomplished to protect those most vulnerable to pellagra. Worse yet, Goldberger's prophecy proved correct. In 1921 in the South the incidence of pellagra increased, as did the number of deaths. There were 2,451 deaths from pellagra in 1921, but this figure is soft because Alabama, Georgia, Arkansas, and Texas, where the disease was known to be on the increase, did not furnish reliable reports. In Missis-

INCIDENCE OF PELLAGRA IN THE STATE OF MISSISSIPPI[a]			
YEARS	CASES BY RACE	NO. OF DEATHS	PELLAGRA MORTALITY RATE
1907–11[b]	White 1387 Black 1156 Race not reported 352		
	Total cases 2,895	1,250	43.17 (per 100 reported cases)

YEARS	CASES BY RACE		MORBIDITY RATE PER 100,000	DEATHS	MORTALITY RATE PER 100,000
1914[c]	White	3,963	476.4	256	30.8
	Black	6,991	654.6	936	87.6
	Total	10,954	575.9	1192	62.7
1921[d]	White	1,970	230.7	82	9.6
	Black	7,932	846.8	602	64.3
	Total	9,902	553.0	684	38.2
1926[e]	White	2,363	276.7	104	12.2
	Black	5,030	537.0	460	49.1
	Total	7,393	412.9	564	31.5
1930[f]	White	3,381	339.1	97	9.7
	Black	6,792	670.3	476	47.0
	Total	10,173	505.5	573	28.5

[a] Population for the state of Mississippi in 1910 was 1,797,000; in 1920, 1,791,000; and in 1930, 2,010,000, according to The Statistical History of the United States from Colonial Times to the Present, compiled by the United States Bureau of the Census (New York: Basic Books, 1976), p. 30.
[b] C. H. Lavinder, "The Prevalence and Geographic Distribution of Pellagra in the United States," Public Health Reports 27 (December 13, 1912), p. 2077.
[c] A Statistical Report of Pellagra in Mississippi and Suggestions to the Legislature Relative to Its Prevention and Cure (Jackson, Mississippi: State Board of Health, 1915), pp. 8, 13; Report of the Board of Health of Mississippi from June 1, 1913, to June 30, 1915 (Jackson, Mississippi: State Board of Health, 1915), pp. 61–67.
[d] Report of the Board of Health of Mississippi from July 1, 1921, to June 30, 1922 (Jackson, Mississippi: State Board of Health, 1923), pp. 48, 56.
[e] Twenty-fifth Biennial Report, Being the Forty-ninth and Fiftieth Annual Reports of the State Board of Health of the State of Mississippi, July 1, 1925, to June 30, 1927 (Jackson, Mississippi: State of Mississippi, 1927), pp. 29, 34–40.
[f] Twenty-seventh Biennial Report, Being the Fifty-third and Fifty-fourth Annual Reports of the State Board of Health of the State of Mississippi, July 1, 1929, to June 30, 1931 (Jackson, Mississippi: State of Mississippi, 1932), pp. 25, 273.

sippi the number of deaths from pellagra in 1921 was 684; in 1920 it had been 544. In South Carolina the death rate for every 100,000 persons was 18.5 in 1921, an increase of 20 percent from the 15.6 per 100,000 of the previous year.[60]

Only Mississippi asked for federal aid, because of the extreme situation of the Delta. With one-fifth of the state's population, the Delta had three-fifths of the state's cases. To meet the crisis, Goldberger and Wheeler developed a two-pronged attack: they made essential foods available, and then encouraged people to eat them. Wheeler suggested that a health officer who understood the Delta and its people be sent to educate planters and tenants in the need for better nutrition.[61]

However, other states continued to resist. In North Carolina the health officer Watson S. Rankin noted that Goldberger's conclusions contradicted data from the Agriculture Department indicating that food supplies in the South were more plentiful than usual. He charged the surgeon general with a "lack of courage" for his failure to admit error in declaring the South in the grip of famine and plague.[62]

The parting shots at Goldberger were not fired until November 1921. At a meeting of the Southern Medical Association at Hot Springs, Arkansas, several public health officers, including Waller Leathers of Mississippi, defended Goldberger and the necessity of a good diet to cure pellagra. However, most of those present still argued that infection was the cause of the disease and that Goldberger's prison farm experiment and transmissibility experiments were meaningless.[63]

Joseph Goldberger defined pellagra as a product of distinct economic and social patterns. His southern audience, outraged by the assertion that conditions inherent in the southern economy and lifestyle were causing the scourge, refused to confront the changes required to wipe out the disease. After all, the poverty and limited access to wholesome food that Goldberger denounced were in some cases the direct result of the industrialization and urbanization that was generating wealth, fueling the emergence of the New South.

Goldberger could never reconcile himself to the South's defensive posture toward criticism of its institutions, especially in the face of evidence and rational argument. It was a posture born of a long tradition of deep hostility toward the North and the federal government. The trend had begun in the years before the Civil War, when southerners had rallied around slavery and countered the critique of abolitionists by defining themselves as a distinguished, harmonious civilization, superior to the contentious, industrial North. Goldberger never understood that the resistance to his dietary advice was part of both the legacy of postwar bitterness and the boosterism for what Progressive southerners called the New South. In the minds of southern businessmen, especially cotton men, the New South was robust, vigorous, and on the rise. As they had during the Rockefeller Foundation's war on hookworm, many southerners resented Goldberger's war on pellagra.[64] They did not want to hear that their diet was making them weak. They did not want potential investors or their former adversaries in the North to have doubts about the viability of the southern labor force and the potential for profitable economic investment in the South.

While Goldberger heard their loud objections to what he had learned about pellagra, his head also echoed with the advice offered him five years earlier by Victor Vaughan and William Welch. Vaughan thought defeating pellagra depended on "securing for the people a properly balanced diet." That advice was economically impractical. Now Goldberger understood that it was politically impractical as well. Welch had advised him to find "individual dietary ingredients less expensive than fresh milk, fresh eggs and meats." The challenge posed by Welch's advice, combined with the political realities amply revealed in the previous two months, drove Goldberger back to his bench at the Hygienic Laboratory in the autumn of 1921.

EIGHT

"Nailing Pellagra's Old Hide to the Barn Door"

In the past, whenever Joseph Goldberger sought answers to pellagra's cause and cure, he got on the road to witness personally how pellagrins lived and what they ate in and outside of institutions such as orphanages, asylums, hospitals, and prisons. He and Edgar Sydenstricker had followed the disease into the villages and homes of mill workers. However, in the late summer of 1921 pellagra's trail did not lead to the train station. It had become a journey of the mind best pursued in the red brick building at Seventh and C Streets in Washington, D.C., the site of the Hygienic Laboratory.[1] Now the tall physician bent over his microscope and opened and closed the doors of animal cages, seeking to accomplish what he had not done before: find the dietary element that prevented pellagra and identify a source of it that was broadly affordable and accessible.

Increasingly when Europeans and their American cousins wanted answers to the reason for human suffering, they turned not to altars but to well-equipped laboratories. In late-nineteenth- and early-twentieth-century Europe and the United States, scientific laboratories were most often associated with institutes or universities. However, in Europe the best researchers were encouraged by their governments or by private donors with laboratory facilities. There was no similar commitment from the U.S. government, and American facilities for medical research paled in comparison to those on the other side of the Atlantic. There were laboratories at only a few emerging graduate schools and at public health agencies in a few states and cities. At the end of the nineteenth century America's best young scientific minds went abroad to study with the likes of Robert Koch in Germany and Louis Pasteur in France.[2] The era when rich and powerful pharmaceutical companies could afford elaborate campuses was decades in the future.

In typical American fashion, necessity was the mother of invention. Cholera epidemics drove the federal government to open a one-room bacteriological laboratory at the Marine Hospital on Staten Island in August 1887. Marine Hospital Service officer Dr. Joseph Kinyoun was in charge. The facility, with its clutter of glassware and microscopes, was called a "laboratory of hygiene" because bacteriological research was being conducted that would supplement the public health arsenal then in use to battle disease—sanitation and quarantine.[3] Washington's Hygienic Laboratory evolved from these modest beginnings into one of America's most important scientific facilities with state-of-the-art equipment. More and more Americans were turning to science to find answers to social ills. Research on venereal disease, enforcement of the Biologics Control Act (1902) regulating the vaccines and antitoxins that might be injected into the human body, a forerunner of the Pure Food and Drug Act (1906), and Goldberger's pellagra research were just a few of the endeavors that addressed social issues and contributed mightily to the growth of the Hygienic Laboratory's reputation during its rapid expansion.

At the time Goldberger walked up the stairs to his small stuffy office in August 1921, the Hygienic Laboratory had more personnel than ever before. The staff of 55 in 1909 had grown to 117 by 1925, with the scientific staff tripling from 15 to 46.[4] In addition to the laboratory facilities in the main building, labs were housed in several smaller ancillary buildings. The largest of these had a huge kitchen, not unlike those in hotels or resorts. Here there were pots and pans and glassware for measuring. There were barrels with foods that could be prepared and fed to the laboratory animals, the dogs and rats kept in cages in another part of the building. As if they were zookeepers, a small staff of boys fed the animals, cleaned their cages, took their temperatures, and assisted Goldberger in every way he asked. The boys had better be on their toes; that August, Goldberger stalked the kitchen and peered into the cages daily.[5]

When the long day of research—of observation and note taking and brain-racking inquiry—was over, Goldberger and his colleagues rejoined an America that had entered a new and exciting era. Characterized by some as the Jazz Age, the 1920s was a time when the music seemed to echo the speed and spirit of a confident era, at least for the white urban middle class. During the next ten years newspapers would trumpet Charles Lindbergh's flight to Paris and Babe Ruth's towering home runs. The first "talking" motion picture, *The Jazz Singer*, released in 1927, tells the story of a Jewish cantor's child who has to choose between following in his father's footsteps in the pulpit and a career in American show business, his non-Jewish girlfriend at his side, a theme and circumstances that would not have been unfamiliar to Goldberger. In contrast to the era, this period in Goldberger's life has been characterized by one historian as the "quiet search."[6] Though more sedentary than previous years, these years were hardly sedate.

One research facility in the South remained crucial to Goldberger's research and required regular visits, the Georgia State Sanitarium at Milledgeville. Because it was not known whether pellagra existed in animals, who could then be the subjects of experiments that would illuminate the same condition in people, human experimentation proceeded. At the asylum a member of his research team, Dr. W. F. Tanner, was adjusting the diets of inmates who had pellagra, mostly but not exclusively mentally ill black women, to test the hypotheses Goldberger was developing in Washington.

Earlier in August, Goldberger had been at his desk when Tanner began an important new phase of their investigation. While Goldberger was preparing the statement he hoped would defuse the wrath of the southern public health officers who would be converging on Washington, Tanner began a more productive assault on the mystery they hoped to solve. Before her supper the patient Oconee Cobb, a thirty-two-year-old white female who had suffered bouts of pellagra in 1913, 1914, and again in October 1920, was given "one-half dram" of the amino acid tryptophan. The regimen would continue before each meal. Nothing else would change. She would receive all her regular medications.[7] Amino acids such as tryptophan are the building blocks of protein. And as Goldberger had observed many times, those whose diets were rich in animal protein did not get pellagra.

Tanner monitored Cobb's symptoms. Her diarrhea, a symptom of pellagra, continued and at first even worsened. However, by the third day her pellagra rash had begun to show slight improvement. On the fifth day the skin looked "nearly normal, except for an appearance of tenderness and loss of elasticity." The backs of her hands and her feet began to clear. An ecstatic Tanner reported, "I might add that the improvement in this patient's skin condition has surpassed anything I have ever seen in a case of pellagra in an equal period of time. It might be well for you to see her as early as you find convenient." Tanner was on the lookout for other patients with advanced cases of pellagra, those whose rashes were unmistakable. Not all received tryptophan. Some were given supplements of milk salts and cod-liver oil. Every day Tanner examined their feet and hands. Only those who received tryptophan got well.[8]

As an unseasonably warm autumn arrived, Goldberger journeyed to Milledgeville and, along with Tanner, took stock of their research. The thirty-three-year-old Tanner had perfect credentials for the position. He was a local, born in Milledgeville, had graduated from the Georgia Military College, and had earned a medical degree from the Atlanta College of Physicians and Surgeons in 1910. He had interned at the sanatorium and then had been assistant physician at the institution for more than two and a half years. He had been involved in pellagra studies since 1915 and had a special interest in the diagnoses of mental diseases. Because advanced pellagra often resulted in dementia and those institutionalized for other mental disorders sometimes contracted pellagra, Tanner was a sound choice to assist Goldberger in this phase of the research. But Goldberger was never enthusiastic about him. Generous in his praise of those he regarded as highly competent, Goldberger thought less of Tanner the longer the two worked together.[9] Still, Tanner understood what needed to be done, and Goldberger depended on him to follow the explicit instructions he sent from the Hygienic Laboratory.

In a letter to the assistant surgeon general, Goldberger spoke optimistically of what he and Tanner had thus far accomplished in this phase of the research: "The trend of the evidence, as you know, has been towards the protein as the essential factor concerned [in preventing pellagra]. We now have evidence which it seems to me leaves no room for doubt as to this. Pellagra may occur in an individual subsisting on a diet complete, so far as it is possible to judge, in all known factors except protein." Then he revealed the exciting new observation: "Our tentative feelers with certain amino acids have been very interesting and very suggestive." However, Goldberger, cautious, lest he overstate what he knew as opposed to what he merely suspected, added, "It is doubtful however whether they can be conclusive except where made as prophylactic tests." Without exaggerating his claims, he assured his superior that the present tests were "sufficiently encouraging to warrant their continuation and if possible to make with certain of them a preventive test."[10]

As important as the pellagra study was to the PHS, insufficient funds were a perennial obstacle to research. Goldberger was so convinced of the rightness of his research direction that he was not above begging his bosses, especially in light of a recent cut in funding: "This brings me to the question of funds. With the present allotment of $20,000—less 10%, or $18,000 net—we can do very little more this fiscal year. Hardly more than mark time. Is there no possibility of scraping up a little more for pellagra this year[?]" All he needed was another $12,500 for a test that could determine which amino acid was the preventive: "With these [funds] it will be possible to feed 10 individuals for 6 months—a period sufficiently long, I think, to give conclusive results." He left his question hanging in the air: "Now, would it be possible for you to scrape up, somehow, this additional sum?" Going further out on a limb than usual when it came to promises about the speed of results, he predicted that with the funding, "the outlook is promising that by the end of the present fiscal year we would have the question of the amino acid deficiency narrowed down within very restricted limits."[11] There is no evidence that he got the funding, and the modest direction taken by his research suggests that he got considerably less than he requested.

Not all the stories from Milledgeville were happy. In October, Tanner delivered some sad news: "Sarah Franklin died yesterday, cause pellagra. She had been eating well, taking all her supplements but steadily refusing the beef at dinner up to the end." Those not getting tryptophan or eating the foods that Goldberger had identified as preventing pellagra did not survive the scourge. When a patient seemed to be failing, Tanner supplemented her diet. Fannie Jones, a forty-five-year-old in one of the black wards, began to get worse in late October. Tanner reported, "Her buttermilk was increased to 40 oz. daily, beginning with dinner today. Two other patients taking the gelatine have been eating poorly and were begun on buttermilk. This leaves only four patients taking the gelatine and milk mineral." Gradually Goldberger and Tanner were learning what would and would not stop pellagra's progression. In a letter to Mary, Goldberger, overly optimistic in his private correspondence, predicted, "We have found a road which if followed another year or two will come close to nailing pellagra's old hide to the barn door."[12]

In January 1922 the Goldberger family was swept by sadness with the passing of Mary's father. Only seventy-two years old, Edgar Farrar died of pneumonia at the family's retreat in Biloxi, Mississippi. Because of his political prominence in New Orleans, his death was front-page news in *The Times-Picayune* and other newspapers. Since his daughter's marriage to Goldberger in 1906, Farrar had remained true to his promise; Joseph Goldberger was always welcome in his home and treated with the affection of a son. When his son-in-law's income did not permit family travel or the modest luxuries of middle-class life, such as a piano in the living room, Edgar Farrar generously opened his checkbook. His second home in Biloxi became the entire family's vacation house. However, Farrar had displayed more than material generosity; he had offered Goldberger an elder's adulation and appreciation for his achievement. While Goldberger's own parents spoke little English and applauded from the sidelines, Farrar understood and discussed with his son-in-law the medical conquests in which he played a part. The compassionate and rational approach to public policy that characterized Progressivism was a bond that overcame the men's differences in region and religion.

True to this Progressive vision, Goldberger continued working hard, trying to identify the substance in the diet that when absent caused the onset of pellagra. However, he had some added responsibilities. That year Surgeon General Cumming ordered a major reorganization of the Public Health Service, including many reassignments. Dr. Rolla Dyer became assistant director of the Hygienic Laboratory, taking charge whenever Director George McCoy was away and assuming responsibility for a reorganization that included dividing up the laboratory's Division of Pathology into three sections: Infectious Disease under Dr. James P. Leake, Pathology under Dr. Gleason C. Lake, and Nutritional Disease

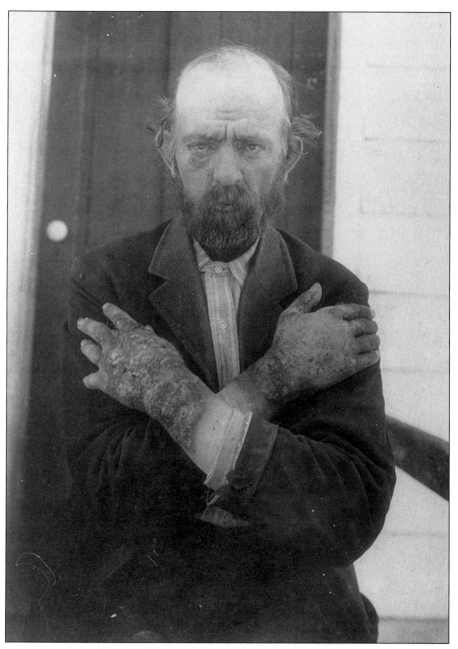

Man with pellagra "gloves." (Courtesy of James C. Babcock Collection, Waring Historical Library, Medical University of South Carolina, Charleston, South Carolina)

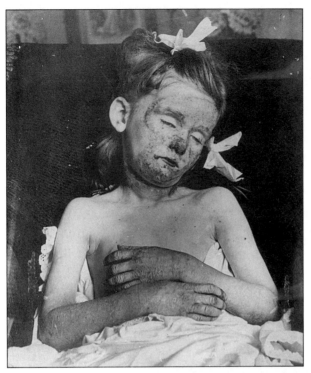

Female child with pellagra, circa 1910. (Courtesy of James C. Babcock Collection, Waring Historical Library, Medical University of South Carolina, Charleston, South Carolina)

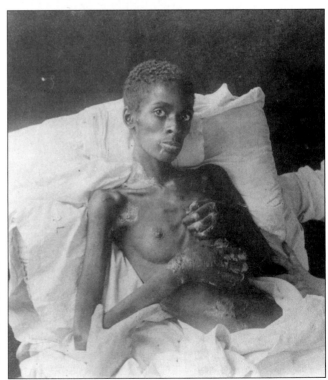

African-American woman with pellagra. (Courtesy of James C. Babcock Collection, Waring Historical Library, Medical University of South Carolina, Charleston, South Carolina)

Dr. George A. Wheeler, Goldberger's most trusted assistant, who was at his side in the mill village studies and the Rankin State Prison Farm experiment. (Courtesy of the National Library of Medicine)

Dr. Milton J. Rosenau, circa 1906. Rosenau directed the Hygienic Laboratory during Gold-berger's early years with the U.S. Marine Hospital Service. The two remained lifelong friends even after Rosenau departed for Harvard's School of Public Health. (Courtesy of the National Library of Medicine)

Dr. John Anderson, who collaborated with Goldberger in fighting typhus in Mexico and conducting research on measles. (Courtesy of the National Library of Medicine)

WHY, WHAT'S THE EXCITEMENT?!

THE SOUTH

HARDING

PELLAGRA CURE

SOMEBODY MUST HAVE PLAYED A JOKE!

A cartoon in *The* (Memphis) *Commercial Appeal*, June 28, 1921, suggesting that President Warren G. Harding was overreacting to allegations by the U.S. Public Health Service that the South was suffering a pellagra crisis.

A mill family at dinner, circa 1920. The children's glasses of milk suggest that they, at least, will not be susceptible to pellagra. (Courtesy of the Office of the U.S. Public Health Service Historian)

Flood devastation in Egremont, Mississippi, May 2, 1927. (Courtesy of the Mississippi Department of Archives and History)

Goldberger's dietary experiments with dogs required food preparation. The Hygienic Laboratory's diet laboratory had a supply of huge pots and gas burners. (Courtesy of the Office of the U.S. Public Health Service Historian)

The Liberty ship SS *Joseph Goldberger,* launched in 1943. (Courtesy of Dr. Donald Sharp)

The Goldberger family on the front steps of their house in Washington, D.C., circa 1920. The children are Mary, Ben, Farrar, and Joseph. (Courtesy of Linda Keiter)

under Dr. Joseph Goldberger.[13] Finally Goldberger was getting a taste of the administrative responsibility he had craved when he applied to be head of the Hygienic Laboratory in 1915.

In the early 1920s the Hygienic Laboratory was a bustling place, and Goldberger was sometimes asked to advise on non-nutritional diseases, especially typhus. In some laboratories investigators were studying how best to control smallpox, diphtheria, and rabies. Others investigated tularemia, poliomyelitis, and Rocky Mountain spotted fever. Goldberger's own experience with dengue fever and yellow fever caused him to be sent into the field whenever a strange fever not easily identified appeared. On his way back from one such trip to Louisiana, he was authorized to stop at Milledgeville.[14]

After the trip Goldberger wrote to the surgeon general explaining his research design and precisely why these eating studies were so important in solving the next part of the pellagra mystery. First, he must know what substances and in what quantities prevented pellagra. Therefore, some asylum inmates were served forty ounces of buttermilk as a supplement to their basic diet and as the only animal protein in it. Another group got only twenty-four ounces, but their diet included "some beef protein." A second study examined the therapeutic value of proteins such as "gelatine, beef, and casein." Goldberger hoped to determine in a general way whether proteins from these sources added to the diet could cure a pellagrous person. Likewise, he hoped to learn how the protein factor was related to pellagra apart from any other dietary factor. He speculated that while gelatin was unlikely to be of value, beef and casein might yield positive results. As for the next step, he explained, "Besides these objectives the study is paving the way for a systematic investigation of the therapeutic value of certain amino acids, an investigation that is expected to aid in the eventual elucidation of the fundamental problem of the cause of the disease."[15]

There was also the matter of the animal model. About five years earlier the nutrition experts Russell Chittenden and Frank Underhill, working at Yale, reported they had produced pellagra-like symptoms in dogs through experimental dietary manipulation. Goldberger and a PHS colleague, Dr. Atherton Seidell, had tried to duplicate the process, but the press of other matters caused them to abandon their trials. A second attempt also floundered because of insufficient personnel at the Hygienic Laboratory. However, in the winter of 1921–1922 Goldberger had visited New Haven to deliver a paper at the Yale Medical Society and while there learned that Underhill and a colleague were studying in greater depth the "Chittenden-Underhill syndrome."[16]

When Goldberger returned from New Haven, he suggested to Assistant Surgeon General Schereschewsky, who was in charge of research, that a cooperative arrangement might be negotiated whereby the Yale researchers received some funding to continue their work at a faster pace. At first the Yale professors declined the offer. However, by the following September the research had become sufficiently promising that Underhill and a collaborator, Lafayette Mendel, were now favorably inclined toward the arrangement if it could bring them a badly needed fifteen hundred to two thousand dollars. Because of the research's direct relevance to pellagra studies, Goldberger vigorously supported the arrangement. The funds would pay for an assistant and the cost of food for the animals at the Yale laboratory. The agreement was made. Meanwhile, Goldberger continued his own research in Washington to identify an animal model.[17]

Goldberger was required to submit to the surgeon general by the late spring of 1923 an outline of his research for the next fiscal year. The brief report opens a window on the state of his thinking and expectations as he pursued the solution to the last part of the pellagra puzzle. He explained to Hugh Cumming that the "fundamental object" of the pellagra program was to "discover the essential dietary factor or factors concerned in the prevention of pellagra and thus in the causation of the disease." He would accomplish that end in several ways. First, he would test the preventive power of certain vitamin-rich foods. He offered butter and cod-liver oil as examples. Perhaps a vitamin was the missing substance. He would also test a vitamin-free protein (casein). The tests would involve supplementing the diets of pellagrins at the Georgia State Sanitarium, with Tanner there to observe the recurrence or non-recurrence of the disease. By the time of his report, Goldberger had realized that the vitamin-rich foods were having little effect. Casein was the object of his interest.[18]

A second phase of the research would take place at the Hygienic Laboratory and involved using rats to check which amino acids were in short supply in a pellagra-producing diet. Here, too, some progress had been made. What Goldberger learned from the rats would be tested by manipulating the diets of humans at Milledgeville.

The third phase of the research was the cooperative arrangement with Underhill and Mendel at Yale. Goldberger needed to know whether dogs could contract pellagra. Therefore, while the Yale researchers continued their work, he would use the Hygienic Laboratory's facilities in a fourth phase of the research program to study dogs suffering with the syndrome identified by Chittenden and Underhill. He would feed the canines diets whose worth in pellagra prevention was being simultaneously tested on humans at Milledgeville. He acknowledged that the Yale experiments and his own work on dogs were duplicative in some ways but insisted that finding a suitable animal model was urgent enough to justify any overlap.

A fifth phase involved preparing pure proteins for use in the experiments. Casein would be used in tests in Georgia and Washington. A sixth phase encompassed anything that might arise that bore on the study, or, as Goldberger phrased it, "miscellaneous epidemiological, clinical and therapeutic observations, principally at the Georgia State Sanitarium and in the practices of physicians reporting cases to Tanner."[19]

The rest of his office's efforts, Goldberger reported, involved combing an older literature, especially books and articles in Italian and Romanian that required translation. Here he hoped to find neglected clues that might unlock the pellagra mystery. Finally, considerable effort was still needed to compile the vast array of data that he, Wheeler, and Sydenstricker had gathered in the mill villages they had studied in 1916.

Goldberger's proposed budget for the ambitious year ahead was twenty thousand dollars. Aside from personnel such as a translator and statistical clerks, needed in the era before high-speed calculators and computers, the research at Yale represented the biggest cost: twenty-five hundred dollars. Not until after World War II would large sums of federal dollars be routinely allotted for research at universities and other privately owned research institutions.

Laboratory research is a slow, plodding process. As the months passed, Goldberger's life narrowed to the path between home and laboratory, punctuated by occasional trips to Georgia to visit with Tanner. In a letter to Mary, who had taken the children to Biloxi for the summer, he described, with a level of detail interesting only to a spouse, how he managed to care for himself, from the details of making breakfast—coffee, a hard-boiled egg, and some whole wheat bread—to where he took his evening meal, the Cosmos Club or a moderately priced Washington eatery.[20]

If his correspondence with Mary included reports of what and where he was eating, his days were also spent thinking about food. As early as 1917 Goldberger and Tanner had learned that neither soybeans nor black-eyed peas (cowpeas) were much good in preventing pellagra. Ubiquitous and popular in poor southern communities, either would have been a convenient and cheap substitute for milk, meat, and eggs. Although Goldberger had once thought otherwise, and even written glowingly to Mary of the value of beans in preventing pellagra, tests now confirmed that he must look further.[21]

What substances must the body have to remain healthy? By the early 1920s most physicians had come to understand the importance of proteins, mineral salts, and vitamins. The work on vitamins was at the cutting edge of nutrition research, and Goldberger's acquaintance with the writings of Funk, McCollum, and others suggests his appreciation of the role that vitamins played in healthy bodies. Vitamins A, B, and C had already been discovered, although water-soluble vitamin B had not yet been included in the B complex. The battle against beriberi and scurvy, well known to physicians and laymen alike, suggested what damage the absence of particular vitamins could do to a body.

Goldberger and Tanner formulated diets to test each category of substance. Mineral salts having the same inorganic elements as a liter of milk were tested. So, too, were the three vitamins then known to nutrition researchers. In no case did their presence prevent the onset of pellagra in Milledgeville patients.[22]

Perhaps the answer lay with proteins. Goldberger had observed that individuals well nourished on foods containing animal protein did not contract pellagra. The work on tryptophan had been encouraging. But amino acids were expensive to distill. Could specific amounts of certain foods be substituted? Goldberger designed his tests to resemble the biological tests developed by Elmer V. McCollum. After Edward Mellanby and others had demonstrated that rickets was caused by a dietary deficiency, McCollum announced that a fat-soluble vitamin, vitamin D, was effective against it. Now Goldberger and Tanner followed McCollum's method of adding one element at a time to their laboratory animals' diet to study its impact.

At Milledgeville, Tanner was ordered by Goldberger to follow the McCollum method. Using small squads of patients, Tanner added fresh beef to the institution's routine, starchy diet. Next he tried adding buttermilk. Both prevented pellagra. Gelatin, butter, and cod-liver oil did not. The latter was especially disappointing, because McCollum had just demonstrated that vitamin D was present in cod-liver oil. However, it proved of no use with pellagra.[23]

While he and Tanner corresponded about which foods to add to the diets of the Milledgeville patients, Goldberger focused increasing attention on finding an animal model. Chittenden and Underhill's experimentation still sounded promising. From veterinarians in the South, Goldberger learned about a disease known as black tongue. The initial canine symptoms were sluggishness and unwillingness to eat. Those were soon followed by an inflamed mouth, vomiting, and diarrhea. Three out of four animals contracting the condition died. Those who tried to treat the animals assumed it was an infectious disease.[24]

Relying on his keen powers of observation, Goldberger noted that black tongue was most frequent in the same parts of the country as pellagra. Underhill and Chittenden had induced symptoms by substituting bread for meat and milk in dogs' diets and watched symptoms develop in as little as four days. As early as January 1922 Goldberger had placed his dogs on a diet similar to the one consumed by poor southerners. It included grits, rice, wheat farina, cowpeas, lard, gelatin, cod-liver oil, milk, and tomato juice. He supplemented the diet with a cake of commercial yeast, designed to stimulate their appetites. During the summer he doubled the yeast, because the dogs were not consuming most of the foods being offered them. Eleven months later some dogs had mange, but none presented symptoms of black tongue.[25]

The following year Goldberger and his longtime assistant George Wheeler reassessed their black-tongue research. Determined to produce black tongue in their laboratory, they dropped the small amounts of milk

and substituted cottonseed oil for cod-liver oil. Knowing that human pellagrins did not have yeast as a routine element in their diets, they discontinued that as well. As they had hoped, the symptoms of black tongue
began to appear. Now they systematically added one food at a time to the
dogs' diets, waiting to see which, if any, would reverse the course of the
disease. Foods, such as meat, that had positive results were included in
the small but critical category of pellagra preventives. Foods were
dropped from consideration if the dogs suffering from black tongue died
after they were added to the diet. The results did not always immediately
fall into one category or another. In some cases the amount of a food
consumed made all the difference. For example, small amounts of soybeans did not prevent the disease; large amounts did. In dogs at least 360
grams were required for soybeans to prevent the disease. Skim milk was
much the same. Other foods, including butter, carrots, rutabagas, egg
yolk, whole corn, cottonseed oil, and cod-liver oil, simply failed the test
regardless of the amount consumed.[26]

The list of preventives included lean beef, pork liver, salmon, wheat
germ, and yeast. Goldberger and Wheeler were most surprised by
brewer's yeast. Brewer's yeast is the microscopic fungi used in the fer-
mentation of beer. Added to their diets only to stimulate the dogs' appetites, the yeast banished black-tongue symptoms very quickly. Canine
victims of black tongue recovered within four and a half days of being
served the yeast. The yeast was the only tested substance that yielded
such marked results. Even very large amounts of butter and cod-liver oil
failed to alleviate symptoms. Casein prevented black tongue's distinctive
dermatitis but did nothing to prevent other symptoms. Would what
healed dogs cure the pellagrous women under Tanner's care at
Milledgeville?[27]

The answer was emphatically yes. Goldberger and Tanner began
their human trial of yeast on May 26, 1923. Only two patients were given
brewer's yeast. Their dramatic recovery encouraged Goldberger to expand the trial to twenty-six patients the following year. Every day patients
were served dried brewer's yeast at supper, usually drenched in syrup to
make it palatable. Several days later the pellagra was in retreat. The reason was not as obvious. In fact, the results with yeast appeared to contradict the dramatic results achieved in 1921 with certain amino acids. Yeast

had so little protein that the success of tryptophan seemed puzzling. At a loss for how to label brewer's yeast, Goldberger began to refer to it as possessing the P-P factor, a shorthand for pellagra preventive. Not any yeast would do. Goldberger and Tanner also tried baker's yeast, but it required very large quantities to achieve the same results.[28]

Goldberger did not know why brewer's yeast cured and prevented pellagra, but it did. And it was cheap. Southerners could face the spring of 1925 without fear. Even the poorest of them could afford brewer's yeast, and Goldberger's results were now being broadly disseminated. Accessibility was a different matter. A pellagra sufferer, Mrs. E. C. Belisle, who wrote to Goldberger from Tampa, Florida, the location of many breweries, begging some brewer's yeast sent C.O.D., epitomized one of the social problems that long strengthened pellagra's grip on the South.[29]

Goldberger did not know it, but through his experimentation he had stumbled onto a complex biochemical relationship. The amino acid tryptophan and the vitamin niacin are related in ways that scientists would not fully understand until the 1930s. Tryptophan, not produced in the human body, is a precursor in the pathway to niacin. Niacin, the common designation for nicotinic acid, prevented pellagra. Goldberger understood none of these relationships. He and Tanner had noted the dramatic curative properties of tryptophan mixed in the foods of Milledgeville patients such as Oconee Cobb. Now he was aware that brewer's yeast had the same effect. He neither understood their relationship nor knew that it was the nicotinic acid in brewer's yeast that made it such a potent pellagra preventive.

Experiments feeding yeast to rats who showed symptoms that Goldberger thought analogous to pellagra led him to speculate about the nature of vitamin B. He observed that restricting the diets of albino rats caused them to have erosions in the mouth, ulcerated tongues, and rashes on ears and paws. He rescued the animals with yeast that had been subjected to heat under pressure in an autoclave. Autoclaved yeast did not prevent polyneuritis and the rats did not grow. If deprived of vitamin B, the rats died, but not from pellagra. However, when the rats were given vitamin B, but not from autoclaved yeast, the symptoms of what Goldberger thought to be pellagra reappeared. Only vitamin B and the autoclaved yeast made the animals healthy. Now Goldberger realized what some other observers had noticed: vitamin B had different parts. In humans the anti-neuritic kind prevented beriberi. He speculated that the second kind possessed the P-P factor. Vitamin B was a complex, part of which prevented pellagra. Although research many years later would demonstrate that the rats' disease was not a rodent version of pellagra, Goldberger had learned much about vitamin B.[30]

Had Goldberger and Tanner continued their research on tryptophan or vitamin B, they might have pushed scientific understanding of the nutritional biochemistry with which they were dealing. Instead, they turned from the mysteries of biochemistry to the more practical and immediate problem of accessibility. Was there not something as accessible as it was inexpensive that might benefit pellagrins? Thus far Goldberger had been unable to identify a pellagra preventive that was as inexpensive as brewer's yeast. In 1923 he tried dry skim milk, but too much of it was required to do the job. By 1924 and 1925 he had returned to beef. Earlier tests had involved a small number of patients. Now he increased them to twenty-six patients, who got seven ounces of ground beef daily, half for lunch and half for supper. None got pellagra, but the skewed diet did produce beriberi, which then required whole cornmeal and cowpeas to cure.[31]

It occurred to Goldberger that the same foods produced in different parts of the country might differ in their pellagra-preventive value. For example, he wondered whether Georgia butter differed from Vermont butter because of the dissimilar quality of the pastures that nourished the cows in each state. Was butter derived from cows fed in the robust pastures of Vermont better able to prevent pellagra than the local butter to which Tanner had access at Milledgeville?[32] It was not.

While Goldberger and Tanner racked their brains trying to decide which food to test next and in what amount, there were other, silent partners in their search. As wards of the state, ones declared mentally incompetent at that, the Milledgeville patients who ate what Tanner served them had little choice about whether they would participate. These women, mostly black but some poor whites, aided in finding a solution to the pellagra mystery. Occasionally one of them balked at eating an item she did not care for. But most complied. Every day they ate corn bread or mush, cowpeas, wheat flour, and lard and drank some tomato juice. Then one item was added to test its value in preventing pellagra: a pound of carrots each day, cooked differently for variety; a pound of rutabagas; wheat germ added to other foods. In every instance the purpose was to find the food or foods that best prevented the horrid symptoms of pellagra. From these trials Goldberger learned that wheat germ and salmon were pellagra preventives. Wheat germ could be added to flour sold to those living in areas affected by pellagra, and canned salmon was both available to and affordable by southerners, who frequently purchased it at local stores.[33]

In 1925 Tanner was transferred to Ellis Island to inspect immigrants, and Goldberger replaced him with George Wheeler. The two colleagues who had done so much fine work together were reunited. Throughout the summer of 1925 and into 1926, the experiments continued, with Goldberger feeding the dogs at the Hygienic Laboratory and Wheeler supervising the dietary adjustments at Milledgeville. Goldberger periodically visited Milledgeville to see that the work was progressing well. Both were equally patient researchers. Goldberger shared hints freely with his longtime colleague, knowing that Wheeler would not object. When Wheeler mentioned that the patients were rebelling against eating so many carrots, Goldberger offered some advice:

> It occurs to me to suggest that it may perhaps be practicable to serve part of the carrots at noon in the food mixture, as you have apparently actually begun, and the other half at supper, possibly stirred into the supper syrup. As you know, the patients are all quite fond of syrup and in the past we have found the syrup a very convenient vehicle for articles of food that by themselves would not be much relished. It may be that the syrup may serve well as a vehicle for the carrots.

He then added diplomatically, "However, as you are on the ground you are in the better position to judge as to the most feasible way of handling it."[34]

At times the stress of keeping the various eating trials on target bubbled to the surface. On one trip to Georgia in April 1925 Goldberger left his briefcase in the cab taking him to the train station and had to ask Mary to call the company and try to track it down because it contained important papers. On the train he consoled himself with a novel purchased at the station, Sinclair Lewis's *Arrowsmith*. The book, which deals with the conflict between physicians seeking to turn medicine in both a scientific and a humanitarian direction and others hoping to make their reputations and fortune, was understandably of "interest" to Goldberger, who found it a more than worthy substitute for the western novels he usually purchased to read on trains and in hotels.[35]

The work schedule was grueling, but even if he was a bit tardy, he always answered his children's notes to him, often written when they were at their grandmother's summer home in Biloxi. In the summer of 1926 he made good on a promise to write the always difficult Farrar a letter. Goldberger told his son how delighted he was to hear that Farrar was behaving himself and causing Mary no grief. He then offered his son a "prescription" for life, one that reflected Goldberger's own most dearly held values: "Take care of your body to keep it healthy and clean; occupy your brain, your mind, with clean wholesome things; treat others fairly and squarely and do it politely and not like a 'Hick.' Then you will be able to stand up straight, look every one straight in the eye and make friends while so doing." Perhaps recalling that youngsters don't much appreciate sermons brimming with parental advice, Goldberger caught himself: "That's all! You can do it. And I believe you will!"[36]

During the next year he could offer his wisdom to Farrar across the dinner table. He remained close to home and laboratory. He also established a growing list of foods that were pellagra preventives. However, brewer's yeast remained the most reliable and inexpensive way to prevent the disease and treat it after onset when economic circumstances made a balanced diet with adequate animal protein impracticable. Yeast's efficacy would be tested in the field in 1927.

In the spring of 1927 thousands of southerners living near the Mississippi River experienced one of the worst floods in the region's history, and the surgeon general ordered Goldberger to head south. This would not be Goldberger's first trip during a Mississippi flood. Five years earlier, in June 1922, Dr. Waller Leathers, executive officer of the Mississippi State Board of Health and one of the more enlightened of the state public health officers, expressed to Surgeon General Cumming concern about pellagra during that year's flood. Goldberger was briefed and taken on a tour of "plantations" in those Delta counties where pellagra was most prevalent, "especially among tenants and particularly among colored people," according to Leathers. Leathers wanted more than advice, however. He wanted the surgeon general to send a PHS representative for an extended stay to study pellagra on the Delta's plantations so that Mississippi might take whatever action was required to reduce its incidence in these counties. The home of such large owners as the famous land baron LeRoy Percy, the Delta lands were some of the most productive in the state. However, pellagra trumped profits when black and white tenants were too sick to farm. Hoping that the plight of southern blacks might move the federal official, Leathers argued, "I am disposed to believe that Mississippi has more pellagra relatively speaking than any other state and we know that about 70 per cent of it occurs among colored people."[37]

Several days later, back at his desk in Washington, Goldberger reported on the trip. He had found little pellagra, but he had also learned that Leathers's concern was not about an existing outbreak but about "a probable increase in pellagra in the overflowed area." Leathers reiterated his desire for a PHS officer to be assigned to the state to study pellagra conditions in the Delta.[38] At the Public Health Service his request was understood as potentially exacerbating federal-state tensions so evident at the Washington meeting in 1921, when Goldberger and the PHS had been lambasted for their dire predictions of rampant pellagra. The surgeon general acted expeditiously to resolve the matter.

Cumming convened a sanitary board of four assistant surgeon generals. It met on July 3, 1922. Although the board did not support Leathers's request for an officer to do a multiyear study of pellagra just in Mississippi, it did recommend that a PHS officer be detailed to the state for three or four months to "make a survey of the situation and aid the State Health Authorities in organizing a campaign against pellagra in the State"; in addition, the officer would plan coordination with federal and state agencies that might help with food distribution during a flood. The board made quite clear that it did not intend to allow Mississippi to thrust the problem into the federal government's lap. It expressed the hope that "having been shown the way it would then become a problem to be attacked by the State itself." To justify its decision, the board explained that it was the policy of PHS to foster and develop local initiatives and that "the corrective work could be undertaken by those social and economic agencies whose special province it is to deal with social and economic conditions."[39] The surgeon general had dodged the bullet, and Goldberger's much-respected assistant, Dr. George Wheeler, was assigned to study conditions in Mississippi. Five years later, in 1927, little had improved, and the flood was much larger than that in 1922.

In the spring of 1927 the seasonal rains were unusually heavy. Overcut forests could not slow the flowing water, which rushed into streams. Tributaries of the Mississippi, filled by mid-April, overflowed their banks. From Oklahoma and Kansas in the West to Illinois and Kentucky in the East, the waters were rising, driving southerners from their homes. Meanwhile, the Mississippi itself was rising higher than it had before. By late April the levees had proved inadequate. The river was carrying in excess of three million cubic feet of water each second. As the river raged and wealthy southern landowners in the Delta blamed inadequate flood control, the poor gathered their meager possessions and fled for their lives.

By the time the waters finally receded, 16,570,627 acres had been flooded in 170 counties covering seven states. Crop losses were enormous, costing $102,562,395. Homes, 162,017 of them, were flooded, and 41,487 structures were totally destroyed. Because water covered everything except church steeples and the roofs of the tallest buildings, 5,934 boats were used by rescuers to save lives and belongings.

From 250 to 500 individuals lost their lives. Many thousands of others did not because of the heroic efforts of the Red Cross, which established 154 camps and fed 311,922 people in their own homes.[40] The Red Cross was not the only agency on the scene. State and local agencies, state National Guard units, railroad companies, and the Rockefeller Foundation all contributed to the relief effort. So, too, did federal agencies. In an era long before the Federal Emergency Management Agency (FEMA), federal agencies such as the Departments of War, Navy, Veterans Affairs, Treasury, Agriculture, and Commerce helped out in limited ways. The U.S. Public Health Service, including Joseph Goldberger, was very much involved.

Throughout the early spring of 1927 Goldberger and his colleagues in

Washington were following the news from the flooded area with horror at the human suffering. In late June, Nan Cox, a Red Cross nurse in Cleveland, Mississippi, wrote to her former teacher Dr. Elmer V. Mc-Collum at the Johns Hopkins School of Hygiene and asked for help. She reported, "Red Cross is rationing the refugees and they are developing Pellagra at a rapid rate as I found out to-day." She described the ration as consisting of salt pork, molasses, cornmeal, flour, dry beans, black-eyed peas, rice, coffee, and sugar. She asked McCollum to "send me a suggestion of canned groceries that will help prevent pellagra and other nutritional diseases, that can be easily handled in the rationing." Fresh food was almost impossible to acquire because, as Cox observed, "most of this territory is still under water and will be for at least a month. Poor transportation and perishable products just cannot be gotten here except at tremendous cost."[41]

McCollum forwarded Cox's note to Goldberger, who scribbled an immediate reply to be sent as a telegram: "Would urge liberal daily inclusion in diet of the yeast preparation named vegex[,] of canned salmon and of canned tomatoes as pellagra preventives."[42] But Goldberger and Sydenstricker needed to assess the pellagra situation for themselves.

In 1927 neither local health agencies with their flood-control planning and disease-prevention planning, nor the Public Health Service was prepared for the large-scale disaster. Goldberger, taking Sydenstricker with him, headed south to advise the Red Cross on how to help stall the escalating number of pellagra cases and to study the disease as it appeared in community after community affected by the flood.[43] The two visited Dyersburg and the surrounding area in Tennessee. From there they went to the afflicted areas in Arkansas. Then it was on to Jackson, Greenwood, and Indianola in Mississippi. They concluded their tour in Louisiana, visiting New Orleans, Baton Rouge, Alexandria, and Monroe. In their account of the investigation the two explained that these areas were selected because they were physically accessible to outsiders and were sufficiently representative so that any conclusions drawn would be applicable to other areas of the flood region as well.

As they had once tramped door to door through South Carolina mill villages, Goldberger and Sydenstricker used cars and boats as well as shoe leather to visit the flooded Delta. Records were not being carefully kept, and of the four states they visited, only Mississippi was keeping morbidity reports. However, even there the data were incomplete. They began their journey in the other states. In some places, such as Dyersburg, Tennessee, and Little Rock, Arkansas, conferences were called so that state and local officials could speak with Goldberger.

In Mississippi, where Goldberger was known and celebrated because of the Rankin experiment, his impending visit made the front page of the *Jackson Daily News*. On July 25, 1927, the main headline read, DELTA IN GRIP OF NEW MENACE FROM PELLAGRA. Right beneath it was the subheadline "Poor Diet Causes Wide Spread of Disease, Goldberger Coming." The man whom some southerners once saw as bearing the unwelcome message that diet, not microbes, was at the root of the pellagra problem was now described by the press as the "world renowned authority on pellagra." Goldberger was a friend coming to their aid in a time of dire need.

On their way to Arkansas, Goldberger and Sydenstricker stopped in Memphis for the night. In his daily letter to Mary, Goldberger wrote that like western Tennessee, "Arkansas has a fine crop of pellagra—plenty of it with lots to spare!" Explaining that the morning paper carried an article about the Red Cross furnishing food to "clear up pellagra," a sad and somewhat weary Goldberger confided to her, "Judging from what we have seen in Tennessee and Arkansas they need it." Mary confessed that the human suffering her husband described had made her weep; the human suffering Goldberger witnessed hardened his determination to relieve it.[44]

Never content with impressions alone, Goldberger and Sydenstricker used what data they had to construct a comparison of the estimated number of pellagra cases and deaths in 1924, 1925, and 1926 with the number they could estimate for 1927 in all the states they visited. There was little question that there had been "a definite and more or less marked tendency to an increase in pellagra in these States during 1925 and 1926 as compared to 1924; the aggregate number of deaths in 1926 [1,850] being fully 80 per cent larger than in 1924 [1,020]." Worse yet, Sydenstricker and Goldberger predicted that by the end of 1927, the number of pellagra deaths in the four states would be 2,300 to 2,500 unless drastic measures were taken. Their projection was that 45,000 to

50,000 in the four states would suffer a recognizable case of pellagra by the end of the year—over half in the overflow area closest to the bulging rivers.[45]

Those were the horrifying numbers, but what did Goldberger and Sydenstricker see as the solution to the tragedy that met their eyes day in and day out? Brewer's yeast. Twelve thousand pounds of brewer's yeast were distributed to southerners in the flood-ravaged area. It did not take much to save lives. Two teaspoonfuls three times a day were the adult dose. One teaspoon three times a day was sufficient for children. Red Cross workers mixed the untasty stuff with milk, molasses, or fruit juice to make it somewhat palatable. Whatever its taste, it worked. Most pellagrins were cured in six to ten weeks.[46]

The cost of preventing the rashes, the diarrhea, and the mental debility? Three cents per day. Goldberger had halted an American tragedy. However, he had had a few accomplices. What Goldberger had learned from his dogs at the Hygienic Laboratory and from the women patients in Georgia who day after day and night after night dutifully ate whatever Tanner or Wheeler served them now had yielded a rich dividend, thousands of lives.

Saving the sick took priority. However, a close second for Goldberger was fully understanding what had happened in the states affected by the great flood of 1927. The Mississippi journalist who heralded Goldberger's coming offered one explanation for the escalating incidence of pellagra, lack of milk: "Vast numbers of cows drowned during the flood left the delta without a milk supply and where cows have been brought in since the flood there is nothing for them to eat. Grass is dead or covered with mud and powdered milk is being shipped into the area by the carload."[47] For Goldberger such answers were insufficient. They did not account for the climbing morbidity rates before the Mississippi washed over its levees.

Back in Washington, Goldberger and Sydenstricker analyzed what they had just witnessed. Even as cleanup continued in the South, they collaborated on a lengthy report for publication in November 1927. Without denying the devastating impact of the flood, they did observe that the overflow area of Tennessee, Arkansas, and Mississippi was one where pellagra was historically prevalent. Their conclusion: "It seems to us highly probable, particularly in view of the depressed economic conditions in this area, associated with the low price of cotton in 1926, that this area would have suffered an increased incidence even had no overflow taken place."[48]

They allowed that the overflow had made matters worse. The number of milk cows was decreased by drowning or sale by owners. Inadequate food for the cows meant less milk as well. Fresh meat and eggs were rare because home-owned poultry was drowned, and the supply of fresh vegetables was diminished by gardens that were flooded or not planted until late in the season. Still, the investigators thought that blaming it all on the flood was an exercise in denial.

What was there, then, about the lower Mississippi River valley that made it pellagra country? The "unprofitable cotton crops of 1925 and 1926" resulted in dietary habits conducive to the onset of pellagra. Chief among them was the reliance on the so-called three-*m* diet—meat, meal, and molasses. Tenant farmers, "both white and colored," subsisted on it. The meat was not the lean beef that Goldberger knew to be a pellagra preventive but salt pork. The meal was cornmeal. The molasses was sorghum or cane. There might also be some wheat flour, some rice, and dried beans. This was the diet of the South's rural poor, and as Goldberger and Sydenstricker had observed years before among the mill workers of the Piedmont, the fare was almost guaranteed to yield a bumper crop of pellagra.[49]

What Goldberger and Sydenstricker had done in 1916 in sketching the patterns of life among mill workers they now did for the impoverished tenant farmers they saw suffering in the Delta and elsewhere near the Mississippi and its tributaries. However, rather than conduct their own extensive surveys, they relied on what they learned from others during their 1927 excursion.

They learned that because greedy landowners wanted tenants to devote every square inch of land to cotton production, too few tenant farmers owned cows. Moreover, tenants, at their economic low point in the late winter and early spring, sometimes found no alternative to selling their cows for cash at just the moment when their diets could use fresh milk.[50]

Similarly, gardens were problematic because they demanded labor that was required in the cotton fields. And the space necessary often seemed excessive to owners bent on maximizing cotton output. Agricultural extension agents and others told Goldberger and Sydenstricker that the tenants themselves were partly to blame because they lacked the habit and ambition to garden and even lacked the skills, knowing far more about caring for cotton plants than tomatoes or peas.[51]

Wild vegetables, fish, and game supplemented the diet when available. However, hunting and fishing were less frequent at those times of year when the cotton needed tending. Canned meats, potatoes, and cabbage were common purchases when the money was available. As Goldberger had learned in his laboratory and sanatorium trials, canned salmon was popular and a pellagra preventive, but many could not afford it when the crop was poor.[52]

Goldberger and Sydenstricker saved their most pointed and acerbic criticism for the agricultural system that kept tenants downtrodden. They observed that "while all agricultural production is more or less speculative, the speculative character of cotton production is even more pronounced than that of most other forms of agriculture." In the South cotton tended to be the "sole crop." It was sold in a market "sensitive to many factors," and a market in which many of the planters were self-conscious speculators, having their serious business interests elsewhere. There was, of course, more than one kind of cotton plantation in Mississippi: small, private farms subdivided among the tenants; large plantations owned by private individuals or corporations; and plantations bought as speculative ventures by those who knew little about such agriculture. The last kind of business venture was especially vulnerable, and when bad weather or boll weevil infestation was compounded by deflating land values, cotton speculators often lost their investment. In 1926 and 1927, when conditions were poor, undercapitalized speculators were ruined. Mortgage holders then made matters worse by either trying to run the plantation themselves or letting the land lie fallow. Caught in the middle, tenants almost always suffered economically. The cash and credit extended to them were most often "the very least possible amount that can be arranged for."[53]

Now Goldberger and Sydenstricker turned from land distribution to a detailed description of a year in the economic life of a Mississippi tenant farmer. In December planters advanced their tenants so-called Christmas money. The money had usually been spent by the end of the holiday. From January 1 to March 1, the only cash that could be spent on food came from odd jobs such as "mending houses and barns, lumbering or working to repair levees." In March began the seasonal arrangement of the planter's advancing each tenant $1 to $1.25 per acre farmed each month. The family income, ranging from fifteen to forty dollars per month, was sometimes supplemented by light labor done by women and children on others' land while the main tasks of planting and cultivating the crop got under way. Cash advances ceased on July 1, with no further income available until the crop was picked and ginned. Once the ginning was over, there were two sources of income in a good year: sale of the cotton lint after the deduction of advances; and sale of the seed, which tenants did not have to share with the owner. In a good year food was plentiful, and, as Goldberger observed, "the tenant tends to extravagance, to purchase beyond the limits of absolute need such things as clothing and cheap automobiles." Therefore, by Christmas "the negros [sic] and most of the white tenants" rarely had money saved.[54]

Whether advances came as credit at a local store or as cash, preferred by most tenants, the system was pernicious. "For the most part, except in unusually favorable years, the tenant is constantly in debt, or on the verge of debt, to the planter or the store." As a result, tenants were "chronically on the verge of deprivation." While some always teetered on the edge, others were steeped in extreme poverty. Who went under? "The less energetic, less capable, and less efficient, 'shiftless' class find themselves on or below the borderline." However, the PHS colleagues were only too aware that even a small decrease in income could force a goodly number of efficient tenants teetering on the border into "the class which actually suffers deprivation." They agreed that such was the case "in 1915, again in 1921, and again in 1924 and 1926." Thus, they concluded, the high incidence of pellagra in the wretched summer of 1927 was the result of a pattern of land distribution and use with dietary repercussions, "the gravity of which has been accentuated by the overflow."[55]

What could be done? Goldberger and Sydenstricker made two recommendations. The first advised public health officials on how to cope with natural disasters that created food shortages. The second took aim at the fragile economic conditions so easily exacerbated by a natural disaster.

Goldberger began the first recommendation by observing that a half pound of lean beef, a half pound of dried cowpeas, a quart of buttermilk, a quart of canned tomatoes, or an ounce of pure yeast each day provided an adult with an adequate supply of the P-P factor. A combination of several of these foods would do, and they were curative as well as preventive. Such foods could banish pellagra after the onset of symptoms. However, in the absence of such foods because of a disaster, relief workers should distribute "dried pure yeast (preferably the killed culture), canned (chum) salmon, canned beef, and canned tomatoes, or adequate funds or credit with which to purchase such a supply."[56]

As for the second recommendation, dealing with broader social conditions, Goldberger and Sydenstricker were well aware that their report led logically to the conclusion "that any attempt to remove the conditions which are fundamentally responsible for the prevalence of pellagra would involve a revolution of dietary habits and of the entire economic and financial system as it now exists."[57]

Having learned the danger of being unguarded, they cloaked their call for this revolution in moderate language crafted to avoid confrontation. They began by observing that their suggestions had already been somewhat embraced by "the Federal Department of Agriculture and [by] the State agricultural colleges and other agencies." Further, they emphasized that they viewed "the situation as a public-health problem," not as an opportunity to offer a more general critique of southern society. Therefore, they recommended that to lessen the deprivation causing pellagra, tenants' income should be stabilized "in such a way as to lessen the effect of seasonal and periodic limitations" on their access to pellagra-preventive food. Second, they advocated "crop diversification" as a means of making food supplies available "throughout the tenant population area and with less seasonal variation." An increase in milk supply in particular would contribute not only to pellagra prevention but also to "the improvement of health in general." How might more milk be made available? Goldberger and Sydenstricker suggested ways in which more general cow ownership among tenants might be accomplished but did not explicitly say that planters must stop opposing such ownership. Instead, they proposed "plantation dairies operated by plantation owners or managers." The milk from these dairies would be sold to tenants "at a minimum price and [would] be included in the ordinary rations bought from the store or commissary." Another suggestion was "community dairies."[58]

Mentioning the Department of Agriculture and other advocates of "more and better gardens," Goldberger and Sydenstricker called for developing ways of planting gardens, including "planting . . . produce in rows in the cotton fields themselves" and initiating "plantation truck patches." They suggested that the produce from such gardens, like the milk, might be sold in the plantation store or commissary.[59]

Increasing the access to cattle, swine, and poultry was also desirable. It would meet the local need for fresh meat and eggs. However, Goldberger and Sydenstricker added that an increase in animal husbandry "would have to be worked out in various ways to conform to local conditions."[60]

What did conforming to local conditions mean? It meant that Goldberger and Sydenstricker did not want to elicit a backlash from planters and politicians hoping to protect their profits and political turf from those they perceived as federal interlopers. Such a reaction could only be counterproductive to improving the health of southern tenant farmers in the region. Therefore, Goldberger and Sydenstricker eschewed the language of collectivism. The profits from community dairies and truck gardens would belong to the plantation owner, but at least wholesome milk and vegetables would be accessible to a greater extent than they were at the time of the flood.

In the end, Goldberger and Sydenstricker, neither of them a Milquetoast by nature, did not sound the call for dramatic change. Likely fearing a reaction that might delay yet again any progress that would improve health and prevent pellagra in the South, they offered a final paragraph to their report on the Mississippi flood of 1927 that is a study in the mealymouthed moderation often raised to a high art in Washington. They described the conditions underlying the devastation they had seen as calling for "study with a view to working out practicable solutions of the economic and agricultural problems involved." All they insisted on was that "in such a study . . . the needs of health must be held in mind as of controlling importance."[61] The experience of the previous decade had taught Goldberger that "hitting the publicity line hard," as he had once promised Mary he would do, came with costs that a more mature and practical Goldberger was unwilling to bear. He now preferred slow progress through persuasion to the satisfaction of denouncing those he considered fools and rascals.

As the flood waters receded, the Red Cross continued to battle human suffering. Pellagra did not recede with the waters. It was a legacy of the disaster that Red Cross workers battled with a combination of nutrition and education in the refugee camps. Goldberger's research provided their ammunition. Yeast distribution was a stopgap measure. Those who managed to reach a refugee camp were served only two meals a day, but the Red Cross workers included pellagra preventives such as milk and meat with the local fare of bread, syrup, and grits.

The areas around the Mississippi and its tributaries were not the only places that experienced flooding in 1927. Heavy rains had caused some flooding in the mountains of eastern Kentucky as well. There, too, Red Cross workers offered foods that prevented pellagra at costs as low as fifteen cents per day. Families were permitted to take food with them from the camps. However, the Red Cross went further, and in cases where families suffered multiple cases, workers collected foods to send home with them. Such packages contained cabbages, dried peas, and canned commodities, including tomatoes and milk. As much as possible fieldworkers sought to supplement the usual corn bread, syrup, and salt pork with pellagra preventives.

Understanding that the most meaningful charity allowed the recipients to provide for themselves, the Red Cross gave cows to some flood victims. These were gifts from private donors and organizations. Dairymen in Louisiana received forty head of cattle from the American Jersey Cattle Club to help them restore themselves to productivity.[62]

Red Cross workers taught pellagra prevention by example, principally through the diet served in the camps. They also gave talks and distributed literature on how to prevent the disease. When the Red Cross withdrew, state and local health workers continued to educate citizens.

If pellagra was prevalent prior to the deluge, as Goldberger and Sydenstricker reported, it remained well after the flood. In some parts of the Delta counties pellagra was ubiquitous. Twelve hundred cases were treated in just two counties of Mississippi over the next two years, and as many as seventy-five pellagrins per day converged on county health officials seeking yeast, food, and some guidance on how to banish their symptoms. Weekly clinics helped some. Access to yeast contributed by the American Legion Auxiliary and the Red Cross helped others. However, in Bolivar County, Sunflower County, and many others in Mississippi the problem of too little milk and meat and too few gardens where fresh vegetables could be grown was not solved. The change for which Goldberger and Sydenstricker had called did not come.

Tragedies leave many legacies. While the flood was still menacing lives, the blues singer Bessie Smith released two recordings about the flood, "Back Water Blues" and "Muddy Water (A Mississippi Moan)." Blind Lemon Jefferson recorded "Rising High Water Blues" around the same time that Goldberger and Sydenstricker were touring the region. Earlier in July, Richard Wright published a short story, "Down by the Riverside," in the African-American newspaper the *Chicago Defender*. It is not surprising that black Americans were among the first to sing and write about the flood. Official Red Cross sources estimated that 53.8 percent of those affected were "negroes." Even so, because of prevailing racism, black southerners were often treated less well than whites, even by the Red Cross.[63] The devastation had not caused racism to take a holiday.

The Red Cross's "Official Report of Relief Operations" documented Goldberger's visit and the value of the yeast treatment he prescribed. Reports by state health officers "uniformly indicate the value of this measure," according to the Red Cross. Dr. Eugene Bishop, the health commissioner of Tennessee, noted:

> A worker from this department made quite a detailed study of the pellagra situation in these three counties (Dyer, Lake and Lauderdale) early in July and before yeast was advocated. He went over the same territory in September, at which time he saw many of the patients visited in July. Practically all of these patients were free of symptoms and he saw no far-advanced pellagra. In ques-

tioning the patients, almost without exception they stated that beneficial results came promptly after beginning the use of yeast.

And most physicians agreed.[64]

Goldberger and Sydenstricker spent much of the autumn of 1927 completing their article on the flood for publication. Goldberger continued research in Milledgeville and Washington, confirming foods as pellagra preventives or negligible in their effect on the disease.

In the early months of 1928 he remained preoccupied with thoughts about the devastation he had seen in Mississippi and the other states affected by the flood. Much of what he and Sydenstricker had witnessed was the result of nature, as the Mississippi River washed away the barriers that men had built to constrain it and reclaimed the alluvial plain. However, when it came to disease and especially pellagra, Goldberger was thoroughly convinced that the culprit was not nature but man. All that it took for pellagra to win in the struggle between disease and humanity was for greed to triumph over altruism and for good men to do nothing or, worse yet, to rationalize the reason for their inaction.

Goldberger wrote to the surgeon general in early 1928 and counseled action. He formally requested that Cumming employ "a suitable person to work in a selected locality in which pellagra is highly endemic." He told Cumming that "although in its essence the problem [of pellagra] is an economic one," food availability among the tenant farmers could be improved by increasing the milk supply through cow ownership and the amount of fresh vegetables through "promoting the cultivation of better gardens." Goldberger hoped that such an individual might work to "restrict the prevalence of pellagra and malnutrition in general" by implementing "the methods best suited for promoting the ends sought." Once again he was suggesting that even within the constraints of politics and practicality, change might be possible. Well aware of the bevy of state and federal agents in the field trying to improve agriculture in the South, Goldberger insisted that his suggestion would place alongside them an individual less focused on agriculture than on change from "the standpoint of health."[65]

If there was political contentiousness between North and South and between state and federal governments, there was also bickering between federal agencies. Goldberger, understanding it all too well, suggested, "To ensure harmonious cooperation with agricultural agents, the proper Bureau of the U.S. Department of Agriculture might be invited to detail one of its agents to the Public Health Service to undertake the study."[66] He never stopped trying to vault over the obstacles to change.

Later in the spring Goldberger received a letter from an old friend whose interests converged with his own. Dr. W. R. Redden had first met him when both were involved in influenza research in 1918. Redden had been in charge of the naval volunteers who participated in the experiments that Goldberger and Rosenau had designed. Now he was the national medical officer of the American Red Cross, his office not far from the Hygienic Laboratory in downtown Washington. The two men had already enjoyed a pleasant phone conversation. Redden explained that he now wished to reiterate in writing what they had discussed on the phone. First he expressed the entire organization's gratitude to Goldberger for his interest and advice during the flood crisis. Specifically, Goldberger's observation that there had been a great deal of pellagra in the overflow areas prior to the flood had allowed the Red Cross to answer critics who blamed the pellagra outbreak on the kind of food it was distributing. Redden also wanted it on record that there were two groups of refugees: the 300,000 individuals in the refugee camps, who could be given wholesome food and yeast; and those on the plantations, where landowners often decided who got Red Cross rations and who did not. Moreover, some tenants had fled and were living in freight cars and on top of levees, where they could not be reached by Red Cross workers. Redden was delighted that Goldberger's words had "indirectly rather than directly" offered him a response to those who sought to blame pellagra among the tenants on the Red Cross. He could quote Goldberger to deflect criticism of the Red Cross.

Redden was equally pleased that Goldberger's discovery of yeast's value in preventing pellagra offered the Red Cross a course of action — supplying yeast to local physicians for distribution to the community. Thanks to Goldberger, the Red Cross did not have to wait for the next crisis to begin battling pellagra, however intractable the long-term economic and social arrangements might be in the rural South.

Letters such as Redden's were filled with gratitude and praise. Now in his fifties, Goldberger was finally receiving professional recognition for his achievements. He had been elected a fellow of the American Association for the Advancement of Science. He was also a fellow of the American Public Health Association and a member of the board of governors of the American College of Physicians. Other honors and memberships reached his desk. As director of the Nutrition Program in the Pathology Division of the Hygienic Laboratory, Goldberger had administrative responsibilities. He was accomplished and was being modestly rewarded by his colleagues.

Goldberger accepted the honors and accolades graciously. However, as his letters from the South during the flood suggest, his greatest reward remained in relieving suffering. The image in a letter from the summer of 1927 that had made tears roll down Mary's cheeks was of a boy trying to plow a field, though his body was racked by pellagra. The sight of the suffering youngster haunted Goldberger.

Ten years after the flood Dr. William DeKleine, acting medical director of the Red Cross during the catastrophe, recalled Goldberger's visit and the dramatic influence that yeast distribution had on pellagra victims. Between 1927 and 1935 the Red Cross distributed over three-quarters of a million packages of seeds to encourage gardening as a way of preventing pellagra. It also distributed 350,000 pounds of yeast. Referring to the pellagra preventive in yeast as vitamin G (for Goldberger), a designation that became increasingly frequent during the late 1920s, DeKleine described yeast's use during the 1927 flood as "a practical public health measure of considerable importance."[67]

Goldberger had spent much of the early 1920s in the Hygienic Laboratory seeking to understand which foods would prevent pellagra. Some of what he learned saved thousands of lives when he was called into the field during the 1927 Mississippi flood. Now, not unlike Cincinnatus, the fifth century B.C. Roman general who returned to the plow after being asked to leave the peace of his farm to preserve Rome from its enemies, Goldberger went back home. He retreated to Washington and to the relative serenity of the Hygienic Laboratory. There, surrounded by his pots and pans and autoclaves and animal cages, he hoped to solve the final mystery, the identity of the pellagra preventive.

NINE

Kaddish for a Hero

If Joseph Goldberger was anxious to exit the public arena in the spring of 1928, Mary Goldberger was equally anxious to enter it. She was actively supporting a bill sponsored by the Democratic senator Joseph Ransdell from her home state of Louisiana to fund an institute for the study of all human diseases, a national institute of health.

Mary Goldberger, despite her husband's many admonitions to pay closer attention to home and children, had become a club woman, head of the Louisiana State Society chapter in Washington. Because of her club activities in this heritage organization, she was contacted by Charles Holmes Herty, adviser to the Chemical Foundation, former president of the Synthetic Organic Chemical Manufacturers Association, and a leader in promoting scientific research in the United States. Herty asked Mary to secure the support of the General Federation of Women's Clubs and get them to attend the Commerce subcommittee hearing on the bill. Mary was delighted to be involved and volunteered to meet with Mrs. Bell Sherman of the National Congress of Parents and Teachers, the leadership of the League of Women Voters, and other groups to gather support for the measure. Perhaps hoping to spur her on to even greater efforts, Herty wrote flatteringly, "Doctor Goldberger did a great service by his scientific work on pellagra, but I believe his wife is going to do a greater service in securing legislation which will provide adequate means and facilities for a host of scientific men like Dr. Goldberger and his associates to do still greater service to our country."[1]

On May 25, 1930, President Herbert Hoover would sign the Ransdell Act into law. The Hygienic Laboratory would become the National Institute of Health, beginning a new era, albeit modestly, in the federal government's relationship to medical research; the large federal budgets for medical research were many years and a world war away.[2] Ironically, the Ransdell Act stipulated that scientists receiving fellowships could not be commissioned officers of the U.S. Public Health Service. Goldberger's research on pellagra would not have been eligible for funding.

As Mary lobbied for the Ransdell bill, her husband continued his medical detective work, pursuing the nutrient missing from the diets of pellagrins. He was increasingly in demand as a speaker as well. On October 31, 1928, he addressed the American Dietetic Association. In simple, direct, nontechnical language he summarized his significant findings with respect to pellagra and offered some conclusions based on fourteen years of research. Distilling the myriad statistics on patients afflicted with the disease, Goldberger told his audience that pellagra was most frequent in children between two and fifteen years of age, a revision of the earlier view that the "adult woman, the housewife," was most often afflicted. He described how "hard times," especially the reduction of family income when food prices were rising, were "very likely to be followed by an increase in the incidence of the disease" while, conversely, increased income and purchasing power led to lower incidence. As for the cause, he now told them with confidence that the two-century-old puzzle was all but solved and that "beyond a reasonable doubt . . . pellagra is a vitamin deficiency disease analogous to scurvy and beriberi."[3]

Hoping to simplify the more complicated question of what was missing from pellagrins' diets, Goldberger explained that he had come to call the as yet unidentified pellagra preventive "factor or vitamin P-P." Perhaps evoking smiles in his audience, he joked that it had come to his attention that some were calling vitamin P-P by the name vitamin G. And though it was not yet fully identified, they knew many of its properties. Citing his studies of dogs and rats, he explained that vitamin B was a complex with at least two factors: "one a heat-sensitive antineuritic or beriberi (polyneuritis) preventive, and the other a heat-resistant factor indistinguishable from the pellagra preventive." Especially interesting, he thought, was that different foods, even those with vitamin B, differed in their success as pellagra preventives. He offered them the example of "lean muscle meat": although it was known to be a poor source of vitamin B, "tests in both human and canine disease [black tongue] show it to be a very good source of P-P."[4]

Far less difficult to identify was why pellagrins, 120,000 individuals in 1927, had diets deficient in pellagra preventives. Goldberger summed it up more concisely than ever before: "The problem of pellagra is in the main a problem of poverty."[5]

Poverty. It was an easy word to understand, but the conditions that gave rise to it were not. Nor were the complicated dietary conditions attendant on it. Earlier in his talk Goldberger had used a convenient device to get his audience to understand where the problem of pellagra was greatest. Rather than denounce the South for its grinding poverty, he asked his audience to imagine a map and some pushpins of the kind used to track cases of an epidemic disease. He said that if they could imagine such a map, most of the pushpins representing pellagra cases would be in the southeast quadrant of the country and in particular areas of particular states. Few pins in Virginia and Florida. Many more in the Carolinas and the Mississippi Delta. If he was coy as to where pellagra was most prevalent, he was less so as to what was most needed to eradicate it: "Improvement in basic economic conditions alone can be expected to heal this festering ulcer in the body of our people." Wisely advising his audience not to expect such change "in a day," he did predict that such a time might arrive sooner rather than later by "the cooperative action of all whose vision enables them to see the great social and economic advantages to be derived from the eradication of the disease."[6] Certainly in states such as Mississippi, death rates for pellagra were already in decline for both whites and blacks (see table on page 197).

Dr. Joseph Goldberger would not live to see that day. Although he did not know it, he had just delivered his last speech. Even as he spoke of pellagra's presence in the American population as a "festering ulcer in the body of our people," a growth of another kind, a malignant tumor, was eating away at his own body. In less than three months he would be dead.

Earlier in the fall, Goldberger had begun to feel ill. His weight dropped, and symptoms of anemia appeared. Physicians at the Naval Hospital could not diagnose the mysterious illness. Unable to learn the cause, they treated the symptoms. But word was spreading that Goldberger could not make it into the Hygienic Laboratory every day. A young assistant, Dr. William Henry Sebrell, who would one day head the National Institutes of Health, continued Goldberger's work in the lab. In November, Goldberger entered the Naval Hospital.

As he was suffering his last illness, Goldberger was nominated once again for the highest honor a man of medicine can receive. His oldest friend in the PHS, Milton Rosenau, wrote, "It has given me special satisfaction to cast my vote for the Nobel Prize for 1929. This does not mean that you will get it, for the judgment is difficult and fortune fickle. I happen to know, and I think I am not divulging a confidence when I tell you, that [Reid] Hunt has voted likewise." Rosenau, understanding the politics of prizes, expressed his regret that he could not get his hands on a list of "American voters, so that we could have the advantage of group judgment." The statement sent to the Nobel Prize Committee and likely drafted by George McCoy, head of the Hygienic Laboratory, discussed every aspect of the pellagra research, concluding:

> It is not an exaggeration to say that many competent observers believe that no more important piece of medical research work has been accomplished in this generation than has been done by Doctor Goldberger. It has put in our hands knowledge which when applied may be expected to lead to the eradication of pellagra. In addition to this immediately practical outcome of his investigations, there has come a broader understanding of human nutrition and diet by the definite establishment of pellagra as one of the deficiency diseases.

Knowing that Nobel committees preferred honoring the discovery of new knowledge to the new applications of old knowledge, McCoy added, "One of the results yielded by these investigations has been the discovery of another nutritive essential—a vitamin preventive of pellagra—Factor P-P or Vitamin G."[7] It was the fifth time Goldberger had been nominated for the Nobel. He did not win.

By December, Goldberger had also begun to lose his battle for life. His condition was grave. From his bed in the Naval Hospital he struggled to survive. Doctors prescribed blood transfusions. In an era before blood banks and the storage of blood plasma, volunteers gave blood directly. Donors lay on a bed or cot near the recipient, and blood from their veins ran directly into the recipient.

When word reached the PHS that Goldberger needed blood, twenty colleagues—physicians and young laboratory assistants—volunteered. So, too, did Mary and the Goldberger children. Fourteen volunteers had blood compatible with Goldberger's. Donors from the Hygienic Laboratory, whose names the surgeon general refused to release, set up a relay system of lying down and giving their blood to Goldberger by the pint, one on Tuesday and another on Thursday, until they had all given, and then they began again.[8] Goldberger found the transfusion process disturbing. He did not like the thought that he was taking from another the fluid that had long been equated with life itself. He preferred not to know whose blood he was receiving; to preserve some anonymity in the process and prevent tearful encounters, he insisted on keeping a towel over his face during the transfusions.[9]

The cohesiveness and esprit de corps of the Public Health Service would have prompted a show of support for any comrade, especially one who had given so much to the service. However, Goldberger was more than admired. He was liked. Dr. Roscoe Spencer of the PHS recalled years later that Goldberger often joined younger colleagues for lunch at the nearby Department of the Interior cafeteria and chatted about experiments. Dr. Grover Kempf, who had worked with Goldberger at the Pellagra Hospital in Spartanburg, recalled him as a "remarkable man," but one who was not universally loved because "he was very strict—not [a] disciplinarian, but in his work, he was very strict in the records and recording of his work, and he demanded close attention to all the details." However, from Kempf's perspective Goldberger was "one of the superior officers of the United States Public Health Service," one who had earned his affection and respect. Years later, Goldberger's son

Joseph recalled that some who feared Goldberger's rigorous standards and discipline in the laboratory referred to him behind his back as "Caesar."[10]

As reports of his illness found their way into newspapers, Mary received letters from all over the nation wishing her husband a full recovery. Typical was the note from Dr. Oscar Dowling, president of the Louisiana Board of Health: "I see by the papers Doctor Goldberger is sick. I am writing to express the hope he is improving and may soon be entirely well. He is too valuable [a] man to be sick. We need more like him."[11]

Trains from New York, Boston, and Perth Amboy brought relatives, including his brothers Leo and Ben and his favorite cousin, Max Rossett. According to Mary's recollections, the heavy atmosphere in the hospital room was lightened by their reminiscences of their youthful adventures in the streets of the Lower East Side. Especially moving was the last good-bye with Goldberger's older half brother Jake, son of his father's first marriage and the individual who, with his brother Max, had preceded the rest of the family to the United States. Jake had lent young Joseph the money for medical school. With all the energy he could muster, Goldberger hugged Jake and sobbed his gratitude.[12]

Not long before he died, Goldberger had highly emotional visits from his most trusted protégé, George Wheeler, and the Harvard pharmacologist who had been so instrumental in the first Nobel nomination, Reid Hunt. So weak now that he could barely be understood, he whispered to Hunt, "We must have philosophy." However, accepting Goldberger's decline philosophically was not something that Hunt or Wheeler could do. Hunt left Goldberger's bedside with tears streaming down his cheeks. Wheeler was bereft with grief. He and Goldberger had been comrades in the war on pellagra from the very beginning. Mary recalled that when Wheeler entered the hospital room, he knelt at Goldberger's bedside and softly said, "My chief."[13] Goldberger learned through Edgar Sydenstricker that all the staff members who assisted in compiling his pellagra data were wishing him well: "I will let you in on a little secret which may amuse you: All of your pellagra statistical group—of both sexes—refer to you (when you are not in ear shot) as 'Joe' and have been doing so for years. So that now whenever we happen upon each other, the invariable first question is 'How is Joe?'"[14] Hoping to cheer his friend, Sydenstricker conveyed the mixture of awe and warmth that Goldberger inspired.

As Goldberger's condition worsened, visits from friends and colleagues were curtailed. The man who had cheated death before knew the gravity of his condition. On January 5, 1929, he dictated a memorandum of his wishes "in case of my death." The document had four "wish[es] and preference[s]." First, the document should be given to his wife. Second, "there should be no funeral service whatsoever." Goldberger had scratched out the word "elaborate" before "funeral" and added in ink the word "whatsoever." Third, he wished his body to be cremated and the ashes strewn on the Potomac River near Haines Pont. Fourth, and finally, he asked that his close friends and colleagues at the Hygienic Laboratory—Arthur Stimson, James P. Leake, and George W. McCoy—aid Mary in carrying out his wishes and preferences. The statement was signed "Jos. Goldberger." The writing has an uncharacteristic quiver, the scrawl of a weak and shaky hand.[15]

The memorandum reached Mary on January 17, 1929. The man she had addressed for decades as "my dearest Joseph" closed his eyes for the final time at 6:29 A.M. Two days earlier, before drifting into a coma, he had held her hand. He asked her not to leave him because she had always been "my rock, my strength." Then he told her, "Mary we must have patience."[16] His patience had made him a successful bench scientist, and his lack of patience had driven him to seek practical ways to save lives in the face of scientific and political opposition. Perhaps he had not always been the most patient of husbands, but he had always been a loving one.

Scientist to the end, Goldberger had requested that his body be autopsied. Physicians discovered the cause of death to be hypernephroma, a rare form of kidney cancer.[17] Goldberger's doctors had not been able to detect the renal carcinoma. They did not know the cause of death until the postmortem.

Mary and Joseph had been married for almost twenty-three years. At her request a death mask was made of her beloved Joseph's face.[18] Then he was cremated in conformity with his wishes.

Friday January 18, 1929, was a dreary and blustery day in Washington,

D.C. A cold, damp wind chilled Mary, her four children, and the small crowd of friends and colleagues who knew and loved Joseph Goldberger and had come to pay their respects. His brothers and sister were present. At sunset they gathered at Haines Point on the banks of the Potomac River.

The ceremony was simple. As Goldberger had requested, there were no flowers or funeral trappings. Abram Simon, chief rabbi of Washington Hebrew Congregation, the largest Reform synagogue in Washington, officiated. Although he had flirted with Unitarianism, Goldberger had never renounced his identity as a Jew. However, like many first-generation immigrant Jews, he had embraced secularism. In Goldberger's case, science was his surrogate faith. There is no record of his ever having attended a synagogue service in Washington, and although *The Washington Post* described Rabbi Simon as "an intimate friend of Dr. Goldberger's," there is no evidence of such a friendship in his correspondence. Perhaps one developed in the last months of Goldberger's life in the privacy of his hospital room. It seems more likely, however, that Mary invited the rabbi to come out of respect for the preferences of the Jewish relatives from Perth Amboy who had unsuccessfully pressed for a traditional Jewish burial. Cremation, while forbidden by Orthodox Jews, is permitted within the Reform tradition.[19]

Rabbi Simon began by turning to the river and reciting the Nineteenth Psalm, one designated "For the leader, A psalm of David." As the rabbi spoke, George McCoy scattered Goldberger's ashes over the Potomac. The location was highly appropriate. Overlooking the river was Goldberger's beloved Hygienic Laboratory, where his mind had battled disease. And it was by studying the Potomac's waters for evidence of typhoid that he had begun his distinguished career so many years before. Now his remains floated gently, briefly upon its surface.

Turning to those assembled, Rabbi Simon chanted the Kaddish in Hebrew, as he said, "for the comfort of those of our faith." He began the haunting chant, "Yis-gad-dal v'yis-kadash, she 'meh rab-bo." Goldberger would not have objected. The Kaddish, recited in the depths of mourning, is an affirmation of faith in the power and goodness of the one living God. With the haunting cadence of the Kaddish drifting into the evening air, the rabbi offered a brief eulogy.

Being a Washington rabbi, Simon had ministered often to the city's movers and shakers of his faith. He acknowledged that this "simple service" had "a national aspect." He celebrated Goldberger's heroism as an epidemic fighter and medical detective, observing, "The United States Public Health Service mourns a man who lent honor to its service. Science pays its tribute of affection to the memory of an unspoiled hero who, ever standing at his post of danger, never faltered in the performance of his duty, however dangerous."[20]

Goldberger, much beloved by Mary and the children, was a public hero, after all, and because it was an era when the designation "hero" was applied without irony, Simon embraced it and elaborated on it elegantly:

> Heroism on the battlefield is easily dramatized, catches the popular eye and wins people's applause. What recognition is there, or what rewards are ample enough to compensate those men of science who track the deadly microbes to their lairs, discover serums for the prevention of contagious diseases, and oft pay the supreme sacrifice for their self-inflicted and self-sustained courage? This is the heroism of peace in a superlative sense. Dr. Goldberger was a self-inoculated carrier of health to countless thousands. Years to come, an adequate appraisal of his service to the human race will be possible.

Having praised Goldberger's achievements, Simon spoke of the man, depicting his intelligence but also his remarkable humility and personal warmth:

> His was a high sense of the beauty and the sacredness of life. No vain ambition or pride in fame lured him from his inconspicuous task. Neither anger nor envy seamed the garment of his soul. Keen of intellect, impatient of falsehood and bombast, he carried to his last breath the rich simplicity of chivalry. A gentleman by instinct, tolerant in faith, lover of truth, cultured and soft-spoken, he captivated us by the rare radiance of his spirit.

The rabbi concluded with a brief statement about how much Goldberger would be missed. "Humanity mourns its friend," he said. And then, referring to the ashes that McCoy had just scattered, he linked the Jewish immigrant doctor to the American history of which he was now a part: "We scatter his precious ashes, these to mingle with the sacred waters which touch the shores of Mount Vernon to join the mighty ocean of the divine brotherhood."[21]

The rabbi's eulogy concluded, the ceremony was over. Surgeon General Hugh Cumming later wrote in an unpublished memoir, "I shall never forget that cold, bleak day."[22] He issued a four-and-a-half-page official eulogy to be circulated within the PHS. The first two paragraphs were especially memorable because they captured the way in which so many of his colleagues regarded Goldberger:

> It happens but rarely that when a man dies, and in our imperfect human way we attempt to evaluate his life in terms of service to humanity, we come to the incontrovertible conclusion that here was a man whose life was productive of a consistent series of useful contributions, and that some of these were of far-reaching benefit to mankind. If we review the biographies of many who are with justice accounted great men, how often do we find to our disappointment that many of their beneficent acts were to an extent counterbalanced by mistakes, or even that some of their deeds which were performed with noble intent have been found susceptible of ignoble applications by others.
>
> The death of Dr. Joseph Goldberger affords one of those rare opportunities to examine a life consistent in its continuous record of useful contributions to medical knowledge in a number of different lines of research, and culminating in a discovery which we believe is destined to take its place among the classic major accomplishments of medical science.

Cumming went on at great length to discuss Goldberger's research and accomplishments. He recited a short history of pellagra and its horrors and what Goldberger's pathbreaking research had done to cure and prevent it. Cumming then reminded all that "the disease which baffled the best medical talent of Europe for two centuries has yielded well within a decade to the researches of one American scientist."

The immigrant boy had become an "American scientist" whose praises were sung by the highest-ranking medical officer in the U.S. government. It was that immigrant past that Cumming exalted in the last lines of his tribute:

It may well be thought that when Dr. Goldberger's parents, sturdy farmer folk living just South of the Carpathians in Hungary, set out for America, they could little foresee what a great contribution their seven-year-old [actually nine-year-old] boy would make to American medicine. And yet we may perhaps trace to certain qualities which he inherited from them the great success in scientific achievement which he realized—qualities of sterling honesty and uprightness, of tireless industry, of unending patience, of orderliness and cleanliness of thought and action which when combined with a lovable sweetness and tolerance and an ever ready and delightful sense of humor went to the making of a truly great man, fitted for great deeds.[23]

Goldberger's death was covered by newspapers not only in New York and Washington but in other parts of the country as well. Southerners greeted his death with sadness. In Columbia, South Carolina, the announcement made the front page. In Natchez, Mississippi, the *Democrat* told readers, "Dr. Goldberger Who Conquered Palagra [*sic*] Dead." In the state capital of Jackson, where Goldberger had worked with orphan children and persuaded Earl Brewer to gamble with his political career, the *Daily Clarion-Ledger* said of him, "Civilization owes a debt of gratitude to this soldier of science who attacked and conquered an unknown enemy." In New Orleans, Mary's hometown, *The Times-Picayune* ran a picture of her husband and a long article.[24]

The Yiddish-language press in New York mourned as well. Always seeking news of a Jewish-American hero to demonstrate the loyalty of immigrants toward their adopted home, editors embraced the Goldberger story and made his demise front-page news. *Forverts* (Jewish Daily Forward), the most popular of such newspapers, lauded him as a "discoverer of important remedies" and a "martyr to science." *Der Tog* (The Day) lavished praise on the "Famous Jewish Doctor." The writers were not always on the mark. *Forverts* told its readers that pellagra came from indigestion. More seriously, the newspaper attributed Goldberger's death to his "experiments to liberate humanity from pellagra."[25]

The Yiddish press was hardly alone in publishing inaccuracies. In the days following Goldberger's funeral, a story began to surface that his body was autopsied because he was the victim of an "unknown disease" or a "mysterious malady" or a mystery "anemia" or a disease "which started during his pellagra studies." It was implied that his body was autopsied to learn more about the disease that he had struggled against and that had in the end conquered him. Mary was asked by a news service specializing in stories about science, the Science Service, to be interviewed and clear up the "mystery" of her beloved husband's death.[26]

With characteristic dignity, she wrote a statement that could be issued as a press release. Acknowledging the "speculation and bewilderment" as to why her husband wanted his body autopsied and then cremated, Mary offered several answers. First, she explained that "as a physician and man of science, he had the scientific attitude of mind toward life. He believed everyone, after death, so far as humanly possible, should be autopsied for the advancement of knowledge. Especially so when there was any doubt as to the cause of death." She called the prejudice against autopsy "medieval." She then took aim at the source of misinformation: "Through miserable error and misunderstanding the Associated Press was at first misinformed with regard to the true cause of death." She then pointed out that with her permission and that of her eldest son, Farrar, now over twenty-one, the correct information was given to the press by Goldberger's physician at the Naval Hospital, Dr. C.O.W. Bunker. Explaining that the cause of death was "hypernephroma of the left kidney, a rare form of malignant tumor," Mary said of her husband, "In life he would be the last man to suppress truth that would shed light in a dark place."[27]

Especially troubling, of course, were the rumors that Goldberger had died of pellagra. After all, if that were true, then pellagra was an infectious disease. Mary called the idea "a shocking misstatement of fact, which was a direct blow to all his years of research on pellagra." Bitterly she called it "meat to his enemies and a good story for a gullible public," adding, "So long as people are going to hide behind a barrier of prejudice, superstition and jungle phylosophy [*sic*], so long will they help to retard the advance against this insidious malady." Those closest to Goldberger did their best to comfort Mary, widow and now guardian of her beloved Joseph's memory. One of Goldberger's close friends at the Hygienic Laboratory, Dr. Arthur Stimson, wrote her a warm and comforting letter. After assuring her that the medical journals got the cause of death correct, he wrote, "Joe's work is in no danger of being discredited,—it was too well done for that . . . Let's not worry about the mistakes of the newspapers or the opinions of a few hill-billy doctors. They will be forgotten in a short time. Joe's work will stand as a permanent contribution to Medicine and science." Rosenau wrote her to say he imagined Goldberger was made of "the kind of material of which patriarchs and prophets were made in other days." Edgar Sydenstricker wrote to make certain she knew of an article in the journal *Science* that suggested that hereafter the P-P factor be formally known as "Vitamin G." He also told her he had hung a picture of Goldberger on his office wall.[28]

The compliments were flattering. However, they nourished the souls, not the bodies, of Goldberger's survivors. Mary was destitute. In an era before Social Security and sophisticated pension systems, widows survived on family savings and the generosity of children or other relatives. With four children to raise and Mary's love of shopping, the Goldbergers had managed to save almost nothing. Knowing her dire economic straits, Goldberger's friends and associates stepped forward immediately to sponsor a special act of Congress that would afford her a pension of $125 per month. Congressman Harold Knutson of Minnesota, chairman of the House Committee on Pensions, wrote to Mary on January 22 and sent her a copy of H.R. 16411, which had already been introduced. The bill read:

> Be it enacted by the Senate and House of Representatives of the United States of America in Congress assembled, That the Secretary of the Interior be, and he is hereby, authorized and directed

to place on the pension roll, subject to the provisions and limitations of the pension laws, the name of Mary H. Goldberger,
widow of Joseph Goldberger, late surgeon, United States Public
Health Service, and pay her a pension at the rate of $125 per
month.[29]

They could not save his life, but Goldberger's friends could still do
something to help him. They grabbed their pens and petitioned Congress. Dr. George McCoy, Anderson's successor as head of the Hygienic
Laboratory, could not take the lead in lobbying for the legislation because he was a federal employee and forbidden to lobby, so he turned to
Rosenau, who enthusiastically started a letter-writing campaign. Consulting the membership lists of the National Academy of Sciences, the
American Academy of Sciences, the American Association of Patholo-
gists and Bacteriologists, and the Association of American Physicians,
Rosenau sent eight hundred letters urging recipients to write to members
of Congress: "Here is a chance for a republic to show recognition and
justice to a public officer who gave his all without thought of gain. It
would be helpful if you would write to your two senators and to your representative in the House and to any other member of Congress you may
know, endorsing the bill and asking their interest." He included the
names of all the members of the Senate Finance Committee. In a final
paragraph he reminded them that both Joseph and Mary had taken risks
for their country: "Dr. Goldberger contracted typhus fever, dengue and
yellow fever while studying these diseases. Both he and his wife subjected themselves to experiments with pellagra in order to test the manner by which this disease may be contracted." Later he wrote to McCoy,
"I never engaged in anything of this sort that has met with such wholehearted approval, enthusiastic support and unanimous response as the
just and modest provisions of Senate bill 5473. I thank you for the privilege of permitting me to take a small part."[30]

Luminaries in medicine and other fields of science supported the
cause. Columbia University's distinguished anthropologist Franz Boas,
Harvard's bacteriologist Hans Zinsser and its eminent physiologist Walter B. Cannon, Cornell's pioneer nutritionist, Graham Lusk, the Rockefeller Institute's Simon Flexner, and William and Charles Mayo at their

clinic in Rochester, Minnesota, were just a few of the many renowned individuals who took the time and effort to draft letters advocating the pension to Congress. William Mayo promised to mention it to his senators in person, adding, "My brother and I and our associates in the Clinic esteemed Dr. Goldberger highly and appreciated the great value of his medical research."[31]

In a personal letter to Utah senator Reed Smoot, Goldberger's collaborator and cherished friend John Anderson explained, "It is impossible to estimate the value to the citizens of the United States of his studies on Pellagra alone, in that he has definitely pointed out how this disease may be prevented, and how cured once developed." A politician could understand lives saved. He could also comprehend valor, especially when compared with the heroism of soldiers, whose widows received pensions. Therefore, Anderson offered an analogy not unlike the one proffered by Rabbi Simon at the memorial service: "Dr. Goldberger has as surely given his life for the benefit of his countrymen as any soldier or sailor who laid down his life in the great war."[32] That sentence would most certainly have brought a smile to the lips of the man who had been rejected by the Navy twice in his life.

In March the surgeon general wrote Mary to inform her that the House version of the bill, giving her a life pension of $125 per month, had been passed by both houses of Congress. In his note Cumming conveyed the relief felt by those who loved and respected Goldberger: "The sense of loss which all the officers of the Public Health Service feel since Dr. Goldberger's death is partly compensated by the knowledge that some provision has been made for you and your children to offset in some slight degree Dr. Goldberger's sacrifice of financial reward during his lifetime for his outstanding scientific achievement."[33] Mary received a copy of the document from the Bureau of Pensions signed on April 3, 1929, ordering that she receive $125 every month to begin retroactively to March 4.

The pension was gratifying but hardly sufficient. Not in 1929. Not with four children in college or intending to go. The boys had already taken loans to pay tuition. However, there was still young Mary to consider. Help came from an unexpected source—Julius Rosenwald, a millionaire philanthropist with a long interest in the South and its poverty.

Rosenwald was born in Springfield, Illinois, in 1862 into a German immigrant family. At age sixteen, he moved to New York and got involved in retail clothing. The Sears, Roebuck mail-order house became a customer, and Rosenwald soon closed his own business to work for Sears. By 1896 he had become vice president. By 1925 he had become chairman of the board and a millionaire. Rosenwald had a special interest in African-Americans and their plight in the postbellum South. He made large donations to the Tuskegee Institute, of which he was a trustee after 1912, and contributed to building over four thousand black schools in fourteen states, as well as many YMCA and YWCA buildings in black communities. The Julius Rosenwald Fund administered the contributions.

Rosenwald, an important figure behind the scenes in Washington and a frequent visitor to the city, had no doubt been following Goldberger's career and the news of his death. On a trip to Washington in March 1929, likely to attend Herbert Hoover's inauguration, he paid a surprise visit to Mrs. Goldberger. Young Joe Goldberger was not home at the time, but neighbors described to him how a big black limousine pulled to the curb in front of the apartment building at 2120 G Street, where the family had moved after Goldberger's death. Sitting at Mary's kitchen table, the millionaire asked her how he could help. She asked only for financial assistance with her daughter's college education, funds that Rosenwald readily provided.[34] Young Mary wrote her benefactor a thank-you note for his most extraordinary gift. In his return letter Rosenwald explained why he cared about her father. It was consistent with the many other acts of generosity he made throughout his life; a businessman who pursued profits, he held in highest admiration those who eschewed personal gain for the greater good of humankind. Wanting to play some small role in their sacrifice, he helped them. Now he wrote to Goldberger's daughter, "I can only repeat what I said to your mother, that it is a privilege to be of service to the family of so distinguished a man as your Father was, who devoted his life for the benefit of others."[35]

Joseph Goldberger had placed the highest value on two aspects of his life: his family and his work. Friends such as George McCoy and Milton Rosenau made sure that a grateful nation kept faith with Goldberger by caring for his family. Admirers such as Julius Rosenwald chipped in. But what of his work? Who would shoulder that burden?

Dr. George Wheeler did not forget his chief. After Goldberger's death, Wheeler continued the pellagra research. He did not discover the nature of the P-P factor. However, he did spend much of the early 1930s defending Goldberger's work against criticism and seeking to identify additional pellagra preventives. The onset of the Great Depression made it more important than ever that vulnerable members of the population have access to pellagra-preventive foods.

Perhaps not surprisingly, Goldberger's doubters remained equally active. Indeed, even as tributes to Goldberger were still being published, speakers at the 1930 annual meeting of the Southern Medical Association were taking potshots at him. Dr. J. Frank Wilson, a Florida physician, suggested that his work was still inconclusive and that it left humanity as much "in the dark" about the disease as when physicians thought it was "caused in some vague manner by corn." Wheeler rose to deliver a vehement defense of the Goldberger approach to diet.[36]

Interestingly, though his own state public health office in South Carolina was implementing policies resonant with Goldberger's findings, James A. Hayne stood up after Wheeler concluded his paper to insist that "we know very little" about pellagra. He fulminated, "Of course, in the United States we have rammed down our throats the ideas of Dr. Goldberger to such an extent that physicians are afraid to say they do not believe them, but in other countries where physicians do not come under the domination of Dr. Goldberger they do not accept his belief." Then, in an especially silly couple of sentences, Hayne compared Goldberger's influence on the American medical establishment to Benito Mussolini's in Italy. Concerned that Mary would read or hear about Hayne's outburst, Wheeler wrote a gentle, soothing letter to her, assuring her that what Hayne had to say "does not amount to anything. He is a chronic opposer and drifts about from pillar to post in an effort to support his position. However, regardless of what he says in open meeting, his policies and practices in his home state are strictly in accordance with the principles laid down by Dr. Goldberger." Wheeler told Mary, "No one takes him seriously in these meetings."[37]

His comforting words to Mary notwithstanding, Wheeler found himself spending much time and energy defending Goldberger's ideas. While most of the attacks were foolish, Wheeler understood that criticism left unanswered might well result in some public health officials' neglecting the dietary advice derived from Goldberger's work. The threat of pellagra remained real and, if left untreated, deadly. Some agreed that the problem was dietary but refused to accept that there was an unknown pellagra preventive. Serious researchers such as Dr. Sidney Bliss at Tulane University presented the greatest challenge. In an article in *Science*, Bliss claimed that pellagra was an iron deficiency and even persuaded the editors at *The Journal of the American Medical Association* that the nutritional deficiency was still an open question. Wheeler was enraged and wrote a sarcastic response that the surgeon general refused to clear for submission.[38]

Nor had the infectious theory of pellagra been permanently banished. A Virginia physician, Dr. Beverly Tucker, advocated reopening the possibility that pellagra was caused by a virus. Proposing a testing program to include animals and criminals on death row, he exhibited his work at the 1935 meeting of the Southern Medical Association, where it was awarded a prize.[39]

Neither Wheeler nor the surgeon general put any stock in such claims. Instead, Wheeler continued to test foods for their P-P value.[40] His research did not identify the pellagra preventive, but it did contribute to saving lives, always his mentor's first priority. As the economic depression of the 1930s worsened, every bit of knowledge concerning foods and the amount required in the diet to prevent pellagra was of crucial importance. So, too, was the distribution of garden seed and yeast undertaken by the Red Cross. Between 1927 and 1937 the Red Cross distributed a half million pounds of yeast, and even that at times fell short of local needs. By 1933 only those most in need were getting yeast from the Red Cross. Local groups of northern reformers, such as those with the American Friends Service Committee, picked up the slack in particular places, but there was much suffering. At times all the Red Cross or local health agencies could do was engage in short-term assistance, such as lending a cow to a pellagra-ridden family. Education materials were published and distributed. Some contained errors, but even those with correct information were inaccessible to the considerable number of illiterate Americans. In 1930 almost 17 percent of South Carolina's population could not read, triple the national average.[41]

Despite the poverty of the depression era, mortality from pellagra declined. Pellagra deaths in 1935 were recorded at 3,543, well below the peak year of 1928 and closer to the 1925 figure of 3,344. It was more than education. Disastrously low cotton prices led to an increase in food production by farmers and mill workers. Some grew enough to sell. Owners who earlier had discouraged wasting land on gardens and cows now favored home food production to reduce the amount of food they would have to supply tenants. Yeast distribution helped still others.

The coming of the New Deal helped, too. Well before President Franklin D. Roosevelt proclaimed the South the "nation's No. 1 economic problem" in 1938, he and his advisers made it clear that they knew there was more at the heart of the South's poverty than the Great Depression. New Dealers understood that the South rested on a foundation of agriculture and remained mired in an anachronistic and crippling farm-tenancy system. However, if they had a comprehensive understanding of the origins of southern poverty, their programs often proved inadequate to tackle a problem grounded in history and culture as much as in economics. The Federal Emergency Relief Administration helped fend off starvation, but food distribution was not calibrated to battle pellagra. Individuals ate what they could to fill their empty bellies. The Resettlement Administration, created in April 1935, launched a plethora of overlapping programs, but the cabinet-level agency attempted to help tenant farmers and sharecroppers buy land and encouraged cooperative efforts in agricultural marketing and equipment buying. Its successor, the Farm Security Administration, continued the struggle and battled pellagra, specifically, through education and medical services programs. Other programs set up as part of the New Deal had the added bonus of effectively suppressing pellagra among southerners. Young men in the Civilian Conservation Corps—all white in the South—got a wholesome, well-balanced diet. Rural electrification in the Tennessee Valley allowed for improved refrigeration. Foods once too perishable to be preserved for very long were now readily available even in hot weather.[42]

As the nation battled the depression and then the Axis powers, Mary

Goldberger raised and educated her children. Thanks to Julius Rosenwald's generosity, daughter Mary went to the University of Wisconsin, where she was a student radical and a critic of capitalism. After raising a family, she had a brief career in social work. The boys pursued their educations at George Washington University. One of them, Joseph, completed his medical education at Tulane University and became an ophthalmologist. His younger brother, Ben, earned a degree in business and after World War II worked on foreign aid through a State Department program to bring business skills to underdeveloped nations. He spent much of his career in Tunisia. The eldest son, Farrar, had earned a degree in civil engineering. He worked in New Orleans with the Sewage and Water Board. Always troubled, he returned to Washington and committed suicide at the age of twenty-four in 1931. The Goldberger family was living on Broad Branch Road in northwest Washington. Farrar's brother Joseph recalled hearing the shot in the next room. The tragedy and the loneliness of a mother with a rapidly emptying nest eventually persuaded Mary to return to her beloved South. She spent the rest of her life in Mississippi.

Until her death in 1959, Mary Goldberger sustained her husband's memory. She cooperated in the production of a short movie about her husband's pellagra work, assisted a young naval officer, Robert Parsons, in writing her husband's biography, and delivered public addresses around the country.[43] According to her son Joseph, Mary, always in need of additional income, hoped to profit from some of these ventures. However, she was largely motivated by a desire to see that her heroic husband was not forgotten. As she had been his helpmate in life, Mary became a kind of professional widow, devoting the remainder of her life to his memory.

As she anxiously and at times impatiently waited for Parsons to finish his biography, Mary Goldberger spoke publicly about her husband's achievements. About two years after Goldberger's death she wrote an article with the encouragement of George McCoy and some of Goldberger's former colleagues at the Hygienic Laboratory. Titled "Science Pigeonholed—Pellagra," the essay became the basis of talks she gave at the University of Texas, Hillman Hospital in Birmingham, Alabama, and the University of Mississippi.[44]

The petite, pretty, bespectacled Mary, her voice betraying her southern roots, stepped to the lectern and recounted her husband's war on pellagra, offering her audiences insight into his soul. In many ways it was the eulogy she had not given on that blustery day in January 1929. It reflected the ideas at the foundation of his beliefs and at the core of their relationship. She began one rough draft with a single sentence that echoed their letters during their courtship and beyond: "All knowledge is sterile not translated into service." She argued that despite all the fine research that produced understanding which made "the earth habitable and life livable," humankind needed "a Moses to lead us into the land of Promise." She said she feared that the work of scientific medicine, such as that done by her husband, might be "pigeonholed for future generations, to be dug out of the ruins of civilization some centuries later." She then told the story of the hunt for the pellagra cure, mentioning her own participation in the filth parties and at times stopping to read directly from letters, including some of her husband's daily correspondence with her. She began at the moment when he returned from his first trip to the South in 1914 and embraced the challenge of pellagra, saying, "The light of battle was in his eyes." Then she described his war—right up to his death.

Mary often concluded her lectures by outlining her own hopes for reform. She said it was a dream of hers to go into one of the "forgotten communities" in the South with a "public health doctor and nurse, a nutritionist, psychologist and social worker, and show the world what can be done with a community." She then lamented, "But that means endowment, and where oh! where is it coming from!" Then, taking a page from her husband, Mary lashed out at those who had the resources to implement change that would save lives: "The chambers of commerce and the babbits of my beloved south *must* realize that there will be no economic regeneration of a country, still bleeding from the wounds of the Civil War, until the 'poor whites' and the ignorant negros [sic] who labor and till the rich soil are helped to a mode of living less benighted than underfed cattle." Turning from her role as aggrieved widow to daughter of the South, she reminded her audience of the credentials entitling her to such a critique: "I have a right to take the South to task, as the daughter of a man whose breath of life was service to his state, and as the widow of a man who risked his all in her service."[45] Goldberger never doubted that he had married a feisty woman.

Three years before Mary died, a version of her remarks was published under the title "Dr. Joseph Goldberger: His Wife's Recollections." She delivered it at the 1955 meeting of the American Dietetic Association in St. Louis, the same group before whom her husband had delivered his last address. In it she added an anecdote she had not used in earlier versions. She told her audience that a few weeks before her husband was taken ill, she and he were out walking and she began to complain about the lack of appreciation and the inadequacy of the honor paid him. Mary recalled that Joseph turned to her, smiling, and said, "I know what I have done, and it is a satisfaction to my soul which no one on earth can take from me."[46]

Was Dr. Joseph Goldberger's soul satisfied at the end of his life? It should have been. In addition to the pathbreaking assault on pellagra, Goldberger's war on disease and deprivation led to victories in the struggle against measles, dengue, typhus, and Schamberg's disease. He was an active combatant against yellow fever, typhoid, and diphtheria. Of all his contributions, the most lasting was his epidemiological research linking how people lived to what made them sick. He made that contribution because he refused to be tied to his desk and insisted on the close observation that can only be done in the community by human investigators with open eyes and open minds.

Yet it was marred satisfaction, for Goldberger died knowing that much more needed to be done to save lives from the scourge of pellagra and that he could not do it. Indeed, no physician could. His frustration is suggested by an encounter he had with the author and scientist Paul De Kruif not long before he left the Hygienic Laboratory for the last time. De Kruif, best known for his 1926 classic, *Microbe Hunters*, a volume of biographies honoring great men of science, wrote a second study, *Hunger Fighters*, that appeared only months before Goldberger's death. An entire chapter of the volume was devoted to Goldberger and was based on interviews De Kruif had conducted at the Hygienic Laboratory. Many years later, in his own autobiography, De Kruif remembered Goldberger as being concerned about who would distribute the yeast that could cure and prevent pellagra among the poorest. "'Who's going to see to that?' asked Goldberger forlornly." After reminding the author that "'pellagra is only ignorance; pellagra is only poverty,'" Goldberger said to De Kruif, "You understand, . . . I'm no economist. I'm only a doctor.'"[47] Their conversation ended, Goldberger headed back to the red brick building and returned to his laboratory.

Epilogue

The final piece of the pellagra puzzle was set in place by researchers at the University of Wisconsin and announced so modestly Joseph Goldberger might have been the scriptwriter. Dr. Conrad A. Elvehjem and his colleagues reported their breakthrough in a letter to the editor of the September 1937 issue of the *Journal of the American Chemical Society*. Elvehjem stated that they found it "most interesting" that black tongue was caused by a deficiency of nicotinic acid, a substance now usually referred to as niacin.[1]

Scientific researchers in agricultural chemistry in Elvehjem's lab had noticed that physicians were curing pellagra with liver extract. They learned that rats on a diet deficient in the P-P factor, as Goldberger had understood it, could be stimulated to grow with nicotinamide and nicotinic acid, both substances synthesized from liver extract. Because there is no rodent equivalent of pellagra, scientists then began working with dogs. After inducing black-tongue disease using a diet developed by Goldberger—yellow corn, casein, cottonseed oil, and mineral supplements—Elvehjem and Carl J. Koehn in the Department of Agricultural Chemistry confirmed that nicotinic acid affected the canines dramatically. Dogs that got a single dose of thirty milligrams were hungry, and with their improved appetite came growth and disappearance of black-tongue lesions. Those that got nicotinamide were cured as well, but much more slowly. Soon scientists at Wisconsin sat down to write their letter to the editor.[2]

Later in 1937 researchers began to use the nicotinic acid treatment on small numbers of pellagrins. In a most dramatic episode at the Duke University hospital, a white farmer with a fifteen-year history of recurrent pellagra was cured. First he was given a diet without the P-P factor as a control. Then, because he would not eat and was beginning to show signs of mental disturbance, nicotinic acid was administered. He received sixty milligrams daily by injection, but his diet was left unchanged. Within a day his appetite returned, and within two days the illusions of persecution he had been suffering disappeared. Within a week he was reacting normally, and his skin lesions began to heal. At the end of two weeks they were gone.[3]

The most impressive research on humans was done in 1938 by Tom Spies at the University of Cincinnati College of Medicine. Beginning conservatively, Spies tested small doses of nicotinic acid on a group of thirteen subjects, none of whom had pellagra. He used a highly diluted solution of nicotinic acid. Doses varied from a few milligrams to two hundred milligrams daily. Those being treated had some flushing and tingling of the skin but no serious side effects. Nor were there adverse reactions when the drug was given intravenously. After establishing that healthy subjects and a few non-pellagrous patients tolerated nicotinic acid well, Spies turned to a selected group of pellagrins. In the test group oral doses and injections of nicotinic acid were administered but not a P-P-rich diet. It worked. Lesions of the mucous membrane, including tongue, mouth, vagina, and anal canal, all healed promptly after treatment. Only pellagrous rashes complicated by secondary infections failed to improve. Three pellagrins died despite the treatment, but they either were already too close to death to be saved or suffered from other conditions as well as pellagra.[4]

Elvehjem identified the curative P-P factor as nicotinic acid in the laboratory. Spies demonstrated that it cured human beings of pellagra and prevented the disease. Now there was no doubt that the poor, even those with limited access to milk, fresh meat, eggs, and green vegetables, could be protected.

Nicotinic acid is part of the vitamin B complex. Physicians all over the United States began efforts to establish a standard dosage. Soon the therapy was being universally administered. Nicotinic acid was effective, and, just as important, it was inexpensive and easily acquired.

Yet another piece of the puzzle slipped into place in 1945. Biochemists at the University of Wisconsin demonstrated that those who blamed corn consumption for pellagra were not as clueless as Goldberger had asserted. Researchers had begun to feed dogs corn grits even as they administered nicotinic acid. They could still cure black tongue, but it took much more nicotinic acid to do so. Dogs fed a diet rich in milk and minerals got less nicotinic acid but grew better faster. In short, corn consumption depressed the level of nicotinic acid retained in the body. White corn, the kind favored in the South, was even more deleterious than yellow corn. The European medical detectives were keener observers than Goldberger had given them credit for being.[5]

A second road not taken by Goldberger would have brought him closer to the biochemical identity of the P-P factor. In 1921 he and Tanner had learned that the Milledgeville patient Oconee Cobb was cured of her symptoms by the amino acid tryptophan. In the spring of 1945 Wisconsin scientists went back to Goldberger's research and supplemented their black-tongued dogs' corn-based diet with tryptophan. Again the dogs resumed normal growth. What did tryptophan have to do with nicotinic acid? Eventually scientists learned that both human beings and animals have the ability to convert tryptophan into nicotinic acid under certain conditions. Pellagra was thus a deficiency of both tryptophan and nicotinic acid. Goldberger had come to the very periphery of the biochemical identity of the P-P factor. However, he did not understand the intervening biochemistry necessary to find the solution. He did not know that other B vitamins, pyridoxine and riboflavin, are involved in the metabolism of tryptophan or that pyridoxine is required to synthesize niacin from tryptophan. Biochemistry was such a new field that Goldberger lacked the tools to analyze fully the ramifications of his research observations.[6]

The discovery of nicotinic acid was significant, but the problem remained of how to get it into the diet of the poor. Efforts to enrich foods with vitamins had begun in the 1920s with the encouragement of distinguished nutritionists, including Elmer V. McCollum, whom Goldberger had so admired. Bread was fortified by most commercial bakers with vitamin D. In 1924 Dr. Harry Steenbock discovered that exposing food to ultraviolet radiation produced vitamin D. Not just bread but milk, meat, cereals, corn, and flour could all be fortified through irradiation. Food enrichment received the endorsement of many prestigious groups, including the American Medical Association.[7]

In early 1941, with Europe already at war, the movement to fortify flour escalated in England and the United States. In Washington the Committee on Medicine of the National Research Council advised that thiamine, part of the vitamin B complex, be added to the white flour purchased for the armed services in order to prevent beriberi. The Food and Drug Administration worked toward establishing recommended nutritional standards for white flour, which were adopted by the Millers' National Federation. The enrichment program included niacin as well as thiamine. A committee of the National Research Council eventually determined that ten times as much niacin as thiamine was necessary if pellagra was to be prevented as well as beriberi. Later another B vitamin, riboflavin, was added. Cost was not an issue. Flour could be vitamin enriched for as little as three cents per twelve-pound bag.[8]

The Russian revolutionary Leon Trotsky once wrote that war was the "locomotive of history." As President Franklin Roosevelt turned his attention to eventual American entry into the war, he linked nutrition to the issue of defense. The administration supported enrichment but made clear that it was not a cure-all for poor diet. After America's entry into the war the U. S. government did not mandate enriching all flour, because of the myriad legal and practical questions it raised. However, in an example of American voluntarism, many millers enriched their flour. In January 1943 a new federal agency, the War Food Administration, required that all commercially produced white bread be fortified with vitamins and minerals for the remainder of the war. The Roosevelt administration found legal justification in its war powers for such an order. Although the mandate expired with the end of the war in 1945, individual states had already begun to mandate flour enrichment.[9] Ironically, South Carolina, whose former chief public health officer James A. Hayne had long been a Goldberger critic, was the first state to mandate enrichment.

Enrichment was a major step toward wiping out pellagra in the United States, but the victory did not occur immediately. In states where it was not mandated, some thought all bread and flour were enriched and did not read the label. Others read the label and objected, because they did not understand the health value of enrichment and thought this was just another scheme to get a few more cents out of consumers. Health departments launched consumer-education campaigns, but these took time, especially in rural America and among the poor. In the South, postwar economic changes resulted in diversification of agriculture, increased industrial development, and gradual unionization. And, much like their fellow middle-class Americans, southerners were swept up in the enthusiasm for vitamin supplements that had begun even before the war. What one scholar has described as "vitamania" swept the country as Americans turned to science, and especially to the vitamins that scientists had discovered, to bring them longer and healthier lives.[10] All contributed to the disappearance of pellagra. By the end of the century, when a medical audience in Charleston, South Carolina, was asked how many had ever seen a case of pellagra, only a few of even the older physicians raised their hands.[11] The last battles in the American theater of Goldberger's war were won in classrooms, on union picket lines, and in supermarkets.

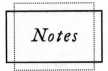

Notes

INTRODUCTION

1. The term "hunger fighters" was coined by Paul De Kruif, *Hunger Fighters* (New York: Harcourt, Brace, 1928).

2. The best volume on pellagra is Elizabeth W. Etheridge, *The Butterfly Caste: A Social History of Pellagra in the South* (Westport, Conn.: Greenwood Publishing, 1972). See also Daphne A. Roe, *A Plague of Corn: The Social History of Pellagra* (Ithaca, N.Y.: Cornell University Press, 1973).

3. Baxter Haynes, "Pellagra from the Viewpoint of the Patient," *International Clinics*, 36th ser., 4 (1926), pp. 76–80.

4. Harry Golden mentioned Goldberger in many publications and even included him in a book about southern Jews; see *Our Southern Landsman* (New York: G. P. Putnam's Sons, 1974), pp. 194–97.

5. Jimmy Carter, *An Hour before Daylight: Memories of a Rural Boyhood* (New York: Simon and Schuster, 2001), p. 53; Pauli Murray, *Proud Shoes: The Story of an American Family*, rev. ed. (Boston: Beacon Press, 1999), pp. 251–54; "It's the Same Old South," lyrics by Ed Eliscu, music by Jay Gorney, recorded by Count Basie with vocal by Jimmy Rushing, Dec. 13, 1940, New York. The song is included on the record *Count Basie Super Chief*, Columbia, 1972.

6. Centers for Disease Control, "Outbreak of Pellagra among Mozambican Refugees—Malawi, 1990," *Morbidity and Mortality Weekly Report* 40 (April 5, 1991), pp. 209–13; Sophie Baquet and Michelle van Her, "A Pellagra Epidemic in Kuito, Angola," www.ennonline.net/fex/10/fa12.html.

1. "ANOTHER POOR JEW"

This chapter's title is taken from an article written by T. Swann Harding for *The Atlantic Monthly* in August 1931, two years after Goldberger's death. Swann's article depicts Goldberger as one of the many impoverished Jewish immigrants who made their adopted home richer by their presence.

1. Elizabeth W. Etheridge, *The Butterfly Caste: A Social History of Pellagra in the South* (Westport, Conn.: Greenwood Publishing, 1972), p. vii, has characterized pellagrins as stigmatized by their membership in this "butterfly caste."

2. Joseph Goldberger, "The Transmissibility of Pellagra: Experimental Attempts at Transmission to the Human Subject," *Public Health Reports* 31 (Nov. 17, 1916), pp. 3159–73.

3. After World War I's political adjustments, Giralt, also known as Giraltovce, was in Czechoslovakia; today it is in Slovakia. On the location of Giralt, see *Vlastivedny slovnik obci na Slovensku* (Dictionary of communities in Slovakia) (Bratislava, Czechoslovakia: Veda, 1977), vol. 1, pp. 392–93. Material on the Jewish community of Giralt was obtained from the Web site http://www.jewishgen.org/shtetlinks/giraltovce/Jewish%20history.htm. For the genealogical information on the Goldberger family I am indebted to several descendants who have labored to piece together family trees, including Eric M. Bloch of Glendale, Wisconsin, who descended from the Guttman (later Goodman) family, into which Samuel Goldberger married.

4. "Passenger Lists of Vessels Arriving at New York, N.Y., 1820–1897," RG 36, M237, roll 472, no. 1505, National Archives. The date 1883 also appears on Samuel Goldberger's citizenship papers, G-431, National Archives & Record Administration, Northeast Region, New York.

5. Friedrich Kapp, *Immigration and the Commissioners of Emigration of the State of New York* (New York: Nation Press, 1870; reprint, New York: Arno Press, 1969), pp. 111–12.

6. The only other volume devoted to Dr. Joseph Goldberger's life is Robert P. Parsons's *Trail to Light: A Biography of Joseph Goldberger* (Indianapolis: Bobbs-Merrill, 1943). The volume lacks any scholarly citations. However, Goldberger's son Joseph recalled in conversations with me that his mother, Mary, spent many hours talking to Parsons in which she provided details of Goldberger's early years. These details were what her husband and other relatives had told her of the family's early years in the United States.

7. Diploma from Male Grammar School no. 4, July 3, 1890, in family collection owned by Dr. Joseph H. Goldberger. A thorough institutional history of the City College of New York is S. Willis Rudy, *The College of the City of New York: A History, 1847–1947* (New York: City College Press, 1949). On the architecture, see Paul David Pearson, *The City College of New York: 150 Years of Academic Architecture* (1997). See also Sherry Gorelick, *City College and the Jewish Poor: Education in New York, 1880–1924* (New Brunswick, N.J.: Rutgers University Press, 1981).

8. Rudy, *College of the City of New York*, p. 33.

9. *The College of the City of New York, Forty-fourth Annual Register*, 1892/93, pp. 16–19, 113.

10. Appointed a police surgeon in November 1907, Murray ascended to chief surgeon in 1918 and retired from the police force in 1926. He was remembered in
obituaries as the physician who sought to improve the health of department
clerks with daily exercises and by opening a departmental dental clinic. In September 1920, when a bomb allegedly thrown by radicals rocked Wall Street, killing thirty persons and injuring an estimated three hundred more, Murray's
medical heroism on the scene saved lives. Certificate of Death for Patrick J. Murray, Department of Health, Borough of Brooklyn, April 3, 1946, certificate no.
7490, New York City Department of Records and Information Services, Municipal Archives. Also see "Dr. P. J. Murray, Hero of Wall Street Bombing," *New
York Times* (April 3, 1946).

11. Flint's father, Austin Flint Sr., was an eminent physician who had been a professor of the principles and practices of medicine and clinical medicine at Bellevue,
a medical college he helped found. By the time Joseph Goldberger entered the
lecture hall to hear him, Austin Flint Jr. had achieved an eminence in his own
right as a professor of physiology and his own son, Austin Flint III, had joined the
faculty in obstetrics. Having studied physiology in Paris with Claude Bernard
and histology with Charles Robin, Flint had prepared himself to be one of the
foremost experts on this side of the Atlantic. He had written a five-volume study,
The Physiology of Man, between 1866 and 1875. See Ronald Elmer Batt, "Austin
Flint, Jr.," in Martin Kaufman, Stuart Galishoff, and Todd Savitt, eds., *Dictionary of American Medical Biography* (Westport, Conn.: Greenwood Press, 1984),
vol. 1, pp. 254–55. Also see entry in Allen Johnson and Dumas Malone, eds., *Dictionary of American Biography* (New York: Scribner's, 1931), vol. 6, pp. 472–73.

12. Parsons, *Trail to Light*, p. 29.

13. "Goldberger Family Tree," compiled by Eric M. Bloch, p. 6. I am grateful to Mr.
Bloch for sharing a copy of this document and the many useful paragraphs it includes on the extended Goldberger family who lived in Perth Amboy, New Jersey.

14. Abraham Flexner, *Medical Education in the United States and Canada: A Re-
port to the Carnegie Foundation for the Advancement of Teaching* (New York:
Carnegie Foundation for the Advancement of Teaching, 1910; reprint, New York:
Arno Press, 1972), p. 275; Jane E. Mottus, "Bellevue Hospital," in Kenneth T.
Jackson, ed., *The Encyclopedia of New York City* (New Haven, Conn.: Yale Uni-
versity Press, 1995), pp. 98–99; Jane E. Mottus, *New York Nightingales: The Emer-
gence of the Nursing Profession at Bellevue and New York Hospital, 1850–1920*
(Ann Arbor, Mich.: UMI Research Press, 1981), p. 18; Kenneth M. Ludmerer,
Learning to Heal: The Development of American Medical Education (New York:
Basic Books, 1985), pp. 146–47; Charles Rosenberg, *The Care of Strangers: The
Rise of America's Hospital System* (New York: Basic Books, 1987), p. 205.

15. Kenneth M. Ludmerer, *A Time to Heal: American Medical Education from the
Turn of the Century to the Era of Managed Care* (New York: Oxford University
Press, 1999), p. 64; Leon Sokoloff, "The Rise and Decline of the Jewish Quota in

Medical School Admissions," *Bulletin of the New York Academy of Medicine* 66 (Nov. 1992), pp. 497–99.

16. Flexner, *Medical Education in the United States and Canada*, p. 270.

17. *Bellevue Hospital Medical College and Carnegie Laboratory*, Spring session 1895, New York University Medical Center Archive.

18. Parsons, *Trail to Light*, pp. 64–65. Early correspondence in the Goldberger Papers in the Southern Historical Collection at the University of North Carolina, Chapel Hill, shows that Goldberger remained in the small office on South Washington Street until he left Wilkes-Barre for his first assignment in the U.S. Marine Hospital Service. His address was listed in the 1898 *Wilkes-Barre Directory*.

19. *Wilkes-Barre of the Present: A Brief Illustrated Sketch* (Wilkes-Barre, Pa.: R. Baur & Son, 1900), p. 25; and *Wilkes-Barre Record Almanac: A Hand Book of Local and General Information, 1907* (Wilkes-Barre, Pa.: *Wilkes-Barre Record*), pp. 42–43.

20. Joseph Goldberger, "Alcoholism," *Transactions of the Luzerne County Medical Society* 6 (1898), pp. 202–6. Goldberger's first paper, delivered earlier that year and published in the same volume, was "The Use of the Saline Solution," pp. 17–26.

21. On Goldberger's earnings in his first two years, see Parsons, *Trail to Light*, pp. 66–67. Goldberger's son Joseph Herman Goldberger shared his recollections in an interview with me in Austin, Texas, on August 11, 1993.

22. Van Reypen to Goldberger, May 3, 1898, Joseph Goldberger Papers, Southern Historical Collection, University of North Carolina Library, Chapel Hill, box 1, folder 1; also see Parsons, *Trail to Light*, pp. 45, 78–79. On the increase of the force, see *Secretary of the Navy's Annual Report for 1898* (see Web site at www.history.navy.mil/wars/spanam/sm98-13.htm). Goldwin Smith is quoted in Albert Isaac Slomovitz, *The Fighting Rabbis: Jewish Military Chaplains and American History* (New York: New York University Press, 1999), p. 27. On Jews' supposed aversion to physical labor, see Le Roy Eltinge, *Psychology of War* (Fort Leavenworth, Kans.: Press of the Army Service Schools, 1915), as quoted in ibid., p. 35. On the attitude of the U.S. Naval Academy, see Leonard Dinnerstein, *Anti-Semitism in America* (New York: Oxford University Press, 1994), p. 87.

23. Walter Wyman to Goldberger, July 18, 1899, Goldberger Papers, box 1, folder 1. The exam results for 1899 were announced in the *Annual Report of the Supervising Surgeon-General of the Marine-Hospital Service of the United States for the Fiscal Year 1900* (Washington, D.C.: Government Printing Office, 1900), pp. 27–28. An account of the ordeal is in Victor Heiser, M.D., *An American Doctor's Odyssey, Adventures in Forty-five Countries* (New York: W.W. Norton, 1936), pp. 10–12.

24. For his first post, see Wyman to Goldberger, July 26, 1899, Goldberger Papers, box 1, folder 1. On the inspection of immigrants, see Alan M. Kraut, *Silent Travelers: Germs, Genes, and the "Immigrant Menace"* (New York: Basic Books, 1994), pp. 62–63.

25. Wyman to Goldberger, April 24, 1900, and Richardson to Goldberger, June 6, 1900, Goldberger Papers, box 1, folder 1.

26. Henry Plauché Dart, "Edgar Howard Farrar: A Sketch of His Life and Times," memorial lecture delivered before the Supreme Court of Louisiana, Oct. 2, 1922 (New Orleans: Andrée Printery, 1922), pp. 4–5.

27. "Widow of Dr. Goldberger Dies in Biloxi Home," *Daily Herald, Gulfport and Biloxi* (Sept. 12, 1959).

28. Richardson to Goldberger, Dec. 29, 1905, Goldberger Papers, box 1, folder 4.

29. Dart, *Edgar Howard Farrar*, pp. 4–5.

30. Ibid., p. 7.

31. For the trip to the opera, see Mary to Goldberger, March 5, 1906, Goldberger Papers, box 1, folder 5; also see Parsons, *Trail to Light*, p. 132. Goldberger reminisced, "Six weeks ago as I write, I kissed my Mary for the first time"; Goldberger to Mary, Jan. 25, 1906, Goldberger Papers, box 1, folder 5. Mary's recollection of the proposal was described to the author by her son Joseph in a note, December 15, 2002.

32. For the Goldbergers' reaction, see the letter transcribed in Parsons, *Trail to Light*, pp. 133–34. A contemporary study of the phenomenon published in 1920 found that between 1908 and 1912, a peak period of immigration from eastern Europe, only 1.17 percent of first- and second-generation Jewish immigrants married non-Jews, the lowest of any major group. However, the same study found that the general rate of intermarriage among newcomers of all groups in that period increased from 11 percent among first-generation white male immigrants to about 33 percent among second-generation white male immigrants. See Julius Drachsler, *Democracy and Assimilation: The Blending of Immigrant Heritages in America* (New York: Macmillan, 1920), pp. 121, 264. Sociologists working in the early twentieth century observed that "mixed marriages increase among Jews as they become Americanized, a process which, on the whole, depends on the length of their residence in America." See Arthur Ruppin, *The Jews in the Modern World* (London: Macmillan, 1934; reprint, New York: Arno Press, 1973), p. 321. According to one study based on marriage records in New York City for the period 1908–1912, "mixed marriages were fewest among Jews from Russia and Poland, more frequent among those from Hungary and Holland, and most frequent among German and French Jews," who had experienced secular society in their own countries prior to departure for the United States. See Drachsler, *Democracy and Assimilation*, p. 121. See also the companion volume by Drachsler, *Intermarriage in New York City: A Statistical Study of the Amalgamation of European Peoples* (New York: Columbia University Press, 1921). An excellent volume on interfaith marriages is Anne C. Rose, *Beloved Strangers: Interfaith Families in Nineteenth-Century America* (Cambridge, Mass.: Harvard University Press, 2001).

33. Joseph Goldberger to Leo Goldberger, Jan. 19, 1906, reprinted in Parsons, *Trail to Light*, p. 133.

34. Ibid., p. 134.

35. Joseph Goldberger to Leo Goldberger, Jan. 26, 1906, reprinted in Parsons, *Trail to Light*, pp. 134–35.
36. Walter Wyman to Edgar Howard Farrar, Dec. 30, 1905, Goldberger Papers, box 1, folder 4.
37. Thomas Farrar Richardson to Goldberger, Dec. 29, 1905, and Thomas Farrar Richardson to Edgar Howard Farrar, Dec. 29, 1905, Goldberger Papers, box 1, folder 4.
38. Charles Levy to Edgar Howard Farrar, n.d. [Feb. 1906], Goldberger Papers, box 1, folder 5.
39. Ibid.
40. Ibid.
41. Ibid.
42. Goldberger to Mary, fragment, n.d. [c. late Jan. 1906], Goldberger Papers, box 1, folder 6; Goldberger to Mary, Jan. 27, 1906, Goldberger Papers, box 1, folder 5.
43. Goldberger to Mary, Jan. 27, 1906, Goldberger Papers, box 1, folder 5.
44. Benny Kraut, "Reform Judaism and the Unitarian Challenge," in Jonathan D. Sarna, ed., *The American Jewish Experience* (New York: Holmes & Meier, 1986), p. 89. See also Benny Kraut, "A Unitarian Rabbi? The Case of Solomon H. Sonnenschein," in Todd M. Endelman, ed., *Jewish Apostasy in the Modern World* (New York: Holmes & Meier, 1987), pp. 272–308. Lewis Godlove to Rabbi Solomon H. Sonnenschein as quoted by Kraut, "Reform Judaism and the Unitarian Challenge," p. 89.
45. For a discussion of Unitarianism, see Sidney E. Ahlstrom, *A Religious History of the American People* (New Haven, Conn.: Yale University Press, 1972), pp. 388–402.
46. *Christian Register* (Jan. 11, 1906); Goldberger to Mary, fragment, n.d. [c. late Jan. 1906], Goldberger Papers, box 1, folder 6.
47. Ibid.
48. Ibid.
49. Ibid.
50. Ibid.
51. Mary to Goldberger, Jan. 24, 1906, Goldberger Papers, box 1, folder 5.
52. Ibid.
53. Goldberger to Mary, fragment, n.d. [c. Feb. 20, 1906], Goldberger Papers, box 1, folder 6.
54. Goldberger to Mary, Feb. 24, 1906, Goldberger Papers, box 1, folder 5.
55. Goldberger to Mary, Feb. 2, 1906, Goldberger Papers, box 1, folder 5.
56. Edgar Howard Farrar to Dr. Jos. Goldberg [*sic*], telegram, Feb. 16, 1906, and Edgar Howard Farrar to Goldberger, Feb. 16, 1906, Goldberger Papers, box 1, folder 5.
57. Goldberger's telegram is not among his papers. He told Mary what he had wired to her father in his letter to her on the evening of February 16. Goldberger to Mary, Feb. 16, 1906, Goldberger Papers, box 1, folder 5. Goldberger to Edgar

Howard Farrar, Feb. 16, 1906, Goldberger Papers, box 1, folder 5. *State and Federal Quarantine Powers: An Address Delivered by Edgar H. Farrar, Esq., of New Orleans before the Quarantine Convention Held at Mobile on February 9, 1898,* Historic New Orleans Collection, Kemper and Leila Williams Foundation, New Orleans.

58. Goldberger to Mary, Feb. 16, 1906, Goldberger Papers, box 1, folder 5.

59. Ibid.; Goldberger to Mary, Feb. 24, 1906, ibid.

60. Goldberger to Mary, Feb. 24, 1906, ibid.

61. Edgar Howard Farrar to Goldberger, Feb. 23, 1906, letter cited in full in Parsons, *Trail to Light,* p. 142.

62. Goldberger to Mary, Feb. 21, 1906, and April 6, 1906, Goldberger Papers, box 1, folder 5.

63. Receipt from Office of Recorder of Births, Marriages, and Deaths, Parish of Orleans, April 20, 1906, Goldberger Papers, box 1, folder 5.

2. MEDICAL MYSTERIES

1. *Sunday Star* (May 6, 1906), p. 1.

2. Ibid.

3. See William Osler, *The Principles and Practice of Medicine,* 6th ed. (New York: D. Appleton, 1905), pp. 57–105. Today the fever is known to result from the release of cytokines as a part of the immune system's response.

4. *Evening Star* (June 26, 1906), p. 12; J. Fraise Richard, letter to the editor, *Evening Star* (July 2, 1906), p. 3; *Evening Star* (July 12, 1906), p. 12.

5. *Evening Star* (July 24, 1906), p. 2.

6. Kenneth F. Kiple, ed., *The Cambridge World History of Human Disease* (New York: Cambridge University Press, 1993), pp. 1100–1. There is a rich literature on yellow fever in the United States, especially in the South. Some recent volumes include Margaret Humphreys, *Yellow Fever and the South* (New Brunswick, N.J.: Rutgers University Press, 1992); John H. Ellis, *Yellow Fever & Public Health in the New South* (Lexington: University Press of Kentucky, 1992); Khaled J. Bloom, *The Mississippi Valley's Great Yellow Fever Epidemic of 1878* (Baton Rouge: Louisiana State University Press, 1993); and Jo Ann Carrigan, *The Saffron Scourge: A History of Yellow Fever in Louisiana, 1796–1905* (Lafayette: Center for Louisiana Studies, 1994).

7. Walter Wyman to Goldberger, April 19, 1902, Joseph Goldberger Papers, Southern Historical Collection, University of North Carolina Library, Chapel Hill, box 1, folder 2.

8. Robert P. Parsons, *Trail to Light: A Biography of Joseph Goldberger* (Indianapolis: Bobbs-Merrill, 1943), p. 104.

9. Frank M. Chapman, "A Naturalist's Journey around Vera Cruz and Tampico," *National Geographic* 25 (May 1914), p. 536.

10. *Register of the Department of State* (Washington, D.C.: Government Printing

Office, Nov. 10, 1913), p. 96. Also see the consular card for Tampico on file at the Department of State Historian's Office. These cards listing consular officials are organized by post and were handwritten during the 1960s.

11. Marlatt to Goldberger, July 26, 1902, Goldberger Papers, box 1, folder 2.

12. Parsons, *Trail to Light*, pp. 110–11.

13. Kiple, ed., *Cambridge World History of Human Disease*, pp. 855–56; Osler, *Principles and Practice of Medicine*, pp. 10–15; and Margaret Humphreys, *Malaria: Poverty, Race, and Public Health in the United States* (Baltimore: Johns Hopkins University Press, 2001), p. 46.

14. A brief biography of Rosenau is in Martin Kaufman, Stuart Galishoff, and Todd L. Savitt, eds., *Dictionary of American Medical Biography* (Westport, Conn.: Greenwood Press, 1984), vol. 2, pp. 649–50.

15. Rosenau to Goldberger, Dec. 17, 1903, Goldberger Papers, box 1, folder 3.

16. Wyman to Goldberger, March 22, 1904, and March 23, 1904, Goldberger Papers, box 1, folder 3.

17. Wyman to Goldberger, March 23, 1904., ibid.

18. Ibid.; and Wyman to Goldberger, April 8, 1904, Goldberger Papers, box 1, folder 3.

19. Goldberger to Wyman, n.d. [c. April or May 1904], Goldberger Papers, box 1, folder 3.

20. Ibid.

21. Ibid.

22. Charles Wardell Stiles and Joseph Goldberger, "A Young Stage of the American Hookworm—*Nector americanus* (Stiles, 1902)—8 to 12 Days after Skin Infection in Rabbits and Dogs," *American Medicine* 11 (Jan. 18, 1906), pp. 63–65.

23. Carrigan, *Saffron Scourge*, pp. 168–69.

24. Ibid., pp. 170–75.

25. Ibid., p. 176.

26. *State and Federal Quarantine Powers: An Address Delivered by Edgar H. Farrar, Esq., of New Orleans before the Quarantine Convention Held at Mobile on February 9, 1898*, Historic New Orleans Collection, Kemper and Leila Williams Foundation, New Orleans.

27. Henry Plauché Dart, *Edgar Howard Farrar: A Sketch of His Life and Times, Delivered before the Supreme Court of Louisiana, Monday, October 2, 1922* (New Orleans: Andrée Printery, 1922), pp. 8–9.

28. *Daily Picayune* (Aug. 5, 23, 1905).

29. *Daily Picayune* (Aug. 4, 1905).

30. *Daily Picayune* (Aug. 5, 1905).

31. *Report of the Louisiana State Board of Health for 1904–1905 to the General Assembly of the State of Louisiana*, pp. 45–48.

32. Rosenau to Goldberger, July 19, 1906, Goldberger Papers, box 1, folder 5.

33. Ibid.

34. Goldberger to Mary, July 23, 1906, and Sept. 3, 1906, Goldberger Papers, box 1, folder 5.

35. Joseph Goldberger, "Sanitary Survey of the Drainage Basin of the Potomac River," *Hygienic Laboratory Bulletin* 35 (1907), pp. 229–53. Goldberger also conducted a study of the bottled water sold in Washington to see if vendors were selling contaminated water; see Joseph Goldberger, "Sanitary Inspection of the Table Waters Vended in Washington, D.C.," *Hygienic Laboratory Bulletin* 35 (1907), pp. 153–64. Also see Joseph Goldberger, "Typhoid 'Bacillus-Carriers,'" *Hygienic Laboratory Bulletin* 35 (1907), pp. 167–74. For the quotation, see Goldberger, "Sanitary Survey," p. 253.

36. Goldberger, "Sanitary Inspection of Table Waters," pp. 160, 162, 153.

37. Goldberger, "Typhoid 'Bacillus-Carriers,'" pp. 167, 168.

38. For a description of the Typhoid Mary case, see Judith Walzer Leavitt, *Typhoid Mary: Captive to the Public's Health* (Boston: Beacon Press, 1996); and Alan M. Kraut, *Silent Travelers: Germs, Genes, and the "Immigrant Menace"* (New York: Basic Books, 1994), pp. 96–104.

39. Certificate of Live Birth no. 144.641, June 28, 1907, Department of Health, Government of the District of Columbia; Lazard to Goldberger, July 8, 1907, and Wyman to Goldberger, July 26, 1907, Goldberger Papers, box 1, folder 7.

40. Osler, *Principles and Practice of Medicine*, p. 157.

41. George Walter McCoy, in Jeannette Barry, comp., *Notable Contributions to Research by Public Health Service Scientists; a Bibliography to 1940*, PHS publication no. 752 (Washington, D.C.: U.S. Department of Health, Education, and Welfare, 1960), pp. 55–62; also see George Walter McCoy, personnel file, U.S. Public Health Service. Wyman to Goldberger, July 27, 1907, Goldberger Papers, box 1, folder 7.

42. Goldberger to Mary, July 30, 1907, Goldberger Papers, box 1, folder 7.

43. Joseph Goldberger and George W. McCoy, "Dengue Fever as Observed in Brownsville, Tex., August, 1907," *Public Health Reports* 22 (Dec. 6, 1907), p. 1757; Goldberger to Mary, Aug. 2, 1907, Goldberger Papers, box 1, folder 7.

44. Osler, *Principles and Practice of Medicine*, pp. 237, 1762.

45. "Inspection at Brownsville," *Daily Express* (San Antonio) (Aug. 2, 1907), p. 1.

46. Goldberger and McCoy, "Dengue Fever as Observed in Brownsville," pp. 1757–58.

47. "Louisiana Has Not Quarantined against Texas," *Daily Express* (San Antonio) (Aug. 8, 1907), p. 5.

48. Goldberger to Mary, Aug. 3, 1907, Goldberger Papers, box 1, folder 7.

49. "Is Pleased with Conditions at Brownsville," *Daily Express* (San Antonio) (Aug. 11, 1907), p. 2.

50. "Oil on Water Sure Death to the Mosquitoes," *Daily Express* (San Antonio) (Aug. 23, 1907), p. 6.

51. Editorial, *Daily Express* (San Antonio) (Aug. 28, 1907), p. 4.

52. Ralph Chester Williams, *The United States Public Health Service* (Washington, D.C.: Commissioned Officers Association of the United States Public Health Service, 1951), pp. 547–48.

53. Goldberger and McCoy, "Dengue Fever as Observed in Brownsville," pp. 1757–62.

54. He and Stiles eventually published "Observations on Two New Parasitic Trematode Worms: *Homalogaster philippinensis, Agamodistomum nanus,*" *Hygienic Laboratory Bulletin* 40 (May 25, 1908), pp. 23–33, based on their work in the lab at this time.

55. Jay F. Schamberg, "An Epidemic of a Peculiar and Unfamiliar Disease of the Skin," *Philadelphia Medical Journal* (July 6, 1901), pp. 5–6. Dr. Jay F. Schamberg and Joseph Goldberger were very much contemporaries. Like Goldberger's friend and mentor Milton Rosenau, Schamberg was a Philadelphian. The son of Gustav Schamberg and Emma Frank, Jay Schamberg was born in 1870. Only four years older than Goldberger, he had married May Ida Bamberger a year before Goldberger wed Mary Farrar. Educated at the University of Pennsylvania, Schamberg earned his medical degree there in 1892 and interned there the following year. He then spent a year in Europe studying dermatology in Vienna, Paris, Berlin, Hamburg, and London. Upon his return, he set up a medical practice in Philadelphia and lectured on infectious eruptive fevers at the University of Pennsylvania. He was also on the dermatology faculty of the Philadelphia Polyclinic College for Graduates in Medicine (later the University of Pennsylvania). Schamberg was in the process of becoming a renowned dermatologist. Biographical information on him can be found in Kaufman, Galishoff, and Savitt, eds., *Dictionary of American Medical Biography,* vol. 2, pp. 664–65.

56. Joseph Goldberger and Jay F. Schamberg, "Epidemic of an Urticarioid Dermatitis due to a Small Mite (*Pediculoides ventricosus*) in the Straw of Mattresses," *Public Health Reports* 24 (July 9, 1909), p. 974. Goldberger and Schamberg published separate final papers on the episode. See Joseph Goldberger, "The Straw Itch (*Dermatitis schambergi*): A Disease New to American Physicians," *Public Health Reports* 25 (June 10, 1910), pp. 779–84; and Jay F. Schamberg, "Grain-Itch (*Acaro-dermatitis urticarioides*): A New Disease in This Country," *Journal of Cutaneous Diseases* 18 (1910).

57. Schamberg to Goldberger, June 23, 1909, Goldberger Papers, box 1, folder 9.

3. DISEASE AND DUTY

1. Edgar Howard Farrar to Mary, April 16, 1909, Joseph Goldberger Papers, Southern Historical Collection, University of North Carolina Library, Chapel Hill, box 1, folder 9. See Craig H. Roell, "The Piano in the American Home," in Jessie H. Foy and Karal Ann Marling, eds., *The Arts in the American Home, 1890–1930* (Knoxville: University of Tennessee Press, 1994), pp. 85–110; Arthur L. Loesser, *Men, Women, and Pianos* (New York: Simon and Schuster, 1954); and Andrew R. Heinze, *Adapting to Abundance: Jewish Immigrants, Mass Consumption, and the Search for American Identity* (New York: Columbia University Press, 1990), p. 138. See also Richard K. Lieberman, *Steinway & Sons* (New Haven, Conn.: Yale University Press, 1995).

2. William Osler, *The Principles and Practice of Medicine*, 6th ed. (New York: D. Appleton, 1905), pp. 105–9.
3. Mark H. Beers and Robert Berkow, *The Merck Manual of Diagnosis and Therapy*, 17th ed. (Whitehouse Station, N.J.: Merck Research Laboratories, 1999), pp. 1228–29.
4. Wyman to Goldberger, Nov. 8, 1909, Goldberger Papers, box 1, folder 9. John Anderson was dark-haired and handsome with a small mustache covering his upper lip. Only a year older than Goldberger, he was born in Fredericksburg, Virginia, on March 14, 1873. A good son of the South, he graduated from the University of Virginia Medical School, and then pursued postgraduate studies in bacteriology at Vienna, Paris, and Liverpool's School of Tropical Medicine. In 1898 he joined the USMHS. In 1902 he was made assistant director of the Hygienic Laboratory, and on October 1, 1909, he succeeded Milton Rosenau as the laboratory's director, a post he would hold until 1915, when he resigned to become the director of the Research and Biological Laboratories of E. R. Squibb and Sons. Anderson was an expert on Rocky Mountain spotted fever. Biographical information on him is available at the National Institutes of Health Web site, http://www.nih.gov/about/almanac97/chapt1/dirbio.htm. The best work on the history of Rocky Mountain spotted fever is Victoria A. Harden, *Rocky Mountain Spotted Fever: A History of a Twentieth-Century Disease* (Baltimore: Johns Hopkins University Press, 1990).
5. Goldberger to Mary, Nov. 14, 1909, Goldberger Papers, box 1, folder 9.
6. John F. Anderson and Joseph Goldberger, "On the Relation of Rocky Mountain Spotted Fever to the Typhus Fever of Mexico," *Public Health Reports* 24 (Dec. 10, 1909), pp. 1861–62; Goldberger to Mary, Dec. 4, 1909, Goldberger Papers, box 1, folder 9.
7. Goldberger to Mary, Dec. 7, 1909, Goldberger Papers, box 1, folder 9.
8. Goldberger to Mary, Dec. 10, 1909, Goldberger Papers, box 1, folder 9.
9. Goldberger to Mary, Dec. 12, 1909, Goldberger Papers, box 1, folder 9. The preliminary note he refers to was published as John F. Anderson and Joseph Goldberger, "A Note on the Etiology of 'Tabardillo,' the Typhus Fever of Mexico," *Public Health Reports* 24 (Dec. 24, 1909), pp. 1941–42.
10. Goldberger to Mary, Dec. 17, 1909, and Dec. 26, 1909, Goldberger Papers, box 1, folder 9.
11. Goldberger personal chart of illness [1910], typescript, pp. 1–2, Goldberger Papers, box 1, folder 10.
12. Ibid., p. 3.
13. Goldberger to Mary, January 22, 1910, Goldberger Papers, box 1, folder 10.
14. John F. Anderson and Joseph Goldberger, "On the Infectivity of Tabardillo or Mexican Typhus for Monkeys and Studies on Its Mode of Transmission," *Public Health Reports* 25 (Feb. 18, 1910), pp. 177–85; John F. Anderson and Joseph Goldberger, "On the Etiology of Tabardillo or Mexican Typhus: An Experimental Investigation," *Journal of Medical Research* 22 (1910), pp. 469–81.

15. Goldberger to Mary, Dec. 4, 1909, Goldberger Papers, box 1, folder 9.
16. Goldberger to Mary, Dec. 9, 1909, Goldberger Papers, box 1, folder 9.
17. The two-thousand-dollar annual salary is an estimate calculated on the compensation scale listed in government regulations for 1897 and 1920; see *Revised Regulations for the Government of the United States Marine-Hospital Service, Approved November 29, 1897* (Washington, D.C.: Government Printing Office, 1897), p. 14, and *Regulations for the Government of the United States Public Health Service, Approved August 29, 1920* (Washington, D.C.: Government Printing Office, 1920), p. 32. Goldberger to Mary, Dec. 9, 1909, Goldberger Papers, box 1, folder 9.
18. Goldberger to Mary, Dec. 21, 1909, Goldberger Papers, box 1, folder 9.
19. Although Joseph often referred to the forthcoming child as "little Mary" during the pregnancy, he was delighted with the son who bore his first name.
20. Nathan E. Brill, "An Acute Infectious Disease of Unknown Origin: A Clinical Study Based on 221 Cases," *American Journal of the Medical Sciences* (April 1910), p. 488. Brill had published two brief reports discussing the resemblance of the disease he observed to typhoid fever much earlier; see Nathan E. Brill, "A Study of 17 Cases of a Disease Clinically Resembling Typhoid Fever, but without the Widal Reaction; Together with a Short Review of the Present Status of Serodiagnosis of Typhoid Fever," *New York Medical Journal* 67 (Jan. 8, 15, 1898), pp. 48, 77.
21. Wyman to Goldberger, May 27, 1910, Goldberger Papers, box 1, folder 10.
22. Nathan E. Brill, "Pathological and Experimental Data Derived from a Further Study of an Acute Infectious Disease of Unknown Origin," *American Journal of the Medical Sciences* (Aug. 1911), pp. 196–218. Anderson and Goldberger described their research in "The Relation of So-Called Brill's Disease to Typhus Fever," *Public Health Reports* 27 (Feb. 2, 1912), pp. 149–60. The research is also described in a coauthored paper that Goldberger read at the New York Academy of Medicine, March 19, 1912, and then published; see John F. Anderson and Joseph Goldberger, "The Experimental Proof of the Identity of Brill's Disease and Typhoid Fever," *New York Medical Journal* (May 11, 1912), pp. 976–81.
23. Wyman to Goldberger, October 17, 1911, Goldberger Papers, box 2, folder 12.
24. Goldberger to Mary, Nov. 10, 1911, and letter marked "Confidential" from Goldberger to Mary, Nov. 22, 1911, Goldberger Papers, box 2, folder 13; Goldberger to Mary, Jan. 5, 1912, Goldberger Papers, box 2, folder 14.
25. Goldberger to Mary, Nov. 25, 1911, Goldberger Papers, box 2, folder 13; Nathan Brill, letter to the editor, *Journal of the American Medical Association* 57 (Dec. 2, 1911), p. 1854.
26. Goldberger to Mary, Dec. 14, 1911, Goldberger Papers, box 2, folder 13.
27. Anderson and Goldberger, "Relation of So-Called Brill's Disease to Typhus Fever," p. 154; and Anderson and Goldberger, "Experimental Proof of the Identity of Brill's Disease and Typhoid Fever."

28. Joseph Goldberger, "Typhus Fever—a Brief Note on Its Prevention," *Public Health Reports* 29, no. 18 (May 1, 1914), pp. 1068–73.

29. Goldberger to Mary, Nov. 26, 1911, Goldberger Papers, box 2, folder 13.

30. Ibid.; Goldberger to Mary, Dec. 11, 1911, Goldberger Papers, box 2, folder 13.

31. Goldberger to Mary, Jan. 10, 1912, Goldberger Papers, box 2, folder 14.

32. Goldberger to Mary, Dec. 6, 1911, and Dec. 10, 1911, Goldberger Papers, box 2, folder 13.

33. Goldberger to Mary, Dec. 10, 1911, Dec. 15, 1911, and Dec. 16, 1911, Goldberger Papers, box 2, folder 13. In modern times circumcision has been widely accepted as a sanitary measure believed by many physicians to have preventive value against penile cancer and sexually transmitted disease. See David L. Goleaher, *Circumcision: A History of the World's Most Controversial Surgery* (New York: Basic Books, 2000) pp. 125–59.

34. Goldberger to Mary, Jan. 5, 1912, Goldberger Papers, box 2, folder 14.

35. Beers and Berkow, *Merck Manual*, pp. 2320–21; Osler, *Principles and Practice of Medicine*, p. 145.

36. Goldberger to Mary, Sept. 12, 1911, Goldberger Papers, box 2, folder 12.

37. John F. Anderson and Joseph Goldberger, "Experimental Measles in the Monkey: A Preliminary Note," *Public Health Reports* 26 (June 9, 1911), pp. 847–48; John F. Anderson and Joseph Goldberger, "The Period of Infectivity of the Blood in Measles," *Journal of the American Medical Association* 57 (July 8, 1911), pp. 113–14; Joseph Goldberger and John F. Anderson, "An Experimental Demonstration of the Presence of the Virus of Measles in the Mixed Buccal and Nasal Secretions," *Journal of the American Medical Association* 57 (Aug. 5, 1911), pp. 476–78; also, in that volume, "The Nature of the Virus of Measles," pp. 971–72; John F. Anderson and Joseph Goldberger, "The Infectivity of the Secretions and the Desqualming Scales of Measles," *Journal of the American Medical Association* 57 (Nov. 11, 1911), pp. 1612–13.

38. Goldberger to Mary, Dec. 14, 1911, Goldberger Papers, box 2, folder 13.

39. Rupert Blue to Goldberger, March 8, 1913, Goldberger Papers, box 2, folder 15.

40. Goldberger to Mary, Oct. 28, 1910, and Nov. 4, 1910, Goldberger Papers, box 1, folder 11.

41. Goldberger to Mary, Nov. 27, 1910, Goldberger Papers, box 1, folder 11.

42. Goldberger to Mary, Dec. 2, 1910, Goldberger Papers, box 1, folder 11.

43. Ibid.

44. Goldberger to Mary, Dec. 12, 1910, and Dec. 14, 1910, Goldberger Papers, box 1, folder 11.

45. *New Orleans Daily Picayune* (Nov. 2, 1911). The term "common malefactor" was used by Henry Plauché Dart in *Edgar Howard Farrar: A Sketch of His Life and Times, Delivered before the Supreme Court of Louisiana, Monday, October 2, 1922* (New Orleans: Andrée Printery, 1922), p. 21.

46. The letter is reprinted in Dart, *Edgar Howard Farrar*, pp. 21–22.

47. Goldberger to Mary, Nov. 7, 1911, Goldberger Papers, box 2, folder 13; Goldberger to Mary, Feb. 10, 1912, Goldberger Papers, box 2, folder 14.
48. Goldberger to Mary, Feb. 12, 1912, Goldberger Papers, box 2, folder 14; Rupert Blue to Goldberger, July 28, 1913, and Nov. 7, 1913, Goldberger Papers, box 2, folder 15.
49. Blue to Goldberger, Dec. 1, 1913, and Dec. 2, 1913, Goldberger Papers, box 2, folder 15.
50. Osler, *Principles and Practice of Medicine*, pp. 192–210; Beers and Berkow, *Merck Manual*, pp. 2303–6. Also see Kenneth F. Kiple, ed., *The Cambridge World History of Human Disease* (New York: Cambridge University Press, 1993), pp. 680–83.
51. *Detroit News* (Nov. 26, 1913), pp. 1, 2.
52. Joseph Goldberger, C. L. Williams, and F. W. Hachtel, "Report of an Investigation of Diphtheria Carriers," *Hygienic Laboratory Bulletin* 101 (Aug. 1915), pp. 29–41.
53. Robert P. Parsons, *Trail to Light: A Biography of Joseph Goldberger* (Indianapolis: Bobbs-Merrill, 1943), pp. 260–73.
54. Blue to Goldberger, Feb. 7, 1914, Goldberger Papers, box 3, folder 16.
55. Ibid.

4. Scourge of the South

1. The classic works on this period in southern history are C. Vann Woodward, *Origins of the New South, 1877–1913* (Baton Rouge: Louisiana State University Press, 1951); and George Brown Tindall, *The Emergence of the New South, 1913–1945* (Baton Rouge: Louisiana State University Press, 1967). The volume that best reflects current scholarship and offers the best overview of the South in this era is Edward L. Ayers, *The Promise of the New South: Life after Reconstruction* (New York: Oxford University Press, 1992). Also quite useful are Howard N. Rabinowitz, *The First New South, 1865–1920* (Arlington Heights, Ill.: Harlan Davidson, 1992); and Dewey W. Grantham, *The South in Modern America: A Region at Odds* (New York: HarperCollins, 1994). See also Pete Daniel, *Standing at the Crossroads: Southern Life in the Twentieth Century* (New York: Hill and Wang, 1986). A fine social history of the New South is William A. Link, *The Paradox of Southern Progressivism, 1880–1930* (Chapel Hill: University of North Carolina Press, 1992). The best discussion of intellectual changes in southern thinking is Daniel Joseph Singal, *The War Within: From Victorian to Modernist Thought in the South, 1919–1945* (Chapel Hill: University of North Carolina Press, 1982).
2. Rabinowitz, *First New South*, pp. 7–8.
3. A classic study of southern geography and economic conditions is Rupert B. Vance, *Human Geography of the South: A Study in Regional Resources and Human Adequacy* (Chapel Hill: University of North Carolina Press, 1935). On the South's poor whites, see J. Wayne Flynt, *Dixie's Forgotten People: The South's Poor Whites* (Bloomington: Indiana University Press, 1980); and J. Wayne Flynt,

Poor but Proud: Alabama's Poor Whites (Tuscaloosa: University of Alabama Press, 1989). Peonage among both white and black laborers is well covered by Pete Daniel, *The Shadow of Slavery* (New York: Oxford University Press, 1972). For an overview of southern economic development after the Civil War, see Gavin Wright, *Old South, New South: Revolutions in the Southern Economy since the Civil War* (New York: Basic Books, 1986).

4. C. H. Lavinder, "The Prevalence and Geographic Distribution of Pellagra in the United States," *Public Health Reports* 27 (Dec. 13, 1912), p. 2080; George M. Niles, "Pellagraphobia: A Word of Caution," *Journal of the American Medical Association* 58 (May 4, 1912), pp. 1341–42.

5. The best description of early work on pellagra and the finest book on the disease overall is Elizabeth W. Etheridge, *The Butterfly Caste: A Social History of Pellagra in the South* (Westport, Conn.: Greenwood Publishing, 1972). Etheridge mentions the changing of the guard when Lavinder departs at his own request (p. 65).

6. The neck rash was named for Don Gaspar Casal, a physician in the Spanish court who identified the disease in 1735 after observing it among peasants in the town of Oviedo in the province of Asturias. He described it as a "disgusting skin disease or *mal de la rosa*" and thought it a peculiar form of leprosy, although he also compared it to scurvy. Casal speculated that it was caused by humidity, fogs, temperature changes, winds, and poor diet. For the general description of the effects of the disease, see Elizabeth W. Etheridge, "Pellagra," in Kenneth F. Kiple, ed., *The Cambridge World History of Human Disease* (New York: Cambridge University Press, 1993), pp. 918–19.

7. For a fine review of this literature, see Etheridge, *Butterfly Caste*, chap. 1.

8. R. M. Grimm, "Pellagra: A Report on Its Epidemiology," *Public Health Reports* 28 (March 7, 14, 1913), p. 513.

9. J. F. Siler, P. E. Garrison, and W. J. MacNeal, *Pellagra: First Progress Report of the Thompson-McFadden Pellagra Commission of the New York Post-graduate Medical School and Hospital* (New York, 1913).

10. Etheridge, *Butterfly Caste*, p. 53; George A. Zeller, "Pellagra—Its Recognition in Illinois and the Measures Taken to Control It," *Transactions of the National Conference on Pellagra Held under the Auspices of the South Carolina State Board of Health at State Hospital for the Insane, Columbia, S.C., November 3 and 4, 1909* (Columbia, S.C.: State Co., 1910), p. 46.

11. *Illinois State Board of Health Monthly Bulletin* 5 (Oct. 1909), pp. 326, 457, 461. The copies, with Goldberger's underlining and comments, are in the Goldberger Collection in the Medical History Division of the National Library of Medicine.

12. *Report of the Pellagra Commission of the State of Illinois, November, 1911* (Springfield: Illinois State Journal Company, 1912), pp. 13, 247.

13. Etheridge, *Butterfly Caste*, pp. 9–11.

14. *Report of the Pellagra Commission*, p. 249.

15. See Kenneth J. Carpenter, *The History of Scurvy & Vitamin C* (New York: Cambridge University Press, 1986).

16. For a discussion of the struggle to legitimize biochemistry as a discipline separate from chemistry, especially the efforts of Russell Chittenden, see Robert H. Kohler, *From Medical Chemistry to Biochemistry: The Making of a Biochemical Discipline* (New York: Cambridge University Press, 1982), p. 286.

17. Casimir Funk, "Studies on Beri-Beri; VII: Chemistry of the Vitamine Fractions from Yeast and Rice Polishings," *Journal of Physiology* 46 (1913), pp. 173–79. Also see Casimir Funk, "The Etiology of Scurvy in Animals, Infantile Scurvy, Ship Beri-Beri, Pellagra," *Journal of State Medicine* 20 (1912), p. 341. For a full exposition of Funk's ideas, see Casimir Funk, *The Vitamines*, authorized translation from the second German edition by Harry Dubin (Baltimore: Williams & Wilkins, 1922).

18. Goldberger to Surgeon General, March 2, 1914, RG 90, box 149, National Archives.

19. Inspection report of Western State Hospital, Staunton, Va., March 21, 1914, Goldberger-Sebrell Collection, Vanderbilt University Library, box 4, file I-27.

20. Goldberger pocket notebook, May 11–12, 1914, Goldberger-Sebrell Collection, box 4, file I-14.

21. Ibid.

22. *Proceedings of the Conference of State and Provincial Boards of Health of North America* (1914), pp. 70–71. Few copies of this document were printed. This copy was found in the Goldberger-Sebrell Collection, box 5.

23. Joseph Goldberger, "The Etiology of Pellagra," *Public Health Reports* 29 (June 26, 1914), p. 1685.

24. Ibid., pp. 1685, 1686.

25. Joseph Goldberger, "The Cause and Prevention of Pellagra," published letter to Surgeon General, *Public Health Reports* 29 (Sept. 11, 1914), p. 2357.

26. Goldberger to Blue, Sept. 21, 1914, RG 90, file 1648, box 153, National Archives.

27. Blue to Secretary of the Treasury, Sept. 25, 1914; Acting Secretary A. H. Glenman to Waring, Sept. 29, 1914; and Glenman to Waring, Sept. 29, 1914, RG 90, file 1648, box 153, National Archives.

28. Goldberger to Mary, Sept. 30, 1914, Joseph Goldberger Papers, Southern Historical Collection, University of North Carolina Library, Chapel Hill, box 2, folder 16.

29. Goldberger to Mary, Oct. 3, 1914, Goldberger Papers, box 2, folder 16.

30. Goldberger to Mary, Sept. 30, 1914, Goldberger Papers, box 2, folder 16.

31. Goldberger to Mary, Oct. 5, 1914, and Sept. 30, 1914, Goldberger Papers, box 2, folder 16.

32. Joseph Goldberger, C. H. Waring, and David G. Willets, "The Treatment and Prevention of Pellagra," *Public Health Reports* 29 (Oct. 23, 1914), pp. 2821–25.

33. Ibid., p. 2822.

34. Ibid., p. 2823.

35. Ibid., pp. 2824–25.

36. Goldberger to Mary, Dec. 19, 1914, Goldberger Papers, box 2, folder 16.
37. Office of the President of Harvard College to Goldberger, Dec. 29, 1914, Goldberger Papers, box 2, folder 17.
38. Rosenau to Goldberger, Jan. 4, 1915, Goldberger Papers, box 2, folder 17.
39. Goldberger to Rosenau, Jan. 7, 1915, Goldberger Papers, box 2, folder 17.
40. Joseph Goldberger, "Diet and Pellagra," Cutter Lecture on Preventive Medicine, delivered at Harvard Medical School, April 2, 1915, typescript, pp. 1, 9, 11, 12, 13–14, Goldberger-Sebrell Collection, box 4, file 1-23.
41. Ibid., p. 29.
42. Ibid.
43. *Savannah Morning News* (July 21, 1915).
44. William J. Cooper Jr. and Thomas E. Terrill, *The American South: A History*, 3rd ed. (Boston: McGraw-Hill, 2002), pp. 584–85; Arthur Link, *Wilson: The Struggle for Neutrality, 1914–1915* (Princeton, N.J.: Princeton University Press, 1960), pp. 91–102.
45. *Savannah Morning News* (July 21, 1915); *Jackson* (Miss.) *Daily News* (March 17, 1915).
46. Joseph Goldberger, C. H. Waring, and David G. Willets, "The Prevention of Pellagra: A Test of Diet among Institutional Inmates," *Public Health Reports* 30 (Oct. 22, 1915), pp. 3120–21.
47. Ibid., p. 3123.
48. Ibid., pp. 3123–31.
49. Ibid., p. 3130.
50. Ibid., pp. 3125–26.
51. Ibid., p. 3126.
52. Ibid., pp. 3126–27.
53. Ibid., p. 3127.
54. *State* (Columbia, S.C., Oct. 21, 1915).
55. "Minutes of the Third Triennial Meeting of the National Association for the Study of Pellagra," MS, James Woods Babcock Papers, University of South Carolina Library, Columbia. The meeting minutes, which have never been published, were made good use of by Etheridge in her description of what transpired, *Butterfly Caste*, pp. 87–89.
56. Goldberger to Mary, Oct. 23, 1915, Goldberger Papers, box 2, folder 18.
57. "Minutes of Third Triennial Meeting," pp. 143–44.
58. Goldberger, "Diet and Pellagra," p. 14.

5. PELLAGRA, PRISONERS, AND PARDONS

1. *New York Times* (Dec. 13, 1983). On the Leo Frank case, see Leonard Dinnerstein, *The Leo Frank Case*, rev. ed. (Athens: University of Georgia Press, 1987); and Jeffrey Melnick, *Black-Jewish Relations on Trial: Leo Frank and Jim Conley in the New South* (Jackson: University Press of Mississippi, 2000).

2. E. H. Galloway, "Pellagra in Mississippi," *Southern Medical Journal* 8 (1915), p. 691; William F. Petersen, "The Mortality from Pellagra in the United States," *Journal of the American Medical Association* 69 (Dec. 22, 1917), p. 2098.

3. Joseph Goldberger, C. H. Waring, and David G. Willets, "The Prevention of Pellagra: A Test of Diet among Institutional Inmates," *Public Health Reports* 30 (Oct. 22, 1915), p. 3119; Richard P. Strong and B. C. Crowell, "The Etiology of Beriberi," *Philippine Journal of Science* 7 (1912), p. 291. The possibility that Goldberger conceived of an eating experiment using convicts as the result of having read Strong's beriberi studies is suggested by Jon Harkness in "Research behind Bars: A History of Nontherapeutic Research on American Prisoners" (Ph.D. diss., University of Wisconsin, Madison, 1996), pp. 17–18. On Goldberger's needing the governor's assistance, see Norman Howard-Jones, "Human Experimentation in Historical and Ethical Perspectives," *Social Science and Medicine* 16 (1982), pp. 1429–30.

4. For discussions of southern Progressivism and social reform, see Edward L. Ayers, *The Promise of the New South: Life after Reconstruction* (New York: Oxford University Press, 1992), pp. 413–22; and William A. Link, *The Paradox of Southern Progressivism, 1880–1930* (Chapel Hill: University of North Carolina Press, 1992).

5. Goldberger to Mary, Jan. 21, 1915, Joseph Goldberger Papers, Southern Historical Collection, University of North Carolina Library, Chapel Hill, box 2, folder 17.

6. Goldberger diary, Jan. 21, 1915, DeWitt Stetten Jr. Museum of Medical Research, National Institutes of Health Historical Office, building 31, Bethesda, Md.

7. Goldberger diary, Jan. 22, 1915, and Jan. 23, 1915.

8. Goldberger diary, Jan. 23, 1915.

9. On Parchman, see David M. Oshinsky, *"Worse Than Slavery": Parchman Farm and the Ordeal of Jim Crow Justice* (New York: Free Press, 1996).

10. Goldberger to Mary, Jan. 28, 1915, Goldberger Papers, box 2, folder 17.

11. W. F. Minor, "They Ate Their Way to Freedom," *Times-Picayune New Orleans States Magazine* (Jan. 9, 1949), p. 8.

12. Among Brewer's friends was the legendary trainman Casey Jones. After the tragic accident that took Jones's life in April 1900 and became immortalized in song, Brewer secured a generous sum for Jones's widow. Basic facts about Brewer's life come from a typescript biography and newspaper clippings, including obituaries in the E. L. Brewer Papers, no. 348, folders 8 and 6, at the Mississippi State Archives in Jackson, and from the entry in Robert Sobel and John Raimo, eds., *Biographical Directory of the Governors of the United States, 1789–1978* (Westport, Conn.: Meckler Books, 1978), p. 823. Brewer's political career is well documented in standard histories of Mississippi, such as Dunbar Rowland's two-volume work, *History of Mississippi: The Heart of the South* (Chicago: S. J. Clarke Publishing Co., 1925), vol. 2, pp. 336–43; and Richard Aubrey McLemore's two-volume *A History of Mississippi* (Jackson: University and College Press of Mississippi, 1973), vol. 2, pp. 54–58. See also Albert D. Kirwan, *Revolt of the Red-*

necks: Mississippi Politics, 1876–1925 (Lexington: University of Kentucky Press, 1951), pp. 232–58; Charles Granville Hamilton, *Progressive Mississippi* (Aberdeen, Miss., 1978), pp. 107–20, 181–85; William F. Holmes, *The White Chief: James Kimble Vardaman* (Baton Rouge: Louisiana State University Press, 1970), pp. 254, 262, 328–29; and Chester M. Morgan, *Redneck Liberal: Theodore G. Bilbo and the New Deal* (Baton Rouge: Louisiana State University Press, 1985), pp. 36–37. A volume titled *Bilbo, Brewer, and Bribery in Mississippi Politics* (1917) is an attack and apologia written by one of Brewer's political nemeses, Gambrell Austin Hobbs.

13. "Dr. Goldberger's Great Work Banishes Pellagra Terror," *Jackson (Miss.) Daily News* (Nov. 2, 1915), p. 1.

14. Minor, "They Ate Their Way to Freedom," p. 8. Whatever precautions Brewer and Goldberger took to avoid criticism on ethical grounds, contemporary physicians and ethicists do not agree on whether or not their behavior satisfied the canons of informed consent, even as understood in 1915. In a September 1994 article in the *Annals of Internal Medicine*, "Joseph Goldberger: An Unsung Hero of American Clinical Epidemiology," Joanne G. Elmore and Alvan R. Feinstein defended Goldberger's behavior as ethical: "At the time of Goldberger's work . . . some of our modern legal and ethical principles had not yet been developed . . . Conducting research on prisoners was a common procedure." However, that explanation hardly satisfied at least one physician, Bradley K. Evans, who accused the authors of being apologists for Goldberger. Evans insisted that whether or not today's standards and procedures were available to Goldberger was beside the point because "ethical principles from religion and physicians—Hippocrates to Claude Bernard—were available to Goldberger, including the oldest standard, never try to harm the patient." Unwilling to let Goldberger off the moral hook, Evans contended that whether or not experiments using human subjects were common or standards of informed consent were protean was irrelevant to calculating the ethical weight of Goldberger's behavior. However, he did allow that he did not know the state of Goldberger's mind concerning the experiments: "Perhaps he thought he had consent, that the prisoners were not patients, that the harm would be small, or that there were overriding social concerns." See Bradley K. Evans, M.D., to the editor, *Annals of Internal Medicine* 122 (Jan. 1995), p. 157. The opening volley in the current debate over informed consent, which has caused some to revisit Goldberger's work, began with Henry K. Beecher, "Ethics and Clinical Research," *New England Journal of Medicine* 74 (1966), pp. 1354–60. See also Ruth R. Faden and Tom L. Beauchamp, *A History and Theory of Informed Consent* (New York: Oxford University Press, 1986); and David J. Rothman, *Strangers at the Bedside: A History of How Law and Bioethics Transformed Medical Decision Making* (New York: Basic Books, 1991).

15. This "liberal" argument for prison experimentation is discussed in Harkness, "Research behind Bars," p. 8. The ethical debate over the use of prisoners continues. See Jonathan D. Moreno, *Deciding Together: Bioethics and Moral Con-*

sensus (New York: Oxford University Press, 1995); and Jonathan D. Moreno, *Undue Risk: Secret State Experiments on Humans* (New York: W. H. Freeman, 2000).

16. Goldberger to Mary, April 24, 1915, Goldberger Papers, box 2, folder 17.

17. Joseph Goldberger and George A. Wheeler, "Experimental Pellagra in the Human Subject Brought about by a Restricted Diet," *Public Heath Reports* 30 (Nov. 12, 1915), p. 3336; "Dr. Goldberger's Great Work Banishes Pellagra Terror," Jackson *Daily News* (Nov. 2, 1915), p. 1.

18. For a discussion of the use of blacks in antebellum medical experimentation, see Todd L. Savitt, "The Use of Blacks for Medical Experimentation and Demonstration in the Old South," *Journal of Southern History* 48 (Aug. 1982), pp. 331–48. Also see W. Michael Byrd and Linda A. Clayton, *An American Health Dilemma: A Medical History of African Americans and the Problem of Race, Beginnings to 1900* (New York: Routledge, 2000), pp. 270–77. The broader issue of medical experimentation and blacks is also treated in James Jones, *Bad Blood: The Tuskegee Syphilis Experiment*, new exp. ed. (New York: Free Press, 1993). See also Susan M. Reverby, ed., *Tuskegee's Truths: Rethinking the Tuskegee Syphilis Study* (Chapel Hill: University of North Carolina Press, 2000), and G. J. Barker-Benfield, *The Horrors of the Half-Known Life: Male Attitudes Toward Women and Sexuality in Nineteenth-Century America* (New York: Harper and Row, 1976), pp, 101–102.

19. Joseph Goldberger and George A. Wheeler, "The Experimental Production of Pellagra in Human Subjects by Means of Diet," *Hygienic Laboratory Bulletin*, no. 120 (Feb. 1920), p. 11. Those serving sentences for murder included Guy R. James, John McDaniel, Alex Gamble, John Shows, D. W. Pitts, and John Brook. W. H. English was serving a life term for criminal assault. Gabe "Ed" Pickering was in the midst of a fifteen-year sentence for manslaughter. E. S. Atkinson and Woodson Atkinson were each serving seven years for embezzlement, and Ira D. Wry was serving five years for bigamy. Neither Brewer nor Goldberger ever formally released the names of the convict volunteers. In his and Wheeler's publications describing the experiments, Goldberger designated the convicts by their initials. However, after the experiment Jackson's *Daily Clarion-Ledger* (Nov. 2, 1915), p. 8, published the prisoners' names.

20. Goldberger and Wheeler, "Experimental Production of Pellagra in Human Subjects," p. 21.

21. Goldberger and Wheeler, "Experimental Pellagra in the Human Subject," p. 3338.

22. Ibid.

23. *Jackson Daily News* (Nov. 2, 1915).

24. James to Brewer, Aug. 4, 1915, RG 27, box 390, folder 159, Mississippi State Archives, Jackson.

25. Rucker to Brewer, Sept. 16, 1915, RG 27, box 390, folder 159, Mississippi State Archives.

26. Goldberger to Mary, April 18, 1915, Goldberger Papers, box 2, folder 17.

27. Goldberger to Mary, April 25, 1915, Goldberger Papers, box 2, folder 17.
28. Ibid.
29. Ibid.
30. Mary to Goldberger, May 22, 1915, Goldberger Papers, box 2, folder 17; Joseph H. Goldberger, interview by author, Austin, Tex., Aug. 11, 1993; Goldberger to Mary, June 17, 1915, Goldberger Papers, box 2, folder 17.
31. Goldberger to Mary, June 20, 1915, and June 24, 1915, Goldberger Papers, box 2, folder 17.
32. Goldberger to Mary, Aug. 25, 1915, Goldberger Papers, box 2, folder 18.
33. Rosenau to Goldberger, Sept. 14, 1915, and Vaughan to Rosenau, Sept. 24, 1915, Goldberger Papers, box 2, folder 18.
34. Goldberger to Mary, Oct. 29, 1915, Goldberger Papers, box 2, folder 18.
35. Goldberger and Wheeler, "Experimental Pellagra in the Human Subject," pp. 3336–39.
36. The groups included Dr. E. H. Galloway, secretary of the Mississippi State Board of Health; Dr. Nolan Stewart, the former superintendent of the Mississippi State Hospital for the Insane at Jackson; Dr. Marcus Haase, professor of dermatology at the Medical College of the University of Tennessee; and Dr. Martin F. Engman, professor of dermatology at Washington University Medical School in St. Louis. In addition to these consultants, Drs. C. R. Stingily and F. L. Watkins of the Mississippi Board of Health and Dr. C. H. Waring, assistant surgeon in the Public Health Service, examined the subjects. Goldberger and Wheeler, "Experimental Pellagra in the Human Subject," pp. 3338–39.
37. Mary to Goldberger, Oct. 27, 1915, and Goldberger to Mary, Oct. 29, 1915, Goldberger Papers, box 2, folder 18.
38. *Jackson Daily News* (Nov. 2, 1915).
39. Ibid.; *Jackson Daily News* (Oct. 2, 1933).
40. Goldberger's letter to Brewer is reprinted in full in Minor, "They Ate Their Way to Freedom," p. 9; *Jackson Daily News* (Nov. 2, 1915).
41. Goldberger to Brewer, Nov. 1, 1915, as reprinted in Minor, "They Ate Their Way to Freedom," p. 9.
42. Rosenau to Goldberger, Nov. 4, 1915, Goldberger Papers, box 2, folder 18.
43. Hunt to Goldberger, Nov. 2, 1915, Goldberger Papers, box 2, folder 18.
44. Edgar Howard Farrar to Goldberger, Nov. 11, 1915, and Mary to Goldberger, Nov. 3, 1915, Goldberger Papers, box 2, folder 18.
45. Transcript of the pellagra symposium discussion, *Southern Medical Journal* 8 (May 1, 1915), pp. 31–42.
46. Goldberger to Mary, Nov. 22, 1915, and Nov. 25, 1915, Goldberger Papers, box 2, folder 18.
47. W. J. MacNeal, "The Alleged Production of Pellagra by an Unbalanced Diet," *Journal of the American Medical Association* 61 (March 25, 1916), pp. 975–77.
48. Joseph Goldberger, "A Reply," *Journal of the American Medical Association* 61 (March 25, 1916), p. 977.

6. "FILTH PARTIES" AND MILL MEALS: MEDICAL SLEUTHING IN LAB AND VILLAGE

1. Goldberger to Mary, fragment, n.d. [c. late Jan. 1906], Joseph Goldberger Papers, Southern Historical Collection, University of North Carolina Library, Chapel Hill, box 1, folder 1.

2. A fine collection of surveys to gather and analyze social data is Martin Bulmer, Kevin Bales, and Kathryn Kish Sklar, eds., *The Social Survey in Historical Perspective, 1880–1940* (New York: Cambridge University Press, 1991). An excellent volume on the social sciences and their relationship to Progressive thought is Dorothy Ross, *The Origins of American Social Science* (New York: Cambridge University Press, 1991).

3. Mary Goldberger, "Science Pigeonholed—Pellagra," typescript, n.d., "Pellagra File," Library of the Mississippi State Board of Health, Mississippi State Archives, Jackson.

4. Alan M. Kraut, *Silent Travelers: Germs, Genes, and the "Immigrant Menace"* (New York: Basic Books, 1994), pp. 96–104. Also see Judith Walzer Leavitt, *Typhoid Mary: Captive to the Public's Health* (Boston: Beacon Press, 1996).

5. Joseph Goldberger, "The Transmissibility of Pellagra: Experimental Attempts at Transmission to the Human Subject," *Public Health Reports* 31 (Nov. 17, 1916), pp. 3159–73. Robert P. Parsons, *Trail to Light: A Biography of Joseph Goldberger* (Indianapolis: Bobbs-Merrill, 1943), p. 311. According to the Goldbergers' son Joseph, much of the material in this volume came from conversations between Parsons and Mary Goldberger; the nurse's reaction is likely from such a conversation. Mary Farrar Goldberger, "Dr. Joseph Goldberger: His Wife's Recollections," *Journal of the American Dietetic Association* 32 (Aug. 1956), p. 726.

6. Goldberger, "Transmissibility of Pellagra," p. 5.

7. Goldberger to Mary, June 25, 1916, Goldberger Papers, box 2, folder 19.

8. Goldberger, "Transmissibility of Pellagra," p. 12.

9. Joseph Goldberger, "The Transmissibility of Pellagra—Experimental Attempts at Transmission to the Human Subject," *Southern Medical Journal* 10 (April 1, 1917), pp. 277–91.

10. "Discussion Symposium on Pellagra," *Southern Medical Journal* 10 (May 1, 1917), p. 387.

11. Ibid.

12. Ibid., p. 384.

13. J. F. Siler, P. E. Garrison, and W. J. MacNeal, "Relation of Pellagra to Location of Domicile in Spartan Mills, S. C., and the Adjacent District," *Archives of Internal Medicine* 20 (Aug. 1917), pp. 258–59n. Also in Elizabeth W. Etheridge, *The Butterfly Caste: A Social History of Pellagra in the South* (Westport, Conn.: Greenwood Publishing, 1972), p. 117.

14. H. F. Harris, *Pellagra* (New York: Macmillan, 1919).

15. Kraut, *Silent Travelers*, passim; William F. Petersen, "The Mortality from Pella-

gra in the United States," *Journal of the American Medical Association* 69 (Dec. 22, 1917), pp. 2096–98; "Report of the Pellagra Commission of the N.M.A.," *Journal of the National Medical Association* 10 (Oct.–Dec. 1918), p. 164.

16. Goldberger to Mary, Dec. 4, 1916, Goldberger Papers, box 2, folder 19; McCollum to Goldberger, Jan. 1, 1917, Goldberger Papers, box 2, folder 20; McLaughlin to Goldberger, Dec. 6, 1915, Goldberger Papers, box 2, folder 18.

17. Biographical data on Sydenstricker were derived from Richard V. Kasius, ed., *The Challenge of Facts: Selected Public Health Papers of Edgar Sydenstricker* (New York: published for the Milbank Memorial Fund by Prodist, 1974), pp. 4–6. Also see obituary, *New York Times* (March 20, 1936). Sydenstricker's PHS work marked the beginning of a long and distinguished career in health research, which later culminated in the scientific directorship of the prestigious Milbank Memorial Fund.

18. There are many useful descriptions of the increasing role of cotton mills in the economic lives of southerners. A fine synthesis that places the rise of textile mills in the context of late-nineteenth-century history is Edward L. Ayers, *The Promise of the New South: Life after Reconstruction* (New York: Oxford University Press, 1992), pp. 111–17. Also see David L. Carlton, *Mill and Town in South Carolina, 1880–1920* (Baton Rouge: Louisiana State University Press, 1982); Jacquelyn Dowd Hall et al., *Like a Family: The Making of a Southern Cotton Mill World* (Chapel Hill: University of North Carolina Press, 1987); and G. C. Waldrep III, *Southern Workers and the Search for Community: Spartanburg County, South Carolina* (Urbana: University of Illinois Press, 2000). Issues of health are treated in Edward H. Beardsley, *A History of Neglect: Health Care for Blacks and Mill Workers in the Twentieth-Century South* (Knoxville: University of Tennessee Press, 1987). Much of the data on the growth of the industry presented here is cited in Howard N. Rabinowitz, *The First New South, 1865–1920* (Arlington Heights, Ill.: Harlan Davidson, 1992), pp. 44–45.

19. Rabinowitz, *First New South*, p. 45.

20. Waldrep, *Southern Workers and the Search for Community*, pp. 16–17.

21. Ibid., p. 15.

22. Ibid., pp. 17–18.

23. William J. Cooper Jr. and Thomas E. Terrill, *The American South: A History*, 3rd ed. (Boston: McGraw-Hill, 2002), p. 477.

24. Rabinowitz, *First New South*, p. 47.

25. Joseph Goldberger, G. A. Wheeler, and Edgar Sydenstricker, "A Study of the Relation of Diet to Pellagra Incidence in Seven Textile-Mill Communities of South Carolina in 1916," *Public Health Reports* 35 (March 19, 1920), pp. 648–713.

26. Ibid., p. 659.

27. Ibid., p. 660.

28. Ibid.

29. Ibid., p. 664.

30. Ibid., p. 706.

31. Ibid., p. 707.
32. Joseph Goldberger, G. A. Wheeler, and Edgar Sydenstricker, "Pellagra Incidence in Relation to Sex, Age, Season, Occupation, and 'Disabling Sickness' in Seven Cotton-Mill Villages of South Carolina during 1916," *Public Health Reports* 35 (July 9, 1920), p. 1663.
33. Ibid.
34. Ibid.
35. Joseph Goldberger, G. A. Wheeler, and R. E. Tarbett, "A Study of the Relation of Factors of a Sanitary Character to Pellagra Incidence in Seven Cotton-Mill Villages of South Carolina in 1916," *Public Health Reports* 35 (July 16, 1920), pp. 1701–2.
36. Ibid., pp. 1711–12.
37. Ibid., p. 1714.
38. Joseph Goldberger, G. A. Wheeler, and Edgar Sydenstricker, "A Study of the Relation of Family Income and Other Economic Factors to Pellagra Incidence in Seven Cotton-Mill Villages of South Carolina in 1916," *Public Health Reports* 35 (Nov. 12, 1920), pp. 2673, 2674, 2677.
39. Ibid., pp. 2677–78. See James W. Jobling and William F. Petersen, "The Epidemiology of Pellagra in Nashville, Tennessee," *Journal of Infectious Disease* 18 (Jan. 1916), pp. 501–67; and James W. Jobling and William F. Petersen, "The Epidemiology of Pellagra in Nashville, Tennessee, II," *Journal of Infectious Disease* 21 (Aug. 1917), pp. 109–31.
40. Goldberger, Wheeler, and Sydenstricker, "Relation of Family Income and Other Economic Factors to Pellagra," p. 2678.
41. Ibid., pp. 2678–80.
42. Ibid., pp. 2680–82.
43. Ibid., p. 2683.
44. Ibid., p. 2686.
45. In twenty-four of the sixty-one families with multiple cases of pellagra, there were two or more cases; and in eight of them, there were three or more cases. Ibid., pp. 2687–88.
46. Ibid., p. 2690.
47. Ibid., p. 2694.
48. Ibid. The comparison of the two villages is on pp. 2697–707 of the report.
49. Ibid., p. 2703.
50. Ibid., pp. 2708–9.
51. Ibid., p. 2709.
52. Edgar Sydenstricker, "The Prevalence of Pellagra: Its Possible Relation to the Rise in the Cost of Food," *Public Health Reports* 30 (Oct. 22, 1915), pp. 3132–48.
53. Ibid., pp. 3147, 3135–36.
54. Ibid., pp. 3137, 3139, 3140.
55. Ibid., p. 3148.

56. Goldberger, Wheeler, and Sydenstricker, "Relation of Diet to Pellagra Incidence," p. 707.

7. COTTON IN CRISIS AND THE POLITICS OF PUBLIC HEALTH

1. Goldberger to Mary, April 7, 1917, Joseph Goldberger Papers, Southern Historical Collection, University of North Carolina Library, Chapel Hill, box 2, folder 20.
2. Goldberger to Mary, May 20, 1917, Goldberger Papers, box 2, folder 20.
3. Goldberger to Mary, June 18, 1917, and June 23, 1917, Goldberger Papers, box 2, folder 20.
4. Data are from William J. Cooper Jr. and Thomas E. Terrill, *The American South: A History*, 2nd ed. (New York: McGraw-Hill, 1996), p. 584.
5. Goldberger to Mary, Aug. 14, 1917, Goldberger Papers, box 2, folder 20.
6. Goldberger to Mary, Sept. 12, 1917, Goldberger Papers, box 2, folder 20.
7. Edsall to Blue, July 23, 1917, RG 90, box 149, National Archives.
8. Ibid.
9. Ibid.
10. Ibid.
11. Goldberger to Mary, July 1, 1917, Goldberger Papers, box 2, folder 20.
12. Ibid.
13. Goldberger to Mary, June 17, 1915, and Mary to Goldberger, May 22, 1915, Goldberger Papers, box 2, folder 17.
14. Goldberger to Mary, March 22, 1917, Goldberger Papers, box 2, folder 20.
15. Goldberger to Mary, July 1, 1917, Goldberger Papers, box 2, folder 20.
16. Goldberger to Mary, July 20, 1918, Goldberger Papers, box 2, folder 21.
17. Goldberger to Mary, March 25, 1917, Goldberger Papers, box 2, folder 20.
18. Vaughan to Blue, Dec. 27, 1917, attached to Blue to Goldberger, Jan. 19, 1918, RG 90, file 1648, box 150, National Archives.
19. Welch to Blue, Jan. 14, 1918, RG 90, file 1648, box 150, National Archives. Goldberger to Sullivan, May 1918, Joseph Goldberger Correspondence, History of Medicine Division, National Library of Medicine, box MSC 195–199, folder C196.
20. Goldberger to Mary, Aug. 6, 1918, Goldberger Papers, box 2, folder 21.
21. Ibid.
22. Goldberger to Mary, Aug. 14, 1918, Goldberger Papers, box 2, folder 21.
23. Goldberger to Mary, Aug. 20, 1918, Goldberger Papers, box 2, folder 21.
24. Goldberger to Surgeon General, Aug. 26, 1918, RG 90, file 1648, box 153, National Archives.
25. Blue to Goldberger, Sept. 28, 1918, and Goldberger to Mary, Nov. 11, 1918, Goldberger Papers, box 2, folder 21.
26. The best book on the influenza epidemic in the United States remains Alfred W. Crosby, *America's Forgotten Pandemic: The Influenza of 1918* (New York: Cambridge University Press, 1989).

27. Ibid., pp. 47, 48.
28. Ibid., pp. 47–50.
29. M. J. Rosenau, W. J. Keegan, Joseph Goldberger, and G. C. Lake, "Experiments upon Volunteers to Determine the Cause and Mode of Spread of Influenza, Boston, November and December, 1918," pp. 5–53, and "Experiments upon Volunteers to Determine the Cause and Mode of Spread of Influenza, Boston, February and March, 1919," pp. 55–97, *Hygienic Bulletin*, no. 123 (Washington, D.C.: Government Printing Office, 1921).
30. Crosby, *America's Forgotten Pandemic*, pp. 279–81.
31. W. J. Keegan, "The Prevailing Pandemic of Influenza," *Journal of the American Medical Association* 71 (Sept. 28, 1917), pp. 1051–55.
32. Crosby, *America's Forgotten Pandemic*, p. 281.
33. Rosenau, Keegan, Goldberger, and Lake, "Experiments November and December, 1918," pp. 12–21.
34. Rosenau, Keegan, Goldberger, and Lake, "Experiments February and March, 1919," p. 96.
35. Wheeler to Surgeon General, July 16, 1919, RG 90, file 1646, box 151, and Goldberger to Surgeon General, April 8, 1919, RG 90, file 1646, box 151A, National Archives.
36. Goldberger to Surgeon General, April 8, 1919, RG 90, file 1646, box 151A, National Archives. John Carroll was born in Kansas and studied with the artist Frank Duveneck. Years after his service with Goldberger, he emerged as a noted portrait painter. See *Bulletin of the Addison Gallery of American Art* (1941), p. 27.
37. Goldberger to Surgeon General, Aug. 11, 1920, RG 90, file 1646, box 153, National Archives.
38. Ibid.
39. Ibid.
40. *Report of the Board of Health of Mississippi, from June 1, 1913, to June 30, 1915* and *Report of the Board of Health of Mississippi, from July 1, 1917, to June 30, 1919*.
41. *Spartanburg Journal* (Dec. 18, 1920).
42. Ibid.
43. Joseph Goldberger, "Memorandum Relative to Pellagra, Evidence Available (July 1, 1921) of Increased Pellagra Prevalence in 1921," attached to Goldberger to Surgeon General, July 18, 1921, RG 90, file 1648, box 152C, National Archives.
44. Goldberger to Schereschewsky, July 9, 1921, RG 90, file 1648, box 152C, National Archives; Goldberger, "Memorandum," p. 7.
45. *New York Times* (July 25, 1921).
46. Harding to Farrand, July 25, 1921, Warren G. Harding Papers, presidential case file 712, Pellagra, folder 1, Ohio Historical Society, Columbus; Harding to Cumming, July 25, 1921, RG 90, file 1648, box 152C, National Archives.
47. *Evening Star*, clipping, n.d., scrapbook 2, Goldberger Papers. Also see *New York Times* (July 26, 1921).

48. "Outline of a Program for Dealing with Existing Pellagra Situation and Mitigating That Threatened for 1922," n.d., RG 90, file 1648, box 152C, National Archives.
49. Byrnes to Harding, July 27, 1921, and July 30, 1921, Harding Papers.
50. *Congressional Record*, 67th Cong., 1st sess. (1921), 4428, 4398, 4478, 4367.
51. *Atlanta Constitution* (July 28, 1921); *New York Times* (July 27 and Aug. 14, 1921).
52. *New York Age* (Aug. 6, 1921).
53. *Minutes of Conference of State Health Officers of the South, August 4–5, 1921*, pp. 3–10, 64–66, RG 90, file 1648, National Archives.
54. Ibid., pp. 19–35.
55. Cumming to Harding, Aug. 9, 1921, RG 90, file 1648, box 152C, National Archives.
56. Ibid.
57. Ibid.
58. Resolutions attached to Ibid.
59. Ibid.
60. U.S. Department of Commerce, Bureau of the Census, *Mortality Statistics, 1921* (Washington, D.C.: Government Printing Office, 1924), p. 67; *Report of the Board of Health of Mississippi, from July 1, 1921, to June 30, 1923*, p. 23; *Forty-second Annual Report of the State Board of Health of South Carolina for the Fiscal Year 1921 to the Legislature of South Carolina*, p. 88.
61. G. A. Wheeler to Mississippi State Board of Health, Sept. 14, 1921, RG 90, file 1648, box 152C, National Archives.
62. *Spartanburg Herald* (Aug. 30, 1921).
63. W. E. Deeks, "The Etiology and Treatment of Pellagra," *Southern Medical Journal* 15 (Nov. 1922), pp. 891–98. Also see "Discussion" in the same volume, pp. 899–905. See also Elizabeth W. Etheridge, *The Butterfly Caste: A Social History of Pellagra in the South* (Westport, Conn.: Greenwood Publishing, 1972), p. 169.
64. James H. Cassedy, "The 'Germ of Laziness' in the South, 1900–1915: Charles Wardell Stiles and the Progressive Paradox," *Bulletin of the History of Medicine* 45 (March/April 1971), pp. 159–69. Also see John Ettling, *The Germ of Laziness: Rockefeller Philanthropy and Public Health in the New South* (Cambridge, Mass.: Harvard University Press, 1981). Southern businessmen and politicians had reacted against the Rockefeller Foundation's crusade against hookworm as an example of northern organizations' intrusion into southern affairs and implication of southern backwardness.

8. "NAILING PELLAGRA'S OLD HIDE TO THE BARN DOOR"

1. For much of the material on the Hygienic Laboratory and the government's role in scientific research I am indebted to Victoria A. Harden, *Inventing the NIH: Federal Biomedical Research Policy, 1887–1937* (Baltimore: Johns Hopkins University Press, 1986).

2. Ibid., p. 9.
3. Ibid., p. 10.
4. Ibid., p. 55.
5. Robert P. Parsons, *Trail to Light: A Biography of Joseph Goldberger* (Indianapolis: Bobbs-Merrill, 1943), pp. 325, 332.
6. Elizabeth W. Etheridge, *The Butterfly Caste: A Social History of Pellagra in the South* (Westport, Conn.: Greenwood Publishing, 1972), pp. 170–86.
7. Tanner to Goldberger, Aug. 5, 1921, Goldberger-Sebrell Collection, Vanderbilt University Library, box 4, file 1-8.
8. Ibid. and Tanner to Goldberger, Aug. 13, 1921, Goldberger-Sebrell Collection, box 4, file 1-8. See also Joseph Goldberger and W. F. Tanner, "Amino-Acid Deficiency Probably the Primary Etiological Factor in Pellagra," *Public Health Reports* 37 (March 3, 1922), pp. 462–87; and Joseph Goldberger and W. F. Tanner, "An Amino-Acid Deficiency as the Primary Etiologic Factor in Pellagra," *Journal of the American Medical Association* 79 (Dec. 23, 1921), pp. 2132–34.
9. Goldberger to Mary, Sept. 23, 1921, Joseph Goldberger Papers, Southern Historical Collection, University of North Carolina Library, Chapel Hill, box 2, folder 22; "Application for Examination for Appointment as Assistant Surgeon," June 16, 1914, confidential personnel file, W. F. Tanner, Division of Commissioned Personnel, U.S. Public Health Service. High ratings on the annual report from Goldberger early in Tanner's career had become check marks most frequently found in the "average" box by the early 1920s. On the 1922 "Confidential Efficiency Report," Goldberger scribbled, "I should rate him as a good average." "Confidential Efficiency Report for W. F. Tanner," July 1–Dec. 31, 1922.
10. Goldberger to Schereschewsky, Sept. 22, 1921, RG 90, file 1648, box 153D, National Archives.
11. Ibid.
12. Tanner to Goldberger, Oct. 5, 1921, and Oct. 26, 1921, Goldberger-Sebrell Collection, box 4, file 1-8; Goldberger to Mary, Sept. 23, 1921, Goldberger Papers, box 2, folder 22.
13. Bess Furman, *A Profile of the United States Public Health Service, 1798–1948* (Washington, D.C.: U.S. Department of Health, Education, and Welfare, 1962), p. 351.
14. Kerr to Goldberger, Sept. 16, 1922, Goldberger Papers, box 2, folder 22.
15. Goldberger to Surgeon General, July 12, 1922, RG 90, file 1648, box 153, National Archives.
16. Russell H. Chittenden and Frank P. Underhill, "The Production in Dogs of a Pathological Condition Which Closely Resembles Human Pellagra," *American Journal of Physiology* 44 (1917), pp. 13–66; Goldberger to Surgeon General, Sept. 30, 1922, RG 90, file 1648, box 153, National Archives.
17. Ibid.; and attached letter and contract, Stimson to Goldberger, Oct. 13, 1922.
18. Goldberger to Surgeon General, June 4, 1923, RG 90, file 1648, box 153, National Archives.
19. Ibid.

20. Goldberger to Mary, July 16, 1923, Goldberger papers, box 2, folder 23.

21. Joseph Goldberger and W. F. Tanner, "A Study of the Pellagra-Preventive Action of Dried Beans, Casein, Dried Milk, and Brewer's Yeast with a Consideration of the Essential Preventive Factors Involved," *Public Health Reports* 40 (Jan. 9, 1925), pp. 54–80. See also Joseph Goldberger and G. A. Wheeler, "A Study of the Pellagra-Preventive Action of the Cowpea (*Vigna sinensis*) and Wheat Germ," *Public Health Reports* 42 (Sept. 30, 1927), pp. 2383–91. Goldberger no longer advised southerners to eat "BEANS," Goldberger to Mary, December 10, 1911, Goldberger Papers, box 2, folder 13.

22. Goldberger and Tanner, "Amino-Acid Deficiency Probably the Primary Etiological Factor in Pellagra."

23. Joseph Goldberger and W. F. Tanner, "A Study of the Prevention and Treatment of Pellagra: Experiments showing the Value of Fresh Meat and Milk, the Therapeutic Failure of Gelatin, and the Preventive Failure of Cod-Liver Oil," *Public Health Reports* 39 (Jan. 18, 1924), pp. 87–107. See Elmer V. McCollum, *A History of Nutrition: The Sequence of Ideas in Nutrition Investigations* (Boston: Houghton Mifflin, 1957), pp. 135–37, 217–34, 271–87.

24. G. A. Wheeler, Joseph Goldberger, and M. R. Blackstock, "On the Probable Identity of the Chittenden-Underhill Pellagra-Like Syndrome in Dogs and 'Black-Tongue,'" *Public Health Reports* 37 (May 5, 1922), pp. 1063–69. Also see Joseph Goldberger and G. A. Wheeler, "Experimental Blacktongue of Dogs and Its Relation to Pellagra," *Public Health Reports* 43 (Jan. 27, 1928), pp. 172–217.

25. Goldberger and Wheeler, "Experimental Blacktongue of Dogs," pp. 172–77.

26. Joseph Goldberger, G. A. Wheeler, R. D. Lillie, and L. M. Rogers, "A Study of the Black Tongue–Preventive Action of 16 Foodstuffs, with Special Reference to the Identity of Black Tongue of Dogs and Pellagra of Man," *Public Health Reports* 43 (June 8, 1928), pp. 1385–454.

27. Ibid. Also see Joseph Goldberger, G. A. Wheeler, R. D. Lillie, and L. M. Rogers, "A Further Study of Experimental Black Tongue with Special Reference to the Black Tongue Preventive in Yeast," *Public Health Reports* 43 (March 23, 1928), pp. 657–94.

28. Goldberger and Tanner, "Preventive Action of Dried Beans."

29. Belisle to Goldberger, March 31, 1926, Goldberger Papers, box 2, folder 23.

30. Joseph Goldberger and R. D. Lillie, "A Note on the Experimental Pellagra-Like Conditions in the Albino Rat," *Public Health Reports* 41 (May 28, 1926), pp. 1025–29.

31. Goldberger and Tanner, "Preventive Action of Dried Beans," pp. 72–73. See also Joseph Goldberger, G. A. Wheeler, R. D. Lillie, and L. M. Rogers, "A Further Study of Butter, Fresh Beef, and Yeast as Pellagra Preventives, with Consideration of Factor P-P of Pellagra (and Black Tongue of Dogs) to Vitamin B," *Public Health Reports* 41 (Feb. 19, 1926), pp. 297–318. Goldberger and Tanner needed more biochemistry than they had at this point. The work of Emil Fischer and his students on coenzymes would be crucial in the years to come.

32. Goldberger, Wheeler, Lillie and Rogers, ibid.

33. Goldberger and Wheeler, "Pellagra Preventive Action of the Cowpea and of Commercial Wheat Germ." Also see Joseph Goldberger and G. A. Wheeler, "A Study of the Pellagra-Preventive Action of Canned Salmon," *Public Health Reports* 44 (Nov. 15, 1929), pp. 2769–71.

34. Goldberger to Wheeler, Nov. 11, 1925, Goldberger-Sebrell Collection, box 4, file I-9.

35. Goldberger to Mary, April, 1, 1925, Goldberger Papers, box 2, folder 23.

36. Goldberger to Farrar, Aug. 11, 1926, Goldberger Papers, box 2, folder 24.

37. Leathers to Cumming, June 1, 1922, RG 90, file 1648, box 153, National Archives. On the flood, see Pete Daniel, *Deep'n As It Come: The 1927 Mississippi River Flood* (New York: Oxford University Press, 1977); and John M. Barry, *Rising Tide: The Great Mississippi Flood of 1927 and How It Changed America* (New York: Simon & Schuster, 1997). On LeRoy Percy and the flood, see Bertram Wyatt-Brown, *The House of Percy: Honor, Melancholy and Imagination in a Southern Family* (New York: Oxford University Press, 1994), pp. 238–40, 242–47. On the history of life on the delta, see James C. Cobb, *The Most Southern Place on Earth: The Mississippi Delta and the Roots of Regional Identity* (New York: Oxford University Press, 1992).

38. Goldberger to Surgeon General, June 7, 1922, RG 90, file 1648, box 153, National Archives.

39. J. W. Schereschewsky, A. J. McLaughlin, B. S. Warren, and R. H. Creel to Surgeon General, July 3, 1922, RG 90, file 1648, box 153, National Archives.

40. The data are from Daniel, *Deep'n As It Come*, p. 10.

41. Cox to McCollum, June 27, 1927, Goldberger-Sebrell Collection, box 4, file I-22.

42. Goldberger to Cox, July 3, 1927, Goldberger-Sebrell Collection, box 4, file I-22.

43. Joseph Goldberger and Edgar Sydenstricker, "Pellagra in the Mississippi Flood Area," *Public Health Reports* 42 (Nov. 4, 1927), pp. 2706–25 and reprint no. 1187.

44. Goldberger to Mary, July 30 [1927], Goldberger Papers, box 3, folder 36; Mary to Goldberger, July 29, 1927, Goldberger Papers, box 2, folder 24.

45. Goldberger and Sydenstricker, "Pellagra in the Mississippi Flood Area," reprint, pp. 4–5.

46. *The Mississippi Valley Flood Disaster of 1927: Official Report of the Relief Operations* (Washington, D.C.: American National Red Cross, 1928), pp. 107–8.

47. *Jackson Daily News* (July 25, 1927).

48. Goldberger and Sydenstricker, "Pellagra in the Mississippi Flood Area," reprint, p. 5.

49. Ibid., p. 7.

50. Ibid., p. 8.

51. Ibid., p. 9.

52. Ibid.

53. Ibid., pp. 10–11.

54. Ibid., p. 13.

55. Ibid., pp. 14–15.

56. Ibid., pp. 17–18.
57. Ibid., p. 18.
58. Ibid., p. 19.
59. Ibid., p. 20.
60. Ibid.
61. Ibid.
62. For this and the previous paragraph, see *Red Cross Courier* 6 (Aug. 15, 1927), p. 4; (Sept. 13, 1927), pp. 6–7; (Sept. 15, 1927), p. 29; (Oct. 1, 1927), p. 14. Also see Etheridge, *Butterfly Caste*, p. 184.
63. Daniel, *Deep'n As It Come*, p. 6; *Mississippi Valley Flood Disaster*, p. 5; Barry, *Rising Tide*, pp. 320–21.
64. Barry, *Rising Tide*, p. 108.
65. Goldberger to Surgeon General, Jan. 17, 1928, Goldberger-Sebrell Collection, box 4, file I-11.
66. Ibid.
67. William DeKleine, "Recent Trends in Pellagra," American Red Cross Archives, "Pellagra" file, reprint from *Quarterly Review* (Jan. 1936), pp. 2–3.

9. KADDISH FOR A HERO

1. Herty to Mary, April 19, 1928, Joseph Goldberger Papers, Southern Historical Collection, University of North Carolina Library, Chapel Hill, box 2, folder 24. See Victoria A. Harden, *Inventing the NIH: Federal Biomedical Research Policy, 1887–1937* (Baltimore: Johns Hopkins University Press, 1986), p. 139.
2. Harden, *Inventing the NIH*, p. 158.
3. Goldberger's last speech was to the American Dietetic Association on October 31, 1928. It was later published as Joseph Goldberger, "Pellagra," *Journal of the American Dietetic Association* 4 (March 1929), pp. 221–27; the quotation is on p. 224.
4. Ibid., p. 226.
5. Ibid., p. 227.
6. Ibid.
7. Rosenau to Goldberger, Nov. 21, 1928, Goldberger Papers, box 2, folder 24; memorandum of work of Dr. Joseph Goldberger in connection with investigation of pellagra, typescript and in handwriting, "Fwd. to Prof. Reid Hunt by Dr. McCoy for nomination for Nobel Prize," Nov. 24, 1928, Goldberger-Sebrell Collection, Vanderbilt University Library, box 5, file I-46.
8. *New York Times* (Dec. 29, 1928).
9. According to Dr. Joseph H. Goldberger, his mother, Mary, had spent many hours with Naval Officer Robert Parsons, Goldberger's first biographer, telling him the details of those last weeks. See Robert P. Parsons, *Trail to Light: A Biography of Joseph Goldberger* (Indianapolis: Bobbs-Merrill, 1943), pp. 332–33.
10. Interview with Dr. Roscoe Spencer, 1964, p. 30, Oral History Collection, Columbia University; interview with Dr. Grover Kempf, Sept. 11, 1977, Oral History 79,

History of Medicine Division, National Library of Medicine, Bethesda, Md. Joseph H. Goldberger to author, December 15, 2002.

11. Dowling to Mary, Dec. 30, 1928, Goldberger Papers, box 2, folder 24.

12. Parsons, *Trail to Light*, pp. 331–32.

13. Ibid., p. 333.

14. Sydenstricker to Goldberger, Dec. 29, 1928, Goldberger Papers, box 2, folder 24.

15. Goldberger, memorandum, Jan. 5, 1929, Goldberger Papers, box 3, folder 25.

16. Certificate of Death for Joseph Goldberger, Health Department of the District of Columbia, record no. 318093, Jan. 17, 1929; Parsons, *Trail to Light*, p. 333.

17. Certificate of Death.

18. The death mask is in the Smithsonian National Museum of American History in Washington, D.C.

19. *Washington Post* (Jan. 18, 1929). Telephone conversation with Dr. Joseph H. Goldberger, Aug. 20, 2002. The journalist Bess Furman wrote, "Efforts of Dr. Goldberger's own family to force traditional funeral services were useless"; see Furman, *A Profile of the United States Public Health Service, 1798–1948* (Washington, D.C.: U.S. Department of Health, Education, and Welfare, 1962), p. 364. Solomon B. Freehof, *Reform Jewish Practice and Its Rabbinic Background* (New York: KTAV Publishing House, 1976), pp. 133–35.

20. Rabbi Simon's entire eulogy is reprinted in Parsons, *Trail to Light*, pp. 334–35.

21. Ibid.

22. "The Memoirs of Dr. Hugh Smith Cumming, Sr.," two-volume unpublished manuscript available on microfilm at the University of Virginia, Charlottesville, p. 350, and quoted in Furman, *Profile of the United States Public Health Service*, p. 364.

23. Hugh S. Cumming, "Joseph Goldberger," n.d., RG 443, Records of National Institutes of Health, 1930–1948, General Records, file 1650 F-G, box 83, National Archives. Also in Goldberger Papers, box 3, folder 25.

24. *State* (Columbia, S.C., Jan. 18, 1929); *Natchez Democrat* (Jan. 18, 1929); *Daily Clarion-Ledger* (Jan. 18, 1929); *Times-Picayune* (Jan. 18, 1929).

25. *Forverts* (Jan. 18, 1929); *Der Tog* (Jan. 18, 1929).

26. Goldberger's final illness was called a "mysterious malady" by the *Times-Picayune*, January 18, 1929. Washington, D.C.'s *Evening Star* of January 18, 1929, called it an "unknown disease." The *New York Times* called it an "anemia, which is one of the symptoms of pellagra." The *Evening World* called it a "fatal illness, which started during his pellagra studies."

27. Mary Goldberger, handwritten statement [1929], Goldberger papers, box 3, folder 25.

28. Stimson to Mary, Feb. 20, 1929, and Rosenau to Mary, Feb. 21, 1929, Goldberger Papers, box 3, folder 29; Sydenstricker to Mary, March 9, 1929, Goldberger Papers, box 3, folder 30.

29. Knutson to Mary, Jan. 22, 1929, and attached copy of H.R. 16411, Goldberger Papers, box 3, folder 25.

30. Rosenau to "Dear Doctor," Feb. 1, 1929, Goldberger Papers, box 3, folder 26; Rosenau to McCoy, Feb. 11, 1929, Goldberger Papers, box 3, folder 28. Rosenau favored the Senate bill because it would have given Mary $150 per month rather than the $125 provided for in the House bill.

31. Mayo to Rosenau, Feb. 8, 1929, Goldberger Papers, box 3, folder 27.

32. Anderson to Smoot, Feb. 7, 1929, Goldberger Papers, box 3, folder 27.

33. Cumming to Mary, March 7, 1929, Goldberger Papers, box 3, folder 30.

34. Joseph H. Goldberger, interview by author, Austin, Tex., Aug. 11, 1993.

35. Rosenwald to Miss Mary Humphreys Goldberger, May 17, 1929, Goldberger Papers, box 3, folder 30.

36. Papers and discussion at the Twenty-third Annual Meeting held in Miami, Florida, Nov. 19–22, 1929, were published in volume 23 of the Southern Medical Journal; J. Frank Wilson, "Arspenamine in the Treatment of Pellagra: Report of One Hundred Cases," Southern Medical Journal 23 (Aug. 1930), pp. 758–63; G. A. Wheeler, "The Prevention of Pellagra," Southern Medical Journal 23 (April 1930), p. 303.

37. "Discussion," Southern Medical Journal 23 (April 1930), p. 304; Wheeler to Mary, April 9, 1930, Goldberger Papers, box 3, folder 31.

38. Sidney Bliss, "Considerations Leading to the View That Pellagra Is an Iron Deficiency Disease," Science 72 (Dec. 5, 1930), pp. 577–78; and Sidney Bliss, "The Increasing Prevalence of Pellagra," Journal of the American Medical Association 96 (Feb. 21, 1931), p. 614; Wheeler to Surgeon General, Feb. 26, 1931, marked "letter not sent," RG 90, general file, 1924–1935, file 2, no. 042532, National Archives.

39. Beverly R. Tucker, "A New Conception of Pellagra," Virginia Medical Monthly 61 (1935), pp. 686–90. See Elizabeth W. Etheridge, The Butterfly Caste: A Social History of Pellagra in the South (Westport, Conn.: Greenwood Publishing, 1972), p. 190.

40. G. A. Wheeler and D. J. Hunt, "The Pellagra-Preventive Value of Green Cabbage, Collards, Mustard Greens, and Kale," Public Health Reports 48 (June 30, 1933), pp. 754–58. G. A. Wheeler, "The Pellagra-Preventive Value of Autoclaved Dried Yeast, Canned Flaked Haddock, and Canned Green Peas," Public Health Reports 48 (June 20, 1933), pp. 67–77.

41. Etheridge, Butterfly Caste, pp. 198–202.

42. Michael R. Grey, New Deal Medicine: The Rural Health Programs of the Farm Security Administration (Baltimore: Johns Hopkins University Press, 1999), pp. 35–38, 204–5.

43. In 1940 MGM produced a brief film, usually shown with one or two full-length feature films, titled A Way in the Wilderness, a line excerpted from Isaiah 43:19 (the first frame mistakenly cites 44:19). The part of Goldberger was played by Shepperd Strudwick, well known to contemporary movie fans and still remembered by old-movie buffs as a fine performer. According to one newspaper account, Strudwick's appearance with makeup and glasses was so close to Goldberger's

that "members of [Goldberger's] family who witnessed the preview were startled." See "Mrs. Goldberger Honored with Picture Preview," n.d., Goldberger Papers, box 3, folder 39.

44. Mary Goldberger, "Science Pigeonholed—Pellagra," typescript, n.d., "Pellagra File," Library of the Mississippi State Board of Health, Mississippi State Archives, Jackson. Later published as "Dr. Joseph Goldberger: His Wife's Recollections," *Journal of the American Dietetic Association* 32 (Aug. 1956), pp. 724–27.

45. The cover note, dated August 29, 1949, explains that the draft was written about two years after Goldberger's death and was used as the basis of talks.

46. Mary Farrar Goldberger, "Dr. Joseph Goldberger: His Wife's Recollections," p. 727.

47. Paul De Kruif, *Hunger Fighters* (New York: Harcourt, Brace, 1928), p. 369; Paul De Kruif, *The Sweeping Wind: A Memoir* (New York: Harcourt, Brace & World, 1962), p. 132.

EPILOGUE

1. C. A. Elvehjem et al., "Relation of Nicotinic Acid and Nicotinic Acid Amide to Canine Black Tongue," *Journal of the American Chemical Society* 59 (1937), pp. 1767–68.

2. Ibid. Also see C. J. Koehn Jr. and C. A. Elvehjem, "Further Studies on the Concentration of the Antipellagra Factor," *Journal of Biological Chemistry* 118 (1937), pp. 693–99. Elvehjem's work and background are described in Elizabeth W. Etheridge, *The Butterfly Caste: A Social History of Pellagra in the South* (Westport, Conn.: Greenwood Publishing, 1972), pp. 207–8.

3. D. T. Smith, J. M. Ruffin, and S. G. Smith, "Pellagra Successfully Treated with Nicotinic Acid," *Journal of the American Medical Association* 109 (1937), pp. 2054–55. Also see Daphne A. Roe, *A Plague of Corn: The Social History of Pellagra* (Ithaca, N.Y.: Cornell University Press, 1973), pp. 123–24.

4. T. D. Spies, C. Cooper, and M. A. Blankenhorn, "The Use of Nicotinic Acid in the Treatment of Pellagra," *Journal of the American Medical Association* 110 (1938), pp. 622–27. Also see T. D. Spies, W. B. Bean, and R. F. Stone, "The Treatment of Subclinical and Classic Pellagra: Use of Nicotinic Acid, Nicotinic Acid Amide, and Sodium Nicotinate with Special Reference to the Vasodilator Action and Effect on Mental Symptoms," *Journal of the American Medical Association* 111 (1938), pp. 584–92. Also see Roe, *A Plague of Corn*, pp. 124–26.

5. W. A. Krehl, L. J. Tepley, and C. A. Elvehjem, "Effect of Corn Grits on Nicotinic Acid Requirements of the Dog," *Proceedings of the Society for Experimental Biology and Medicine* 58 (April 1945), pp. 336–37; and, by the same authors, "Corn as an Etiological Factor in Production of a Nicotinic Acid Deficiency in the Rat," *Science* 101 (March 16, 1945), p. 283.

6. W. A. Krehl, L. J. Tepley, P. S. Sarma, and C. A. Elvehjem, "Growth-Retarding Effect of Corn in Nicotinic Acid-Low Ration and Its Counteraction by Trypto-

phan," *Science* 101 (May 11, 1945), p. 490. Also see Etheridge, *Butterfly Caste*, p. 216, and Konrad Bloch, *Blondes in Venetian Paintings, the Nine-Banded Armadillo, and Other Essays in Biochemistry* (New Haven: Yale University Press, 1994), pp. 185–207.

7. Etheridge, *Butterfly Caste*, pp. 211–12.

8. Ibid., pp. 212–14.

9. Ibid., p. 214. Also see Suzanne White, "Chemistry and Controversy: Regulating the Use of Chemicals in Foods, 1883–1959" (Ph.D. diss., Emory University, 1994), pp. 254–308; Suzanne White Junod, "Food Standards in the United States: The Case of the Peanut Butter and Jelly Sandwich," in David F. Smith and Jim Phillips, eds., *Food, Science, Policy, and Regulation in the Twentieth Century: International and Comparative Perspectives* (New York: Routledge, 2000), pp. 167–88; and Suzanne White Junod, "Whose Standards Should Prevail? Quaker Oats' Battle over 'Bottled Sunshine,'" *FDLI Update* (March/April 1999), p. 12.

10. Rima D. Apple, *Vitamania: Vitamins in American Culture* (New Brunswick, N.J.: Rutgers University Press, 1996).

11. I asked this question of an audience after delivering the annual Warren A. Sawyer Lecture sponsored by the Waring Historical Library at the Medical University of South Carolina, Feb. 12, 1998.

There are several collections of Joseph Goldberger papers. The largest one, which includes the extensive correspondence with Mary, is the Joseph Goldberger Papers in the Southern Historical Collection at the Wilson Library, University of North Carolina, Chapel Hill. Unfortunately, while Mary saved most of Joseph's letters, he did not do the same with hers, so there are very few of her letters to him. A second collection of considerable importance is the Joseph Goldberger–W. H. Sebrell Jr. Collection at the Annette and Irwin Eskind Biomedical Library, Vanderbilt University, in Nashville. Dr. William Henry Sebrell Jr. was one of Goldberger's assistants at the Hygienic Laboratory during the last years of Goldberger's life. In addition to Goldberger's professional correspondence the collection has useful article reprints on pellagra, including articles in languages other than English and copies of Goldberger's articles in *Public Health Reports* and elsewhere. Especially interesting is a pocket notebook in which Goldberger scribbled during his first trip south to visit institutions with a high incidence of pellagra. A wealth of material on pellagra and a fine collection of photographs are in the James W. Babcock Papers at the Waring Historical Library at the Medical University of South Carolina, Charleston. There is also a modest collection of Goldberger letters in the Wade Hampton Frost Collection at the Alan Mason Chesney Medical Archives of the Johns Hopkins Medical Institutions.

The records of the U.S. Public Health Service, which include Goldberger's official correspondence, are in Record Group 90 of the National Archives. Goldberger's thought processes at the beginning of the pellagra investigation can best be understood by reading what he read. Fortunately, many of the journals to which he referred, bearing his underlinings and marginalia, are available in the historical collection of the National Library of Medicine. Fragments of a journal are also available at the DeWitt Stetten Jr. Museum of Medical Research at the National Institutes of Health.

Materials on the Rankin State Prison Farm experiment and the Mississippi flood are available at the Mississippi Department of Archives and History in Jackson. Those interested in the former will find the pardon and suspension files of special interest. Further material on the flood of 1927 can be found in the Hazel Braugh Records Center and Archives in Falls Church, Virginia.

Dark rumors that anti-Semitism kept Goldberger from a prestigious appointment at Yale surfaced after his death. I investigated these in collections at the Yale Manuscripts and Archives Library, including James Rowland Angell's presidential and personal papers, the Charles-Edward Amory Winslow Papers, and the Milton C. Winternitz papers. I also benefited from reading the Edgar Sydenstricker collection and the William T. Sedgwick Papers at Yale. The rumors cannot be substantiated from the available documents.

Oral histories of several of Goldberger's colleagues in the U.S. Public Health Service are available in the Oral History Collection in Butler Library at Columbia University in New York.

In 1943 Robert P. Parsons, a naval physician who had encountered Goldberger during the influenza research conducted at a naval station in the Boston area during World War I, published a biography, *Trail to Light*. It lacks scholarly citations, although several letters and documents are published in full. Parsons drew much of his information on Goldberger's personal life from many hours of conversation with Mary Goldberger. No transcripts exist. However, some of the material can be verified from letters and other documents in the papers collections cited above.

The best single volume on pellagra is Elizabeth W. Etheridge's *The Butterfly Caste: A Social History of Pellagra in the South* (1972). Also valuable is Daphne A. Roe's *A Plague of Corn: The Social History of Pel-*

lagra (1973). Some of Goldberger's many publications on pellagra were compiled in a volume, *Goldberger on Pellagra*, edited by Milton Terris (1964). A volume of articles on the disease by Goldberger and many others is *Pellagra*, edited by Kenneth J. Carpenter (1981). Few scholars have fully comprehended Goldberger's unique contribution to public health in the United States, especially the lasting value of the pioneering epidemiological studies that he and Edgar Sydenstricker conducted in seven South Carolina mill villages in 1916. The late George Rosen did. His paragraphs on Goldberger's work in *A History of Public Health* (1958) discuss clearly the relationship of economic and social factors to disease that Goldberger hoped to demonstrate. Another useful source is Charles Rosenberg's brief biographical sketch of Goldberger in *The Dictionary of Scientific Biography* (1972).

Index